CRISIS of the RAJ

Published for Dartmouth College by
University Press of New England
Hanover and London, 1986

Wayne G. Broehl, Jr.

CRISIS of the RAJ

The Revolt of 1857
through British Lieutenants' Eyes

University Press of New England

Brandeis University	*University of New Hampshire*
Brown University	*University of Rhode Island*
Clark University	*Tufts University*
University of Connecticut	*University of Vermont*
Dartmouth College	

Printed in the United States of America

Library of Congress Cataloging in Publication Data

Broehl, Wayne G.
   Crisis of the Raj.

   Bibliography: p.
   Includes index.
   1. India—History—Sepoy Rebellion, 1857–1858.
I. Title.
D S478.B76   1986   954.03'17   86–4067
I S B N 0–87451–374–X

Map and Illustration Credits

Map 1 adapted from Michael Edwardes, *Battles of the Indian Mutiny* (New York: Macmillan, 1963); used with the permission of the copyright holder, BT Batsford Limited, London.

Map 2 from Fred. Roberts, *Letters Written During the Indian Mutiny* (London: Macmillan, 1924).

Illustrations 1 and 3 from *Narrative of the Indian Revolt, from Its Outbreak to the Capture of Lucknow by Sir Colin Campbell* (London: Vickers, 1858).

Illustrations 2 and 8 from Thomas Frost (ed.), *Complete Narrative of the Mutiny in India, from Its Commencement to the Present Time*, 3d ed. (London: Read, 1858).

All remaining illustrations from Charles Ball, *The History of the Indian Mutiny: Giving a Detailed Account of the Sepoy Insurrection in India; and a Concise History of the Great Military Events Which Have Tended to Consolidate British Empire in Hindostan*, 2 vols. (London: London Printing & Publishing Co., 1858).

Contents

Acknowledgments

This book, the product of an extensive research project at the Amos Tuck School of Business Administration at Dartmouth College, was accomplished over a fifteen-year period, with a large number of people involved at one stage or another. My debts to these people are profound. First, I am grateful to the Trustees of Dartmouth College for extensive financial support of this project throughout, under the aegis of the Research Program at the Amos Tuck School. My colleague at Tuck, Victor McGee, has been a particularly important collaborator and has joined with me in preparing this book's extensive appendix on the use of computer-based content analysis for such research. My colleagues from the Department of Psychiatry at the Dartmouth Medical School, Stanley Rosenberg, Thomas Oxman, and Paula Schnurr, were also involved substantially in the content analysis dimension of this study. In addition, Professor Schnurr provided important insights for the hypotheses drawn in the concluding chapter.

A number of Tuck School students and their wives also participated in this project over the years. I especially want to recognize Kate Baxter, Donald Derrick, Elizabeth Derrick, Marianne Ehinger, Thomas Johnson, Jason Klein, Kathleen McDonald, Mark McDonald, V'Ella Warren, Priscilla Wayne, and Vincent Wayne.

As always, my debts to librarians in the research libraries in this country, in England, and in India require ample recognition. I especially wish to thank the staffs of the India Office Library of the British Library, the National Army Museum in London, the Manuscript Division of the British Museum, the Manuscript Division of the Library of Congress, and the always-wonderful staffs of Baker Library and Feldberg Library at Dartmouth College. My long-standing administrative colleagues, Suzanne Sweet, Ellie Lackey, and Joan Adams, were involved with me throughout the study. I also appreciate the unique input of both knowledge and materials from the grandson of one of the lieutenants, George Cracklow.

Last, and most important, I am eternally grateful to my late son Michael and to my wife, Jean, for their support of this project. Both worked extensively on the materials of the project, and their contributions throughout are manifold.

Hanover, New Hampshire   W.G.B.
January 1986

CRISIS of the RAJ

Introduction

Seldom in history has an event so captured the imaginations of people as the Indian Mutiny of 1857 (Indian nationalist writers call it "The First War of Independence" or "The People's Uprising"). When the Indian soldiers in the British army in India—the "Sepoys"—rebelled against their officers in Meerut in May of that year, in the process brutally murdering a number of these officers, their wives, and their children, they set in motion an uprising that spread all through the north of India. The British contingent in Delhi was overrun; once more horrible carnage was wreaked upon the English residents, men, women, and children alike. The important military garrisons at Cawnpore and Lucknow were put under siege.

Though perhaps two-thirds of the army in the country stayed reasonably loyal—there were only sporadic incidents in the Madras and Calcutta "presidencies"—the severity of the attacks on the bastions in the North West Provinces (Oudh and Rohilkhand) and in the Punjab and Rajputana soon raised the specter that the British might be driven off the continent altogether, just one hundred years after the Battle of Plassey. England, under Robert Clive, had gained suzerainty over the Indian subcontinent in the events surrounding that battle. Though the battle itself had not been totally decisive, there had been shadowy threats for years that the natives would forcibly take back their country from the British "on the one-hundredth anniversary of Plassey." And indeed, in various British outposts scattered throughout the north of India, the enlisted men turned against their British officer masters, killing them and their wives and children.

There was a savagery about these murders that profoundly shook the assumptions and sensibilities of the English people; the British press exacerbated the situation with sensationalist reporting that twisted the already ugly facts. The British soldiers in the campaign retaliated in kind, summarily executing Indian prisoners and adding their own variations of unspeakable acts. It was a brutal war throughout, with many atrocities on both sides.

A decisive series of military battles now ensued. First, Delhi was retaken by the British. Their main force arrived at Cawnpore soon after, only to find that almost the entire garrison had been butchered (with the bodies of many dozens of the women and children stuffed down a well). Lucknow's siege was lifted in November, but the key city was not retaken until March 1858. A whole series of lesser skirmishes over the remainder of that year finally brought the mutiny to an end. In the process, though, the delicate fabric of interpersonal trust that many on both sides had assumed to exist had been torn asunder; indeed, the very premises of British colonialism throughout the world had been challenged and fundamentally altered.

The British held India for another eighty-nine years, until Lord Louis Mountbatten, as Britain's last viceroy, engineered the independence of both India and the bifurcated Pakistan that had to be split off at the insistence of the Moslem leaders. During these four-score-plus years of post-mutiny rule, Britain instituted important administrative changes while continuing to extract plentiful economic rewards from its relationship as imperial master. Nevertheless, the events of 1857 and 1858 were a psychological watershed for British imperialism and colonialism.

It is not difficult to see why the mutiny has intrigued people over all these years. Human drama infiltrates into every part of this story: it is laced throughout with heroism and cruelty, suspense and intrigue. Here are romantic tales galore, great dramas that are the stuff of narrative historians; and writers and polemicists have exploited these stories in countless books. There is more than just melodrama, however, for serious scholars have analyzed the mutiny with equal eagerness, interesting themselves in its economic and social underpinnings, the potential implications of a "popular movement" among the Indian peoples, and the lessons for not only the British and Indian people but the many others concerned with the multifaceted face of world colonialism over the past several hundred years.

This book has a smaller canvas. Here the story is seen through the eyes of a small group of young British lieutenants going through that stirring set of battles. It is a study of the psychoso-ciological tensions that affected these young people—a group of intelligent and able men who were only partially in control of their destinies, yet had the ambitions, the achievement motivation, pos-sibly the group skills and personal innovation, to strive and struggle through the dramatic events they experienced. We will come to learn a good deal about these four men (and the mother of one of them)—to see their frustrations, their loneliness, their anomie, their failures. At the same time their enthusiasms, their successes, their hopes and dreams, come through constantly, giving a poi-gnancy to their story that transcends the "facts" themselves.

The stuff of this study is an extensive series of letters from the lieutenants back to their families during the height of the hostilities. Three went through the key battles together, almost in tandem; the fourth was in the headquarters group nearby. All sat down to write at just about the same time, generally after one of these great en-gagements. These are not memoirs written months or years later, nor journals later edited and brought "up to snuff." These are letters written on the battlefield, under the most trying of conditions; they express the full gamut of the young lieutenants' emotions as they moved through this startling phase of their lives. Each writes in his own style (and the mother in hers), and these lexical differences appear to come from distinct, deeply ingrained personal values and convictions. This fascinating set of letters also gives us a rich trove of raw material for a look at leadership, both strong and weak.

These four young men had some remarkable similarities. They were within six months of one another in age, all born in 1832 and thus all twenty-five in the first year of the mutiny. All had been born in India; three had military fathers, and one was descended from a family of civil servants in India. Three of the four had gone through the famous Addiscombe Military Seminary at Croydon, England, before coming out to India to serve in the early 1850s.

But there were also profound differences among the four. Lt. Frederick Roberts won the coveted British military award, the Vic-toria Cross, in the course of the mutiny and then went on over the next forty years to an outstanding military career that culminated in his becoming the commander in chief of the British army (in which role he became a central player in the Boer War). In his letters Roberts clearly evidences a keen sense of organizational acumen, combined with enthusiasm, courage, and a strong dose of the soldier's fatalism; he appears temperate in spite of the provocations of the vindictive war, willing to think strategically about long-term objectives rather than extracting immediate vengeance. He seems to have had an unerring instinct for being in the right place at the right time—and being *seen* (the "ubiquitous Roberts," said one dispatch).[1] There are thirty letters written by Roberts back to his family during the years 1857 and 1858.

The second data set is fifty-eight letters from Lt. George Cracklow, who went through Addiscombe with Roberts, departed for India at the same time as Roberts, and went through the same battles. He, on the other hand, had a very different subsequent life: he was nominated for the Victoria Cross but did not receive it, suffered a stroke in 1862 that incapacitated him, and left the service in 1864, dying in 1878. Cracklow's letters also exhibit a soldier's courage, but laced with vengeful images and harsh judgments; his view of the world appears sensitive but profoundly pessimistic, angry, authoritarian; he seems impressionable, frustrated by his lack of recognition; he combines moral righteousness with Draconian solutions, all this infiltrated with tinges of racism.

The third lieutenant, Arthur Lang, was at Addiscombe with Roberts and Cracklow; he graduated a year after the other two, gaining in the process the Pollack Medal as the top member of his class. Lang was trained as an engineer at Addiscombe, the only one of the four to achieve this highest-ranking position there. His letters reflect this matter-of-fact, analytical training. He, too, was courageous, but in his letters he appears less concerned about public glory than the others. The judgments he recorded are generally antiseptic and cool; many of them are quite blunt and brusque, but they are not often tinged with the fervor and passion of Cracklow's. It was Lang whose father was a civil servant, and Lang continued the tradition by becoming a public works engineer after the mutiny (still as a military man; the final rank he held was colonel). His career was modest. One of his obituaries stated, "As an engineer he made no particular mark in India. . . . The projects which more particularly commanded public attention were those of railways and great irrigation canals, and Colonel Lang . . . was in the buildings and roads branch, which lent itself less to the distribution of honours and distinction."[2] He died in 1916 at age eighty-four. There are over one hundred Lang letters, some of them quite short; these have been consolidated into thirty-four composite letters for the purposes of this study.

The fourth man, Thomas Watson, began his military career in India in the same year as Cracklow and Roberts; he left ninety-five letters. He was not an Addiscombe graduate but gained his commission by direct petition from his mother, the widow of a British lieutenant colonel who also had served in India. Watson's letters chronicle his duller job back at the headquarters office, following each battle from a distance where only the sounds could be heard. Watson's writing, which differs sharply from that of the other three, mirrors his preoccupation with his widowed mother, living at a hill station in north India during the mutiny. His older brother and younger married sister, incidentally, were also in the country at this time; both brother and brother-in-law were British officers (as had been another older brother, who had died in 1844 at age twenty-six). Watson's letters picture a man resigned to a functionary role, isolated, depressed, preoccupied with the perquisites of the job, the minutiae of daily cantonment life. Watson stayed in the Indian Service, rising slowly to the rank of lieutenant colonel before his retirement (in Tasmania).

Lieutenant Watson's mother was profoundly devout, moralistic in relation not only to the Indians but to her British friends and acquaintances. She appears fearful and suspicious (her self-imposed isolation was an anomaly at the tightly knit hill stations). Quite conscious about her physical surroundings, she exhorted her son with all of her own anxieties and concerns—a litany of loneliness and frustration. We have thirty-four of her letters.

As one reads these five sets of letters, the differences among the correspondents seem very striking on an intuitive level. Though the four men went through the war together, they ended with very divergent later careers. Their backgrounds, too, present contrasts. Roberts's father was a general in the British army, Cracklow's a captain, and Watson's a lieutenant colonel, all three serving in India. Roberts's and Lang's fathers were living at the time of the mutiny; Cracklow's had died when the boy was one year old; and Watson's had died when the son was just two. The Roberts family was upper class, the Cracklow family lower middle class, the Lang and Watson families somewhere in between.

However much we may infer from extensive quotations, sound history depends not alone on intuition but on analysis as well. We instinctively sense that these four men were very different people, and we can even qualitatively describe their separate typologies. We would likely hypothesize also that the woman's writing is distinctly different from the men's. But we also might desire to supplement subjective judgments with a more objective, more quantitative, way of developing these typologies.

Therefore, this book also draws on an intriguing new method of study whose name is content analysis. A particular branch of this content analysis field is explored here—the use of the computer to analyze the content of particular texts. All the letters of these five participants have been entered into a computer and treated to a sophisticated content analysis program that considers them along ninety-seven separate psychosociological parameters. The resulting glimpses further help to explain some of the critical differences hinted at in the texts themselves. In sum, a set of powerful analytical tools has been applied to a body of already-interesting material to give further insight into psychosociological leadership attributes. This fresh view of historical method is elaborated in data in the Appendixes.

With the richness provided by this addition, we can more readily draw conclusions about the dominant psychological profiles of the four young officers. We now find Cracklow more precisely pictured—as a detached, compulsive, aggressive person, not as strong as Roberts on the leadership qualities that eventually made the latter a beloved commanding general, the "Bobs" of Rudyard Kipling's poem. Roberts also evidences those qualities of hard work, achievement motivation, and organizational perceptiveness that would bring him through the ranks to the top post of the British armed forces. Lang's writing mirrors his administrative preoccupation, a bureaucratic thread that would permeate his later life. Watson, on the other hand, focuses on a narrower world: his widowed mother, the cantonment and its petty problems, the struggle to make ends meet on a lieutenant's pittance. His organizational skills were expended planning for a better life for his mother in the here and now. He lacked the competitiveness, the combativeness, characteristic (in separate ways) of Cracklow and Roberts, and neither did he have the practicality of Lang. The statistical results, then, give a good fit to our qualitative readings of the letters; the computer has given us increased confidence in our instinctive, subjective judgments.

Indeed, the results from the computer programs on each of the letter writers are quite evocative, driving us back to the letters once more, with new clues and hypotheses to test. What triggers aggression and hostility in soldiers in combat? (What is Cracklow communicating to his subordinates—indeed, to his family—by his harsh rhetoric?) Can positive qualities of leadership be interlaced with such hostility? How does the articulation of racist or class-conscious thinking affect leadership qualities? Can achievement imagery be isolated in such textual material, and can analysis of it validate Harvard psychologist David McClelland's hypothesis that its cognitive reinforcement can inculcate achievement motivation? Can the experiences, the formal records, established at seminal earlier institutions help to explain later psychological manifestations? (For example, all four men attended public school, but only two, Roberts and Lang, were registered at prestigious "inner-five" institutions; Roberts, Cracklow, and Lang also graduated from a well-known military academy, Lang producing a superior record, whereas Watson did not train at such an institution.) Do early letters contain precursors of later problems? Can incipient physical or psychiatric problems be spotted by persistent themes and repeated use of key words? (E.g., can Cracklow's mercurial personality give clues to his later stroke; is Cracklow [perhaps Watson, too] a misogynist; is Watson's indecision the sign of a leadership malaise?)

But we are in danger of getting ahead of our story. The events now to be described relating to the mutiny will frame the story particularly around the lives of these four men and one woman. The book will retell much of the great mutiny lore, though it is not intended to be one further military analysis of the campaigns. Similarly, we will be analyzing at a number of stages the Victorian mind-set that made British imperial colonialism such a unique institution. Again, though, this is not per se a study of the Victorian period of England's imperial and colonial history. The venue is India, and this country's puzzling and enigmatic ethos will inevitably color our thinking. Yet the locale could conceivably be different— the study does not depend on Indian history itself.

There will be new insights here on all of these subjects, and perhaps some further judgments to add to the many analyses of militarism, Victorianism, and imperial India. Extensive research in the National Archives of India, in the India Office Library and the National Army Museum in London, and in the Library of Congress has uncovered fresh materials that are incorporated here. But, to repeat, the primary focus is on the lives of these five people as they found themselves in traumatic juxtaposition in a sudden, tension-filled situation. If we can understand their differences, we can then throw some new light onto human responses under stress, not alone in the military but also in other walks of life.

Chapter 1
Victoria's Heyday

J. B. Priestley used the title I have chosen for this chapter as the name for one of his recent books, on Victoria's reign during the 1850s. This was "no catchpenny title," he avowed, for the decade not only was a happy one for the young monarch personally but also brought to fruition a number of forces from previous decades that came together for that long nineteenth-century period we now call Victorianism. The historian G. M. Young called it "the Victorian Noon Time" and maintained that if he had to choose a period for his next life it would be this one. Priestley chronicled the decade's outstanding features: It was an England "rich, powerful, and comparatively tranquil," small in population but "unrivaled" in industrial production and foreign trade. Its army might be small—"shockingly organized," said Priestley—but its navy "could not be challenged." It regarded the various upheavals on the Continent "with amused complacency." The reform movement of the two previous decades had repealed the hateful Corn Law, so "Coal and Cotton did not have to compel young children to work until they dropped from exhaustion." There was factory inspection now, even a Public Health Act. It was a period of calm and compromise, with the upper class and middle class closer to each other than in the past (but still practicing, as the English could do best in those days, a smug brand of social snobbery). There were still terrible problems going unsolved; Charles Dickens, Anthony Trollope, and many others wrote movingly of them. But the 1850s began on a positive enough note to prompt Young to make his euphoric comment about his afterlife.[1]

Now to narrow our focus: two young men entered Addiscombe

Military Seminary in that first year of the decade, and a friend joined them there a year later. Three of our lieutenants—Frederick Roberts, George Cracklow, and Arthur Lang—began their adult lives as cadets at the well-known institution dedicated to training professional soldiers for service in India.

Addiscombe made a unique and noteworthy contribution to India over its half-century life (from 1809 to 1861).[2] Here the East India Company trained its military officers: its graduates went out only to India, as employees of "John Company," the colloquial name the Indians gave to this proprietary organization. Addiscombe graduates were mercenaries, employed as a private military force by a private company. Though the earliest British forces in India were largely private, raised by the forerunners of "the Company," there soon were also royal forces under the Crown. There evolved over many years an always-complex, often-murky relationship between the royal and the Company military forces, complicated by the relationship of both of these military arms to the civilian administrators. By the mid-nineteenth century the Company's own military organization was professionalized and placed under contemporary standards of discipline and rules governing the relationship between Queen's officers and Company's officers. In effect, the Company troops were now fully covered by British military law. Yet the relationships remained complicated and quite often acrimonious. As one of the famous military leaders of the nineteenth century put it: "From the time of the establishment of a local army there had existed an absurd and unfortunate jealousy between the officers of the Queen's and Company's services . . . this ill-feeling influenced not only fellow-countrymen, but relations, even brothers, if they belonged to different services . . . it is difficult to understand how so puerile a sentiment could have been so long indulged in by officers who no doubt consider themselves sensible Englishmen."[3]

Addiscombe came to play a special role in this heightened professionalism of the Company officers. From its halls as graduates came some of the great names of nineteenth-century India: Henry Lawrence, Robert Napier, Baird Smith—not only soldiers but administrators who brought to India the resoluteness of leadership that seemed necessary in a country so complex and variegated. Twice every year during this period, between forty and fifty young men left the seminary (a part of the name they seemed universally to dislike), took up their appointments with the company, and left by packet boat for what would be at least a ten-year assignment, perhaps a lifetime.

The school was located at Addiscombe Place, near Croydon outside London. At the center of the campus was a mansion, an Elizabethan-style edifice built in 1702, which had had a number of illustrious owners before its purchase by the East India Company. By the time Cracklow and Roberts entered in early 1850 the extensive grounds included not only several barracks buildings but also a drawing and lecture hall called the "Chapel" ("it could not well have been less like one," commented one of its graduates.)[4] There was also a separate dining hall and an assortment of service buildings—a bakehouse, a dairy, a laundry, even a brewhouse. Then in 1843 a noteworthy addition came with the construction of a large sand-modeling hall, sixty feet by fifty feet, the entire inside of which was covered with a fine sand to a depth of about thirty inches. The sand was kept moistened with water and could be built up and shaped in any way. Thus a cadet could plan and actually construct a particular battle plan that would stay perfect for many weeks. Roberts, Cracklow, and Lang were fortunate in that the two years they resided in Addiscombe saw a new gymnasium and a separate building for "fives and racquets" also added.

It was not the buildings, though, that gave Addiscombe its special ethos; it was the entire institution. The military and civilian faculty, almost every member of which was a noteworthy character in his own right, lived together with a student body of young, ambitious, English schoolboys under a tight set of rubrics and mores uniquely designed to give a special Indian fillip to military training.

A boy applied to Addiscombe somewhere between the ages of fourteen and eighteen, with various testimonials about health and moral character and with certain prerequisites in mathematics, English, and so on: "He is also required to construe and parse Caesar's Commentaries correctly. He must likewise possess a correct knowledge of all of the rules of Arithmetic usually taught in schools, especially the rule of three, compound proportion, practice, interest, vulgar and decimal Fractions, and the extraction of the square root."[5] Once the "gentleman cadet" was admitted, his parents or guardians were required to pay fifty pounds per term (of which there were two each year).

Now the work, and the unexpected accompaniments, began in earnest. It was the latter in particular—the tricks and the highjinks, the anecdotes and the legends—that combined to give Addiscombe its special reputation and character. We see these in rich array as we follow George Cracklow, Fred Roberts, and Arthur Lang (who entered one term later, in June 1850) through their time at Addiscombe.

Their lieutenant governor (the head officer of the seminary) was Major General Sir Ephraim Stannus. He was a splendid-looking man, with a bushy head of white hair and a tall, soldierlike presence. Stannus had had a distinguished career in India, returning to head Addiscombe in 1834. The distinguishing feature of his personal style was his choleric temper and his use of strong language. Our three young cadets soon learned of this explosive quirk through an age-old schoolboy complaint: the food. "The great cause of excitement," related one of their contemporaries, "centred in the meat supply, which was so bad, that for a good part of the term the cadets absolutely refused to touch their dinners. This culminated in such scenes both in the study-rooms and dining-hall, that Stannus, who was known to have the choicest vocabulary of blessings in the whole service at disposal, came down to lecture the cadets at dinner one day, when, as it so happened, a son of the Chairman of the Court of Directors was acting Senior Corporal. Stannus stormed for a good twenty minutes in something stronger than scripture language, till the clock pointing to the fateful 20 past 1, the Senior Corporal jumped up, and calling all to 'tention,' roared out almost into the old Colonel's ear, the usual form of Grace— 'For what we have received, thank God! Quick march!' all that we had received, no meat being touched, being the Lieut.-Governor's ornate lecture. Furious at this, and not daring to send the Corporal (connected as he was) to the 'Black Hole,' Stannus came down raging on parade next morning, and working himself into a red-hot fury told us 'we were a pack of d——d babies, and that he had a d——d good mind to pack us all off straight to our d——d parents; but he would give us one chance more; he was sure that at least a few gentlemen might be left in the term, and these he would exempt if they fell out of the ranks.' Roaring out at last—'Those who have had nothing to say to these disgraceful proceedings will take two paces to the front! March!'"

The whole company as one took two paces forward, all the while looking as innocent as any lamb. This proved too much for Stannus's temper. The cadets ranked in lines at that time. "For a moment he glared like a wild animal, then rushed along the ranks swearing and brandishing in their faces a big stick which he carried; then hurled it at the nearest window, and turning to the Corporal in charge, shouted—'God d——n you, Sir! March the class off quick or I shall do some one an injury.'" At this point speech failed him, and he dashed off the parade to the mansion, apoplectic. After reflecting that he still had the whole term on his hands, and would have to send perhaps forty cadets to their homes, he changed his mind and ordered extra drill for the remainder of the term, some two months.[6]

Under Stannus were seventeen faculty members, "Professors, Masters, etc." There were five for mathematics and classics, all ministers. Five more were military officers, two for fortification and artillery, one each for military drawing, military surveying, and sword exercises. There were teachers of science, a French teacher, and last, but certainly not least, two teachers of "oriental languages" (i.e., Hindustani). Roberts, Cracklow, and Lang soon came to know one of these latter well, Charles ("Chaw") Bowles, of whom it was said, "no cadet can possibly have forgotten his oddities."[7] While the three were at Addiscombe, a marvelous character sketch of Chaw, which can hardly be improved upon, came out in an anonymous book: "The forenoon's study was a 'Chaw' study. In other words the Professor of Hindustani instructed the senior class in that language at that hour. A stiff, precise, austere man, little moved by sentiment or enthusiasm, the Professor year by year, nay, term by term had repeated word for word, without shadow of deviation, the same stereotyped phrases, whether for the purpose of rebuke or punishment, or the rendering of a passage in the Selections.

"When Mr. Bowles first joined as professor at Addiscombe he was but 19 years of age, and hence hardly older than some of the senior cadets. He had never been in India, and had an unfortunately pronounced way of rendering the language. It was in this way that he obtained his sobriquet, for he was in the habit of pronouncing 'char,' the Hindustani for 'four,' in a broad manner as 'Chaw,' and his name being Charles, the nickname stuck to him while at Addiscombe for 30 years.

"Occasionally a cadet would ask him innocently the Hindustani for 94, 'Chaw' would instantly fall into the trap and say, with a smack of his lips at the beginning and end, 'char-ran-we,' pronounced by him 'chaw ran away.'

Many tricks were attempted against Bowles; one, called "the Great Mouse Affair," occurred in the time of Roberts, Cracklow, and Lang. One of their fellow students related it: "The cadets were about to enjoy the privilege of an hour or two's instruction in Hindustani from Professor Bowles, whom everyone liked and everyone worried. As the cadets marched into the class-room a mouse was viewed, and the cadets broke off, chased, and captured the animal. What to do with it? was the next question; something to make fun, of course, but now? 'Tie it to 'Chaw's stool,' suggested some genius. The idea was accepted with rapture—string was found, and the mouse tied by the leg to the stool. Perfect silence reigned as the Master of Oriental literature stalked up the room, nearly every cadet being absorbed in his endeavour to discover what 'Baital,' who, so far as I remember, was always obtruding his remains, really had said. It happened that the mouse was so tied that it was only squeezed—and squeezed gently—when Bowles sat upright; when he leant forward as he did when writing or reading, the mouse was free and silent. In a slow sonorous way 'Chaw' said, 'Mr. Corporal, some one is making a squeaking noise.' Of course, no one on this occasion would confess to making the squeaking noise; but after it had occurred again once or twice; 'Chaw' Bowles acted on his own judgment and ordered out the set of six at my desk. I was thus prevented from seeing the rest of the play which lasted for some time until the Professor, leaning further back than usual in his just indignation at not discovering the maker of the 'squeaking noise,' produced one last and extra powerful squeal from the wretched mouse. This attracted Bowles' attention to the real performer whose death-agonies he witnessed. He was more touched by the little animal's sufferings (for he was a most kind-hearted man) than annoyed at having been trifled with. However, he reported the case to the Lieut.-Governor, and all our leave, etc., were stopped until further orders, or until the culprits confessed.

"As time wore on the jest appeared less humorous and the results more tedious, and one day on parade it was intimated that the class would open their hearts on the subject. I forgot the order of confession, but one cadet stepped two paces to the front and said, 'I saw the mouse, Sir,' Another penitent promptly came to the front and said, 'So did I, Sir.' Then for a change a third said, 'I caught the mouse, Sir,' and this went on until every cadet had confessed to 'finding the string,' 'holding the mouse,' 'tying its leg,' etc., etc. How the orderly officer, Captain Couchman, kept his countenance all the time I cannot think. In the end a definite period of extra drill was named, and we served out our time."[8]

If Bowles was seen as a bit eccentric, Rev. Jonathan Cape "may be considered the most remarkable member of the staff of the College during the whole course of its existence." Cape was senior professor in mathematics, spent thirty-nine years at Addiscombe, and in many ways was the antithesis of Bowles. He appeared to the cadets, according to a biographer, as a cold, unsympathetic person but was universally respected for his calmness and firmness. He seemed able to maintain strict discipline with the least possible effort, and it was reputed that no cadet ever attempted a joke with him a second time. His fearsomeness in the entrance examinations was renowned, and his teaching in mathematics was precise and comprehensive (he, in fact, had published a major two-volume text, one in great demand in the various schools training men for work in India). He was a bachelor and "therefore well-off and fully appreciated a good dinner. He had been, so it is said, rather a 'gay dog,' and was once nearly engaged, but on bidding adieu to his lady-love, he was caught kissing the parlour-maid in his passage through the hall. I've seen this done in plays, and am glad it is supposed to have happened once in real life. But by us Jonathan Cape was much respected and feared as the arbitrator of our fates."[9]

In addition to the faculty there was a complement of military officers over the cadets—a staff captain, orderly officers, and a cadre of sergeants. The staff captain during our three cadets' terms was Maj. T. Ritherdon. Though he had spent only a short three years in actual service he was allowed the rank of a captain when he joined the seminary, and he spent all the rest of his service at Addiscombe. "Notwithstanding this," noted a biographer, "he afterwards attained in some mysterious manner the rank of Major." The anonymous storyteller again captures personality quirks well: "He maintained in spite of his exceptional career, or perhaps in consequence of it, a stiffer demeanour and more rigorous notions of military discipline than if he had spent a lifetime in camp. He was a portly and pompous man, and when he appeared at the forenoon paradel, he strutted to and fro with the air of a leader of armies. He obtained the sobriquet of 'Old Staff.' The circular swing of his right leg, the clank of his steel scabbard and spurs, and his stentorian words of command were grand to see and hear; but the effect on the saucy cadet whom they were intended to overawe was not always the one desired. Cadets brought before him for some scrape, who wished to secure his favourable consideration of their case, said that if they called him Colonel Ritherdon they were pretty sure to get off with a slight punishment." When Stannus died suddenly of a heart attack in Roberts's and Cracklow's second term, Ritherdon applied for the top post, "but the Court of Directors wisely decided that his appointment was far from desirable." Ritherdon then quit.[10]

It would indeed have been surprising had not the sergeants been remembered—and their appearance and demeanor ensured that they would be unforgettable. The most noted during the Roberts/Cracklow/Lang days was Sergeant Murray, alias "Squasher." He was a short, pudgy man, "somewhat fond of his glass." Although reputed to be kindhearted, he was also considered to be cranky and was alleged to have at times reported irregularities to the orderly officer, "which he would not have done had he been in his right mind." One of his duties was to superintend the cadets on extra drill, with the latter always endeavoring to go around the parade ground as fast as possible, so as to keep Squasher on the trot, "an exercise for which he was eminently unfit."[11]

A famous Squasher practical joke occurred during Roberts's and Cracklow's first term. At that time the sergeants always watched the cadets closely to try to prevent them from entering public houses to obtain liquor. The perpetrator of the trick related the story in this way: "One day as cadet S and I were 'doubling' into Croydon without leave, with the view of securing the billiard table at the King's Arms, behind us were other cadets on the same errand who had leave to visit Croydon. To our great annoyance, on approaching the railway bridge, we found 'Squasher' on his beat walking towards Croydon, and just about to cross the bridge. The situation was very awkward for us, for of course our names were not in the list which 'Squasher' had with him of those permitted to visit Croydon that afternoon; and if we made a detour, or 'fell back' till he had got over the bridge or some way on, we should have lost the table, for those behind would have passed us. As it happened to be a rainy day, and a shower was still falling, 'Squasher,' to protect himself, had put on a cloak. I may here mention that he was somewhat deaf. Well, on seeing him I said to S——, 'What shall we do?' He replied, 'Leave him to me,' and we 'doubled' on as silently as possible. When just at the top of the bridge S got at 'Squasher's' cloak tail, lifted it up over his shako and bonneted him, and we then ran as fast as we could into the field by the Railway Inn and straight across to the King's Arms. By the time he recovered from the shock we were nearly out of his sight, and he was unable to identify us. We managed to get back by the next parade hour without being discovered, and gave 'Squasher' a wide berth for the next few days, and when I ventured to chaff him on the subject, he got very angry and said, 'Oh! I thought you was one of them. I knowed your run, I did, for you was in my squad, but I couldn't swear to you.' He never knew who it was that bonneted him. It was too serious a thing to disclose." [12]

If the public houses were kept off limits most of the time, the cadets could at least travel across the campus to the small cottage of "Mother" Rose, where they could buy milk, eggs, bread, and butter and where they could use the spare room as a species of club. There they could converse and smoke in a comfortable manner. It was a small room and was most often jammed with as many as fifteen or twenty cadets, so that the atmosphere of tobacco was so dense that one could hardly see to the other end of the room. Mother Rose exerted a profound influence on the cadets over more than a thirty-year period; she was "the friend of everybody." [13]

There was also a small cadre of townspeople who were allowed in the seminary. One of the oddest was "Tarts" (whose real name was Joe Rudge); he had a small shop in the town of Croydon and was also allowed to come daily to Addiscombe to purvey his wares ("light refreshments") in a little den under the staircase near the Fortification Hall. Though he tried to run his business for cash, the cadets were always out of money, and he kept a running account with many of the young men, always able to remember to the penny what each owed him (though he could not read or write). An apocryphal story often told about Tarts involved an Addiscombe graduate on home leave from India, who upon revisiting Addiscombe and seeing Tarts said, "Well, 'Tarts,' you don't remember me." "Oh, yes, Sir, I do," replied Tarts—"you owes me 5 £."[14]

With such a cast of characters, both within the organization and at its fringes, it is a small wonder that the cadets left Addiscombe's gates with lasting memories.

Still, the raison d'être of any educational institution is the training of students. At Addiscombe, despite all the pranks and jokes, there was deadly serious study of all those dimensions of the upcoming assignment to India, military and civilian, that could be expected to be the lot of Addiscombe graduates. Of the forty or so graduates of each class, the top half-dozen would be selected to the prestige service, the engineers, where even their pay would be slightly higher. Those selected stayed in England eighteen months longer, for further training at Chatham Naval College. The next dozen or so would be given another sought-after service, the artillery. The remaining cadets would then be assigned to the ubiquitous infantry. Both of the latter groups typically left for India within three months of graduation. Thus the competition at the seminary was keen, and the instruction rigorous.

George Cracklow had entered with excellent recommendations from Mr. Day, his old headmaster at the preparatory school carrying the latter's name at Briston Hill; Day testified to Cracklow's obedient conduct and diligent habits and prognosticated that he would be "very quick and active." Cracklow did not disappoint his mentor, either; he moved at Addiscombe from "moderate" to "satisfactory" and then to "great" over the months in his statistics course and was "great" or "very great" in most of the months of analytical trigonometry (though in August of 1850 he fell all the way to the bottom of his class of forty in mathematics, the only man to have "satisfactory"). He maintained a steady record of "great" in the course in application. When graduation came in December 1851, he was one of sixteen out of the forty to have a First Class in military drawing. This was a two-man project, the execution of a drawing of the Hill Fort of Wasiota.[15]

His partner for this major project, and his close friend through the Addiscombe years, was Frederick Roberts. The backgrounds of Cracklow and Roberts are amazingly close in some respects. As noted earlier, they were both born in India, and in the same year, 1832 (Cracklow was a month the senior). Both were sons of army officers stationed in India. Here, though, the pattern sharply diverges. George Cracklow's father (also named George) was from an obscure family (his grandfather had been a hat maker in Southwark, London); he rose only to the rank of captain. Roberts, on the other hand, was the son of Col. (later Gen.) Abraham Roberts, a renowned military leader who had served in Indian campaigns that spanned a full fifty years (and who, after retirement, received from Queen Victoria first the order of Knight Commander of the Bath and then the Grand Cross of the Bath). The Roberts family was a famous one, having been settled in Waterford, Ireland, for many generations. Fred Roberts's great-grandfather was a first-rank architect there, his grandfather a respected clergyman. George Cracklow had gone, as noted, to the small preparatory school of E. H. Day; Fred Roberts had been enrolled first at Eton, then at Sandhurst, before coming to Addiscombe.[16]

Roberts, nicknamed by his sisters Sir Timothy Valliant, was a small and delicate child. As a baby in India, he had nearly died from an attack of "brain fever" and had been given up by the doctors. His father was credited with saving his life by resorting to a curious native remedy. He had seen hill women, when at work in the fields, leave their babies by a stream and induce sleep by arranging for a gentle and continuous flow of water over their heads. The father now applied a similar soporific to young Fred, with apparently similar success. When he recovered, though, Fred had permanently lost the sight of his right eye.

Though Abraham Roberts was an officer, he had not yet obtained command of a regiment—and seventeen other officers were ahead of him in the seniority-based promotion ladder—at the time Fred went to Eton. The latter was an expensive place, and his father tried to get Fred a direct commission for India. He failed, and the son was sent to Sandhurst, where, had he finished, he would have gone into the queen's service. Sandhurst also proving to be too expensive, young Roberts was sent to Addiscombe as a "second choice." Fred was disappointed and wrote his father, "If you and Mama wish me to go to Addiscombe I will go there willingly [though] I would certainly prefer the Queen's Service." This view of Addiscombe mirrored a common feeling that the seminary was not "top drawer"; there was a saying in vogue at this time that the directors of the East India Company sent their clever sons into the Indian Civil Service, their stupid sons into the company's cavalry, and their poor relations to Addiscombe.[17]

Roberts was just a step ahead of Cracklow all the way through on grades. When Cracklow was "moderate," Roberts was "great." When Cracklow was "great," Roberts was "very great." Still, neither of them was right at the top of their class (though neither was among the three cadets restricted for six months for "idleness" during their first term).

Six months after Roberts and Cracklow entered, Arthur Lang came to the seminary as a new "Greener" (the first of the four terms was the "Green" term). At the age of "13¾" (as his biographer precisely put it), he came to England from India to attend Rugby School, going on three years later to Cheltenham College. At Addiscombe, Lang was at the top of his class right from the start—"by far the most conspicuous and distinguished man of his batch," said his biographer. He stood well over six feet, with an active, athletic figure. He quickly rose to prominence on the athletic fields and later captained both the cricket eleven and the football fifteen. He also became fast friends with Roberts and Cracklow.[18]

Cracklow and Roberts graduated from Addiscombe in December 1851. Both had done reasonably well in their academic subjects, and their First Class in the military drawing gave them one of the awards. But none of the major academic honors came to either; they were clearly down in the middle of the class in total performance. Lang already had surfaced as one of the leaders of the school; though only a third-termer on the day of the Roberts/Cracklow graduation, he won Second Class in mathematics, fortification, Latin, and Hindustani. As noted earlier, on his graduation he won the coveted Pollack Medal, the prestigious award for the top member of a graduating class.

However, the three cadets were not as much interested in these academic accomplishments as they were in the final results—their assignments to the various services. At the Roberts/Cracklow graduation, six of the forty went to the engineers. Abraham Roberts had promised his son one hundred pounds and a gold watch if he made the engineers, and Fred had written back, "I should be ashamed of myself were I not to get the engineers." But the few "Greats" in the grades took their toll; the next sixteen graduates were to go to the artillery, and George Cracklow and Fred Roberts were in this second group, "the remaining," as the London *Times* article on the graduation ceremonies then noted, "being alloted to the Infantry."[19] A few months later, Lang did make the engineers.

The speeches at the Roberts/Cracklow graduation were duly reported in full in the *Times* and were frank and pointed concerning some of the pitfalls the young men would soon be facing. The honorary chairman began: "In India, the duties entrusted to military officers are frequently of an important and very onerous character . . . in such positions officers are frequently thrown entirely on their own resources. They may be removed a great distance from headquarters and obliged to act with promptness and decision in difficult matters without reference to higher authority." He then went on to inveigh against intemperance as "the fruitful source of nine-tenths of the wretchedness and misery that exist. I am sorry to say that as regards Europeans in India it is not less so, but with this aggravation, that the descent to ruin and degradation is ten-fold more rapid." The chairman then took a swipe at "that nauseous habit of smoking," calling it a "filthy and unwholesome practice [that] often leads to the more dangerous excess I have just alluded to." His next caveat was about excessive spending habits—"extravagance must lead to debt, and nothing will prove more fatal to your comfort and future prospects than such embarrassment." Then he put his finger on one of the real threats of India: the monotony of life in the garrison. The chairman painted a vivid picture of the pernicious threats of gambling and betting and added that "immoral and dissolute conduct will render you an object of general dislike and distrust."

The archbishop of Canterbury was asked to add a few words and was quoted by the *Times* as saying that "they were going among many who, not knowing the principles of Christianity, would form their opinion of its precepts from the conduct of those . . . whom he was addressing." They were urged "never to forget the privileges they had inherited of being English Christians."

This messianic role was drummed into the India-bound British officer at every turn. "Indian life develops all that is proudest and most manly in the British character," commented one officer. "The Englishman there feels that he is a member of an imperial and conquering race. To rule men in his daily business."[20] Rightly did the Indian religious leaders sense that this overpowering attitude of superiority and scornful lack of understanding would easily slip into overt proselytizing and thus threaten to destroy the Eastern faiths. The concept of Christian conqueror spilled over effortlessly into a pervasive role image of the English officer as a father figure, all-knowing and paternalistic; this, too, was also strongly urged that evening by the chairman, whose words must have dimly rung in the ears of those forty graduates when they faced the mutiny six years later: "Such is the character of the Native soldier, with reference to his bearing toward his European officer, that he is proverbial for his susceptibility of the most attached and grateful feelings, particularly toward those who treat him with kindness and consideration. You will easily understand how much your own efficiency as officers will depend upon the degree of influence you can gain over those under your command . . . this hold over the minds and affections of those under your command is the most powerful element of strength in the possession of good officers; to insure its permanency you must maintain it also by the moral effect of your own character and example." With this ringing charge, the graduates went forth to their great adventure.

Chapter 2
"Curry and Rice"
Cantonment Life in Pre-Mutiny India

"Forty years ago, the departure of a cadet for India," wrote Frederick Roberts in 1897 in his two-volume autobiography, *Forty-one Years in India*, "was a much more serious affair than it is at present. Under the regulations then in force, leave, except on medical certificate, could only be obtained once during the whole of an officer's service, and ten years had to be spent in India before that leave could be taken. Small wonder, then, that I felt as if I were bidding England farewell for ever, when I set sail from Southampton with Calcutta for my destination." George Cracklow and Roberts had gone out to India in early 1852 by separate ships, shortly after their graduation. Both took the route that first involved a steamer to Alexandria, then a canal boat to Cairo. Here the typical pattern was to lay up for a couple of days at Sheppard's Hotel before taking the overland route across the desert some ninety miles to make connection with one of the Red Sea steamers at Suez (almost always one of the Peninsula and Orient ships renowned as "posh"; their cabins on the "port out, starboard home" side were favored, because they got less sun than the others). The two lieutenants' next route was down to Aden, then straight around the southern tip of India to the major south Indian port, Madras. The last leg of the voyage ended in Calcutta.[1]

Cracklow and Roberts were both assigned to the large military station in that city, the famous Dum Dum cantonment. The quarters there were crowded and badly ventilated, and the sanitary arrangements were, according to Roberts, "as deplorable as the state of the water supply . . . the only efficient scavengers were the huge birds of prey called adjutants, and so great was the dependence placed upon the exertions of these unclean creatures that the young cadets were warned that any injury done to them would be treated as gross misconduct. The inevitable result of this state of affairs was endemic sickness, and a death-rate of over 10% per annum." About the only incident to relieve the dreary days and weeks of cantonment drill was the onslaught of a cyclone, which did substantial damage both to the town of Calcutta and to the cantonment. "Dum Dum in ruins was even more dreary than before the cyclone," lamented Roberts, and both of the young officers longed for a post in a more salubrious climate, most especially somewhere on the North West Frontier. In the summer of 1853 both had their wishes fulfilled. Roberts was posted to Lahore as aide to his father, who had just been appointed to command the division with the rank of major general (the old soldier was forced to retire the next year, though, owing to failing health). Cracklow's assignment was a smaller cantonment, Sialkot, also on the North West Frontier.

Thomas Watson, our fourth lieutenant, already was there. We did not meet him in the last chapter, for he never attended Addiscombe or, indeed, any other military academy. Watson, upon recommendation of a director of the East India Company, had been "examined" by the the full body of directors in London in the summer of 1850 on his military and academic skills and had then been cleared for a direct appointment as a cadet in the army in India, with his training to be obtained on the job as soon as he reported in India a few months thence. He was eighteen years of age at this time; he had also been born in 1832, just a couple of months before Roberts and Cracklow.

Appointments such as this were essentially patronage, though in this case with some logic to it, inasmuch as Watson's father had been a lieutenant colonel in the British army in India. (The purchase system was also in effect at that time throughout the British army; commissions for ranks as high as lieutenant colonel were traded "over the counter" at quite substantial amounts of money: from £500 for a second lieutenant up to £7,250 for a lieutenant colonel.)[2]

Watson's mother, Sarah, was instrumental in her young son's appointment. Our first view of her, at the time of Watson's examination, gives us some early clues to her temperament and personality. Sarah Watson was in England in 1850, about ready to travel back to India, where she had lived for many years. Her daughter and her son Thomas were to accompany her. Thus she had a vested interest in the precise time when Thomas Watson was to receive his formal appointment as cadet and report for duty in India, and she tried to postpone the date of appointment to fit her own needs. "We wish to have his protection in society for sometime after our arrival," she wrote the directors. Yet she wanted to have it both ways: "It is an important object to us not to defer his receiving it longer than to enable him to spend a little time with me and his sister."

The three went out to India, to find that the bureaucracy of the Company did not bring the appointment at the exact moment when Sarah Watson wished it. She wrote the directors again: "You are so kind and so fully aware of the importance of a single day's further loss of time that I know you will comply with my earnest request to send it by the Marseilles mail of the 24th February." Now she was sorry that she had not been more prompt to agree with the directors at the start: "I feel anxious at not having taken your advice that the appointment should immediately be on its being given in November."

Belatedly, well beyond the date she had tried to engineer, Thomas Watson was appointed a cadet. Within a few months he was posted to his first assignment, a post with a Native Infantry regiment (the 46th) in Meerut, fifty miles northeast of Delhi. (A Native Infantry unit was British-officered, with Indian troops.) Watson thus was being trained on the job within the regiment itself; he carried the title of ensign until late 1856, when he became a lieutenant.[3]

Arthur Lang, the last of the four lieutenants to reach India, was immediately posted to the North West Frontier on his arrival in July 1854. His first post was as assistant executive engineer in the Minister of Works Department. He began with the Rawal Pindi Division and then a year later was appointed executive engineer and superintendent of civil buildings in Lahore. This is the area of northwestern India known then and now as the Punjab.[4]

In those days, the Punjab was particularly backward. Great events had occurred there in the 1840s. This was the territory of the fabled Sikh nation, under the genius of Ranjit Singh's leadership. By 1820 he had consolidated the many disparate fiefdoms into a powerful state—but he had trained no successor. When he died in 1839 a whole series of murders of self-appointed heirs-apparent finally led the British to step in militarily in the First and Second Sikh Wars. By 1848 the Punjab had been annexed by Britain. This led to a civil rule of a most innovative and effective variety by the two famous British brothers John and Henry Lawrence. It was a time (as Henry put it) for "firmness, promptness, conciliation and prudence."[5]

A contemporary writer has called this period in the civil administration of the Lawrences "the rule of the Titans." They did indeed do a magnificent job of setting in motion the administrative machinery to bring a rebellious and far-flung area into the orbit of British law and order. The brothers picked the cream of the crop of graduates from Haileybury, the prestigious East India Company administrative training college in England, supplemented this group with the very best of the officers in the East India Company military services, and posted them as magistrates and collectors to travel the circuit all over the Punjab area. These men were models of the type of British civil servant found in those years all through India: the hardy, independent man who could make his life alone, out in the field administering justice and maintaining the revenues of the Crown.

John Beames, a contemporary of John Lawrence and himself a district officer (a magistrate), felt that Lawrence had too harsh a view of this post: "His ideal of a district officer was a hard, active man in boots and breeches, who almost lived in a saddle, worked all day and nearly all night, ate and drank when and where he could, had no family ties, no wife or children to hamper him, and whose whole establishment consisted of a camp bed, an odd table and chair or so and a small box of clothes such as could be slung on a camel . . . personal government was the only form of rule which the rude and simple Punjabis could understand, therefore, the ideal Magistrate must show himself to all his people continuously, must decide cases either sitting on horseback in the village gateway or under a tree outside the village walls, write his decision on his knee, while munching a native chupatty or a fowl cooked in a hole in the ground and then mount his horse and be off."[6]

Charles Aitchison, another magistrate of that period, said that he felt "ubiquitous": "If in the remotest part of the District there occurred a cow-riot or an affray or a murder or a big burglary, the Deputy-Commissioner or an Assistant had to be on the spot. If cholera broke out, every village affected had to be visited. No remission of revenue was ever granted without a personal inspection of the land and the crops. Nothing that affected the welfare of the District or the contentment of the people was too insignificant for personal attention. It was an unwritten law that the Civil Officers should see things with their own eyes, do things with their own hands, and enquire into things for themselves."[7]

In contrast, the military life in this peacetime period of our four lieutenants was not marked by independence and self-sufficiency. One of Cracklow's fellow officers commented on the transition from England to India: "Well, well, Gunner Thomas Smith, like privates Brown, Jones, and Robinson who had gone before him, drops imperceptibly into Indian ways; and ere many weeks have sped he finds out that it is better fun confining himself to the operation of eating his dinner than having to eat and cook it too; he learns with wonderful promptness the value of a bheestie [water carrier], and he acquires a taste for the pleasures of repose in a shorter time than could possibly have been expected . . . It is pitiable to see the state of helplessness to which some soldiers—'old stagers' in India, arrive—a helplessness fostered by traditional fallacies, and founded on erroneous and ruinous precedents. Doubtless there are many things that the English soldier has been accustomed to do at home which become impossibilities in India, and for the performance of which he must depend greatly on natives; doubtless a large, and to the eye of a European, an overwhelming staff of natives must, from the very peculiar character of Indian warfare, from the exigencies of the climate, and many other minor cause, be constantly in attendance on every English regiment; doubtless it is not only prudent but necessary to protect our friend Thomas Smith as much as possible from the fatal effects of the sun, unless you wish a week after his arrival in the country to accompany him with 'arms reversed,' and a band wailing forth the sad music of the 'Dead March in Saul' to his last resting-place on earth."[8]

Even more so than the British enlisted men, the British officer was served and indulged by large contingents of servants; another one of Cracklow's fellow officers, Lt. Oliver Jones, a naval post-captain who had voluntarily come out to India to work with the artillery, described the system: "Every officer has from four to twelve servants, and the men also have several attached to each company, for a private in India cannot draw his own water, nor cook his own victuals, nor could he, till lately, clean his own boots, nor shave his own chin, but shoe-cleaners and barbers were attached to each regiment."⁹ As another contemporary observer put it, "He must not go out in the sunshine, he must travel in a palki instead of on horseback, he must be punkaed, and tattied and God knows what else, he must have a *khansamaun* [house steward], a *kitmutgar* [table server], a sirdar bearer and bearers, and hosts of other servants, one for his pipe, another for his umbrella, another for his bottle, another for his chair, etc., all to do the work of one man."¹⁰

Still, the main business for our four lieutenants and their fellow subalterns was, of course, soldiering. Cracklow came to Sialkot in late 1852 and took charge of a troop in a Foot Artillery company in the Bengal Artillery, and in the process came under the command of an army officer, Capt. (later Maj. Gen.) George Bourchier, who subsequently had great influence on him. Bourchier was thirty-six years old, eleven years senior to Cracklow. A graduate, too, of Addiscombe, he had come to India in 1839, in time to be involved in the two wars with the Sikhs in the 1840s. This is the man who trained Cracklow and his unit over the five years of cantonment life at Sialkot and who took them into the mutiny. To our great good fortune in reconstructing the lives of the four lieutenants during this period, George Bourchier wrote a controversial book documenting the beginnings of the mutiny and the first year of its progress. This book, *Eight Months' Campaign against the Bengal Sepoy Army during the Mutiny of 1857*, is an articulate and opinion-filled version of how the war looked to one man¹¹—and it documents in particular the life of George Cracklow. More will be heard from Bourchier as our story unfolds.

*   *   *

"I would far prefer the Infantry to Cavalry, but *the* service is no doubt the *Artillery!* Whether up on the Batteries with the heavy guns or in the open with the light ones, you are sure to see most of the fun. I never met such brave plucky fellows as our gunners, nothing alarms, nothing disconcerts them, and then you have the satisfaction of knowing that all are looking to the Artillery, foes as well as friends respect it . . . let me be a *'Gunner'*!!"[12]

These were the words of Fred Roberts, but they could just as well have been written by Cracklow or probably just about any one of the other young subalterns. For the artillery was thought by many to be the plum, the one place where one could get "real action." We need to know something more about the artillery, for this service looms large in the subsequent story, and Cracklow and Roberts remained in it through most of the course of the mutiny.[13]

The Bengal Artillery was divided into two separate troops, the Foot Artillery and the Horse Artillery.[14] The first of these terms was a bit of a misnomer: it was not that the guns were so light as to be carried on foot (as had been the case in earlier days) but, quite the opposite, that the guns were too heavy to be pulled by horse. The armament of the usual Foot Artillery battery was five nine-pound guns and one twenty-four-pound howitzer. These were pulled by either 130 or so bullocks or sometimes an equivalent number of horses. Often the howitzers of this size and larger—the siege guns—were pulled by elephant. The Horse Artillery troop generally had as armament five six-pound guns and one twelve-pound howitzer. Each of these had a team of six horses for the gun and another team of six horses for the wagon. There were generally about fourteen men assigned to a gun and its ammunition wagon, with some of these also having spare gun teams accompanying them. Generally a lieutenant had two or three guns under his command. If the particular unit was Native Artillery, everyone except the officer and perhaps two or three noncommissioned officers would be Indian. If it was a European troop, then it would be called Bengal, not Native, Artillery, and all except perhaps the two limber gunners would be European. However, all troops, European included, had a full detail of Indian lascars (gun and carriage cleaners), syces (stable helpers and grooms), and grass cutters (collectors of forage for the animals).

The basic difference between the Foot Artillery and the Horse Artillery was obviously the much-heightened mobility of the latter. Gun barrels were still very heavy at this time (for example, the bronze nine-pounder weighed thirteen hundred pounds, and a cast-iron barrel of the same size weighed twenty-six hundred). The famous English ordnance engineer William Armstrong was at this very time developing his new so-called built-up barrels, formed by rolling up iron bars in spiral coils and then welding them longitudinally. Armstrong had this technique perfected by 1859, and by the early 1860s the whole of England's field artillery units were using this new, lighter weapon (the built-up nine-pounder weighed only six hundred pounds). However, the British artillerymen fought through the mutiny with the older, heavier guns.

Mobility and rapidity of strike have always been key dimensions of military strategy. In the earlier battles fought in India, Afghanistan, and Nepal, as well as in the 1857 mutiny, the ability to send a rapidly moving troop of six-pound guns drawn by the superb horses available in that part of the world gave the armies tremendous striking power. There grew up a real mystique about being in the Bengal or Native Artillery. Both officers and men had great pride in their equipment and animals and unabashed self-confidence in their own abilities. There was dash—even slapdash—about the way the Bengal Artillery went about its business. For example, few of the Indian guns had sights attached to them. Oliver Jones commented: "I was much surprised at the heavy field-guns in India not being sighted, and asked a distinguished officer in the Bengal Artillery how it was? He said he did not think it of any consequence—that they got the range with one or two shots and this did very well! The Royal Artillery, however, fitted all the guns which came into their charge with sights. I do not know whether the Bengal Artillery thought better of their rough-and-ready plan or not."

Jones described the army in the field: "There is a bazaar also which follows every corps, and which is under the control of the commanding officer. It supplies all the things which are required by soldiers on a campaign, such as soap, tobacco, &c.; also gram for the horses, a kind of vetch, which is their principal food, and which they much prefer to oats; and many other things which it would be very inconvenient to carry about with one . . .

"The number of servants every officer is obliged to keep in India is a great addition to the impediments of any army, especially where food has to be carried, as was the case in Oudh. No one tried to do with fewer than I did, but I had got up to nine, and had I remained in India much longer, I should have been obliged to have two or three more." George Cracklow confided to his mother, "I am not very fond of the natives and so have as few as possible." But "few" in this case was half a dozen.[15]

Jones continued the story of his troop of servants: "True that five of them belong to my horses, for usually every horse has its groom and grass-cutter; I made two syces do for three horses; but for myself, I had Mr. Malakoff, who was as good as two or three, for he was cook, butler, valet, and first-lieutenant, a coolie, a bheestie, or water-carrier, and a dhobie, or washerman, and a camel-driver, who had two camels in charge. The grass-cutter sallies out at early daylight, provided with an instrument not unlike a bricklayer's trowel in shape, though one edge is very sharp, with which he scrapes up the grass close to the earth; and it is marvellous what a quantity he will collect from ground as brown and burnt-up, and apparently as innocent of any herbage as the bare palm of one's hand.

"The grass which the horses prefer, and, indeed, which is best for keeping them in condition, is very dry, short, and crispy, almost resembling moss, which he shaves off the ground, roots and all. Should the grass-cutter bring any of a coarser or longer description, of any with the slightest appearance of greenness, the syce—who would not himself cut a blade of grass for your horse were it starving—would most certainly reject it, and send the grass-cutter for more, and very likely give him a good licking in the bargain.

"There certainly is a good deal of club-law among the natives; and every one of them thinks he has a right way to *wop* any other who is the least beneath him in caste, situation, or service . . . All of these servants are not so serious an expense as it might be thought, for their wages vary from twelve to four rupees a month, for which they have to feed and clothe themselves. I found that my nine servants and three horses did not cost me more than one fine young gentleman, who did me the honour to call himself my groom and valet, and one horse did in England.

"Besides my horses and camels, I had a goat and half a dozen fowls, which gave me a plentiful supply of milk and eggs; it was a curious fact, that these beasts and birds always knew their own tents and belongings, and never strayed to any one else's domains, nor did other people's, and some had pigeons besides the fowls and goats; but they always kept to their own master's tents. The hens were very particular when and where they chose to lay their eggs. Sir William Peel had one which selected a corner of his tent, behind a particular portmanteau, and used to produce its daily *ovation* soon after the march was over and the tent pitched, but never would do so until the portmanteau was placed in the proper corner . . .

"The servants are generally of different castes, and will neither cook nor eat together; nor indeed will they let one another, still less their masters, approach their cooking-places. One day, while my syce was cooking his dinner, one of the officers took a bit of burning wood from the fire to light his cigar; of course the dinner was defiled, much to the grief of the syce, and to the benefit of the Matey, who, being the lowest of the low, eats after anybody, and, I believe, after everything, and who was soon demolishing the savoury currie which the indignant syce turned over to him.

"Their kitchen and *batterie de cuisine* are very simple; they scoop out a hole in the ground, about eighteen inches long by twelve broad, three sides of which they surround with a little mud wall about six inches high, in this they make a little fire with a few chips and two or three bits of dried cow-dung, which is much used for fuel in India; around this fireplace they sweep a space of about five feet across, which they keep clear, and which forms a sanctuary which no one not of their own caste can pass without defiling the victuals; two or three lotahs, or metal pots, are their cooking utensils, and with these small means it is astonishing what good things they will produce.

"In addition to the servants, &c., belonging to the officers and regiments, there are ten dhoolies [covered cots on litters, carried by two or four men] attached to each hundred men; each dhoolie having five (four and a spare one) bearers, so that a regiment has from four to five hundred of these people with it. Also, the field-hospital of the force has a small army of dhoolies and dhoolie-bearers. And moreover, and above all these, there is the commissariat, who have to carry provisions and necessaries innumerable for the forces, and whose beasts, servants, &c. &c., nearly double the 'impedimenta' of the army; yet it must be said of it that it is the most wonderfully organized department; and it had only to appear in Orders that such a division was to march to-morrow at daylight with a month's (or whatever time might be stated) provisions, and by the time denoted every camel, elephant, or bullock-wagon would be in its place ready for the march—a state of perfection seldom attained by the commissariat of any country."

If life in the field had its attractions, life in the cantonments was, in the words of one historian, "trivial and silly."[16] For years, and especially in the period marked by men like the Lawrences and other innovative civil administrators, it was the ambition of many young military men to get a staff appointment with one of these leaders, which would be, incidentally, a better-paid post. It might be a job as a political assistant or perhaps a staff appointment back at headquarters. This drain of manpower had heightened, and many top-rated men were lost to the regiment for good.

For those remaining, there was little opportunity for professional advancement; seniority ruled. There was an opportunity for a small pay differential if one could pass an examination in Hindustani. But George Cracklow, for one, had to force himself to study in the stultifying, enervating climate: "I will have another try at the Hindoostanee, though anything more distasteful to me could hardly be. The next examination will be in July. It is rather a bad time for study during the whole of the hot weather but the longer it is put off the worse it becomes. My own difficulty is the writing. I am a capital hand at the vernacular and I dare say shall manage the business easily enough if I can only make up my mind to stick to it."

Those who stayed with the line troops felt that they were mediocrities. Pay was low, promotion agonizingly slow. Leave policies were unauspicious, opportunities for return on home leave to England few and far between. Perhaps worst of all was the very tedium and boredom so characteristic of garrison life in that period.

A contemporary writer put this malaise well: "The moral effects of the Indian climate are far more dangerous than the physical. We place the half-educated lad with perhaps but very imperfectly developed ideas of religion, probably with no experience in himself of the virtue of self-denial, in a position where to be chaste and temperate requires a struggle which might well appall a member of a religious brotherhood earnest in attempts to subdue the frailities of human nature. It is impossible altogether to avoid this, . . . to mitigate the force of the temptation to immorality to which the soldier in India is exposed. The long tedious hours of the Indian summer day, which must be spent indoors [because of the heat], are often wearisome enough to the man of intellect and cultivated taste. Even with the resources of music and painting in addition to those of literature and society, the time often hangs heavily indeed upon the educated though unemployed man; what must it be to the soldier in a crowded barrack, who has no resource but to lie on his bed and gaze on the barren, ugly, white-washed walls or keep up a mo-notonous conversation with his comrade—monotonous from the absence of any topic of interest, or change of scene, or intervals of solitude to invigorate the mind by thought?"

The writer goes on just as the honorable chairman had done at Addiscombe. The first step is to "the pipe and the strongest Cav-endish tobacco," and "from incessant smoking comes incessant thirst and this leads to drinking." Resort is had to the canteen, but "the allowance procurable there is limited and the shops of the spirit-dealers in the bazaar who surreptitiously supply the Euro-pean soldiers with the most pernicious substitute for rum and gin, is the next place visited; and failing these, the general shops always have on hand a large stock of what is called eau-de-cologne, which is sold at three or four shillings a dozen and in reality is nothing but gin put in old eau-de-cologne bottles slightly scented with some perfume." This finally leads to "the indulgence of those pas-sions which a life of idleness and vacuity of mind is peculiarly cal-culated to encourage. The ravages of disease upon the constitution of the soldier in India from this cause are fearful to contemplate."[17]

Heavy drinking often led to abuse of servants. Beatings were common, and officers generally could inflict them with impunity (though it is interesting that as early as 1809 an officer whose butler had quit without warning was chastised for such an action: "I took him into a room and gave him a thorough horsewhipping for which I have been in danger of coming before the Judges for con-tempt of the petty court. I have been obliged to buy the rascal off with 150 days—and then called butcher & a breaker of compacts with the petty court in the bargain—a murrain go with it all!").

Discipline within the armies was also difficult to maintain in such an environment; stern and often brutal measures were resorted to in order to keep the lines taut. Flogging was widespread. At one time unlimited lashes had been widely allowed, but a ruling in 1832 restricted a district or general courtmartial to three hundred lashes, and the number was further constrained to fifty in 1850. This harsh penalty was more often used against British enlisted men than Indian. "Hardly anyone thought British soldiers could be managed without it; it was needed to keep down drunkenness, insubordination and theft." The Indian troops were less often flogged, for this punishment carried for them a penalty of degradation and disgrace that the British soldier did not feel.

Indeed, flogging seemed only the natural corollary to the endemic "birching" that was one of the cornerstones of English public school self-government. Bullying and ragging were ways of life in the English public school. John Chandos, in his fascinating book *Boys Together: English Public Schools, 1800–1864*, comments: "What today would be accounted grievous bodily harm, or worse, abounded. Little short of death seems to have been taken much notice of, and not always that." Hazing, exquisite in form in the public school in this period, was seen as part and parcel of a pattern of self-government by the students in these schools, a pattern that created men who were "resourceful and adaptable, calm under pressure, and practical in judgment." Much depended upon the quality of leadership among the senior class. If the captain of a dormitory, the student leader, was himself a bully, the pattern became endemic. Sometimes it was the other way: a strong captain would protect against the excesses. At Rugby in 1840, for example, one particular house had the worst reputation for bullying and general demoralization but was "saved and restored to order," wrote Chandos, "by the Draconian rule of a very strong captain of the house called Hodson who later carried his methods to a dramatic climax in India." Hodson did become a hero (controversial, though) in the mutiny and in the process became a striking role model for young lieutenants like our four. We will have reference to this "dramatic climax" later in the book.

With all of the excesses, however, the public school discipline system was still looked upon as efficacious. A typical view was expressed by Sir James Fitzjames Stephen, reviewing the just-published *Tom Brown's Schooldays* in the *Edinburgh Review* in 1858. Stephen first declared that he was thankful to have left Eton and then went on: "We do not believe that any system was ever invented so real, so healthy and so bracing to the mind and body . . . the entire absence of any restraint or supervision, except during the hours actually passed at lessons [was] the best possible security against boys forming illusions about the life which lies beyond their own observation"; they have been "brought into contact from a very early age . . . with real men, real passions and real things."

Public school bullying was at least peer-to-peer; all came out of the public schools as "gentlemen." In the British army, though, the system became explicitly sanctioned and was superior-to-subordinate. Despite the widespread use of flogging in the army, by the early 1850s, at the time of our four lieutenants' muster, it had begun to come under considerable attack as counterproductive. Fred Roberts was witness to an instance shortly after he arrived in the Punjab, and his comments captured the feelings of many: "The parade to which I refer was ordered for the punishment of two men who had been sentenced to fifty lashes each for selling their kits . . . They were fine, handsome young Horse Artillerymen, and it was hateful to see them thus treated. Besides, one felt it was productive of harm rather than good, for it tended to destroy the man's self respect, and to make them completely reckless."[18]

Army life was often doubly lonely because of the lack of female companionship, and especially so in the imperial India of the nineteenth century. Indeed, at the beginning of the century being married was the exception for anyone below the rank of major. In the earlier days of the British in India, open cohabitation with Indian women was not uncommon. By the 1830s the trip back and forth to England was less arduous, and more Englishwomen made the trip, many of them single and looking for matrimonial prizes (these latter were called the "Fishing Fleet"; those who later journeyed back to England without husband or fiancé were known as "Returned Empties"). It did not take the English gentlewomen long to cast opprobrium on the liaisons of their Englishmen and "native" women. In a fascinating little pamphlet written in 1857, an anonymous Bengal artilleryman decried those who lamented the old days of cohabitation and said of the English: "No people on earth can better distinguish the gentleman from the sham." Not a gentleman—one of the most severe accusations a Victorian could make!

Despite the increasing numbers of women out to visit in the cantonments and hill stations, it remained most difficult for the younger officers to contemplate an actual marriage (all four of our young lieutenants were single). In truth, the number of married men was by regulation limited to around 12 percent during this period, though by the midpoint in the nineteenth century John Lawrence, for one, became a warm advocate of a plan allowing an increase. The reasons for the low marriage rate were partly logistic—housing was minimal and rude—and partly sanitary. The death toll on families was inordinately high through all of the 1800s, for the soldiers themselves and especially for their wives and children. Some health hazard was undoubtedly inevitable; as one writer put it, "It is well to face the facts bravely, and admit that some penalty, in the shape of sickness and mortality, must be paid as the price of tropical possessions."

An additional complication, an intractable one unless one had family money, was the low pay of the young officers. George Cracklow complained to his mother in early 1857: "The fact is I have been living as cheaply as possible in order to afford myself the camera and a new concertina that I have just bought. You say in your letter you believe I can take my furlough in two years more. This is not the case as the Directors have again altered the regulations. At present it does not appear to me to be a matter of much import as I have saved no money nor do I see any chance of ever doing so. I can just live on my pay, but can't save a pile. In fact, I consider I have done very well not to be very much in debt, as most of my contemporaries are. As for going home, at present it appears perfectly impossible as I can never have enough money to pay my passage home and out again and it would be of no use going home unless I had enough to live as comfortably. The wretched 120 a year they give us when in England would be hardly sufficient to keep soul and body together." (Apparently it was hard to hide these debts, typically incurred in expenditures for liquor and gambling. Cracklow commented in 1854 about a friend who had become engaged: "He must be rather a bad bet, as he is by all accounts very much in debt and has nothing but his pay.")

For these, and probably other reasons, Cracklow seemed leery of the notion that he himself might marry: "I don't intend getting married until I can afford it. Such misery as I see among ¾ of the married people in this country is a caution not to be lost. However, my resolutions are not likely to be put to the test as I am perfect proof against the charms of the antiquated spinsters of this station." Lang, as we shall see, was *not* perfect proof against the charms of the "spinsters" of his station—or at least one of them.

Quarters were a perennial issue—there simply were not enough of good quality to go around. Cracklow's letter continues: ". . . heard from that old brute Brind and he won't let me have the quarters I had applied for. I have been talking to old Gaitskell about how at dinner and I think he is going to let me have one of the spare rooms in the mess. He is a very kind old fellow and does his best to oblige me. We are just sitting after dinner at mess and he is puffing away on his hookah. He's the only man in the station who smokes one, which is rather a blessing, as it's a most horribly sucking thing. I had a long talk with him the other day. He said he knew my father in England before he came to this country."

The historian Philip Woodruff further describes this housing: "The bungalow [is] shared by four subalterns near the mess . . . Here everything is severely functional; in the central room, a keep of the fortress, there are half-a-dozen hammock-like chairs with arm-pieces prolonged so that the weary legs can be propped up on them as the weary body reclines; there is an attachment screwed on to the right-arm piece which swings out to hold a glass. Not much else, unless perhaps a tiger-skin, a few panther skins on the floor, a few horns on the wall, a rack of hog-spears. In the bedroom, the bed is a wooden frame on four legs, with no headboard or footboard, strung with coarse tape. There is no mattress, but a cool reed mat to lie on; a brass bowl on three bamboos, a metal uniform case and a wooden chest bound with metal, a folding chair, a straw chair, a small mirror—that is the bedroom furniture. No pictures, no curtains, no drawers, bare whitewashed walls; a striped cotton mat on the brick floor. It is not the thing for a young man to find money for comfort or decoration; anything he has should be spent on horses, a gun or a rifle."[19]

Trivia, humdrum. This was the stuff of cantonment life in the early 1850s. Sialkot, Cracklow's small outpost, sixty miles toward the mountains from Lahore, was probably the least lively of the four posts of our quartet. This was a new cantonment, first opened in 1850. Life here had been quiet during these first years, and the records are filled with the minutiae of a mundane and uneventful life; the Reverend Mr. Sloggett, the chaplain at Wuzeerabad, attempted to get a new church built at Sialkot (in 1850 he petitioned the governor-general to give him a quantity of Sikh iron, "consisting of useless musket barrels and damaged sword blades," for the roof of the church); a letter came forward in 1851 from Surgeon MacKinnon to collect a bill from John Inglis (who was going on sick leave to England) for Rs 20/3 to pay for quinine previously obtained for "his private use"; in 1853 there was a reduction of Rs 80 in the rent-roll of the district and a refund of Rs 240 "on account of a well released to Sirdar Shumsher Sing, Sindhanwalla." By 1854 the church was in being; the chaplain pressed again for further government contributions, to hang punkahs (fans) from the ceiling. The government paid again, "but desires to intimate that no further contribution will be made by Government on account of the Sialkot Church." Even this was not final: in early 1857 the government was pressed to contribute Rs 150 for a communion plate. In 1853 the north and south boundaries of the cantonment were extended; the cultivators were getting "as close as 380 yards" at one point, and the Special Medical Commission saw this encroachment as a threat "with reference to the health of the troops." The land was purchased, and the cantonment extended. Likewise, additional lands were taken in these years for roads, for bridges, and for a wide range of minor physical improvements for the cantonment itself.[20]

In contrast, the stations of Fred Roberts and Arthur Lang were larger and, relatively speaking, more lively. Roberts was at Peshawar, the most northwest of the major outposts in the north (just over the line from Afghanistan). The Peshawar cantonment had been laid out by Sir Colin Campbell, who had commanded there when the place was first occupied by the British in 1849. It was not the ideal layout: Campbell had crowded everyone, European and native troops alike, into as small a place as possible so that the station could be more easily protected from the raids of the infamous Afridis and other robber tribes, who inhabited the neighboring mountains. Roberts commented, "From this point of view alone was Sir Colin's action excusable; but the result of this overcrowding was what it always is, especially in a tropical climate like that of India, and for long years Peshawar was a name of terror to the English soldier from its proverbial unhealthiness." Despite these disadvantages, Roberts reported that he was very happy there: "There was a good deal of excitement and adventure . . . the mess was a good one, and . . . as nice a set of fellows as were to be found in the army."

Lahore, Lang's post, was about halfway between Peshawar and Delhi, again a large post in a large town. Here there was a rather more substantial social life; Lang reported of an evening dance at a Christmastime party in 1856: "We went rather fashionably late . . . English canvass tightly stretched & rubbed with waxed candles formed the dancing floor and was very strong and slippery. Every lady in Meean Meer [the cantonment name] seemed there, and several made their debut, Miss Knolles, Miss Hepburn, Miss Cautley & c. Everybody seemed to enjoy themselves & kept it up till late. I danced very little, only with three or four ladies. There was a grand supper." A week later a new party captured Lang: "After dinner we drove over to the 81st Mess and at about 9:30 the ball began and was kept up with great spirit until about 4. The floor was excellent and the playing very good—2 bands. It was not nearly so warm as I'd expected as a cool breeze blew in and the weather was stormy. We were in white trousers. The Misses Smith were a great acquisition and danced very well. Although so many ladies were absent the ball went off capitally." Lang was preoccupied, though, with his work. He reported in April of 1857: "I wrote officially today to be made pucka [permanent] Executive of the Lahore Division. I hope that they will appreciate my claims. I have officiated here for upwards of eight months. That is a long spell at one station for such a wandering party. In that time I have never been ten miles out of Cantonments."

Of Thomas Watson's life in his initial station, Meerut, we literally know nothing. The first letters we have about this most elusive of the four lieutenants come from his mother, in early 1857. She was living at Umballa and just ready to leave for Simla, one of the famous British hill stations some 150 miles north of Delhi, in the foothills of the Himalayas. Watson, upon promotion to lieutenant in early 1856, had been reassigned to Sialkot, joining Cracklow in that small outpost. His mother's smothering protectiveness comes through loudly in our first contact with the Watson family: "You never seem out of my thoughts. *Do, I entreat* you, take great care of your health. I *fear* it will greatly suffer if you do not take a regular good tiffin [luncheon] . . . a long fast & a heavy meal at night are *so bad*—if once a person gets dyspepsia, like dear George, it is hard work to get well of it & do devote *regular hours* in the day to study—read the English poets."

We have no direct evidence of Watson's feelings toward Sialkot, though strong circumstantial evidence suggests that he did not like it, his mother writing in January 1857, "Your last letters do not look as if they have been opened but still I am anxious at your writing so freely your thoughts about your Regt." These are scraps, but by the end of this year, 1857, we will know a great deal more about Thomas Watson and his mother.

Given the sameness of life in the cantonments, the occasional leave was welcomed with delight. These were generally of three to four months in duration (though Roberts got six), long enough to take a substantial trip. Rather than heading back to the more civilized regions around Delhi, both Roberts and Cracklow chose to take their trips up into the high Himalayas, in combination hunting and mountain-climbing safaris. Roberts took his leave in April 1854, traveling straight toward the mountains to the tiny tribal town of Khagan, "almost buried in snow." Roberts described it: "The scenery was magnificent, and became every moment more wonderful as we slowly climbed the steep ascent in front of us; range after range the snow-capped mountains disclosed themselves to our view, rising higher and higher into the air, until at last, towering above all, Nanga Parbat in all her spotless beauty was revealed to our astonished and delighted gaze . . . we could not get beyond Khagan. Our coolies refused to go further, alleging as their reasons the danger to be dreaded from avalanches in that month; but I suspect that fear of hostility from the tribes farther North had more to do with their reluctance to proceed."

Roberts and his companion, another lieutenant, stayed in Khagan a number of days trying to find and shoot the elusive ibex but never saw one. After his return, Roberts became more and more debilitated by a chronic fever he had contracted after his return, one he called "Peshawar fever," and was given an eight months' leave on medical certificate. Again he took a long hike, this time in more felicitous terrain, and spent a number of weeks in the beautiful Vale of Kashmir.

Cracklow also attacked the high Himalayas, on two separate trips. The first, in 1854, was generally successful, though he had difficulty at several points with high floodwaters. In describing one case, he was unwittingly giving us an early example of what one might call his pigheadedness (or, perhaps, just British schoolboy pluck): "At this place they told me it was impossible for me to go on the road, for nearly the whole distance was under water and by this time it was quite dark. However, I was determined to get in if it could possibly be done and set off. Of course, I lost my way, but at last managed to get in after wandering for 5 hours with the water up to my saddle girth and having had to swim 2 nullahs, in which the water was running like a millstream. My swimming did me good service. The horse took the first of these places very well and as it had been raining the whole day long and I had been wet through since six in the morning it did not much matter, the getting of a fresh wetting. But at the second he got frightened and tried to turn back and exhausted himself in struggling instead of swimming straight on. At last I found that he could do nothing with my weight on his back so I slipped off and had a pretty tough swim for it, as my clothes, a great thick coat and trousers encumbered me very much. After being carried down a good way I got over and managed to catch the horse and be in by 11 o'clock that night and hence never felt the slightest ill effects from my wetting."

On his second trip illness intruded: "We started in the first week of last month and got on very well for about 20 marches, when I got a bad attack of rheumatism brought on by marching day after day in the snow and was obliged to halt. It came on first in the soles of my feet, then got into my ankle joint—then to my knees and ultimately into my back. I expected to have got well in a few days and to have been able to go on but it became worse day after day until I was unable to move. To make matters worse a bad attack of diarrhea came on and altogether I became rather seriously ill. I was lying at a miserable little Tartar village called Laina Yarru. Had some medicine but did not really know how to use it and made myself rather worse than better by swallowing a lot of opium pills which nearly put an end to me. After lying there 9 days the diarrhea ceased and Manderson (my chum) then got a machine rigged up on which I could be carried. The road is not a very good one, just room for one man to pass another and leads up and down and along the sides of the most tremendous hill along the most horrible looking precipices and over a wild desolate nearly uninhabited country. I was at the mercy of 8 wild Tartar coolies who seemed to take delight in swinging me about and shaking me till I howled with pain. Of course I could not make them understand a word I said and they had it all their own way, seeming to think that the only thing to be done was to get over the mountains as quickly as possible. We came double marches and arrived here quite clear of the heat but very pulled down."

Later in this letter Cracklow expanded on his hunting, before the onslaught of his illness: "We had capital shooting all along. Until I got ill I got my own share. 4 large red deers and 4 cubs. 3 of the large red stags called in these parts the Bara Singal (from their twelve tiered horns) and several other smaller animals and since my return I have shot 3 very large black bears but which are thought very little of as they are so common over the whole area. This is even a very small bag in comparison with what most of the fellows up here have made . . . It is rather better than I expected, having a companion for the shooting, as the niggras are not to be depended upon."[21]

We must pause in the midst of this spectacular and exciting trip, for George Cracklow has telegraphed his view of the native by the use of a word common in the usage of a great many English at that time—"niggra." Despite much evidence attesting to the mutual respect between the European and the Sepoy, there is constant, telling evidence that this relationship was universally couched by the English in terms of their racial superiority to the Sepoy. S. N. Sen, in his recent book *Eighteen Fifty-seven*, quotes an anonymous resident of northwest India as saying: "The Sepoy is esteemed an inferior creature. He is sworn at. He is treated roughly. He is spoken of as a 'nigger.' He is addressed as a 'suar' or pig, an epithet most opprobrious to a respectable Native, especially the Mussalman [Muslim] and which cuts him to the quick." A British captain, J. G. Medley, reiterates the same theme in a book written in 1858, during the mutiny: "Subalterns, fresh from school, often called natives 'niggers,' and addressed the *argumentum ad hominem* rather oftener than was, perhaps, needful." In his highly evocative book *Curry and Rice*, written in 1856, George R. Atkinson lampoons the whole establishment in "Our Station," in the process again putting the "natives" in their place. He describes one of the English judges there as "so desperately absorbed with his official duties that we see but little of him . . . niggers—no, ten thousand pardons, not niggers, I mean natives—sons of the soil—Orientals—Asiatics—are his source of happiness."[22]

Thus the rule was that of superiority, a superiority of race, position, knowledge, gentility—all of those English virtues of the Victorian era. The Asian was the bête noire of the Englishman, and pervasive racism the order of the day. This was clearly George Cracklow's view, and his letters reiterate this attitude toward the native over and over again (indeed, in a letter of 1854 he called the Indian people "animals"). With the full panoply of their feelings of superiority girding them about as a cloak, it is little wonder that the British in India found the shattering of this complacent superiority during the mutiny so traumatic in effect.

*   *   *

The next chapter will chronicle an irrevocable change in British India—the mutiny of 1857. A few brief comments about the pre-1857 British military institution itself and the mind-set of our four lieutenants (and the mother) seem now in order.

In that one-hundred-year span between the Battle of Plassey in 1757 and the year 1857 the British military in India had fought many campaigns, most of them successful, a few disastrous. Before the turn of the century there were the wars in the south against Hyder Ali and his son Tippoo Sahib (the "Tiger of Mysore"); in the nineteenth century there were campaigns against the Marathas, the successful encirclement of the Pindaries in 1816, and the stupid war against Afghanistan that culminated in early 1842 in a ghastly retreat and slaughter of the British forces. There also had been many expeditions to lands near India—Malaya, Persia, China, Burma. In these wars the British soldier fought with ferocity and intelligence that sometimes was not matched by similarly astute leadership from the generals. Still, the British army in India was judged a first-rate fighting force, the envy of most of the nations of the world.

Yet there were serious weaknesses, too. Some stemmed from the inherent difficulty of recruiting and maintaining a colonial force almost halfway around the world from Britain. In the first half of the nineteenth century, a number of the armies on the European continent grew rapidly, not only in size but in professionalism, until they were cohesive and effectively administered. Not so with the Victorian army of England. It still remained a heterogeneous set of individual units—almost fiefdoms—led by general officers who often claimed their posts by heredity right and/or purchase rather than professional qualification. Indeed, the army merely mirrored the class-bound society of Victorian England. An overwhelming percentage of the generals came from the aristocracy and the landed gentry. Economic interests of both these groups often led to a complex conflict-of-interest pattern of behavior that mixed military and personal concerns.

The dry rot in the younger officer ranks was alleged to be equally widespread. One of the broadsides written in the midst of the mutiny railed that "we see British officers of these noble regiments generally reduced to a few youths, learning their profession from the very men they are sent to command and overawe; spending their time in amusements, or, worse, in idleness."[23] In these junior ranks there was at least more of a mixture of the privileged and the middle class. Different camps held strong opinions about whether these young men should be drawn from the military academies (Sandhurst, Woolrich, Chatham, Addiscombe) or whether they should come from the public schools. The bias toward the latter was strong. The desired qualities were those of general education: "character" and those indefinable elements that combined to make up the English "gentleman." It was what came to be known as the "amateur ideal," a "notion," wrote Gwyn Harries-Jenkins in his book *The Army in Victorian Society,* "that manners, signifying virtue, and classical culture, signifying a well-turned mind, were better credentials for leadership than any amount of expert practical training."[24]

This conclusion drives us back again to looking at the English public school as a profound influence on the Victorian army. When a royal commission was set up in 1861 to investigate the key public schools (what came to be known as the Clarendon Commission), the revelations about fagging and ragging, and the generally primitive behaviors they taught, were laid on the record. Yet, surprisingly, the public schools came out of this three-year investigation with all those implicit values of the English gentleman reinforced once more. If some of the young officers in the British army had the profound experience of public school and others did not, there must have been powerful psychological schisms bred of the bimodal pattern. We will see much of this in studying the four lieutenants. Roberts had a year at Eton, Lang was a graduate of Rugby. While neither was of the aristocracy, there is no doubt that both were in the upper classes; one father, it will be remembered, was prominent in the military, the other a respected civil servant. Lieutenants Watson and Cracklow, on the other hand, did not have benefit of one of these inner-five prestige grammar schools (Winchester, Eton, Westminster, Harrow, and Rugby). They had come through preparatory schools of much more modest stature.

Juxtaposed against the public schools in the public's mind were the military academies, and the latter almost always came off second best. The results of the Crimean War had exacerbated the critics' attacks—there had been all too many less-than-admirable decisions by the military in that controversial war. In this period *Punch* and other media accused the services of "military jocularity" and identified them with authoritarianism, inhumanity, coercion, and rampant social conservativism. The discipline and the military training in the academies—Sandhurst, Woolrich, Chatham, and Addiscombe—were seen as leading not to heightened professionalism but to narrow parochialism. Inasmuch as they were closed communities, the necessary "character" simply could not be achieved in them (so said the critics). The chain of logic then linked some of the slippage in the Crimean experience to these manifestations. There is some inconsistency in this argument, inasmuch as several of the poor decisions there were made by generals with little professional military training. Still, the view persisted throughout the nineteenth century that the military was not up to its task because it was too authoritarian and narrow.

In light of these expressed concerns, we return once again to the four lieutenants. Three of these, as noted, were professionally trained at Addiscombe; and the fourth, Watson, was not only not an inner-five grammar school graduate but did not attend Addiscombe, either. As we learn much more about these four young men in succeeding chapters, we are going to be nagged by a number of half-answered questions and half-seen glimmerings about their personalities. Their educational underpinnings will be key concerns for us.

There are also special remarks that must be appended about the Victorian army in its particular venue of India. The distance from England, the pernicious climate, the long, boring assignments broken only every ten years or so by a visit back to England—all these combined to make India a more complex assignment than just about any of the others in the British armed forces. Yet there was a widespread belief among critics of the British military establishment that the forces in India lived a sybaritic life. Cited by these skeptics were the patterns of large stables of horses, expensive messes, long leaves to visit hill stations, great big-game shooting excursions, and so on. The vast horde of servants served only to confirm some of these suspicions. The young British officer, on the other hand, felt that he was underpaid and overworked and treated to an all-too-spartan single-sex life.

As the year 1857 approached, further complications had surfaced. The advent of more and more Englishwomen in India in the period from about 1830 on tightened the social mores into that special structure we now call "Victorianism." The pervasive racism of the British colonialists became more deeply embedded. While Victorian writers on race did frequently make a distinction between the dusky Indian and the black Negro, with the former in a higher position on the race ladder, there was still a strongly held stereotype about the savage sexual lusts of the nonwhite person. In Jamaica, for example, there seemed to be an overt fear of black lust toward white women. The Jamaican insurrection in 1865 reinforced this belief and fear. In pre-mutiny India there were only occasional undertones of any sexual threat as explicit as this.[25]

What was more often seen was treatment of the Indian as inferior and unintelligent and, especially, pagan. This latter was perhaps the dominant theme. British Christianity was very messianic in the first half of the nineteenth century, particularly attacking the Hindu and Muslim beliefs in India, religions with profoundly held value systems that had been in place for many hundreds of years. The caste system in India was particularly abhorred by many of the liberals in England; they were especially aghast at the Hindu practice of suttee, in which a widow would immolate herself on her husband's funeral pyre.

A missionary letter back to England in 1822 put this intolerance bluntly: "We would have liked to show you . . . the thousands of his subjects who, emancipated from the bondage of Satan, were prostrating themselves before the same throne of grace as that at which British Christians bow . . . But ah! The Crescent of the Eastern Imposter still flies over Hindostan in darkness grosser than that which sometimes obscures the luminary which it is intended to

represent. Braminical flames from the widow's pile or from nocturnal ceremonies produce in moral India a volcanic glare destructive
to all within its reach, appalling to every spectator & extending to
the horizon a brown gloom . . . India is in moral night . . . superstition, like the Angel of Death, still spreads her raven wings over
this immense territory . . . But we continue our exertions knowing
that like the disciples of Jerusalem we are required to wait for the
descent of the Holy Spirit, when superstition with rapid flight shall
escape from the abodes of men & the crescent shall be eclipsed."[26]

Given these rigid values, widely held by the British in India, the
potential for tension within the British military forces there is apparent. On the one hand, the officers and British noncommissioned
officers led their troops with a rigidity and harsh discipline that
brought both strong loyalties among the enlisted men and much
antipathy. Many of these enlisted men were in the native regiments,
that is, were Indians reporting to British—the Indian conquered
reporting to the white conquerors. Indian soldiers, especially those
from the Sikh nation and the Gurkhas (the latter mostly from Nepal), have been legendary throughout the history of the subcontinent. Most British officers in 1857 swore by their Indian troops and
felt them to be loyal to the extreme and willing to take any orders.
There was disbelief among most commanders that *their own* troops
would ever mutiny. Yet there had been mutinies from time to time
in the first half of the nineteenth century, before the 1857 debacle.

On the other hand, there were features about the British rule
that rubbed sensibilities raw in the Indian communities. Most profound was the widely held and accurate belief that the British were
out to eliminate all other religions except Christianity. At the start
of the next chapter we will elaborate on one of the most seemingly
pernicious of all of these proselytizing efforts, namely, the use of
the new Enfield rifle and its infamous paper cartridge, coated with,
according to the Hindu, cow fat, and according to the Muslim, pig
fat. This was the supposed powder keg of the mutiny. Yet as we
have seen, there were a host of other tensions between the Indian
and the British communities, of such profound import as to belie
any belief that the British and the Indian people were in any sense
one. The British military in India exemplified, perhaps as no other
group, these anomalies.

Chapter 3
Devil's Wind
The Indian Mutiny Begins

It was May 10, 1857, when "the wind that blew" started down from Meerut, burst through Delhi, and swept on through Rohilkhand and Oudh, engulfing in the process Lucknow and Cawnpore. Scarcely any area of northern and central India lying along the route of the Grand Trunk Road, stretching from Peshawar far up in Kashmir to Calcutta in the east, was not under threat of attack, siege, massacre, atrocity.

What had caused this uprising? A popularly held belief put much weight on the decision of the British to replace the hoary "Brown Bess" with the Enfield rifle. Militarily, the Enfield was certainly an excellent choice; its longer range and infinitely greater accuracy had served England well in the Crimean War just concluded in 1856. The rifle required a greased cartridge, to be bitten at the end of its paper covering by the rifleman himself before insertion into the gun barrel. The original cartridges came from England, but fresh batches began to be manufactured at Dum Dum cantonment, near Calcutta. Things went well for the new piece of ordnance until, suddenly, a rumor surfaced and spread like wildfire: the grease contained animal fat from a pig and/or a cow. If it was the former, it would be held unclean by the Muslim Sepoys. If the latter it involved an animal sacred to the Hindu, and allowing any part of the animal into one's body was ritual defilement. Loss of caste automatically brought ostracization from family and friends.

In truth, the British command was not certain itself just what the ingredients of the grease were; the inspector-general of ordnance and magazines at Ft. William wrote on January 29, 1857: "As soon as I heard of objections . . . I enquired at the arsenal as to the nature of the composition that had been used, and found it was precisely that which the instructions received from the Court of Directors directed to be used—viz., a mixture of tallow and bees-wax. No extraordinary precaution seems to have been taken to ensure the absence of any objectionable fat . . . it is certainly to be regretted that the ammunition was not prepared expressly without any grease at all, but the subject did not occur to me."[1]

Whatever was truth, the rumor was greeted with horror by most of the Sepoy troops, and soon increasing numbers refused to use the rifle. There were scattered outbreaks of mutiny beginning in January of 1857, amid the rumors of Dum Dum's greased cartridges, and it seemed wise to take the strong measure of disbanding several native regiments. Still, there was no real belief that "Jack" Sepoy would ever openly revolt.

Meerut changed all of this, altering India forever. In late April, when the Native Cavalry had refused to use the greased cartridges, a native courtmartial had quickly handed out long sentences of imprisonment. On May 9, the British divisional commander sternly ordered the eighty-five ringleaders shackled in leg-irons and marched down the lines of the remaining troops under a broiling sun. The effect on the rest of the native troops was one of outrage and stunned horror. The next day they broke into open revolt, seized the jail, and freed the eight-five men—and then stepped over the line of no return by murdering a number of British officers and their families.

The shock of open revolt was so great that the remaining British on the post were momentarily immobilized, and the mutineers escaped the city. Incredulous telegrams back and forth among the garrisons in the north gave the rebels additional lead time (the presence of the telegraph connecting the garrisons was an immeasurable help to the British in the subsequent hostilities). It seemed inconceivable that the rebels could have gone very far in the intense May Indian sun. But the startled British soon realized that the mutineers had unbelievably force-marched straight on to Delhi, formerly the great capital of the Mogul Empire and still the home of its king, Bahadur Shah (presumably under the short tether of the British). Tether or not, although the king made a feeble, frightened

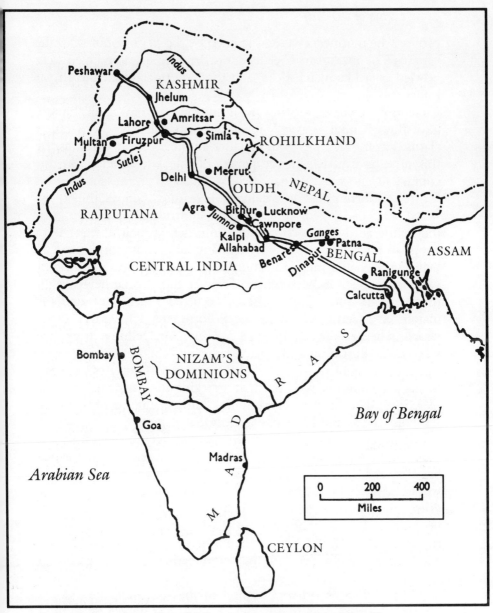

India theaters of war. (Parallel lines indicate Grand Trunk Road.)

protest, the mutineers were welcomed by the city's populace as the vanguard of liberation. The city's few British officers and men were bowled over like matchsticks, and the king reestablished as titular leader.

George Cracklow, writing his mother eleven days later, bluntly gave the essential facts: "I am afraid you will have been rather alarmed at not hearing from me after all the accounts you must by this time have had from the papers of the state of affairs in this country just now . . . We have been in rather an unpleasant position for the last fortnight. Those delightful creatures, Sepoys, the honest Jacks! in praise of whom sufficient could not be said have been mutinying all over the country and murdering their officers. I am happy to say we have not as yet had anything of the sort here . . . I believe they had arranged to murder us on the 9th by attacking us when assembled at mess, when of course they would have caught us unarmed. But a slight mistake occurred which frustrated the matter. At Meerut they were not as fortunate. They attacked the people when at Church and killed several. At Delhi we hear they killed every European in the place, ladies and children not excepted. They caught a Tartar—I am proud to say is an Officer of my regiment—Willoughby, who on their attacking the magazine at Delhi blew it up with his own hands killing himself and 300 of them. I'll send his wife a month's pay to a memorial to him."[2]

The fabled Delhi had indeed fallen completely to the mutineers; most of the remaining English civilians and Indian Christians had been hunted down and killed, with a few taking what they hoped would be refuge in the palace and others escaping out of town. The grim military message was partially true—the great arsenal had been claimed. Willoughby and eight others had heroically defended the bastion until hundreds of the mutineers swarmed over the walls and then lit the powder train that led directly into the magazine. A tremendous explosion ensued, killing five of the nine, with Willoughby and three others escaping in the confusion. Cracklow's information that Willoughby had perished was widely believed at that time: the British were taking a fearful pounding and needed a hero to bolster the sinking feeling among many that they were but a small band entirely surrounded by hordes of bloodthirsty mutineers bent on their death.

The exact facts were probably not important at that point—a live

Willoughby was scarcely less heroic. The explosion did take with it many dozens of the mutineers, but unfortunately for the British, the main sections of the arsenal remained intact. Three thousand barrels of powder fell into the mutineers' hands, enough to arm a major campaign.

When Delhi fell, it was not just a stunning military victory, a coup that left the British in a precarious position, but also a psychological triumph of immeasurable sustenance to the rebel cause. Whether or not there was at that point a widespread conspiracy, linking the myriad Indian kingdoms and protectorates under united rebel leaders, the capture of Delhi instantly converted a barracks revolt into a full-scale rebellion.

This was late spring, the height of the hot season, and the commander in chief of the army, Gen. George Anson, and his staff were comfortably ensconced at the hill station of Simla. The terrible news of Delhi came by telegraph as far as Umballa, but it was not until the following day that Anson was able to take some action. The governor-general, Lord Canning (Earl Charles John), and the civil authority were in Calcutta, a thousand miles away. Their return message to Anson was, essentially, "retake Delhi." When Anson arrived in Umballa on May 15, he began to gather forces to move toward Delhi. The situation was complicated by a pitiful lack of transport—after the Sikh War nine years earlier, most of the army transport had been disbanded under the assumption that the army would contract for civilian services. The Anson forces were short on medical supplies and many miles away from an arsenal, far to the north. Faced with these formidable obstacles, Anson began to move his troops down to Karnal, hoping to arrive there by the end of the month. On May 22, though, Anson succumbed to cholera, turning over his command to Sir Henry Barnard, a veteran of the Crimean War, just before his death. Barnard immediately ordered a march to Delhi, where he expected to join forces with a unit from Meerut under the command of Archdale Wilson.

The situation facing these commanders in that month of May 1857 was indeed grim. Throughout the North West Provinces the disturbances had spread fast. At Aligarh the 9th Native Infantry had mutinied and rushed off to join the rebels at Delhi. There was also a mutiny at Moradabad, where the native troops followed a pattern soon to become typical: they waited a few weeks to see if the British seemed to be losing and then mutinied in early June. At Shahjahanpur the Sepoys had attacked the church while divine service was going on, and there were many deaths. Mutinies at Bareilly, at Rohini, at Etawah, and a number of other stations in the provinces followed. Further west, in Rajputana, there were fewer British posts, yet several had serious outbreaks. The mutineers did not choose to fight at Nasirabad, but there were killings of British officers at Mhow. Other stations in these more out-of-the-way areas also had serious problems. Further east, in Oudh, the major establishments at Cawnpore and Lucknow both were under siege. Though some of the native troops had stayed firm at the start, increasing defections began to occur. Usually it was the mutineers that rose first, in the process encouraging the local toughs—the budmashes—to join (there were always disgruntled elements, ready to take advantage or to settle a grudge from some past action of a British civil or military authority). In a few spots civil rebellion preceded the mutiny, with British factories, missions, and business houses sacked, often to destroy the books of accounts under which the natives were financially beholden to the East India Company.

Now, for a moment, let us hold these broader forces and events in suspension and narrow our focus to one additional critically important area, the Punjab. This was the problem province before the mutiny, the home of the warlike Sikhs, annexed only in 1849. There were some sixty-thousand men cantoned at the various stations, from Umballa up to Peshawar. Something less than half of these were Europeans, Punjabis, and Sikhs. The British had finally conquered the Sikhs in the two wars (1845–1846 and 1848), using native troops that were predominantly high-caste Hindus from Oudh and further east—the "Purbiahs." The latter sneered at the Sikhs as lower caste because the Sikhs did not observe their minute rules about cleanliness and the ritual preparation of food. In turn, the Purbiahs were hated by the Sikhs. Further, in one of those curious turnabouts often seen in history, the British began to favor the Sikhs as their choice for soldiers. The latter were not only tall and manly, with real military bearing, but also were intensely loyal to the British. This mutual respect between British and Sikhs held throughout the mutiny. In the Punjab, though, the tension between the Sikhs and the Purbiahs was intense, adding to the already-present problems.

Our four young lieutenants all were stationed in the Punjab. Fred Roberts, at Peshawar, was the farthest up, just short of the Afghanistan border. George Cracklow and Thomas Watson, at Sialkot, were some 150 miles further south (but off the main trunk road about 40 miles). Arthur Lang was at the cantonment at Meean Meer, just outside the major city of Lahore. We have seen sharp differences among these four young men already, but how did they respond to the mutiny?

Cracklow's personal reactions, in his first mutiny letter to his mother on May 22, were strong: "The government appears to be fast asleep doing nothing but thinking of courtmartials instead of blowing these brutes away from the guns . . . In the meanwhile these people are running us madly all over the whole country . . . had a hard time of it marching all night and grilling in the sun all day, but will be amply repaid if we only get a rap at these niggers. I am in capital health and spirits, dearest mother and hope you will not fidget yourself about me."

Roberts's first mutiny letter, on May 14, reported the same events, though with a more dispassionate, organizationally directed thread: "Yesterday news came from Lahore that the Native Infantry had been disarmed. A Council of War was held here when it was decided to separate the Native Infantry here, sending them to different forts and outposts where they can't do much harm, and dispatching a force at once towards Jhelum . . . to assemble and act whenever occasion may require." Roberts, too, ventilated some personal judgments: "I am in high glee at the thoughts of service, but most sincerely wish it were in a better cause, and not against our own soldiers . . . The most decided measures and strenuous exertions will only save India now. We have some good men on this frontier—Edwardes, Nicholson, Cotton, Chamberlain, etc. Old Reed . . . has one good quality, namely: listening to reason, which is better than being obstinate, when ability is not combined . . . I would anticipate no very great calamity were every division of the army as well off for sensible heads as this one is, but some of our older officers are perfect children, quite unable to take care of themselves."[3]

Quite incongruously, the Peshawar post had just had a dance. Roberts reported it in this first letter to the family after the start of the mutiny: "We had a Grand Masons' ball the other evening—the very best party of the season. The W.M. [Roberts himself] proposed the ladies!! And no end of an eloquent speech."

Roberts seemed instinctly to sense the strategic situation in his next letter, in late May: "I have only time for a few lines just to tell you how jolly I am . . . horrible Blackguards the Sepoys are they not? The mutiny has not gained ground and it is, thank God, only amongst the soldiers. If the country were to rise, we should have to hold our own in different parts of the dominion . . . sacrificing all the tame stations." His own personal ambitions also consistently preoccupied him: "A large force under Chamberlain assembles at Wuzeerabad, of which I am going as *Quartermaster-General!* Hurrah!!! . . . Then I think Quartermaster-General's department is pretty certain!! Eh, My own darling mother."

The Meerut mutiny seemed less of a surprise to Lang than to Cracklow and Roberts. In early April he had reported on a disarming of the native troops in Calcutta and commented, "There really must be a severe example, for the disaffection seems spreading and the 'hoi polloi' imagine that govt. are afraid." Reporting on a murder of one of the officers at one of the stations a few days later, he commented once more, "A terrible example is really required." As to the disarming at Calcutta, he noted that the native troops there were "being awed" by the European regiments: "They were not so foolish as to attempt any sort of row, especially as General Hearsey is no timid trifler."

In mid-April, on the occasion of a visit by John Lawrence to Lahore, another mutiny at another outstation had been reported. Here Lang imputed a religious distinction to the unrest: "I wish they would cease to enlist Brahmins, and indeed Poorbyas at all more than they can help . . . raise Ghoorkas, Sikhs, Punjabees, Dogras, any men but regular Hindoos with their idiotic caste rules." That evening there was another dance at the cantonment, and it was "remarkably cool for this time of year. We had no punkahs and the dancing was kept up with as much energy as in the cold weather. Sir John Lawrence came for about a half-hour and looked very miserable." A few days later Herbert Edwardes, the commissioner of Peshawar, visited Lang's church, and Lang loosed a racist barb in his letter to his mother: "He looks like a Jew, I think, with his aquiline nose and beard—he does not look the great man he is."

When the news of Meerut came, on May 12, Lang wrote a long

letter to the family. The seriousness of what had happened was manifest to him: "I can't believe that the Anglo-Saxon is going to be turned out of India, but if feathers weight more on the scale, down it will go." The shocking news brought quick action by Lang's commander. "The Brigadier is going to disarm the Native troops tomorrow here! This is a fearfully responsible act. Tomorrow morning is to be a full parade, the Europeans and Artillery will be loaded as they were yesterday and who knows but that the three Native Infantry and the Cavalry Regiment won't fight? . . . All the officers are indignant and fully trust their regiments."

The European officers commanding native troops faced a special dilemma; they themselves had trained their troops, and it seemed inconceivable to most that their men would ever rebel against them personally. The next morning, the disarming began. First the brigadier addressed the troops. Lang reported: "He softsawdered, saying what splendid regiments they were, how he loved them, how he longed to win their further honour and to keep their name unsullied and so he was going to order them to show their loyalty in obeying his orders and in laying down their arms." Then came the critical moment when the actual order was given. "I looked at the unfortunate N.I. officers amongst their men. We could have escaped with but one volley, for we were on horseback and would have joined the Horse Artillery but what would they have done." Lang continued: "Out rode Gardiner, commanding the Grenadiers 'order the 16th to pile arms.' Gardiner turns around 'Grenadiers shoulder arms.' Done. 'Ground arms.' Done. 'Pile arms.' A moment's hesitation, a few men begin to pile; a look at the black artillery muzzles must have been decisive. All piled arms." The men were quickly marched away. The clusters of guns were immediately picked up in carts held behind the regiments for this purpose, and the disarmament was over. Lang, though, was a skeptic about the disarming. "If these men get maddened (for this is a disgrace, however much softsawder the Brigadier may give) and choose to run amuck among us, they will have done awful mischief before they can be stopped."

Despite the disarming, there was near-panic among the women and children and among the civilian employees. The brigadier made available the central fort, and the populace of the cantonment flocked in. Lang reported that some of the ladies were apparently "going daft with fright, even in that safe place, guarded by high walls and Europeans." Lang frequently disparaged feelings of fear in others, and he denigrated the precipitous withdrawal of most of the Europeans from the cantonment: "The Montgomerys alone stand firm in their isolated place and quite right they are too, I think." Another theme that he harped on was his belief that some of the higher officers were timid and "funked." "I think we at least should not feel the fear which some of our nervous parties indulge themselves in. The ladies are safely secured in barracks (and don't the dear creatures quarrel!)"

The new chain of events seemed to exhilarate Lang. "This is truly an exciting time . . . I find it suits me beautifully. I feel always in very good spirits, sleep like a top, have a grand appetite . . . in fact the state of things I am very happy to find braces me up instead of depressing me or unstringing my nerves. I am very glad to have this experience. The result shows me that a campaign would suit me, a fact I was not sure of . . . I find that actual danger or expectation of it, calms and 'irons me' at once."

By the end of the month, the situation at Lahore had eased so much that Lang reported having ices and tea with Colonel Boileau's daughters (he was courting one, Sarah). Though the mall had been deserted in the first few days, Lang reported on May 28 that it "looked almost like its former self, so many carriages, etc. were out. I joined Frank Boileau and his sisters, just as in the old days, for a 'light brigade gallop.'" Rumors, though, were still rampant, pushed along by the "croakers" (Lang's term). By the second week of June, a number of outstation people had come to Peshawar, including several contingents of European and some native troops (the latter almost exclusively Sikhs and Punjabis); it looked to Lang "like a great fair now, full of troops . . . the bands play again in the evening and people are much more courageous."

The confluence of troops was for the purpose of putting together a "movable column" that would progress down from Peshawar through the Punjab, bringing order on its way, to end at Delhi (where a small contingent of European troops had already gathered). While a large post like Lahore might feel some increased security, as reported by Lang, the overall situation in the Punjab was deteriorating by the day. Time was of the essence. With Delhi lost and no telling what next, it was critically important to link up the small garrisons, with their combined British and armed loyal native forces, as soon as possible. Thus came this new concept of the movable column. Cracklow excitedly wrote: "Just time for another word. Camels have just come and we start tonight at 10 o'clock and march 30 miles to Mujarabad where we join the 24th Lancers and another battery and proceed to Lahore to join the flying column. Good bye." This flying column was a fast-moving, relatively lightly armed unit, capable of much greater flexibility than the traditional siege train unit drawn by elephant and bullock. The "No. 17 Light Field Battery" was movable, and its commander, Capt. George Bourchier, with Lieutenant Cracklow and the men of the unit, was asked to join.

Lang looked forward to being involved in this column and continued to maintain his equanimity about the situation: "I myself in the finest health and condition and spirits possible . . . patience must ever long be the word." He had continued his active sports life, boxing, playing "singlestick," riding. Some Sepoys had been captured in the area, and Lang reported the results: "I got an agreeable order to run up a rough gallows to accommodate twelve men at once, in the shortest possible time, so had to rush off to the Godown and invent a neat thing in gallows and set men to work."[4]

Fred Roberts had also been sent down from Peshawar to join this column, in his new, important job as quartermaster general; he wrote on May 26: "Been hard at work ever since getting the troops over the Jhelum and Chenab. All are now in motion on Lahore."

Bringing these crack troops down from the Punjab via the movable column was a calculated risk; as George Bourchier put it, "That noble policy of denuding the Punjab to rescue the North-Western Province (and which may be said to have been the salvation of India) was in progress." Bourchier was particularly uneasy about the precarious position of the troops and families left behind in Sialkot. "Sir John Lawrence implored Brigadier Brind not to fancy that the political horizon was growing clearer . . . the interests of individual stations must not be allowed to interfere with the salvation of the country. Yet even with this warning, and the fact that it had been found necessary to disarm the troops at Meean Meer, the 46th Native Infantry and a wing of the 9th Cavalry remained armed at Sialkot until after the withdrawal of the European troops, when to disarm them was impossible."

Roberts also worried; his concern was about Peshawar. There was always the possibility that the amir of Kabul (Dost Mohammed Khan) might take advantage of the slim number of Europeans at this last-of-the-line outpost and attack. He continued, "However, ere many months we will have such a force of Europeans in the Country that I hope all these petty Rajahs will rise, so that we may make one sweep, and wind up by taking *Cashmere!* where I shall be very happy to spend every hot weather roaming about the beautiful places there."

Bourchier particularly faulted Brind at Sialkot, alleging that the commander "would not believe that the infection had spread to the regiments under his command." Bourchier had put his finger on one of the factors that had allowed the mutiny to develop so quickly: "This infatuation was not singular: nothing in the history of the revolution seems more wonderful than the temper evinced by every officer of the Native army, if you only hit it at the probability of *his* corps going wrong; while the same man would willingly allow that no other was safe; the truth of the old proverb that 'every crow thinks it own bairn the whitest,' was fully evinced; but gradually every bairn showed, as he slipped away from the parent hand, that he is not a bit better than his neighbours."[5]

Sialkot was also the post of Thomas Watson, and we now need to pick up the threads of his and his mother's lives. The first extant letter, in January 1857, is from her, written as she stopped at Amritsar on her way to the hill station at Simla, two hundred miles or so to the south. She and her son had been living in their own bungalow in the Sialkot cantonment, and she lamented, "My own beloved son, how I hate leaving you!" She sent many instructions: "Do have tiffin every day *on your own table* . . . if you do not, your health may severely suffer from the *long fast* and late dinner." It had not been an easy journey for her; she reported from her next stop at Umballa: "For the first time I felt knocked up—I believe because I got fidgety the last few hours and did not rest or lie down but sat up the whole 12 hours (or nearer 13) that I was on the way . . . I seem to want to be at home with you." Again she picked at Thomas concerning lunch: "I entreat you take great care of your health. I fear it will greatly suffer if you do not take a regular *good tiffin*. A long fast and a heavy meal at night are so bad." She continued to keep her finger in the social life of Sialkot and admonished Thomas:

"I hope you will not go to that wedding—she doesn't deserve that you should, for she is, to say the least, a coquette."

Her next surviving letter, on June 4, was well into the mutiny itself. She was at Simla. Her thoughts were by then on Watson's safety, though Sialkot seemed quite removed from the hostilities at this time. Watson was now apparently involved in local reconnaissance trips around Sialkot, and she worried about his "long rides." With no overt hostilities to trouble her, she concentrated on lesser concerns: "My own son! God in his mercy preserve you!! It is agony to me to think of you exposed to such a sun." Apparently Watson had written her some harsh thoughts about the Sepoys, for she admonished him, "I am sorry, my darling son, when I find how violently you sometimes feel toward these wretches." She cautioned him on "revengeful feelings" and hoped that the mutineers would be punished "as an act of justice." She prayed that God "will hide you under the shadow of his love that you may be safe . . . that he will keep you as the apple of his eye."

Her smothering religious faith was often phrased in tortured prose, filled with admonitions and pious exhortations to her son: "If our own merciful God sees fit to preserve us and restore peace, surely we can say greater is he that is for us than any that can be against us. The angel of the Lord encompasses round about them that fear him and delivereth them. Oh, let us keep close to God in prayer and watchfulness and in reading his word. The comfort of the scriptures is precious now—let us read them much and often." An almost identical paragraph appears in a letter written by Harcourt Anson, a brevet major, to his wife, also at a hill station in northwest India: "You are sensible and religious enough, I know, not to feel unwarrantable anxiety about me. I have the liveliest joy and trust in my precious Saviour and pray to him daily to give me grace and strength not to fear what man may do unto me. What a sweet, precious bond is community of religious principle and sentiment . . . I am reading Job, Gospel of St. John and Hebrews and drink in grace, mercy and peace every morning."

As to the mutineers, Sarah Watson continued her religiosity: "May our mighty God ever confound their devices and put them to confusion." Given the relative security of Sialkot, she seemed oblivious to some of the larger forces occurring: "I hope that the house looks cheerful. I hope you always have flowers in the drawing room and the best [rugs] are on the sitting room floor. I want everything around you to be cheerful and pleasant looking."

Watson wrote back that "the regiment is as good and staunch as possible." Hearing that his mother seemed to be staying by herself too much, he admonished her to see people and move more in society: "You would then forget your causes for anxiety." He wrote his thoughts about the mutineers: "With what burning feelings of revenge do I meditate on all this. Never, never can the smallest feeling of respect for the Sepoys again enter my heart." Hearing that the British were executing captured Sepoys by tying them to muzzles of cannon and then discharging the latter—what came to be called "blowing from guns"—his mother reacted with horror: "How terrible. Would that the misled and unoffending might have been separated from the ringleaders." In the same letter, she showed again her disbelief that the Hindus were ringleaders: "Mrs. Maxwell says she has had a stack of letters from Peshawar and that the Sepoys who escaped into the Swat valley have been compelled to become Mussalmen and treated inhumanely." She worried about Watson's clothing. "Your muftis [non-duty clothes] are safe. I ached so when I saw you had forgotten them. I will look and let you know which neckties you have left here." The mutiny seemed far away for both mother and son.

Not so, though, at Lahore, where other major disarmings now took place. There remained a large number of native units still under arms, some deemed fully loyal and fighting alongside the British to suppress the mutiny, others left back in cantonments as question marks. Most of the British officers in these native units continued to feel that their own men would not turn against them. Bourchier railed at what he saw as softheartedness: "Whether more stringent measures might not have crushed the mutiny at its outset is a point now past arguing upon. Few were willing to believe that the tornado was more than a transient cloud. More than one regiment . . . was disbanded; the General and his mutinous sepoys parted, shedding 'idle tears,' the former to return to temporize with those who as yet were not in open mutiny, the latter to join their brethren at Delhi." Many nineteenth-century British writers were harsh in their judgments about what they saw as a lack of resoluteness in the leaders; for example, George W. Forrest, the noted historian, spoke for many as he faulted one of the generals: "Major-

General Hearsey with all his experiences of the East failed to understand that concessions made to the murmurs and threats of an ignorant race only increase their perversity and folly."[6]

Fred Roberts, too, would brook no compromising: "All confidence in the Native army is at an end . . . the 19th N.I. were disbanded, as you will have read, for gross mutiny, but our imbecile Government, instead of treating the men as mutineers, paid them up, let them keep their *uniforms*!! and saw them safely across the river. The General Officer, poor fellow!! on reading the order to dismiss them shed tears!! . . . it is too disgusting to see the insane things officers do—enough to ruin any Army, and the craven-hearted fellows seem to think they have nothing to do but make up stories and frighten the poor women out of their wits."[7]

Soon severe problems of morale surfaced among those native troops who had gone through the disarming, and John Lawrence himself finally decided to direct a public commendation to the men of one of these units to buoy up their pride. His wording gives us interesting clues about the British mentality at this highly sensitive moment: "I have heard with much pleasure that at the order of Colonel Wilkie, your commandant, the Native officers and men of the Fourth Regiment gave up their arms without murmur and without hesitation and that since that day all have behaved like loyal and good soldiers. I consider that thus acting you have given me of the strongest proofs that soldiers can give of their obedience and fidelity. A soldier's weapons ought to be under certain circumstances dearer to him than his life, but this is when he is in front of his enemy. To surrender them, however, at the order of his superiors is a high mark of his sense of duty. If you continue to act in this manner, Government will certainly restore to you these arms and deem you more than ever worthy to be entrusted with them." Thus far, Lawrence's logic seemed congruent with the individual soldier's beliefs in discipline and responsibility. But then Lawrence became patronizing and paternalistic, exhibiting once more the implicit racism that was so prevalent in the thinking at this time: "Government did not take away your arms because you behaved ill, but because other regiments of Hindoostanie soldiers have done so. Government wished to save you from the danger of such bad example. When peace and security are restored and you have recovered your arms it will still be remembered to your credit that you surrendered them at the call of your officers without being overawed by cannon or European soldiers."[8]

The ease with which the disarmings were accomplished in those first weeks of the mutiny built a false sense of security, obscuring the true feelings of the Indian soldiers. As the flying column moved down through the Punjab in early June there were more skirmishes with mutinous units of troops and more difficulties within the British lines themselves, with surly behavior and other recalcitrant acts. The British officers became increasingly uneasy about their ability to maintain a presence among their own native troops and among the civilians and so turned toward increasingly harsh methods of reprisal in an attempt to frighten any potential backsliders.

Early in June at Anarkullee two Sepoys of one of the units in the movable column itself were heard to be talking of mutiny and were quickly arrested. Neville Chamberlain, the commander of the column, felt that quick action was crucial, that delay at this moment might be catastrophic. Roberts, now on Chamberlain's staff, described what happened next: "Although Drum-Head Courts-Martial were then supposed to be obsolete, he decided to revive, for this occasion, that very useful means of disposing, in time of war, of grave cases of crime. The Brigadier thought it desirable that the Court-Martial should be composed of Native, rather than British officers, as being likely to be looked upon by the prisoners as a more impartial tribunal, under the peculiar circumstances in which we were placed. This was made possible by the arrival of the 1st Punjab Infantry—Coke's Rifles—a grand regiment under a grand commander . . . composed chiefly of Sikhs and Pathans, and possessing Native officers of undoubted loyalty . . . the Subadar-Major of the Corps was a man called Mir Jaffir, a most gallant Afghan soldier . . . who was made president of the Court-Martial. The prisoner was found guilty of mutiny and sentenced to death. Chamberlain decided that they should be blown away from guns in the presence of their own comrades, as being the most awe-inspiring means of carrying the sentence into effect."

This was the most feared punishment of all to both Hindus and Muslims; William Butler, a missionary, explained why: "What the Sepoys objected to in it was the dishonour done to the body, its integrity being destroyed, so that the *Shraad* could not be performed for them. The *Shraad* is a funeral ceremony, which all caste

Hindoos invest with the highest significance, as essential to their having a happy transmigration; the dissipation of the mortal remains of a man thus executed would necessarily render its importance impossible, and so expose the disembodied ghost . . . to a wandering, indefinite condition in the other world, which they regard as dreadful; and, to avoid this liability, when condemned to die they would plead, as a mercy, to be hung or shot with a musket—any mode—but not to be blown away."[9]

George Cracklow's own guns were chosen this first time for the grisly task, and he told his mother the whole story: "I was ordered to take the guns to the front, the Brigadier then came and told me what was required. The men were to be blown away. In a few minutes the prisoners were marched up to the guns, their irons knocked off and lashed to the muzzles with drag ropes, the muzzles pointing just between their shoulders. The Brigadier made a short speech to the men telling them why these fellows were condemned to death, and that he would serve any man the same he found unfaithful to his salt. The trumpet sounded 'limber up' (which was the signal agreed on). I shut my eyes for half a second and the guns exploded with one report. I could hardly see for the smoke for about 2 seconds when down came something with a thud about 5 yards from me. This was the head and neck of one of the men. You can't imagine such a horrible sight. On each side of the guns about 10 yards lay the arms torn out at the shoulders. Under the muzzle and between the wheels lay the remainder of the bodies with the entrails scattered about. The heads had flown up in the air and fallen in rear of the guns. I could never have imagined bodies would go to pieces so easily." A fellow officer commented: "Quite untouched their faces were, and quite quiet . . . I am afraid we were all very bloodthirsty, as almost everyone had a smile of gratified revenge on his lips."[10]

These executions apparently upset a few of the more squeamish, but in the main they had remarkably universal support among the troops. Roberts probably spoke for most of the young officers when he commented: "It is rather a horrible sight, but in these times we cannot be particular. Drum-Head Courts-Martial are the order of the day in every station, and had they begun this regime a little earlier, one-half of the destruction and mutiny would have been saved . . . at Jullundhur . . . even when the men did mutiny and were consulting about attacking the guns, Brigadier Johnstone would not allow them to fire. Isn't it horrible, mother dear? Very nearly the whole of one Regiment could have been blown to pieces, instead of which they got off and cut up several Officers."[11]

Cracklow, too, appeared to be quite satisfied with the proceedings. "Chamberlain is a splendid fellow . . . not to be trifled with. If they had had a man of his stamp at Barrack-Pore, where the mutinies first broke out, he would have stopped the business at once. At present there is no saying when it will end, since 22 or 23 Native Infantry regiments and two or 3 cavalry have mutinied and I believe all the others will willingly join them when they get the opportunity. As it is now I really believe they think we are afraid of them, and with some cause, for the wavering counsels and delay in punishing the villains has given them good reason for such an opinion. However, they will have cause to alter their judgments if they come across Chamberlain's force."[12]

Cracklow seemed to become more callous as the days passed with more vengeance-oriented tasks: "Since my last letter to you we have been marching about the country in the undignified occupation of executioner general to the Punjab. I myself have become a regular Jack Vetch and think no more of stringing up or blowing away half a dozen mutineers before breakfast than I do of eating the same meal."

Shortly after Cracklow's experience with the blowing from guns, this "first tragedy," as Bourchier put it, the same awful punishment was done on a mass-production basis in Peshawar. A group of 120 mutineers had been condemned to death, all to be blown to bits in front of cannon. At the last minute, as an act of mercy, the number was cut by two-thirds to 40. The entire garrison at Peshawar was drawn up on the parade ground, and before an enormous crowd of awed onlookers, the men were tied to the front of cannon and the pieces armed and fired at once. All the bodies disintegrated before the horror-struck eyes of the multitude. One of the English historians, in commenting on this event, used reasoning similar to that of Bourchier: "It was a wonderful display of moral force, and it made a deep and abiding impression. There was this great virtue in it, that however unintelligible the process by which so great a result had been achieved, it was easy to understand the fact itself . . . the British had conquered because they were not afraid . . . It is hard to say, how many lives—the lives of men of all races—were saved by the seeming severity of this early execution."[13] Apparently, it did not occur to any of the British that it might have been the other way, as much cause as effect: that the stern punishments might have led to severity of response by the rebels.

As May turned to June, life at the Lahore fort was becoming more tense. Lang now grumbled about the buildup of troops and commented on June 9, "I shall not be sorry when that movable column is off, for I think a great part of it is highly objectionable and more to be looked on as foes than friends." There continued to be false alarms about uprisings within the local troops; Lang blamed "those bugbears who have caused such a lot of false reports and such alarm to our croaking cowards." Security was stepped up, and Lang reported that "not a nigger is allowed to move between 10:00 P.M. and gunfire." One of the cavalry troops suspected another of mutinying and raced in, swept out the horses, and took them back to their own lines. On June 7 a number of the units were split, with the Sikhs, Punjabis, and hill men reassigned to the movable column. On June 9 word came that the troops at Jullundur had mutinied and left for Delhi. The movable column took out after them but never was able to make contact.

By mid-June more specific details had reached the Punjab about the massacres at Meerut and Delhi. "One is choked with indignation," wrote Lang, "at the cruelty with which the poor women have been treated. I hope no quarter, no mercy, will be the cry when we have the upper hand." In another letter at this time, Lang cloaked his comments in a religious wrapping: "Britains never shall be slaves . . . and we are not going to be kicked out of India . . . it comes to a religious war of Christians versus Mahommedans and Hindoos, and we know which must win."

As the days went by, Lang's optimistic tone began to change: "Our enemies increase daily, fresh barbarities happen, and no reinforcements can come to our poor army before Delhi. Yesterday news was bad, for it tells the strength of our enemy. Every day do they come out and every day under a scorching June sun have our poor fellows to fight through the hottest hours." He ended his letter on this day with a plaintive desire: "I wish a Cortez, or Pizarro, with a large force and unlimited power, were let loose against these scoundrels."

The British newspapers in India provided a veritable bath of gory details about Delhi, Lang wrote: "More details, and some which I wouldn't write, and which the editors ought to be prevented from publishing, considering that poor frightened ladies all read. I immediately tore paragraphs out of mine before lending them. Our soldiers who know these things are quite mad—they want to stick every native they see."

The actual facts *were* very ugly. Many dozens of not only Englishmen but Englishwomen and children had been murdered in cold blood. These facts, awful enough in their own right, were rapidly embellished by rumor and imagination to include vivid descriptions of rape and torture that became prurient in their concentration on the "dishonouring" of British women. There were undoubtedly instances of rape; the very brutality on both sides would lead some men to it. The evidence sifted after the mutiny, however, failed to support almost all of the legion of rumors.

Cracklow, in contrast to both Roberts and Lang, seemed wholly to believe any story of excesses; early in the mutiny, on May 27, he wrote: "We got sad news from Delhi. The Sepoys have ravished and murdered some 50 ladies who had taken refuge in the palace. Some they rubbed with oil and then set fire to. News of the same description from Aligarh. I live in hopes of letting the first charge of grape I fire into a regiment of Sepoys. We shall give them a lesson that they'll remember to the last days of their lives." Later, in August, he told his mother: "The fearful tragedies that have been enacted all over the country beggar description. At Gwalior after violating the ladies they laid them over guns and then flogged them and then blew them away." Sen, in *Eighteen Fifty-seven*, spoke specifically about this Gwalior mutiny: "The sepoys were not indiscriminant in their slaughter of Christians. Women were allowed to go unharmed but men were not spared as a rule."

Despite the increasingly ominous news, Lang's social and personal life continued apace. His mother apparently was becoming too nosy about his incipient romance with Sarah Boileau; he chastised her in his next letter: "None of your chaff about ye trials of ye domestic bachelor! I scorn to write the 8th time a geneaology of Colonel Boileau of the Artillery . . . I won't tell any more about him or his sons and daughters or where you knew him or of his wife, who is a very pleasant ladylike kind of person, or of Mademoiselles Sarah and Grace, or of Frank Boileau . . . or four more boys, 2 at home and 2 cheeky youngsters out here, who call me 'Lang' and otherwise irritate me! So you needn't ask any more questions about them." He lectured his mother, too, on her long-held attitude toward India: "Do you love them, mother? One month in India now would change your opinion of a lifetime; we on the spot can hear of nothing every day but base ingratitude and conceit, and fiendish cruelty and you'll not say 'the mild inoffensive Hindoo' again!"

Lang's mundane tasks at the fort in the face of the great events swirling around him increasingly irritated him. In late June he reported, "I am running up partition walls in the lady's barracks . . . and these, as you may fancy, are troublesome, ladies being difficult to please in such matters and given to think others better off than themselves." He volunteered for duty at Delhi; several of his friends had already received such orders. "I hope I may be in time," he wrote. "What a change . . . to this luxurious dawdling cantonment life. I dare say I shall wish myself back in Mme. Boileau's drawing room, playing 'La Ci Darem' and such like. But . . . this is no time for men to be idling and shirking . . . I shall be much more useful there than I am here in inglorious ease and security."

Day after day passed with no reassignment, and he vented his impatience: "I shall be late for the fighting, only in time for fever and cholera and demolishing the walls of Delhi in the rains. So to preserve myself from suicide I went over with Frank to Colonel Boileau's and stayed there until they went to barracks." He cautioned his mother not to worry about him; his own troops had been "quietly disarmed." He continued, "In reality I have been very happy and comfortable here—too much so." A few days later he reiterated his frustration: "I am all ready to be off at a minute's notice, and meanwhile go on in a careless, peaceful, station way . . . knowing that perhaps at Lahore and Peshawar alone the security of life and property exists, and that I have no right to be safe and comfortable." Still, he wanted to go on his own terms—that is, as a professional man—rather than just leading a troop of men; when one of his friends was given a troop of two hundred Sikhs and left for Delhi, Lang commented, "I certainly don't envy him; I wouldn't go down that way for anything."

Lang continued to rail at the "croakers," who daily seemed to report the worst in new defections and so on. "I wish I were commanding here," he wrote; "I would take up the extermination policy advocated by the *Friend of India*, instead of keeping all the Europeans in a state of everlasting suspense and killing the women by inches. I'd have the whole native force out here and order them within a quarter of an hour to give me up ringleaders, one out of every ten men. Otherwise volleys of grape and musquetry should rid the station of these nightmares and strike a gentle warning into the bosoms of troops at other stations. This long delay before Delhi . . . has cost the lives of hundreds of our countrymen and women . . . and must lead, if still protracted, to the desertion of Sikhs, Punjabis and all who have not white faces in the country."[14]

As if to reinforce Lang's words, the very next day a much more ominous event occurred. Cracklow's letter of July 14 reported it: "Disarmed the 59th L.S. and on the 9th I think it was got intelligence from Sialkot that the Native troop remaining there had mutinyed, killing Brind the Brigadier and several other Europeans and after pillaging the whole station had bolted towards Gordaspore on their way to Delhi." No longer were they strangers or only acquaintances to Cracklow; his close friends of several years—Brind, the commander, Graham, the surgeon—were dead. A Scotch missionary, Rev. Thomas Hunter, was ruthlessly slaughtered, along with his wife and daughter, while trying to get away in a carriage. The message to the movable column reported that a few English had escaped to the Sialkot fort, while the mutineers released all the prisoners in the jail, plundered the Treasury, destroyed the offices and homes of the British, and then departed abruptly in the direction of Delhi.

The 46th Native Infantry was the only remaining Native Infantry regiment now at the post. Its Sepoys were principally Hindu. There was also a cavalry unit, chiefly Muslim. At the beginning, there had also been several European units (Bourchier and Cracklow's included), but these had been stripped away for the movable column. Thus most of the troops remaining at Sialkot were native. Thomas Watson was one of the 46th's officers, the only one of our four lieutenants to be attached to a native troop.

Brind, the commander, was one of those who believed implicitly in his troops; as the cantonment magistrate, Capt. Gregory Rich, put it later, "He unfortunately had too much confidence in the loyalty of the troops under his command and refused to subject his Sepoys to the dishonour of taking away their arms." Once the European troops left, there arose much controversy around the cantonment about this stand. In one of those twists of fate, Hunter, who was soon to lose his life, had himself formed a self-defense brigade. Brind opposed this action "and even opposed prayer-meetings, which he denounced as conventicles and used all his authority to suppress. At one time he went so far as to threaten to hang Mr. Boyle, the Chaplain." A number of women and children and male civilians did leave Sialkot for Lahore, but the Hunters and others decided to stay.

With many intimations in early July that things had gone awry, on July 9 the native troops finally rose against the British. The cavalry unit seemed to be the instigators, but the infantry unit also joined in. Brind heard shots and immediately ordered his horse, saying that he would go out and quell the disturbance. Rich reported, "According to some accounts he then rode out among the mutinous troops, a number of which were waiting for him outside, and calling them 'his children' begged them to return to their allegiance." The answer of the Sepoys was a shot in Brind's back. Rich continued: "The General turned on the men, but his pistols had been previously unloaded by his khansamah [cook] and clicked harmlessly. He then seized the barrel of his pistol, and riding the trooper down, broke his jaw with the butt end of his weapon." Several other officers came up at this time and, under fire, rode with Brind back to the fort. Twelve hours later the commander died.

Meanwhile, Dr. John Graham, the superintending surgeon for the post, had been warned of the uprising and called to his daughter to come out "for a ride," in order not to upset the servants. His daughter dallied and, as Rich put it, "after a too deliberate preparation, ordered their buggy." As they rode out toward the fort the Sepoys overtook them and shot the doctor. Rich, wringing the maximum out of his story, continued: "This young lady . . . when she reached the fort that day her anguish was past description. She blamed herself entirely for the death of her father—which might not have occurred had she spent less time over her toilet in the morning—and on noticing that a pair of diamond bracelets were stained with his blood, she dashed them from her sight in horror."[15]

There were several other murders and many close calls that day before the small band of Europeans were able to reach the relative safety of the fort, an old building that belonged to Rajah Tej Singh, an old Sikh general. The fact that the fort was the rallying point had been kept secret, for the only gate into it was through one of the narrow streets of Sialkot.

At the time of the Sialkot mutiny Thomas Watson's mother was at Simla, where her reclusive behavior had seemed to increase: "There are several people here who would be friendly if I would bring myself to call on them, but my heart shrinks from it. I feel calmer in my room." Even after she heard about the mutiny at Sialkot she still talked about food and clothes: "I hope you have comfortable board and a good bed my darling son. Did the mess servants remain? . . . Flannel shirts are most valuable." She worried about the damage done to their home: "Our loss of property is great to us, my own beloved son . . . Let us not bestow one sigh upon it. At the same time, if anything can be saved or recovered, you will doubtless do so. The Bible in which your honoured father wrote the names and birth of our children and his and our beloved pictures I would like to recover if such were possible . . . Please, my own son, secure whatever books were left. They were the only things specified as safe in your first letter." When she learned that Thomas was out with a levy chasing mutineers, she was extremely worried: "Oh how I long to hear that you are no longer out after those wretches. I do trust that by the mercy of God you are by this time safe and quiet at Sialkot . . . I have gone through deep agony at the bare thought of the possibility of your being engaged in an encounter with any of these desperate and treacherous wretches . . . I humbly trust it was not necessary for your party to give one hostile shot." A few days later she cautioned him once again: "Do not do imprudent things, and take care of your health for your poor mother's sake." Later in the same letter she continued on a more practical note: "Darling son, do not be another night without a pillow. Your bearer can sew up a bag and stuff it with clean cotton, not that dirty stuff they sell as tree cotton. It is so bad for the head not to be raised and comfortable in sleep." Again she mentioned her isolation: "Mrs. Ousley is very kind—I see no one else."

One of the peculiarities of the Sialkot revolt was the apparent complicity of the servants of the British. Rev. J. Cave Browne commented a few months later: "In almost all other stations domestic servants had been either faithful or at least neutral, but here they were clearly privy to the whole plot; and with only a very few exceptions, every servant, whether Mussulman or Hindoo, proved false. In some cases, not even the claims of fifteen or twenty years' service with a family restrained them from now deserting their masters, or from being the first to help themselves in the general scramble."

In the face of the brutalness of the uprising at Sialkot, with numbers of officers and civilians killed, the treatment of the officers of the 46th Native Infantry was an anomaly. Rich tells the story: "The 46th were inclined to be loyal to their officers, if not to their Colours. When their officers rushed to the lines to try to restore order, they were quite defenceless, as the arms of most of them had been taken away by their servants during the night. But the regiment refused to take advantage of their condition and satisfied themselves with hustling off three of the officers and shutting up the others for safety's sake in the regimental quarter-guard. There they were protected all day with a strong guard of the steadiest men."

Rich continued with a curious vignette: "These sanguine rebels cooly offered their Commanding Officer, Colonel Farquharson, to his great amusement, Rs. 2000 per month, and Captain Caulfield Rs. 1000 per month, if they would remain with them and lead them to Delhi against the English. They also promised them six months leave in the hills every hot weather, and only to be stationed in the best Cantonments once the English had been defeated." The officers, refusing the offer, were kept under confinement the entire day and in the evening were led to the fort with their families by the mutineers before the latter marched off on the road to Delhi.

We cannot be certain of Thomas Watson's role in these events (he wrote his mother the day after, on July 12, but this letter is missing). His mother's reply, on July 15, gives us circumstantial corroboration that he was not among those imprisoned: "What wonderful mercy and interposition of providence attended your steps this morning, so fearfully daring and imprudent as many of them were." In later months there was increasing criticism in the press and informally in cantonments of officers who unduly trusted their men until too late, with killings of women and children resulting;

the Sialkot officers garnered many of these barbs. A later letter from Watson's mother, in mid-October, referred to "vindictive accusations" against Watson: "May those who made it be ashamed to their very hearts and you, my dear, soon cleared . . . Of the thousands and millions who knew of the intended outbreak not one warned or communicated to a single Englishman or Christian is in itself a perfect refutation of the preposterous objections." She continued: "While you were soundly sleeping on your bed . . . Captain Caulfield was protected by the men; while your property was destroyed, his was untouched! With an almost native wife it was far more likely that he had intimation than you had but we know *nobody* had warning given him. God will defend you from your enemies . . . I humbly trust that your honest mind eases you far above such men."

The charges levied against Watson, whatever they were, continued to surface over the next weeks, for in late November he wrote his mother again: "I have taken no further steps about Caulfield's accusations which he denies having made. The old Colonel will, I think, avoid making any answer if I ask him about it. Still, I think perhaps I ought to write him. My reason for not having done so has been from a wish to dismiss the very unpleasant subject from my thoughts."

There are several mysteries in this set of letters. Why was some criticism directed specifically at Thomas Watson? What was meant by the term "almost native" as applied to Captain Caulfield's wife? (She was probably Anglo-Indian; was there an implication that he had dual loyalties?) Why was Thomas Watson's property destroyed, even though he *was* a member of the 46th Native Infantry? Part of the answer to at least this last question may lie in the fact that Caulfield was a line officer, directly involved with the men in a leadership role, while Watson was a support staff officer, assigned as a quartermaster at Sialkot; his primary job was as finance officer, paying wages and guarding the Treasury. This was a sedentary job in the main and linked directly only to a few of the native troops. Even in periods of high activity, it was an assignment that had little excitement to it. But most of the enigmas in these allegations remain: something happened that day that some felt reflected badly on Thomas Watson.[16]

Up to this time the movable column had had little luck in engaging any sizeable force of the mutineers. This presumably highly mobile unit had had to be content with capturing stray mutineers who had gone back to their villages. Now the large number of troops, on their way somewhere in a body from the fresh mutiny at Sialkot, became a prime target for the column.

A new general had just been given command of the unit, the soon-famous John Nicholson, just promoted and given this command over the heads of many senior officers (some of whom showed their jealousy, it was said, by calling him "Mr. Nicholson" behind his back). Nicholson's presence was an electric one, and this young officer soon forged a unique role in the turning of the mutiny.

Cracklow was already in the movable column but almost got left behind for what potentially might be its first big engagement: "Three of our pieces were to be left at Amritsur and I was ordered to remain in charge of them. I could not stand this, being left behind the first time there was a chance of the battery seeing service so I went to the General and begged him to let me go, which he kindly did at last."

Nicholson, determined to make a decisive move in his new command, force-marched the movable column toward Gordaspore, an out-of-the-way post north and east of Lahore, where the Sialkot mutineers were rumored to be heading. Cracklow described it: "We started at 9 o'clock on the night of the 10th and marched all night until 10 o'clock the next day when we got in very much exhausted with fatigue and the heat, which was something terrific, having done 42 miles; several horses fell dead on the road and the men suffered a great deal. We camped down in our wood and were just beginning to feel pretty jolly when it came on to rain tremendously and as we had no tents up here of course we were drenched in a few minutes and all together spent rather an uncomfortable night. I luckily had a bit of bread in one of my holsters and this with a drink of water set me all right."

A fortuitous circumstance kept the mutineers from learning of the attacking column. Cave Browne told the story: "That evening Nicholson was walking down the lines of the 52d Light Infantry to speak to Colonel Campbell, when his keen eye detected, among the crowds of villagers who were pouring into camp with milk, eggs, vegetables, &c., for sale, two men whose bearing attracted his notice. 'Call the sergeant-major of the 52d' he said. 'Sergeant Major, these two men are sepoys of the 46th—have them secured.' The order was instantly obeyed, and the men confessed that they were, and had come to raise 2d Irregulars at Gordaspore. Had these men not been noticed, the tidings of the Column having arrived would have flown like lightning into the rebel camp; they would probably have doubled back and . . . escaped."

Bourchier's comments on this forced march give us a keen sense of the excitement that all the men felt: "Yet under these circumstances, trying as they were, the spirit of fun was not extinct; the Artillery made extemporary awnings of branches of trees over their gun-carriages and waggons, giving them the appearance of carts 'got up' for a day at Hampstead; officers crowned with wreaths of green leaves, were 'chaffed' by their comrades for adopting head-dresses à la Norma."

The battle put an end to posturing. Cracklow told it well: "The next morning about 9 we started after the mutineers who were about 10 miles off, having crossed the river Beas and being quite unaware of our vicinity. The heat was something tremendous. After marching two hours we came up with them . . . drawn up in front of the village in line, with the Cavalry on their flanks." The battle began with a Nicholson error (at least in Cracklow's eyes): "Our General made a great mistake. Instead of letting us (the artillery I mean) pitch into them some 500 or 600 yards off when we could have cut them to bits without none of ours getting hurt, he marched us up to something like 250 yards of them within musket range when the beggars immediately fired into us before we had time to muster or load . . . As soon as the firing commenced a perfect hail of balls came into us. My horse was shot under me and my syce who was standing close to his head was hit in the arm with a musket ball. As I was laying my gun a man was shot within a yard of me and another ball shattered to pieces on the tire of the gun wheel. Just as I had laid my gun for the second round I heard a shout behind me and on turning round found that their cavalry had charged the battery and were sabering away right and left."

Cave Browne was there; he told of the opening enemy charge: "Gnashing their teeth, and worked up to the utmost with intoxicating drugs, they cut right and left at the gunners and drivers . . . and a tremendous volley from the whole line, delivered simultaneously, as if on parade at Sialkot, made things at first look very ugly." Cracklow was one of those in trouble: "As I had no horse, mine being shot, I stood very little chance so I rushed to where my horse lay about 10 yards off and got my pistols out of the holsters. I just got hold of them when down came a trooper at me. I was a little too quick for him. Just as he was cutting at me I fired my pistol at him. Hit him under the sword arm about the middle of the reds and had the satisfaction of seeing him throw up his arms, give a shout and fall off. When I had polished this gentleman off I had a shot at another and am not quite sure whether I hit or missed him. He gave a lurch in his saddle and galloped off as hard as he could. I think he must have got it as I took a very deliberate pot at him.

"We walked into them in fine style when we did commence. They kept up a very hot fire for about 20 minutes and then fled towards the river, we after them . . . I was left on one side of the river with my 3 pieces to barrage an 18 p^n which they had on the opposite side. But am sorry to say could make no impression on it as they had it and their gunners behind a bank of sand, only just the muzzle of the gun out . . . We killed about 100, at least that number of bodies were found. Lots were, of course, wounded and drowned. We captured their colours and half of their baggage. Several people found articles of their own property which those blackguards had pillaged at Sialkot. I suppose all my little goods and chattels are gone forever that I left behind."

The mind-set of the column was profoundly influenced by their leader, Nicholson; a message from him that day is revealing of his attitude: "11½ a.m. My dear Dickson. Cross the river if Adams thinks you can do so without risk. I don't understand why any mutineer has been allowed to remain alive in that village. Desire Boswell to kill them all at once or else to make over the command of the party at the Serai to you and come into camp." In other words, any less vindictive attitude by a subordinate left him subject to being relieved of his command.

Cracklow also wrote his mother more personally about the battle: "I must now tell you about myself a little. First on returning from the river I came over the piece of ground that I had fired my first round of grape into and saw that the effect of it had been very good as there were 12 gentlemen lying on their backs, most fright-

fully mangled . . . Bourchier and I got off all safely. I would have
given anything I possessed for a Colts revolver. I could have killed
a man for every barrel. I had only a pair of single barrelled pistols
which I got lent me a day or two before. However, they saved my
life.

"I am the most extraordinary figure you can imagine. My face
burnt black and all the skin peeling off. We had no uniform. Anyone wears whatever they can lay their hands on, mine consists of a
pair of trousers dyed blue, a coloured shirt and a turban, a sword
belt with a tremendous big sharp sword and a brace of pistols and
a tin pot. This is the most useful article of the whole lot, I think.
The thirst one suffers from is something terrible and the tin pot
comes into use very often after the battle . . . Now my dear
Mummy, don't begin to fidget yourself about me. I am in perfect
health and take great care of myself, I assure you. I have become
quite accustomed to the heat . . . I have never been better in my
life."

Despite the losses inflicted on the mutineers, there remained a
great body, who now were falling back toward the Ravi River at
Trimoo Ghat, a mile or so from where the first battle was fought.
According to one report by R. Montgomery, who was the judicial
commissioner for the Punjab and was attached directly to Nicholson's staff, quite a few of the enemy cavalry, "after galloping off to
a distance, abandoned their horses and throwing arms and uniforms attempted to escape through the country by personating
peaceful subjects." The main body of the rebels attempted to retreat
across the river, but the water had risen very substantially since the
early morning and many were swept away by the stream and
drowned. However, a determined remnant took up a position on a
large island in the middle of the river and positioned one enormous
old iron artillery piece that they had brought with them from Sialkot. Cracklow described the ensuing fray: "The 52nd were taken
down about a mile below the mutineers' position and put across in
boats. Only six were procurable and these only held 50 men each
. . . rather a tedious matter, as the stream was very strong and carried them down a long way each trip. I was back with three guns
of our battery opposite the mutineers' positions with orders to engage their attention from what was going on down below and if
possible silence the gun as soon as it became light enough to see

the emplacement. We commenced firing and found ourselves short. Their gun, a long 18p[n], the Sialkot cantonment gun, was placed behind a double parapet under which the blackguards dived every time we fired, whilst we were out on the open bank of the river and formed an excellent mark for them. One light field gun could not be used very effectively at the distance, some 1200 yards and all our attempts to dismount were ineffective.

"We succeeded in diverting their attention from the 52nd who got over without molestation . . . When the mutineers did discover that our men were on the island they trained the gunmount from us onto them. This exposed its entire broadside to us and most fortunately one of our shots took effect on the left side of the tail. This shot from the great distance had so little force with it as to be unable to dismount the gun but it injured it so much that it could not be depressed for helping to injure the 52nd who were advancing. Although the mutineers continued to fire at the 52nd until the gun was taken, not one of their shots took effect as the gun was so much elevated as to throw every round over their heads. We from the opposite side could not see this and could not help any time the gun was fired giving a groan for our poor fellows who we thought were losing the contest . . . they fought like men without a hope. After the gun was taken there was a little fight in a village and of the mutineers some hundred took to the water and were shot like dogs. Some few who got to the bank were driven back again into the water and shot like so many dogs."[17]

Montgomery was allowed as a civilian to go along that day and excitedly reported to his superior: "About seven o'clock, when the greater part of the Infantry was crossed, Nicholson himself went over and advanced, attended by half a dozen of Sowars, only to reconnoitre the enemy's position. He then went back and brought up the Infantry . . . It was helter-skelter with the mutineers. A few stood at the guns or were under the bank near it. These were speedily disposed of. The rest ran to the head of the island and were followed up by our fellows and took to the water . . . My first and very brief campaign is over. It is more exciting and interesting, a good deal more than hearing appeals."[18]

Cracklow's enigmatic comment in his letter, "shot like so many dogs," was a terse reminder of another example of harsh penalty by the British. Nearly all of the fugitives from this battle at Trimoo

Ghat made their way single-mindedly in one direction: northeast, toward the territories of Goolab Singh, the maharajah of Kashmir. Nicholson's forces rapidly overtook a large number of these, and most of them, to use the euphemism of Montgomery in his report, were "captured and executed by order of General Nicholson." Montgomery concluded: "I feel convinced that not 50 altogether will ever get to their homes . . . The mutineers were accompanied by a very large body of camp followers being public and private servants, artisans, shopkeepers and others. All the males of these, and in some instances, the women and children have been sent back to Sialkot to be recognized and if convicted of plundering or of culpable direction of service, to be punished."

Plunder there was, aplenty. The mutineers had carried with them from Sialkot everything they could get their hands on—"buggies, carriages, horses, plates, clothing, ladies dresses, every possible thing you could imagine," Cracklow wrote. All was now stacked up, ready to be returned to the ransacked post. "I sent my servant over to see if he could recover any of the property I left behind. Not a thing is to be found. It appears the villagers came down on the cantonment after the docile Sepoys (as the *Times* calls them) had left and carried off everything . . . I found one returning veterinary surgeon who had just come over from Sialkot with a couple of my shirts. He told me he had lost all his own and had picked these out of a heap of plunder that was lying in the middle of the barracks square at Sialkot."

Thus George Cracklow, with Nicholson and Bourchier, had experienced his first real taste of battle in the mutiny. It was a considerable success. But what next? Delhi, Cawnpore, Lucknow—all these were still in enemy hands.

Roberts missed this battle, having gained permission from Nicholson to go on down to Delhi ahead of the movable column. "I fully expected being kicked out of the Staff and sent to duty with the Artillery," he wrote his mother on arrival there on June 26, "and was not a little agreeably surprised when I was offered two appointments, one, quartermaster general with the Cavalry Brigade and the other, deputy assistant adjutant general under Sir H. Barnard. Well, I chose the former, being in my own line. *All* the Artillery Captains, imagining I would join the Corps again, asked for me for their troops, so I felt quite proud. Dear mother, you don't think I am conceited telling you all this. I know it will please you, the General and dear little Harriet, to hear such good news, and I feel anything but conceit, dearest, only wondering at my luck in getting on so well."[19]

The Sialkot mutiny instantly put Lahore back to a siege mentality. "All ladies secured in barracks," Lang reported, "their guard doubled . . . Larkins ordered to let his Sikhs fire into any party of natives number 10 or more who may appear." Fortunately for Lang's romance with Sarah Boileau, "Mrs. Boileau's quarters are not so uncomfortable, being one of the end Sergeant's quarters, so that they are much more private than parties who have little partitioned rooms in the big wards, with kutcha partition-walls, only six feet high. These latter parties can't be jolly and private."

But now Lang's orders came through for Delhi. He had just time for a few days of letter writing and tidying up, in the process loosing a few barbs at the "old muffs" at Delhi and railing again to his mother about the English press and its treatment of the mutiny: "The Punjab is to be almost denuded of its troops to enable our side to hold its own before Delhi, and all this time we read sickening twaddle . . . where old women write their views on the component parts of the Indian army, our great supremacy over our conquered subjects, our might never to be endangered . . . and all such sort of trash." The Boileau quarters must have been private enough, for almost as an afterthought, Lang teased his mother with a one-liner at the end of his letter: "I hope you will be happy to hear that I am engaged; if you knew Sarah Boileau you would certainly be so." A few days later he wrote, "When shall I see her dear face again? These are sad days for partings." The next day he was gone.

Within twenty-four hours Lang had caught up with the movable column, just in time to find Bourchier and Cracklow trying to get their guns across the swollen Beas River: "Had a chat and a cup of tea with them and got my cart sent across with one of their howitzers." These rivers in the Punjab—the Ravi, the Beas, the Sutlej— were extremely tricky to cross with heavy equipment, especially in the rainy season. The combination of rushing water from the heavy rains and the hidden reefs made the endeavor quite delicate. Cracklow told of the difficulties that day: "The rains are nearly over and the river is very full, generally about a mile broad. The work of getting all the pieces, waggons, horses, camels and carts into the boats is hardly imaginable." Lang also got into a predicament: "Stuck again. I shall not get into Jullunder till noon. Luckily, the sky is covered with clouds. Such a row! Officers swearing, niggers shrieking and shouting, horses, camels, men and dhoolies passing down to the ghats [riverbanks]."

A day or so later, Lang left the movable column and struck off on his own toward Delhi. His excitement at the upcoming assignment was great: "Your next letter from your son will be from a pucka soldier. When I have been once or twice under regular fire and seen men knocked over right and left of me, I shall feel I can say I am a soldier and no carpet-knight." He signed his letter, "From your most affectionate son, A.M. Lang, who tomorrow will be field engineer, 'avenging army,' camp before Delhi, the doomed city of the Moghuls, etc., etc." Two days later he arrived at Delhi. One of the first friends he saw there was Fred Roberts, who had been in Delhi just three weeks but already had been injured in a skirmish.[20]

The British forces before Delhi had been under constant attack from the enormous force of rebels in the city. Roberts had been immediately involved in these clashes from his arrival on June 29 and within a few days had been wounded. He described the sequence of events to his mother: "Seeing a Howitzer almost disabled, for want of men, I dismounted, remembering that, altho' on the Staff, I was a 'gunner,' and set to work. However, we were soon ordered to retire, and the word to 'limber up' was given. I got on my horse again, and turning round to look after the horses in the limbers, who were very unsteady from the firing, I got shot in the back, just where my waistbelt goes. Most fortunately, thro' God's mercy, I had a small leather pouch on my belt. The bullet went just thro' the middle of this, thro' my trousers and shirt and made a small hole in my back. I can scarcely describe the feeling I had, mother dear, altho' we could not, I believe, have been under a heavier fire (9 men besides myself and Thomson, who was the Officer with the other gun, were knocked over in a few minutes out of 2 guns' crews). From the excitement, I suppose, I quite forgot about the chance of being hit, and when I got this awful crack on my back for a second did not know what it was. Feeling a little faint, I dismounted. Wriford of the Fusiliers, thinking I was mortally wounded, sent a couple of men to take hold of me. However, after getting a glass of water, I thought I could ride, and was not so very much hurt after all, so I mounted and rode alongside the guns to the rear. There is little doubt what the result would have been had I not had the pouch on. As it is, I am nearly well, and but for the damp weather, would probably have been . . . Fortunately, the ball just missed the spine, so I suffer hardly any pain. Am I not a lucky fellow my own mother, and has not God been merciful to me, I can never be sufficiently thankful."

A few days later, Roberts wrote of the death of one of his cousins, Lieutenant Greensill, accidentally killed by his own men on a night patrol, "so sad losing a life in such a way. What with being killed, dying of wounds and Cholera we have already a melancholy long list." Roberts was fatalistic, though, about these losses: "One does not mind Officers being killed so much, it is more or less expected to be the fate of soldiers, but these poor women and children—it makes one's very blood run cold to think what they have suffered. I only trust the ruffians have had the mercy to kill those that have fallen into their hands and not taken with them as we hear some have done. Such atrocities have never, I fancy, been so universally committed. Our enemies, the Afghans and Sikhs respected our wives and children, but these cowardly wretches delight in torturing them." Roberts then added a derisive comment reminiscent of Lang: "Yet I'll venture to say the English papers and Members of the Parliament will try to excuse them and put the blame on everyone else but the proper scoundrels."[21]

Meanwhile, the movable column was fighting its way through the monsoon-soaked countryside, on its way to Delhi. Bourchier had been able to get a short leave to rush up to Simla to see his family. But so rapidly was the movable column advancing toward Delhi that he almost missed catching up with it. "Sooner would I have lost my commission than have allowed my battery to march into Delhi without me," noted the embarrassed captain later. He had to travel 168 miles in twenty-five hours to reach the rapidly moving troops. Cracklow was unhappy that his commander had been able to get back and confided his disappointment to his mother: "Bourchier returned yesterday, I am sorry to say, as I was in great hopes he would not have been able to catch us up, and that I should have had the opportunity of taking the battery into action."

The last few miles of the road into Delhi were a great shock to the troops, many of whom had been in the fair city just a few months before. Bourchier described it: "From Alipore to the camp, death in every shape greeted our approach; even the trees, hacked about for the camel's food, had a most desolate appearance, throwing their naked boughs towards Heaven as if invoking pity for themselves or punishment on their destroyers." The stench of rotting corpses, animal and human, was everywhere; in one hollow alone there was discovered, a few days after the column had passed, sixty-five animal carcasses heaped together in a mountain of putrefaction.

When the Nicholson forces finally arrived at the British camp on August 14, they found the army more in the position of the besieged than of the siegers, "an entrenched camp," Bourchier called it, "holding the forces within the city in check, and from time to time repelling their numerous sorties."

Back at Sialkot, Thomas Watson continued to go out on the local levy activity, hunting for stray mutineers: "Most heartily sick am I of this sort of life, though I dare say cantonments would not be the more pleasant." Worried about his house in Sialkot, he sent instructions back from the field to his servants to mend the roof if it leaked. There was talk at this time of raising further levies to go farther afield. Watson commented: "Knowing so little as I feel I do regarding regimental matters, I should feel very nervous at taking a command of such a kind."

On August 7 Watson's mother learned that he, too, had been able to obtain leave, to visit her in Simla. She wrote: "I did not think my heart could feel such pleasure . . . God almighty bless and keep and preserve you and be with you on this journey undertaken in such love and goodness."[22] It seems surprising that Bourchier and Watson would have been able to obtain leave right in the middle of the most serious stage of the mutiny, just before the great attack at Delhi. Bourchier had returned quickly, to catch up with his unit before this attack. Watson, too, was to go to Delhi, but his leave carried him past the time of that critical battle.

The massacre at Delhi

Barbarous murder of the women and children at Delhi

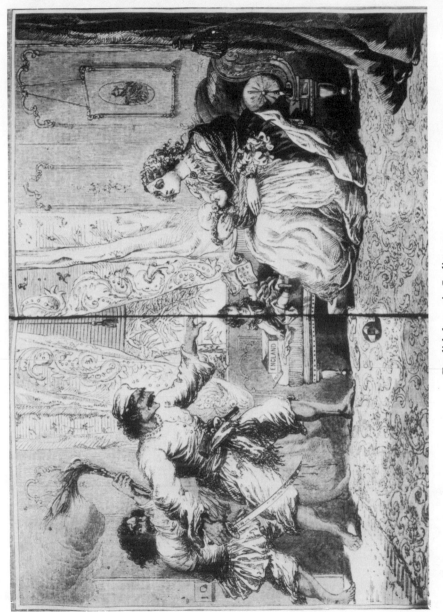

English home in India, 1857

Dr. Graham shot in his buggy by the Sialkot mutineers

Attack on the Sialkot mutineers by General Nicholson's irregular cavalry

Blowing mutinous Sepoys from the guns

Massacre in the boats off Cawnpore

Murder of the English at Cawnpore

Massacre at Cawnpore

Miss Wheeler defending herself against the Sepoys at Cawnpore

The Nana Sahib with his escort, leaving Lucknow to meet the rebel force advancing from Malwa

Mutinous Sepoys dividing spoil

Chapter 4
The Battle for Delhi

"Here we are before Delhi," wrote Cracklow on August 26, "with as little chance of taking the place just at present as we had three months ago. We find it impossible to make a march or in fact do anything with the troop." The camp was ravaged with sickness—cholera was now rampant—and shortages in rations and medical supplies exacerbated the situation. The task facing the already thinned British forces was daunting. "It is very much more formidable than people think," wrote Fred Roberts.

The recapture of Delhi, if possible, clearly was the goal of uppermost priority to the British. Not only was the capital city a veritable bastion of military might, it was the symbol of Sepoy resistance, a psychological flagstaff of inestimable meaning to the insurgents.

The awesomeness of the walled compound was truly overwhelming. Over the centuries of battles and defenses, the city had become a mighty fort within a massive walled enclosure that extended for over seven miles (with the River Jumna forming another two-mile side). The walls facing outward to the land were thick masonry, about twenty-five feet high, interspersed with enclosed battlements, each holding about a dozen artillery pieces. Along the outside of the walls was the equivalent of a medieval moat, a dry ditch some twenty feet deep and twenty-five feet wide. Its walls were in excellent repair: the British challenger outside previously had made certain of that! Though walls of this thickness would have presented no particular challenge to heavy artillery, there were no such pieces available at this moment. Sir Henry Barnard (himself new to the command, after General Anson had died of cholera in late May) found himself under tremendous pressure from both his superiors in Calcutta and his own troops (aflamed anew each day as further details of atrocities, real and imagined, flew through the camp) to take the town forthwith. Fragments of reports—garbled, incomplete, often contradictory—were filtering in from posts further south (most especially some almost unbelievable stories about Cawnpore). "Nothing has ever happened in the world like this," wrote Roberts, "and I hope such a fearful tragedy may never come again. It makes one very melancholy hearing day after day of some old friend being no more, and in my mind has excited such a feeling of horror that I would undergo cheerfully any privation, any amount of work, living in the hopes of a *revenge* on these cruel murderers. This feeling is shared by every European in camp."[1]

Roberts, Cracklow, and Lang now were reunited once again. It was a chance to catch up face-to-face with numbers of their old classmates and friends who had been stationed in various posts around the North West Frontier and other parts of the Punjab, all reunited in the attack force before Delhi. Letters were filled with news of all of these friends: "Caroline Hay's brother is here. He is the image of his mother and equally mad. In the recent rows his wigs were all stolen and as he has not, nor ever had, I believe, any hair, he cuts a most comical figure." Although Countess Roberts, in editing Fred Roberts's letters, seldom indulged in censorship, she did in a couple of cases here: "———, who married ——— ———, is also here. He is, I'm sorry to say, a drunken young snob . . . poor little———. They say she is such a nice girl and dotes on this blockhead. It would be almost a mercy were he killed here, for he will most certainly have to leave the Army some day, unless he changes, and that I should say he is not likely to do so."[2]

The seriousness of the situation preoccupied all three. Cracklow described his territory on the ridge where the British were stationed: "The whole of the ground between us and the city is covered with trees, old walled gardens and ruined houses. This affords excellent shelter to the Pandies, who fight very well behind a wall but never think of coming out into the open. Our men don't understand this kind of work and always rush at them and we in consequence lose a good many." In another letter he reverted to the same theme: "They never advance in line, charge or do anything boldly, but content themselves with creeping around walls and trees and

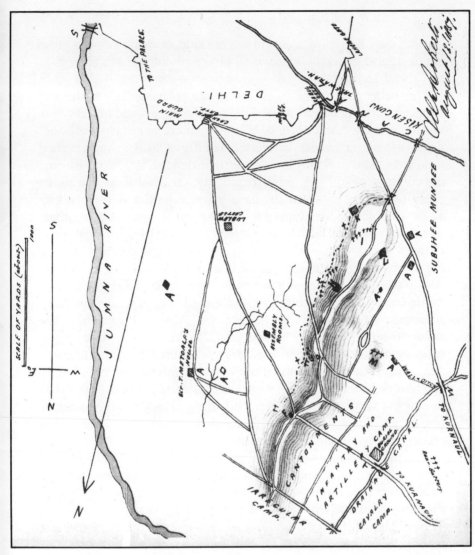

Fred Roberts pictures Delhi before the great battle.

A. INFANTRY. PIQUETS.

F. SIGNAL TOWER.
— 2 H.R. Guns.

G. MOSQUE.
— 4 H.R. GUNS.

H. HINDOO RAO'S HOUSE.
8 Heavy-Light Guns
& Strong Infantry Piquet.

J. HEAVY BATTERY
— 12 Heavy Guns.

K. SAMMY HOUSE.
an advanced Piquet.

L. CROW'S NEST
— 2 5½ Inch Mortars.

M. MOUND BATTERY
3 - 18 PR.S

T. MY TENT. !!!

W. BRIDGE.
destroyed by the ENGLISH.

X. BREAST WORK.

sniping our men from a distance. This kind of work they are great hands at and generally manage to kill or disable an officer or two and about 20 men daily."[3]

This belief that the mutineers were not "playing fair" in the war surfaced in many letters penned by British soldiers and officers during the mutiny. "According to the rules laid down in civilized warfare," one officer wrote, "artillery never fire at artillery (unless they can catch them in flank) but direct their delicate attentions toward the columns of infantry, while deploying, etc.; but these rascals, in every fight here . . . seem to have peppered away at the artillery alone, disabling guns, waggons, etc. in great style and leaving their infantry to meet ours." The mutineers, knowing of this British penchant for fair play, sometimes in a fray would demand a one-on-one combat; an officer told of one example: "Young lieutenant A—— was hailed by a swordsman on foot, who challenged him to single combat, but protested against any opponent taking the dirty advantage of using pistols. Lieutenant A—— chivalrously and rashly, though he had a loaded pistol in his holster, rode at the fellow with his sword, and was severely wounded by him in three places, one cut dividing the ulnar nerve, paralyzed his sword-arm, and he would certainly have been killed directly afterwards, but that one of his Mooltanee horsemen rode up and attacked the footman (rather an unfair thing in single combat, bye-the-bye), saving his officer's life by killing his opponent."[4]

The presence of so many officers in one place soon heightened the invidious comparisons between and among them. Most seemed to be jockeying, in one way or another, for roles that would advance their careers. Cracklow continued to express jealousy and negative feelings about some of his fellow officers: "They have been obliged to call for volunteers from the N.I. for the artillery, as there are so few artillery officers available. The Court of Directors will now see the absurdity of their last move in increasing the native infantry and cavalry as they did in refusing to do anything for us . . . there will be no lack of volunteers for the artillery, as all of the officers of native regiments who have not been murdered are assembled here, and will of course be too glad of any employment, though they will get very little use as artillery officers, as they know nothing of the work. I expect if we get through this business safely, when it is all over they will complete the injustice that has always been shown to our regiments by putting these fellows over our heads."

Cracklow exhibited a detachment from his associates that almost bordered on aloofness. For example, he wrote in early August: "I hope, dearest mother, you will not think me conceited in sending you a copy of a letter which was sent to Bourchier by an officer of some standing in the Regt. but I know my dear old mommy that you will be pleased to hear anything that reflects to my advantage and therefore I send it. It may probably be the means of getting me into the Horse Artillery and if it does it will gratify me immensely to have obtained my chief wish *entirely without obligation to any man* [emphasis is mine]."

Roberts was much more ebullient about his chances, already thinking far beyond just the Battle of Delhi: "Please God, before I write again, I shall have ridden thro' Delhi, and then I hope to join some force going either towards Rohilkhand and Oudh or Gwalior—all new countries to me, and all of which I am very anxious to see; and then, if I may look so far, after the fun is over, to return to Peshawar permanent in the department. Won't that be nice, my mother? I am afraid, according to the new rules, brevets can't be promised to subalterns as formerly, but there are plenty of other rewards, and what I want more than any other is the Victoria Cross. Oh! If I can only manage that, how jolly I should be." (This famous award for "very outstanding deeds of gallantry in the presence of the enemy" was instituted in 1856 but had been made retroactive to the autumn of 1854, thus covering the Crimean War. Just over one hundred of these coveted "V.C.'s" had been awarded in that conflict; now, at this point in the mutiny, practically everyone wanted "the Cross.")

Lang took a more studied view of everything, his focus typically on the narrower bounds of the professional engineer. When he first arrived at Delhi, he was put to work supervising the construction of an abbatis, using elephants to pull the huge felled trees into place. "Sulking Pandies in the thick jungly gardens beyond fired a few shots at us but to no purpose." One of his early assignments was a night effort to cut grass and trees: "All this at first, when clear moonlight shone over all the scene, was very exciting, novel and pleasant, but when at twelve the moon went down and all was dark and the sappers (the new Punjab, raw, undisciplined dogs) trusting to the dark, the thick cover, and the scattered position, took to sulking from bullets and work by hiding in the grass . . . the work ceased to be jolly."

In early August Lang supervised an innovative attempt to bomb the enemy's "bridge of boats" across the Jumna by constructing "a great heavy raft of big casques and trees and setting it off . . . to drift down to the bridge of boats." Lang, ever the professional, wrote, "But I am anything but sanguine as to the usefulness of it; there are so many currents and so many shallows and islands and half-sunken trees, that it is a very great chance anything reaching that bridge, however careful and judiciously it may have been started." They sent two "infernal machines," as they called them, down the river without success: one struck an island and exploded; the second did reach the bridge but failed to explode. Lang suspected that part of the problem was that some of his servants were in communication with the enemy: "When the first infernal machine was started for the bridge, none knew of the project but engineers, officers and a few sappers; yet on that day not a grass cutter crossed the bridge—all were sent to forage on this side, and men evidently waited for these things and knew how to handle them without danger."

Lang's duty assignments were very wearing (and dangerous), but he seemed to shrug them off—as he put it, "the work steeled the mind." He took great proprietary interest in his own jobs and objected to a pattern where "an officer is at Hindu Rao's one tour, at Metcalfe's the next, then at Pagoda, then at Right Battery, and so on, changing about so frequently they see the beginning, ends or middle of works, and cannot have the interest in them, which they would feel when they are continually returning to the same work at short intervals." Lang had a clinical, yet surprisingly lyrical, view of his surroundings. Witness his description of Delhi when he first arrived at the camp: "Exceptionally pretty, the lines of white tents, beyond the green swampy meadows, stretching along the foot of the 'ridge,' . . . from the top of the Flagstaff battery had really the most lovely view; anywhere, you could call it lovely, but to a man fresh from the level, brown, Punjab, it was doubly so."[5]

As June wore into July, then August, the initiative for a British attack on the fortress seemed to ebb away. Each day native forces entered the city from the southern approaches, which right from the start were under native control. Most every day brought a skirmish, and it was an ominous portent of things to come when in one of these small battles the British soldier was found wanting. Maj. Harcourt Anson told of it: "A number charged our picquet; some of our men behaved very badly, absolutely running away and leaving their officer Stillman, to cut his way through the enemy." A courtmartial of two Sepoy prisoners had been interrupted by this battle, and Anson reported its denouement: "The members betook themselves to their respective posts. On reassembling, they asked where the prisoners were. 'Oh!' says the Provost-Marshall, 'Not knowing when you might return, I, to save all further trouble, shot the prisoners directly after you left.'"

By August 14 Lang was reporting increased enemy penetration toward the British positions: "'Pandi' holds ground which once was ours; my first piece of duty here was to construct an abbatis at the very end of Metcalfe's stables, and now that ground and right up to the stables is held by 'Pandi' and the stables themselves are nearly untenable . . . Against our right, too, he advanced and is getting breastworks run up very near to us at the 'Pagoda' picquet and Crow's Nest." Nicholson's movable column (with Bourchier and Cracklow) arrived at about this time, spoiling for a battle. "I hope General Wilson will muster up moral courage enough to order the attack," Lang wrote, "and that this most unsatisfactory dilly-dallying before Delhi may cease."

The troops on the ridge now had their fourth commanding general. Henry Barnard, Anson's replacement, had died of cholera; Gen. T. Reid had become incapacitated; and Archdale Wilson had taken the reins. At the beginning Wilson seemed quite suited for the assignment; Roberts wrote, "Our present commander, Wilson of the Artillery, is pretty tough and I hope he may have better luck." But Roberts and Lang both changed their minds as the weeks ensued. Roberts wrote of a common feeling: "When Wilson first took over the command he did very well—far better than either of his two predecessors. We Artillery men especially were proud of having an officer of our own regiment at the head of the Delhi field force. But ten weeks of responsibility tolled heavily upon him. The strain was tremendous and there was no doubt he was quite broken down by the beginning of September."[6]

Wilson wanted to wait until the siege train of heavy guns arrived; when he learned of a large force coming out of the city on August 25 (presumably to intercept the siege train), he immediately dispatched Nicholson to engage it. Amid a torrential monsoon rain, Nicholson led a force of some twenty-five hundred men and sixteen guns and in a short, hour-long battle at Najafgarh, fifteen miles west of Delhi, defeated some six thousand mutineers, capturing all their guns and killing over eight hundred soldiers. "The rebels offered a desperate resistance," wrote one of the officers accompanying Nicholson, "and a bloody hand-to-hand encounter ensued, in which the towering form and death-dealing arm of Nicholson were conspicuous." Still, despite this morale-building battle, the raw fact remained that Delhi was still held intact, the British remaining too weak for a frontal attack.

A further incident involving "chivalry" happened here at Najafgarh; and one of the officers in the battle brought the story back. "One Sepoy ran the gauntlet down the line untouched. Two European soldiers ran out at him. 'One at a time,' he cried and instantly one of the Europeans halted and ordered arms. The other rushed at the Sepoy, their bayonets crossed, a short struggle ended when the European dashed his bayonet with such force through the Sepoy's body that he threw him up some 8 feet into the air. A cheer from the line greeted this single combat."

For the first time, Cracklow's battery did not get into the action; he was belatedly dispatched only to clean up: "After the fight I went out with horses to bring in the captured guns (we were not with the force as our guns were all armed in Piquet) . . . a very hot ride of about 15 miles across country and very hard work to get the guns in, as the country was a regular morass, in which the guns stuck about every 100 yards. The heat and exposure brought on a slight attack of diarrhea and fever and I have barely got over it yet."

Roberts also missed the engagement: "I was told off to go as Quartermaster-General to the party, but Nicholson says, much as he would like to have me, he would not consent to my accompanying him, as he felt sure I was not strong enough just now for hard work. I was sadly disappointed, but immediately on his return, he came to see me and spoke so kindly and said he wanted me to be well for the grand business, and that I might rely on his never leaving me behind." Roberts concluded: "A man in every sense of the word. He is very kind to me, and, as you see, mother dear, a true friend to me . . . a precious conceited fellow, am I not, mother, telling you all these stories of myself."

Nicholson was also revered by Cracklow, though from more of a distance: "Our General Nicholson, 'old Nick' as the men call him, is an uncommonly fine fellow. He is about 38 years of age, a fine, tall, powerful man full of dash and pluck . . . As long as we are with him we will sure to be in the thick of it as he'll take care to be well to the front."

Roberts, friendly as he was with Lang, nevertheless had the line officer's view of such staff activities as engineering; he wrote his father: "Altho' you used so often to advise, my dear old father, my working hard and getting into the Engineers while at Addiscombe, instead of leading the idle, careless life I used to there, I can assure that, had I the offer, I would not change for anything. In a Station and during times of peace our Engineers lead a life I should detest, building barracks and keeping accounts, and, on service I far prefer Artillery work, not but that at times our Engineers are perhaps exposed to greater danger. They do their business well, whatever it is, and a finer Corps there can not be, but let me be a 'Gunner!!'"

Roberts also was not backward about criticizing the upper echelon of the government and the East India Company: "The Court of Directors seemed to be doing their best to be kicked out, making speeches and abusing their officers . . . it was surely their business to have taken care that a new system was introduced, and not allowed such men to remain in the army. They are trying a nasty, cowardly dodge which will ruin themselves. The officers are not to blame. The whole mutiny from beginning to end is almost unaccountable, but if anyone is to blame, it is the Indian government, made up of men who have never been out of Calcutta all their lives and who know positively nothing of native soldiers."

Yet when it came to tactics and strategy in the field, Roberts seemed judicious and thoughtful; for example, he was more realistic about the dangers of premature attack at Delhi than most of his colleagues: "Several cry out to take Delhi, without any more delay, as if we were not one and all anxious to do so, but the fate of all India depends on our success. Were a failure to be the result, God only knows what would take place."[7]

The long-awaited siege train was now in sight. On September 3

Bourchier and Cracklow's troops were sent out to meet them (up to this point the long line of guns and ammunition wagons had been guarded only by a small detachment of the Beloochi Battalion). "The stink of dead cattle along the road for the first seven miles was even worse than when we came into Delhi three weeks before," commented Bourchier. "The rest of the trip was like a holiday, the contrast to the fresh country air being grateful to the senses after the tainted atmosphere we had been inhaling." A few miles later they met up with the long train, stretching away into the distance more than eight miles. The large guns were dragged by ponderous elephants while the ammunition wagons were pulled by an enormous convoy of oxcarts. The wearying journey at a snail's pace brought them to the Delhi camp just before dawn of the following day, and most of the garrison turned out to watch them stream in, each of the enormous twenty-four pound guns being drawn by two elephants, who pulled along their burden like some little toy.

These huge artillery pieces now had to be set in place, a noisy, dangerous task, with each being laboriously towed into position by forty bullocks, all the time under fire. The location finally picked was inside the Customs House enclosure, for a low wall there gave at least some protection. Since this was only about 160 yards away from the wall of the fort itself, the enemy emplacements in and near the Water Bastion poured a withering fire on the bullocks and men. Thirty-nine men were killed or severely wounded during the grisly night it took to accomplish the emplacements. Commenting on this event later, a military historian called it "an operation that can rarely be equalled in war."[8]

"On the 8th the first battery opened fire," reported Cracklow, "and we are firing steadily on." Only four guns at a time could be employed, as the embrasures required constant repair, and the breach had not been made by the time of Cracklow's letter on September 11: "We all expected that the breach would have been completed and that we should have gone in on the 12th. But owing to delays in the Engineering department we shall not be able to attack until the 15th. You will, I hope, hear of the fall of the cursed place by this mail."

Roberts also watched intensely what was happening at the breach: "Our work here is nearly done . . . this is *the* Battery, in advance of all others and to make the principal breach—it is manned by the 'pets' i.e., all Staff Officers,—and short work we will make of it . . . Delhi will, with God's help, be ours . . . Once we are in, a Column starts in pursuit, and with this I am going as Quarter-master-General!! Am I not lucky, mother dear, altho' only officiat-ing, I am sent before the others in the same Department. I fancy we shall make first of all for Agra and then bend our steps to Cen-tral India or Oudh . . . if the rascals will only fight, many may not survive to tell the tale." Roberts then continued on a more personal note: "My own mother, I wish I could see you once again. I do not anticipate any great struggle, some lives must be sacrificed, and it may please God to take mine. I am ready and willing to give it. No one ever died in a better cause."

Cracklow seemed more ebullient than usual: "I never was in bet-ter health and spirits in my life or had less property to bother wor-rying about." Lang was typically fatalistic, commenting a week or so before the breaching: "God grant that I may feel . . . how pow-erless I am and how petty is this world and all my earthly hopes and plans . . . How very hard and thankless our natural hearts are." Yet Lang, too, waxed optimistic toward the upcoming clash: "We have been sharpening our swords, kukries and dirks—my 'favourite fighting sword' Excalibur has now an edge like a razor and a surface like a mirror." In his matter-of-fact way, he stated flatly, without emotion: "I mean to make my will now in favour of Dacres, who will not be exposed during the next week as we shall be, and who will take charge of my things, and prevent everything I have here being rummaged about and sold by auction. I should hate all my traps put up for sale in a camp auction, before at least some friend had weeded out a good many articles."

As the breaching efforts continued, the tension in the British camp reached a frenzy. Cracklow's own two guns were called up to help demolish the musketry parapet on either side of the breach, and two guns from the Horse Artillery under Lieutenant Blunt kept up a continuous bombardment behind the walls. Lang penned a note hurriedly on September 12: "This is splendid, no nonsense about it. We are fighting close up, hurrying on the most rapid of sieges, working recklessly under fire without approaches or paral-lels; our big smashing guns roar out together in salvoes and crash into the crumbling walls. It does one good to hear and watch a

salvo of 24-pounder guns, pounding the walls, and making the
'deadly breach.'"

By the next day the breach seemed complete, from where the
British could see it. Yet confirmation up close was needed, and now
Lang was given a fearsome assignment: to creep up on to the top
of the glacis, inspect the breach, and report back. He told the story:
"In the evening Nicholson and Taylor came down and ordered me
to inspect the breach after it got dark. I preferred going when I
could see . . . Taking four riflemen, crossed the road leading to the
river in front of the custom house and slunk up through some trees
to the foot of the glacis . . . I ran up the glacis and sat on the edge
of the counterscarp, and examined the appearance. The counterscarp is an earthen slope very steep about 18 feet deep, a dish of 20
or 25 feet leads to a berm wall 8 feet high. Then opposite the curtain
the berm is about 15 feet . . . I ran back, fired at, and coming in was
fired at by our own sentries."

That evening he and George Medley were ordered back for another look, in order to get actual measurements. Medley wrote of
this attempt: "In five minutes we found ourselves on the edge of
the ditch, the dark mass of the Cashmere Bastion immediately on
the other side, and the breach distinctly discernible. Not a soul was
in sight. The counterscarp was sixteen feet deep, and steep; Lang
slid down first, I passed down the ladder, taking two men out of
the six, descended after him, leaving the other four on the top to
cover our retreat. Two minutes more and we should have been at
the top of the breach; but quiet as we had been, the enemy was on
the watch, and we heard several men running from the left towards
the breach. We therefore reascended, though with some difficulty,
and throwing ourselves down on the grass, waited in silence for
what was to happen. A number of figures immediately appeared at
the top of the breach, their forms clearly discernible against the
bright sky, and not twenty yards distant. We, however, were in the
deep shade, and they could not apparently see us . . . After waiting
therefore some minutes longer, I gave a signal, the whole of us
jumped up at once, and ran back toward their own ground. Directly we were discovered, a volley was sent after us; the balls came
whizzing about our ears, but no one was touched." The two trips
were plucky acts indeed, and many later mutiny books told and

retold the story.⁹ Still, this was just preliminary to the great assault itself. Now the word came—it was to be the next morning.

As the moment of the great battle approached, Cracklow worried: "The Pandies are exceedingly plucky and fight like fiends and we shall have no easy job with them . . . I expect the Pandies will make a tremendous fight of it in the city, as they fight uncommonly well behind walls. However, British pluck will I have no doubt, carry the day as it has hundreds of others against equal odds." Roberts commented, too, and with uncommon prescience: "I only trust all the women and children will have been removed, for once inside, few will be spared. It will be an extraordinary day for those that see the end of it, if the Pandies only wait to fight, but I sometimes think the greater part will be off with the plunder they have got, and we shall then have to follow them up somewhere else."

Cracklow's trust in "British pluck" was yet again testimony to the faith and sense of manifest destiny typically found among the British officers. Roberts's optimism the night before the assault on the city exemplified this confidence: "I feel as if all would go well. I never remember being in better spirits or so thoroughly jolly . . . I can scarcely realize that this is the last night I have to spend in my tent before these horrid Walls, the next 2 or 3 in the Batteries and then I hope many miles beyond, following up and punishing these fiends wherever we may meet them."

The task that faced them in the assault on Delhi was fearful, and Archdale Wilson was wavering on just when to plan the key assault, hoping for reinforcements from the south. But Roberts mirrored most of the men's feelings when he commented the day before the assault: "I am right glad there was no chance of assistance from below—or our General [Wilson] would have waited to a certainty, and before any troops could have joined us, our own Force would have been ruined by disease." Wilson was, by his own admission, terribly fatigued, and the toll of the insistent pressure from the governor-general in Calcutta to "take Delhi forthwith," a viewpoint that continued to be expressed privately by many of his own officers, seemed to make him even more indecisive. He penned a long letter to his chief engineer with the evident intent of being able to use it as self-justification with the governor-general if the attack failed: "A letter has been received from the Governor-General urging our immediately taking Delhi, and he seems angry that it was not done long ago. I wish to explain to him the true state of affairs: that Delhi is seven miles in circumference, filled with an immense fanatical Mussalman population, garrisoned by full 40,000 soldiers armed and disciplined by ourselves, with 114 pieces of heavy artillery mounted on the walls, with the largest magazine of shot, shell and ammunition in the Upper Provinces at their disposal, besides some sixty pieces of field artillery, all of our own manufacture, and manned by artillerymen drilled and taught by ourselves; that the Fort itself has been made so strong by perfect flanking defences erected by our own Engineers, and a glacis which prevents our guns breaking the walls lower than eight feet from the top without the labour of a regular siege and sap . . . an attempt to blow in the gates and escalade the walls was twice contemplated, but that it was considered, from the state of preparation against such an attack on the part of the rebels, such an attempt would inevitably have failed and have caused the most irreparable disaster to our cause: and that even if we had succeeded in forcing our way into the place, the small force disposable for the attack would have been most certainly lost in the numerous streets of so large a city, and have been cut to pieces . . . The force under my command is, and has been since the day we took our position, actually besieged by the mutineers who, from the immense extent of suburbs . . . have such cover for their attacks that it has been very difficult to repel them . . . every such attack upon them has entailed a heavy loss upon our troops, which we can ill spare, and which has done us little good."[10]

Had Wilson known how bad the morale of the mutineers in the city was, he might have felt a bit more confident. Back in early August the *Delhi News* was full of bravado: "It is being announced in the open Durbar that the name of the English has been effaced from the map of Hindoostan . . . Those foolish few who expect the English to return are utterly deceived . . . Should the English venture to leave London, they will inevitably lose their own country . . . The British have no friends, whereas many are eager to obey the King's behests." Now, though, by the time of the siege-gun assault, the squabbles among the various forces in the city were putting the king in a difficult position: "They were most fierce and insolent in their demands. The King declared he had no pay to give them. The troops rejoined that in that case, they would plunder both the Palace and the city and massacre all the Court. Upon this, the King rose and threw down the cossock on which he usually sits in Durbar and gave orders that all of the property of the Court, the horses, elephants, caparisons and even the ornaments of the Begums should be immediately made over to them and then turning his face toward Mecca he burst into tears, exclaiming he was well punished for his sins. Had he been included in the massacre of the English he might have been spared this humiliation. During these passionate cries, the whole Court and the Begums were moved to tears, and even the soldiers were ashamed of their violence, excusing themselves on account of the extreme distress and hunger to which they were reduced."[11]

Wilson, however, was operating on the incomplete intelligence available to him from outside the walls. Pressed increasingly by his own officers (Nicholson in the vanguard of the group exhorting action), Wilson finally gave orders for the final assault plan to be effected, commenting: "It is evident to me that the results of the proposed operations will be thrown on the hazard of a die; but, under the circumstances in which I am placed, I am willing to try this hazard—the more so as I cannot suggest any other plan to meet our difficulties."[12]

The battle plan was a straightforward one, worked out by Richard Baird Smith, the chief engineer. There were five columns, each containing approximately a thousand men. The first three columns, under Nicholson's overall command, were to attack the northern walls at the points closest to the river, where the monsoon-swollen waters offered one flank secure from counterattack. The key spot here was the Kashmir Gate. Meanwhile, the Fourth Column was to capture the dangerous suburb of Kishangunj and thus protect Nicholson's right flank, and to enter the Kabul Gate when the Nicholson forces had secured it from within. The Fifth Column was to stay in reserve, just out of range.

The daring Lang/Medley reconnaisance having brought news that the breaches in the wall appeared large enough for the attacking columns to force their way through, early in the morning of the fourteenth the fateful attack began. Wilson's "hazard of the die" would soon be known. It began on a macabre note (as reported by

Cracklow): "These brutes had managed to get hold of an European some short time before we stormed and they hung him naked in front of the breach. He was killed by our own guns, poor fellow."

The eye of the battle had to be at and around the Kashmir Gate itself. The breach had been made to the river side of the gate, and this was now to be the first challenge. That terrifying, age-old moment had come when men had to move straight forward into merciless fire and place their will and courage against that same determination from the defenders. As the ditch had to be crossed before the breach itself could be assaulted, the first men rushed forward with scaling ladders. "Man after man was struck down," told one officer later, "and the enemy, with yells and curses, kept up a terrific fire, even catching up stones from the breech in their fury, and, dashing them down, dared the assailants to come on."

Now the crucial step: "The storming parties pushed on, two ladders were thrown into the ditch, and a brave officer, Fitzgerald . . . who was killed directly afterwards, was the first to mount . . . As soon as I saw my first ladder down, I slid into the ditch, mounted up the escarp and scrambled up the breach, followed by the soldiers." In a flash they were inside—and Delhi was pierced. Sappers quickly blew the gate itself, and two columns, "like a swarm of bees . . . then like hounds topping the fence," fanned out into the town.

Lang and Medley were in Nicholson's Column One; Medley was to enter at the Kashmir breach and Lang to go up the face of the Kashmir bastion, leading the 250 men of the 1st Fusiliers. Lang described those terrifying moments at the charnel point: "At the Custom House road we turned to the left and made up the glacis to the right face of the bastion. It was most gloriously exciting; the bullets seemed to pass like a hissing sheet of lead over us, and the noise of the cheering &c. company was so great that I nearly lost my men, who doubled too far down the road before I could turn them, so they got more fire on the glacis than they needed. The edge of the ditch reached, down we slipped; just as I slid down, on my left I saw Medley and the 75th beginning to swarm their breach, and on my right I saw a column of smoke ascend and heard the explosion of the blowing in of the Kashmir Gate.

"Up went a little ladder, but once on the berm we instantly saw that there was no place for placing our long ladders, so up we scrambled just a steep crumbling wall of masonry. I have seen it since in cold blood, and wondered how we got up at all. I was just falling backwards on our own bayonets when a Ghoorkha pushed me up luckily, and presently over we were . . . tearing down the ramp into the main guard behind the Kashmir Gate. Here was a little confusion; no one exactly was sure of the way. Nicholson and Taylor ran up towards Skinner's house—wrong way—Pemberton and I and Captain Hay and a few more led sharp to the right, under the ramparts along narrow lanes . . . such a place, but on we rushed, shouting and cheering, while the grape and musketry from each bend and from every street leading from our left, and from rampart and housetop, knocked down men and officers.

"It was exciting to madness and I felt no feeling except to rush on and hit. I only wondered how much longer I could possibly go unhit, when the whole air seemed full of bullets. We took tower after tower, and gun after gun, never stopping. On the Mori I shouted out to line the parapet and gave three cheers; bad advice! for we were fired on from our own batteries. We tore strips of white, red and blue from dead 'Pandies" clothes, and put up an impromptu flag and then rushed along again."

After having been so careful to have his sword, Excalibur, polished and sharpened, Lang found that for some reason he was ineffective with it: "In some bend or in some tower caught fellows who were late in flying. I cut at several, but never gave a death blow; to my surprise, I didn't seem able to cut hard but it was of no consequence, as Ghoorkhas' kukri and Europeans' bayonet instantly did the business."

In the midst of his account of the pitched battle, written on September 15, at the height of the fray, he incongruously gave a lyrical description of the city: "Some of the houses are very pretty; courts in the centre of them with little canals and fountains, and very pretty shrubs, flowers, and creepers, balconied rooms, gorgeous in barbaric style of gilding and glass; immense mirrors, thick rich carpets and comfortable chairs, elegant furniture, and a scent of attar all about; strange it seemed to see these rooms full of rough soldiers, Europeans and Sikhs."

Cracklow chronicled his own adventures that day: "A column of ours . . . composed chiefly of native troop, Sikhs, Goorkhas, etc. . . . these brutes after making a very feeble assault bolted like anything and we . . . were sent up to stop the enemy from following them too far . . . it is very little use artillery and cavalry charging stone walls but we blazed away at them for some time and killed a few . . . we were under fire for some 2 hours and the artillery lost 40 men killed and wounded. After this brilliant!! affair we were ordered back."[13] The pullback was necessary because of a shocking eventuality. The first order of priority had been to take the Kabul Gate from the inside, in order to admit the Fourth Column, expected to be right outside. But the latter was not there. Why not?

The Fourth Column had been composed of miscellaneous detachments deputed from no less than eight different regiments collected from picket all across the front—the Crow's Nest, Subzee Mundi, the Mound, and Fakir's Tomb outposts. "This was a faulty formation," criticized one officer, "as detached bodies of men are never so effective as an entire Regiment, and in this case specially so, as Reid's Column was called upon to attack a very formidable position, which the enemy had been vigorously strengthening for weeks past, and to reduce which a very much stronger force, with an efficient Artillery was absolutely necessary." Major Reid, the commander, had just under nine hundred men from these regiments, with a reserve of the twelve hundred infantry of the Jammu native forces in reserve.

His men were ready for the thrust into Kishangunj by 5:00 A.M., but the four Horse Artillery guns that were to accompany him had not yet arrived. When they finally did, they had sufficient gunners to man only one gun. Taking an infantry regiment into a battle of this nature with only one gun was contrary to all that Reid had been taught, so he decided to wait until additional gunners came up. At this point he sent a party of about four hundred of the Jammu troops around to the right to occupy a small village there and protect his flank. Before the missing gunners could come up to the main force, this contingent of Jammu troops had stumbled into trouble. First they had come upon a stone wall, which had had to be leveled by gunfire. The noise alerted the enemy, and as the Jammu troops proceeded down the small road, some two thousand men lining both sides of the road behind the walls and the thick trees opened fire on them.

Reid made a quick decision, ordering his main force forward, earlier than he intended, before the artillery backup had arrived.

But the ruckus on the right from the near-ambush of the Jammu troops had already alerted the mutineers back in the town. Thousands of them poured out to take on Reid's main column. Kishangunj had a loopholed wall around much of it, and this eighteen-foot-high impediment gave tremendous tactical advantage to the defenders. Nevertheless, the main attacking force was definitely holding its own when Reid suddenly was struck in the head by a bullet. Taken for dead, he was rushed to the rear. There followed long moments of indecision and disorder before the question which officer should succeed him was finally answered. Lawrence, the captain, taking over, described the situation: "I found the leading detachments of the different regiments comprised in the column in the utmost confusion. A great portion of them had entirely broken away to the right and were shut out from view in the jungle. Such as remained, chiefly men of the Goorka battalions, the Guides and a very few Europeans were mingled together and it was utterly impossible to reform them and renew the attack on the battalions."

Meanwhile, the situation with the Jammu troops on the right was worsening. Lawrence reported: "The Jammu troops, seeing the confusion and trap, and being themselves exposed to heavy fire, could not be prevailed on to advance. They also broke into the jungle to the right from which they commenced their heavy fire on the enemy . . . At this time the enemy were within fifty paces of the position taken by the Jammu men." Putting it in blunter terms, the Jammu troops had panicked and bolted. For a terrible moment it seemed that the enemy would break through on the right, circle the Fourth Column, and drive right onto the rear of the other three columns, already exposed with long lines out into the city.

Fortunately, Wilson had a contingency plan. He had kept Brig. Hope Grant's cavalry in close proximity for just such an eventuality. Now they were drawn up in sight of the enemy along the walls of Mori Bastion (near the Kabul Gate). In effect, they were to act as decoy to allow the infantry to retreat. Lieutenant MacDowell, the cavalry unit's second-in-command, described the next moments: "We went there at the gallop, bang through our own batteries, the gunners cheering us as we leapt over the sandbags, etc., and halted under the Moree Bastion under as heavy a fire of round shot, grape and canister, as I have ever been under in my life." They were then ordered to continue to sit in their saddles, in direct sight of the enemy, as a fire of death rained into them. One of the contemporary observers struck the note of what was clearly high heroics: "Gallantly they stood, conscious that thus exposing their lives without the power of retaliating, they were serving the common cause." Hope Grant, in a letter written a few days later, struck the same posture of unquestioning British pluck: "The conduct of all my force, both European and natives, was admirable—the unflinching coolness and steadiness of the 9th Lancers being especially conspicuous. Nothing daunted by their numerous casualties, these gallant soldiers held their trying position with a patient endurance; and on my praising them for their good behavior, they declared their readiness to stand the fire as long as I chose."[14]

Lawrence, in his report on the battle, was at pains to ensure that the finger of blame did not point at the Jammu troops: "I may here add that I attribute the fact the the Jamoo troops keeping together as they did and not at once retiring when they saw all the Europeans beaten back, to the unremitting exertions of Captain Mocatta, the only European officer with them. Without presuming to reflect upon the authorities by whom this attack was planned and organized, I consider myself called upon to give my opinion that its failures are mainly attributed to the defective organization of the Fourth Column and to the total want of information as to the strength of the enemy likely to be opposed to it. In support of this opinion I will merely state that the Fourth Column, whose duty it was to take two if not three batteries situated within separate walled enclosures most difficult of access kept defended by large bodies of well-trained soldiers, was composed of 800 ill-disciplined, ill-armed men and 800 of our own troops."

Captain Dwyer, officer under Lawrence that day and in charge of one of the troops on the right, added: "This advance, I am sorry to say, was not effected notwithstanding the utmost exertions on the part of Lieutenant Tenant of the Engineers, Lieutenants Graham and Manderson and myself. A small body of Infantry could not be collected to support the guns as the whole of it had almost from the commencement proceeded to skirmish in very extended order contrary to my repeated orders. On the order for the guns to limber up being given, no horses could be got for which the guns were being worked. The horses had been made over to grass cutters, who took most of them away altogether. 5 or 6 horses I saw killed. The rest were never brought back and I was informed that they also had been killed. The attempt to secure the edyah was, I regret, a complete failure."

In retrospect, analysts have harshly judged a number of the decisions of that day, particularly the inability of the Jammu native troops to maintain discipline under fire. A few historians glossed over the amazing story as merely a study in heroism; one officer later wrote: "Though this deed of the 600 before the walls of Delhi had not been sung by the Poet Laureate and it is not so world famous as that of the other 600 at Balaclava, it fully deserved to be bracketed with it as an example of heroism, self-sacrificing devotion." But most analysts were much more severe in their judgments; as one of them put it: "The wait became a costly piece of passive heroics. They remained mounted, drawn up in line under fire, with the textbook object of preventing any possible flank attack . . . they sat motionless, as if on parade, only the horses tossing their heads wearily and whinnying and pawing the ground at the hail of roundshot and grape . . . it was a fearful, meaningless test of discipline. In front of the horsemen stretched a row of gardens in which it was impossible for them to maneuver. They dared not now retire—even if the order was given—for then they would lose their guns; and they could not take back their guns as well for fear of losing the position and laying the rest of the Artillery and the Infantry fighting inside the walls open to the danger they were supposed to prevent."

Everyone agreed that the cavalry stood up splendidly to this entirely unnecessary massacre, and one officer wrote when it was all over that "Hodson sat like a man carved in stone, and as calm and apparently as unconcerned as the sentries at the Horse Guards." Hugh Gough, Hodson's second-in-command, wrote later: "It was a most crucial test of discipline and endurance to stand there for hours, losing good men every minute and being able to make no return . . . This again for me was a 'first experience.' Being steadily shot at is just at first a most unpleasant one, but as I got a little more accustomed to it, it seemed not much worse than being out in the rain without an umbrella; and after a time I lighted my pipe and took matters very easily. It certainly was a critical time, but the

movement had the desired effect, and as heavily as our brigade
suffered, it was satisfactory to know that we had done our duty and
had borne a good, if passive, share in the day's fighting."[15]

The "cool Hodson" was none other than William Hodson, who
as a captain in the senior class at Rugby School in England in 1840
had used Draconian measures to put down excessive fagging. Hodson had had a checkered career in India. On the one hand, he was
a brilliant horseman and as a cavalry lieutenant a superb leader of
native troops. He was particularly revered by the Sikhs. Earlier he
had been with the Guide Corps, but four years before the mutiny
he had left this crack organization under suspicion of having mis-
appropriated regimental funds. In the intervening period he had
killed a native officer whom he claimed was a mutineer, though
many believe that a more likely motive was that Hodson owed him
money. When the mutiny began, Hodson was given his own cavalry unit, called more formally "Hodson's Horse" but also self-
proclaimed as "the plungers." Sen, in his book *Eighteen Fifty-seven*,
described Hodson as "the *beau ideal* of the hearty Punjab riders,
but like Nicholson, he also belonged to a bygone age. In the
Middle Ages he would have made a good *condottiere* and would
have excelled as a partisan leader. But in the nineteenth century his
easy conscience and elastic standard of honour was an enigma to
those who admired his warlike virtues. In serving his country he
did not miss an opportunity of serving his personal interests, and
he did not neglect the chance of making a penny, honest or dishon-
est . . . his bravery and indefatigable industry earned him the
friendship of many good men but his callous cruelty equally re-
pulsed many potential wellwishers."

Hodson's impassive bravery with the Fourth Column was one
more example of the positive side of his leadership. It was this side
that appealed so much to young lieutenants like Cracklow, Lang,
and Roberts, giving rise to an admiration that even accepted a brutal incident involving Hodson a few days later (to be described in
a moment).

Roberts, watching the whole debacle of the Fourth Column, was
appalled. He wrote his father a few days later: "The Cavalry and
H.A. all this time were creating a diversion outside the Walls, rather
a mad act, I think for they suffered most severely having to retire,
and did little or no good." In his memoirs, written many years later,

Roberts tempered this harsh judgment considerably, and it is to the great credit of his daughter, Countess Roberts, who edited his mutiny letters for publication, that she left the original blunt statement in, only adding a footnote: "Writing with a fuller knowledge, Lord Roberts in his book gives an account of the good work performed by the Cavalry and Horse Artillery on this occasion."[16]

At this critical juncture Wilson was able to detach Bourchier's and Cracklow's guns from the First and Second columns and send them back to relieve Hope Grant's cavalry. With the aid of their added firepower Wilson was able to stabilize the flank—though the original objective, the taking of the Kabul Gate, remained unachieved. Bourchier's timely efforts gained the unit another commendation.

The situation posed inside the gates by the Fourth Column's botch in plans became quite untenable. Lang reported the chain of events: "Brig. Jones came up and called for the engineer officer and asked where the Kabul Gate was; I told him, and he declared that his orders were to stop at the Kabul, and that we ought not to be on so far. We were all shouting for advance; but not a bit; all we could gain was to be allowed to hold our ground. But this was not so easy; as long as we rushed on, cheering and never stopping, all went well; but the check was sad; the men crouching behind corners, and in the archways which support the ramparts, gradually nursed a panic, one by one they tried to get back."

Nicholson quickly learned of the aborted effort of the Fourth Column, but he resolved to press forward into the city anyway. Facing him was an ominous narrow lane with the enemy on both sides and two cannons at the end. Harcourt Anson witnessed the next events and linked them with a similar happening earlier that day: "I am sorry to say that we failed in an attack on the Lahore Gate, through some unaccountable backwardness of our 8th and 75th, who could not be persuaded to advance, though Lieutenant Briscoe, of the 75th sacrificed himself (being killed by a shower of grape) in a vain endeavour to arouse them. Nicholson's Europeans showed a similar recreancy on the 14th when ordered to storm the Burn Bastion. He called upon them repeatedly to advance, and finding they did not, turned around to harangue them, and had got as far as "I never should have thought that Europeans would have quailed before niggers, or words to that effect, when he, poor, gallant fellow, fell mortally wounded." Lang corroborated the accusation: "The men who had once refused, refused again, and, turning, left Nicholson and Pemberton behind, who had to run before the pursuing 'Pandies.' I felt quite disspirited when I saw poor Gen. Nicholson, to whom we all trusted to get us on, brought back as we feared mortally wounded." Moments later eight other officers and fifty men were killed, and the troop fell back.

Thus it appeared that it was British cowardice, rather than enemy action, that had brought about what was to be the death of Nicholson eight days later. Cracklow disparagingly spoke of this behavior in his next letter to his mother: "You will probably see them crowing in the papers about the gallant conduct of the British soldiers, so don't believe a word of it. Even when they were sober, they behaved some of them with the most rank cowardice . . . They on several occasions bolted from less than their own number of niggers. I saw it myself once and have had several instances given me by other officers. They could not be got to advance, and the great number of casualties among the officers is a consequence of their having had to expose themselves so much in trying to urge their men on."[17]

Nicholson's failure to take the lane where he was shot in turn endangered the other column, and it, too, fell back. The telegrams being sent out during that afternoon mirrored everyone's anxieties: "2 p.m.—hard fighting still continues; we hold the Kashmir and Moree Gates and bastions and part of the main streets. Our losses are I fear heavy"; "2:30 p.m.—we hold the line of the city from Kabul Gate to College Gardens. Our loss has been severe but we hope during the evening and night to make good progress. Brig. General Nicholson severely wounded"; "3:15 p.m., some of the mutineers have attempted to cross the bridge-of-boats but were stopped by the fire of light field guns, that the first Bengal Fusiliers had charged a battery four times and ultimately captured the guns, and that the city and bazaars are gradually falling into our hands"; "7 p.m., our position is the same as last reported and no attempt to make any progress tonight. Our mortars and battering guns have been taken in and are firing against Salingurh Palace and the town. The guns and mortars captured on the bastions have been turned against the mutineers. They continue to offer the most determined resistance. Our loss is very severe, particularly officers." Night came with the British still precariously holding onto their foothold in the city, but at a fearful cost—sixty-six officers and over eleven hundred men killed and wounded. The loss of Nicholson was particularly devastating.

Cracklow's dig at the sobriety of the British soldiers had reference to one of the ugliest incidents in the battle for Delhi. As he described it: "The walls had been breached, and up to this point the men behaved very well. But most unfortunately just under the breach they discovered a shed full of bottled beer, and wines of all descriptions. This they at once commenced to drinking and were in a short time nearly all in a state of intoxication. They could not be got to advance or do anything. Instead of our clearing the place and taking possession of the whole city, we got little more than one-fourth of it and could hardly hold that. Liquor was to be had in such quantities that outside the walls champagne was selling for 2 annas a bottle."

It so happened that the area near the Kashmir Gate was peopled by the liquor merchants. Huge stocks of European beer and wine were quickly "liberated" by the British soldiers, who dearly loved their drink under good or bad conditions. Some historians even advanced the thesis that the enemy had deliberately left the spirits there to tempt and then becloud the soldiers. This claim seems to be quite farfetched, especially inasmuch as the mutineers did not follow up with an attack.

They could have, to be sure, for the British soldiers went on a veritable orgy of drinking, despite the fact that all sorts of key objectives—the Jamid Mosque, the deadly Burn Bastion, and Lahore Gate among them—still were firmly in enemy hands. William Hodson, the flamboyant cavalry officer, described the carousing soldiers as "utterly demoralized by hard work and hard drink." Lang talked of the drunkenness, too, and reported a grisly event: "Though hundreds of rupees' worth of beer, wines and spirits are smashed, still the men get drunk . . . 10 men were caught while lying drunk in a house, bound, tortured, and cut to pieces. Yet this does not deter our men." Another officer put the tactical stakes succinctly: "Those had hitherto proved themselves heroes now wallowed in the gutters, helpless and imbecile. Most providentially the enemy did not seize upon that moment for a vigourous onslaught. If they had done so, it would probably have been successful and the British

Empire in India would have been staggered under a crushing and shameful blow from the worst and most persistent foe of its Army, strong drink."

Interestingly, Roberts mentioned the drinking in his mutiny letters only in passing: "Several of our men got drunk." In his 1897 book, *Forty-One Years in India,* he glossed over the realities again: "A report was circulated that a large number of our men had fallen into the trap laid for them by the Native shopkeepers, and were disgracefully drunk. I heard that a few men, overcome by heat and hard work, had given way to temptation but I did not see a single drunken man throughout the day of the assault, although . . . I visited every position held by our troops within the walls of the city." Though both Cracklow and Lang prominently highlighted the cowardice of some of the European troops, Roberts gave it no mention whatever in his letters at the time or in his later book. It probably would have been very hard for him to write his father, a retired general, about such sensitive matters, both reflecting badly on the professionalism of the British soldier.

The orgy of drinking continued for at least a day or two (Cracklow said three full days). Belatedly, Wilson ordered all stocks destroyed, a move that led one officer to rail: "It was deplorable to see hundreds of bottles of wine and brandy, which were sadly needed for our sick, shattered, and their contents sinking into the ground." Bourchier added piously, "Yet although the passions of the troops were, by drink and revenge, worked up to burning heat, not a case, it is believed, was heard of a woman or child having been intentionally hurt—all credit to them."[18]

Given all of the setbacks, General Wilson's first instinct—the fact seems clearly established—was to pull back out of the town to the ridgeline they had held for so many weeks. But his officers argued with him, and a headquarters was set up in the church. The following day was used for consolidating the British positions (the enemy was apparently in no condition to counterattack) and also for that most ancient of soldier actions, plundering. A great many of the residents of the city had fled helter-skelter, and their possessions were littered all over, mixed in with previous loot from the murdered English. "Yesterday, upon one of the Batteries," wrote Roberts to his mother on September 16, "I found a portmanteau with 'Miss Jennings' on it. Her Father was a Clergyman. She was an extremely pretty girl, and was murdered coming out of Church on the 11th of May."

The magazine, with huge quantities of ammunition, was easily captured on the sixteenth; one of the telegrams back to Lahore that day commented, "Notwithstanding the enormous quantity expended by the rebels during the three months last, no impression appears to have been made on the huge piles still left." The same telegram noted, hopefully, "Brig. General Nicholson is a little better." (Fred Roberts, however, had seen Nicholson that day "with death on his face"; the general died on September 22.)

By this time the infantry had lost so many officers that Roberts was drafted to lead one of the units. "I soon found it was impossible to rush ahead. The only chance was to get possession of house after house, and try and command the ramparts between the two gates . . . we were able, by our Riflemen, to keep the rebels out of a strong Bastion (The Burn) between the two gates. Hunting about, I found a lane with a door exactly opposite the ramp leading up to the Bastion. This answered famously, so as soon as it was dark, I got the Officer commanding the piquet to bring 50 Europeans and some few Sikhs for the purpose of taking possession of the Work. The soldiers from want of rest and having been beaten back once or twice were, I am sorry to say, anything but eager for a fight. I told them the Bastion was empty, but that a sentry or two might be below who would have to be knocked over. Out we went, and as I thought, a few shots were fired right into our faces from some Sepoys under the Walls. This over, all was our own, but to my surprise I found the Officer in Command of the party and myself were the only two present, every other one had bolted. We went back and spoke to them, not a little disgusted, but I soon got them round, and away we went and took the place as jolly as possible."

Lang was with Roberts; he also gave his version: "Meeting Taylor and Fred Roberts there, I went with them down a street to the right and we began to make our way, breaking into houses, across or down lanes, occupying and loopholing, commanding houses, till we commanded the interior of the Burn Bastion . . . just after we had rushed into the Bastion (at dusk) up strolled a 'Pandi' up the ramp. At the top an officer clapped a hand on his shoulders saying 'kaun hai'? (who is it?). The startled scoundrel, with a ludicrous expression of dismay, asked 'yih Angrezi guard hai'? (is this an English guard?). Our friend was disarmed and shot; he was a Ghazi, and had been out spying and came back to tell his friends that 50 Europeans and 50 Sikhs were coming; rather late his information!"

Roberts also wrote his family about an incident in which he had been involved the previous day: "I was just in time this morning to save the lives of 2 poor Native women. They were both wounded and had concealed themselves in a little house. Another hour, and both, I believe, would have died from exhaustion; when I gave them some water they were so grateful, for they seemed to expect I should kill them."

By September 18 the dispatches from Wilson's headquarters sounded more optimistic; large numbers of the enemy were abandoning the city down the Muttra road toward Gwalior. On the nineteenth, Burn Bastion fell, and while the palace had not yet been taken there were rumors that the king had gone to his old fort on the Agra road and that the palace was being emptied. There was a thirst for revenge against the king and his family; Roberts quoted the prevailing view: "It has been proved beyond a doubt that the King's son shot several European men and women with his own hand. Yet, even with this, there are some people who talk about a pardon for the 'poor misguided King and his family.'" To most of the men, the victory seemed incomplete without the capture of the king and his sons. William Hodson, the flamboyant cavalry leader, asked General Wilson to let him go out of the city, follow the king's entourage, and bring him back. Wilson gave grudging permission, and Hodson quickly found the king and the queen, with their youngest son, at the tomb of Humayun, five miles south of the palace. After several hours of tense negotiations, Hodson standing outside the tomb and the king hidden inside, the latter agreed to surrender on Hodson's promise that his life would be spared.

This was only part of the royal family, though; two grown sons and a grandson still were to be found. Again Hodson persuaded Wilson to give him fiat to bring them in. He had one hundred men. Lieutenant MacDowell was the only European along with Hodson that day; he wrote later: "We halted half a mile from the place [where the Princes were with about three thousand followers]. Close by were about 3,000 more, all armed, so it was rather a ticklish bit of work. We . . . sent in to say the princes must give themselves up unconditionally, or take the consequences. A long half hour elapsed, when a messenger came out to say the princes wished to know if their lives would be promised them if they came out. 'Unconditional surrender,' was the answer. Again we waited . . . We heard the shouts of fanatics . . . begging the princes to lead them on against us . . . At length, . . . , they resolved to give themselves up."

Hodson and MacDowell, after sending the princes back toward Delhi under guard, rode up the stairs of the tomb to face the enormous crowd. Hodson pointed his carbine at the crowd and said, "The first man that moves is dead." Then he ordered the mob to lay down their arms. "There was a murmur," MacDowell wrote. "He reiterated the command and (God knows why, I can never understand it) they commenced doing so." Once the rather large cache of swords and rifles was taken from the crowd, Hodson and MacDowell caught up with the troop leading the princes in. About a mile from the walls, Hodson stopped the cart carrying the princes. Fearing that the crowd would take them back, he told MacDowell, "I think we had better shoot them here. We shall never get them in." Forthwith, Hodson ordered the three princes to remove their upper garments, then took his carbine and himself shot each of the three dead. The bodies were brought back to Delhi and laid in a prominent place on the main street, the Chandni Chowk, where they were left for many hours for the remaining inhabitants to view.

Hodson's own words on that day, in a letter to his family, give some further clues about his personality: "Today, more fortunate still, I have seized and destroyed the King's two sons and a grandson (the famous, or rather infamous, Abu Bukt), the villains who ordered the massacre of our women and children, and stood by and witnessed the foul barbarity; their bodies are now lying on the spot where those of the unfortunate ladies were exposed. I am very tired, but very much satisfied with my day's work."

While the first reaction of the British troops was elation at this surprising event, later there was severe castigation of Hodson for what seemed to many to be a blatant act of murder. For the young, impressionable junior officers, Hodson remained a great hero, though Roberts did have second thoughts many years later, expressed in his book *Forty-One Years in India*: "My own feeling . . . is one of sorrow that such a brilliant soldier should have laid himself open to so much adverse criticism. Moreover, I do not think that, under any circumstances, he should have done the deed himself, or ordered it to be done in that summary manner, unless there had been evident signs of attempt at a rescue. But it must be understood that there was no breach of faith on Hodson's part . . . he steadily refused to give any promise to the Princes that their lives should be spared; he did, however, undoubtedly by this act give colour to the accusations of blood-thirstiness which his detractors were not slow to make."

The next day Lahore Gate was in British hands, and on the same day the Jamid Mosque was easily captured. Quickly, the palace gates were blown. "In we all rushed," wrote Roberts, who led one of the units, "killing every man we came across, which, however were but few. That night Headquarters was moved to the Palace, and we dined in the King's small Durbar room."[19] Wilson himself moved in, and he finally admitted some optimism by having a salute of guns fired on the twenty-first. Though there were still many hundreds of mutineers hiding about the city and its environs, a potential threat always, it was clear that Delhi had been retaken.

Thus something like five thousand men had captured a walled city defended by forty thousand armed troops. But the losses on both sides had been appalling. From the British forces a total of over thirty-eight hundred troops, British and Indian, were killed, missing, or wounded between May 30 and the final capture of the city on September 20. G. W. Forrest, the military historian, compared the losses at Delhi with those in the Crimean War, just a couple of years before. The latter had been thought to be the most lethal war that the British had fought, but Forrest's figures showed that the Battle of Delhi—from September 8 to September 20—was far worse. Over 21 percent of the total troops involved were killed in this short period; the artillery and infantry were the two heaviest sufferers. "All our best Officers are knocked over," wrote Roberts, "and we are commanded by a muff of a fellow named Greathed, who knows nothing." (Cracklow had equally uncomplimentary comments about Greathed.) Roberts was rather opportunistic about these losses, however, and saw some personal advancements stemming from them: "I am so glad I came to Delhi. Such service I may never see again, and I have done my best to profit by it. I have been most favourably mentioned in Dispatches and may get a

Brevet Majority!! . . . Do you think Major Fred Roberts will do? For the present perhaps!!"

Despite the ghastly bloodbath, though, Bourchier was led to comment piously: "The demon of destruction seemed to have enjoyed a perfect revel . . . While the Church was completely gutted and riddled by shot and shell, its gilt cross was still untouched, and as seen of a bright morning from the ridge, glittering in the rising sun, seemed beckoning us onwards, with the full assurance that the religion of the Cross should still, even in that city, soar high over Mahomedan bigotry and cruelty."[20]

Chapter 5
Agra's Smug Garrison, Cawnpore's Well

"Deeply sensible . . . that a victory not followed up is a victory thrown away" (as one of General Wilson's many severe critics put it), Wilson gave his troops only two days' rest in Delhi and then dispatched a major segment under the command of Colonel Greathed to chase the mutineers. Cracklow, Roberts, and Lang all were in the contingent. "Never did boys escape from the clutches of a schoolmaster with greater glee than we experienced on the 21st of September, when we received our orders," wrote George Bourchier, who also was with them.

Cracklow now had his wish—to leave Bourchier's heavy artillery unit for the considerably more dashing and glamorous Horse Artillery. He confided his politicking to his mother: "Just before starting I found out that there was a vacancy in one of the troops composing our force. As this was too good an opportunity to let slip, I determined to have a try for it. I went to Bourchier. He was very kind, saying that he would be very sorry to lose me but that he would not stand in my way. He gave me a most complimentary letter and mentioned that General Nicholson had spoken very highly of my conduct, and also enclosed the letter of which I sent you a copy.

"Off I set to the General and found him at tiffin in the palace of the King's private apartments. He did not seem much inclined to accede at first so I gave him the letter and this set the matter all right at once."

Roberts, if anything, felt even more excitement about the war (and his own career), telling his mother a few days after the Battle of Delhi: "The Brevet Majority is looking up, I think! Our Brigadier mentioned me very handsomely in his Dispatch yesterday. Jolly is it not? Then when I come home and see you all, how happy we will be. I could not have missed this service for anything; such a chance I may never have again." A few days later, again mentioning coming home, he added, "I may then perhaps find a Mrs. Roberts."

Lang continued in his matter-of-fact and more philosophic vein: "At least we shall, while marching, have fresh air and change, and a week hence it will be October, which I look on as the first of the cold weather months—it is certainly so in the Punjab. This time last year we had begun cricket at Lahore: when shall we have those jolly days again? . . . I hope, however, peace and civilization will soon come."

India certainly did not resemble civilization that first day, when the column assembled on the morning of the twenty-fourth to bid adieu to what had become "the City of the Dead." Lang worked all night to get ready to move: "It was not till 3 A.M. that I could get my servants and camels (which they crushed down with their bundles of loot) to start." Roberts described the almost unspeakable scene that greeted the column: "Not a living creature was to be seen. Dead bodies were strewn about in all directions, in every attitude that the death-struggle had caused them to assume . . . We marched in silence, or involuntarily spoke in whispers, as though fearing to disturb those ghastly remains of humanity. The sights we encountered were horrible and sickening to the last degree. Here a dog gnawed at an uncovered limb; there a vulture, disturbed by our approach from its loathsome meal, but too completely gorged to fly, fluttered away to a safer distance . . . the positions of the bodies were appallingly lifelike. Some lay with their arms uplifted as if beckoning, and, indeed, the whole scene was weird and terrible beyond description. Our horses seemed to feel the horror of it as much as we did, for they shook and snorted in evident terror."[1]

The ghastly toll of lives in the battle just completed had sickened everyone; the mushrooming stories of atrocities (many of them true, many more only rumor) inflamed the blood lust of the troops. Bourchier's purple prose struck the mood: "Let us pause a moment and consider, was it ever to be expected that Musselmen, after it suited their interests, would keep faith with those whom they consider infidels, when to be instrumental in their destruction is a meritorious act in the eyes of their accursed religion? The only comfort one of these miscreants possessed was to this effect: 'I die happy: I have seen English women polluted in the streets of Delhi.'" Bourchier's attitude toward the Muslim was especially bitter; he referred to "the savage propensities of the Musselman; who, while to gain his end he would invariably cringe in abject, nay loathsome, servility before his master, but let him but obtain his object and a little power, and he will twirl his mustaches and laugh in his sleeve at the credulity of those who fancy that aught but interest and pay kept him in the employment of Feringhee heretics."

Many of the officers now began to take swipes at the civil authorities for the latter's presumed softness. Bourchier made no bones about what he thought was necessary: "A roving commission, with unlimited powers and martial law." Presumably this would be military justice, so that "villages tainted with rebellion and murder would not be spared, only from fear that the coffers of the State might suffer a temporary deficit." Roberts mirrored much the same feeling when he wrote his mother in late September: "For a year or two, I would like to have charge of some very bad district to see if I could not break them in. Our civilians have ruined India by not punishing Natives sufficiently, and by allowing all the rascals in the country to hold high offices in their Kutcherries."[2]

The civil authorities, even in these very early stages of the mutiny (before Cawnpore and Lucknow had been relieved), *were* surprisingly conciliatory. For example, A. Brandreth, the secretary of the government in Calcutta in October 1857, wrote shortly after the fall of Delhi: "The Chief Commissioner advocated that defensive arrangements should be confined to the palace and that quarter of Delhi in which the Palace stands . . . it would be sound policy to allow the inhabitants to return. Delhi has long been the entrepot of great trade and a place of much social and political importance. Its possession would be in the Chief Commissioner's judgment in every point of view prove more useful to us than its destruction. However guilty some of its inhabitants have been, it cannot be denied, he believes, by any impartial person that the majority would not be connected with the late insurrection and that a large number would even have sided with us had they possessed the

power. They were . . . in the hands of a merciless and lawless soldiery. They have suffered prodigiously and it would appear good
policy to allow them, those that have survived, to return to their
homes."

Later in the fall another Brandreth letter disclosed heightening
tensions between the civil and the military authorities: "Many able
officers have advocated what the Chief Commissioner thinks is a
mistaken policy. This is to dismantle places like the forts at Agra,
Delhi and Peshawar and construct for ourselves small forts at a
distance from these cities. The Chief Commissioner thinks we may
learn something by a careful consideration of the policy which Native princes formerly adopted. They almost invariably placed their
forts so as to serve two purposes. The first, to defend themselves
from outside enemies, the second with a view of overawing their
own subjects. We have further to reflect the latter object, but surely
as strangers and foreigners it is even more incumbent on us to
observe the latter precaution. The object of a government is not to
destroy a town, but to prevent its inhabitants from rising in rebellion. By placing a fort at a distance from a town we lose half of its
advantages. We can, it is true, protect ourselves in this manner and
eventually suppress insurrection, but it is at least as important to
have the means of preventing, as well as punishing, rebellion."[3]

As the column headed away from Delhi the fresher atmosphere
of the countryside began to raise the men's spirits. Nonetheless, the
baggage cattle had been for so long on scanty and bad forage in
Delhi that they were in poor condition. The camels especially could
scarcely carry their loads, and many of them died. So slow was the
column that an extra day had to be taken in camp for the baggage
column to catch up. When it did, Greathed looked more closely at
the animals and found that they were badly overloaded, chiefly
from, as Bourchier said, "the quantity of plunder and trash that the
camp followers had brought out of Delhi." (Bourchier was not
frank enough to add that the camp followers were generally the
servants of the officers!) Greathed gave the troops a short period to
dispose of the surplus and then effected a second search. Whatever
was found in the shape of plunder at that point was summarily
burned.

Just at daylight on September 28 Greathed's scouts made contact
with an enemy cavalry picket; by the way the latter acted, Greathed

divined that an enemy main body might be near. One was—at a small town a mile ahead called Bulandshahr. It turned out to be a quite large force of mutineers from Jhansi and Nowgong, reinforced by local rebels. A sharp but short battle ensued, lasting only that morning. This encounter, the Battle of Bulandshahr, was only a minor clash on the road to the major battles ahead—Agra, Cawnpore, Lucknow. But for George Cracklow, Bulandshahr provided one of the most frightening moments in the entire mutiny.

The rebels occupied a set of entrenched, well-protected positions. The main force was in the center of the town, in an old *serai*, the ancient form of caravan hostel. Thomas Laurence, a writer in the 1850s, described the layout of this particular form of *serai*: "Imagine to yourself four ranges of thatched buildings meeting at right angles and forming a square, and enclosing a large space of open ground, which is kept for the accommodation of carriages, elephants, camels, horses, mules, bullocks etc. . . . the surrounding ranges, which somewhat resemble barracks, consist of apartments of about eight feet or ten feet square, and the hire of them is half an anna for the night for each . . . any number of travellers may jointly occupy a room . . . the *serais* are the property of private individuals . . . these parties, who are generally females, and of the Mahomedan caste, are called *Mehtranees* . . . and if they have husbands . . . are called *Mehters* . . . each *Mehtranee* has in her charge six or eight rooms or a whole range, and she is expected to look to all the necessities and comforts of the traveller who occupies any of her rooms. She even acts as his mistress for the night, or supplies him with one, which is more frequently the case."

The Bulandshahr *serai*, a many-roomed, solidly built edifice, seemed especially formidable. Near it also was a well-constructed jail, offering further protection. In front of the town, at the convergence of two roads, was a set of breastworks, and on each side were woods. Even more dangerous, because they provided better cover, were high crops on all sides, just coming into the harvest season. From a tactical standpoint, an attack on Bulandshahr was no easy assignment.

Greathed, eager for a definitive clash with as many of the mutineers as he could press to stand and fight, decided to plough right into the fray. He sent four guns of the Horse Artillery with Captain Remmington down one of the two roads before the town and

Bourchier's six guns down the other toward the breastwork. The infantry spread out among the gardens and crops. As Remmington pounded the enemy from the front, Bourchier moved up to a position where he could catch the now precarious breastwork in a crossfire. The enemy rushed pell mell back to the town.

Meanwhile, the cavalry had circled around to the left, accompanied by Cracklow and his two guns. Here they were met with an unexpected, murderous fire from houses at the edge of the *serai*. Cracklow and his small, two-gun, twelve-man unit took the fire head on. One gun's crew was immediately, devastatingly downed, and the other was almost as badly decimated. Only Sgt. A. Diamond and Gunner R. FitzGerald, along with Cracklow on his horse, survived the fusillade unharmed. In the face of continuous heavy fire at point-blank range, Diamond and FitzGerald single-handedly emplaced the gun and, as rapidly as they could reload, poured a fire into the houses. Two infantry units were ordered up to attack, but, "singular to say" (these were Hope Grant's words), "they would not go at it. Some panic came over them." Once again timidity had endangered a unit. An agonizing fifteen minutes of indecision ensued, with Diamond and FitzGerald frozen in the exposed position and Cracklow isolated on his horse to one side. Finally the 9th Lancers were ordered up. They soon drove down through the town, scattered the rebels, and rescued Diamond, FitzGerald, and Cracklow.

Cracklow, describing this terrifying moment, explained to his mother why he stayed with his horse: "I was obliged to stick on his back. Had I anyone to take my horse, I should have been down serving the gun myself, and might perhaps have come in for the same. The affair was noticed by several Lancer officers, who have sent in a letter along with Major Turner's application, and I think there is little doubt of the men getting the Cross."

Apparently, when Cracklow on horseback had run directly into the enemy's fire and the first gun was immobilized, the horse grooms (the syces) had run off. The remaining gun immediately came under the same withering fire. One man was killed and four of the remaining six wounded, so that only Diamond and Fitz-Gerald were left. Clearly, it is most difficult for two men to load and fire an artillery piece, but the two soldiers were able to do so, seemingly oblivious to the heavy fire directly into them. With the syces nowhere to be seen, Cracklow had to make a split-second decision—whether he should try to tie his horse and join Fitz-Gerald and Diamond or remain where he was. He had lost not one but two horses in the same way at Trimoo Ghat, and his decision at this moment was to stay mounted. After the throat-catching lag resulting from the recalcitrance of the first two infantry units, the Lancers finally rescued the three of them, and the little "battle within a battle" was over.

A number of dispatches went forward after the battle commending the three men. Major Turner, the commander of all of the artillery in the unit, called the actions of Diamond and FitzGerald "very gallant conduct" and that of George Cracklow "gallant conduct." Major Ouvry, the commander of the cavalry unit that had rescued the three, also sent forward a commendation, mentioning only Cracklow himself. The war was still young at this point, with just over four months of hostilities behind them. The glories of battle, the commendations, the awards were still the coveted trophies. Cracklow's reference to "the Cross" referred to that most prestigious of all awards, the Victoria Cross. Cracklow had accurately assessed Diamond's and FitzGerald's heroism: a few months later both were awarded the distinction. Cracklow had to be content with the commendations, soon buried away in the written dispatches on the Battle of Bulandshahr.

Lang, who was with the main group, described his feelings to his family. At first he felt ebullience: "'Now,' said the guide, '500 yards ahead are the enemy.' Round swung Murray's two guns and 'Load with Ball,' called out Remmington! Joyful sound! Again the blood danced in one's veins like mercury and I could have laughed with pleasure . . . But no sooner was the word out of his mouth when 'bang' went 'Pandy's' gun, and 'whishhh' came the 9-pounder ball ricocheting like a cricket ball along the smooth hard road: delightful; for just a week we had ceased to hear the perpetual sound of ball."

Soon, though, the timorousness of the troops surfaced once again, a laxity that always infuriated Lang: "After some time our Infantry, with a great deal of cheering and no results, and a great deal of Delhi musquetry, took a couple of guns which 'Pandy' had abandoned!" At least Cracklow had worked his gun "in a most plucky style," Lang concluded.

Roberts, too, had an exciting moment, when he was sent back into Bulandshahr later that afternoon: "On going through a nasty street in the city a strong body of the enemy, who had been concealed in houses, made a stand and opened a heavy fire on us. We charged, and I had the misfortune to have a very fine charger shot right between his eyes—lucky his head was in the way or I should have caught it—and as we were only a few yards off, I have no doubt it would have inflicted a very nasty wound. It was the first morning I had ever ridden him—a favourite horse of poor General Nicholson's, which I bought after his death. The poor brute is still alive, but in a very bad way, so I now have 2 horses *hors de combat*. A great nuisance, for it is impossible to get others. I fortunately started with 4."[4]

Greathed did single out Roberts in his dispatch that day, and Major Ouvry noted that he desired to bring Roberts "conspicuously to the attention" of Greathed. Bourchier found Roberts "ubiquitous" all day. But that was as far as it went in the way of rewards for Roberts, too.

The battle had lasted just over four hours. Greathed's forces had captured three guns and a quantity of baggage and ammunition, and Lang noted that "Major Eld has been appointed prize agent to the combined forces for the plunder taken yesterday. We took 13 guns, all very good brass, and very heavy metal." The enemy had lost about three hundred men, a sizable setback but certainly not decisive for the larger war. The half-day skirmish had cost the British six enlisted men killed and six officers and thirty-five men wounded. There were some ugly incidents hidden in these figures. As a participant in the battle described these events: "The enemy were driven off, but not before they had managed to cut up several of our followers and also killing two men of our sick in the doolies which happened to be near the spot. One man, by name of King, of our regiment, was shot and frightfully cut to pieces, the other fellow belonged to the 8th Foot, he was killed in a similar manner, afterwards being set on fire by igniting his clothes."

Perhaps it was easy for one historian, writing after the fact, to comment grandly about George Cracklow's battery: "Their loss, though heavy, was not out of proportion to the results obtained by their dash."[5] To Cracklow, though, with most of the men in his brand-new command killed or injured, it might not have seemed quite so much "in proportion." The war had not only its climactic battles like Delhi but also its smaller skirmishes like Bulandshahr, and death was a product of both. Cracklow's natural ebullience and zest for battle continued to appear in his letters. But in his letter about Bulandshahr he seemed aware for the first time of the immensity of the conflict; he concluded ruefully: "I think by the time this business is all over, I shall have seen about as much of it as most people—ever since the 25th of May and now we seem only commencing."

Yet the appointment of a prize agent and the promise of personal financial rewards seemed particularly to buoy up Cracklow: "If I get all safe through this business I am a made man. They say a subaltern's prize for Delhi will be 500. This with my H.A. pay would enable me someday or other, please God, to come home comfortably. But I am counting my chickens before they're hatched. There is many a scrimmage yet to get through."

The fort at Malagarh had been the initial objective when Greathed left Delhi. But with the blow given the mutineers at Bulandshahr, they had also given up Malagarh and fled. Lang and a couple of his fellow engineer officers, together with a party of sappers, were deputed there to demolish the fort. "How delighted I felt when I saw the fort and knew it was deserted and that we had not to take it," Lang wrote. "Our light guns would have been no avail against the high thick earthen ramparts." (Here he drew a picture of it for the family.)

Lang's close friend Duncan Home, a lieutenant in the engineers, was with him (Home had been instrumental in blowing the Kashmir Gate on that first day of the Delhi attack; later he would receive the Victoria Cross for this achievement). After the short, fierce battle at Bulandshahr, the taking of Malagarh seemed quite pleasant. "This is our third day here," Lang wrote on October 1, "and our occupation is the demolition of this Fort. We live very well on plunder, on the geese, ducks, and pigeons . . . beautiful beer, unlimited in quantity, cones on cones of lump sugar and numberless great bottles of rosewater with which we bathe! In fact we are living in style, conquerors and marauders." The ebullient young officers took this dangerous work quite casually: "They are great fun, these explosions," reported Lang. "We try to get Gough or any visitors into places where they will get doses of earth and dust, without being really hurt."

Two days later, though, a ghastly development made a mockery of these words. Lang forced himself to write of it: "The last mine to be blown in was the counterscarp, by which we should make a broad smooth road into the place. Home so enjoyed these explosions, laughing always as he watched us clear off. Baker, Stevenson and I rushed up on the ruins of the bastion and saw Home run laughing up to the mine; he put his hand out and to our horror instantaneously the mine sprung. Down we rushed, put every man to work to scrape and dig. Sergeant Robson, a few feet from poor Home, had been knocked down and bruised, but was not really injured, but of poor Home for a minute or two, we saw no traces. I looked around a little distance and about 20 yards off in the hollow of a well I recognised his body, all mangled and covered with dust. Poor fellow, his legs were broken in two places, his arms broken and one nearly torn off. His death must have been instantaneous. It was like a horrid dream from which I longed to wake. I could not realise that the laughing, merry Home, so full of life and happiness just before, was now dead. He escaped the dangers of the blowing in of the Kashmir Gate, to meet his end before a deserted fort."[6]

The column pressed on to Khurja, arriving on October 3. When the troops entered the town, they were greeted by a macabre sight. Bourchier reported it: "As we entered . . . a skeleton was stuck up on the roadside, exposed to public gaze, against a wall. The head had been severed from the body, and cuts in the shin-bones were apparent, inflicted by some sharp instrument; and, in the opinion of a medical committee, this skeleton was that of a European female." Roberts, too, mentioned the incident in the book he wrote in 1897, *Forty-One Years in India*: ". . . a skeleton, ostentatiously placed against the side of a bridge leading to an encamping-ground . . . headless and the bones hacked and broken." Roberts repeated the same "evidence" about the provenance: "It was pronounced by more than one doctor to be the skeleton of a European woman."

Bourchier's reference to "a medical committee" apparently was sufficiently enigmatic to allow him to get by with such a sweeping generalization. To be sure, it could be readily ascertained that a skeleton was female. Whether one could so quickly determine whether the skeleton was Indian or European is considerably more doubtful. Bourchier, Roberts, and Cracklow undoubtedly saw a skeleton in Khurja. After all, corpses were everywhere. There was no further corroborating evidence concerning this skeleton, but the flimsy backup was enough to build it into an atrocity story.

The sight of the skeleton, and particularly the explanation of it by an official of the town—that it was just an old man who had recently died of hunger—so incensed Bourchier that he railed around the camp that night advocating a complete cleanup of the whole town. Surely, he reasoned, there were arms and mutineers hidden all over. But the cooler head of Greathed prevailed, and the next morning the column moved out. "So much for immaculate Koorjah!" was Bourchier's parting shot.[7]

There was nothing that infuriated the British soldiers more than the thought that an Englishwoman might have been violated in the mutiny—raped and/or abducted by native soldiers. In the many extensive hearings held by the British after the war was over, this subject preoccupied a great many, and hundreds of people were interviewed about the stories of such ill-treatment. Remarkably, given the brutality on both sides, there appear to have been very few such instances throughout the entire war.

One of these rumors, however, came to a real-life climax right at this point and directly involved the Greathed column and Roberts. Just before the column left Bulandshahr a spy had reported to him that an English lady was a prisoner in a village about twenty miles away and that she was anxious to be rescued. Roberts did not put much stock in the story and insisted that the spy bring some proof to him. When the column reached Khurja, the same spy reappeared and presented Roberts with a piece of paper on which was written "Miss Martindale." Given such a tangible scrap of evidence, it became incumbent to check out the story, and Roberts was sent, along with a small detachment of cavalry, to search the village in question. They timed their arrival to appear at the boundaries of the village just at dawn. The soldiers pounced upon the enclave from all sides but found only a few women and children around. Apparently, despite their elaborate attempts at secrecy, someone had alerted the village. The next step was to search the surrounding crops, and here they found many of the villagers and some soldiers hidden among them.

At this moment, to everyone's surprise, the case broke wide open; Roberts tells the story: "They one and all denied that there was the slightest truth in the story, and as it appeared a waste of time to further prosecute the fruitless search, we were on the point of starting to rejoin our camp, when there was a cry from our troopers of 'Mem sahib hai!' (Here is the lady), and presently an excessively dusky girl about sixteen years of age appeared, clad in Native dress. We had some difficulty in getting the young woman to tell us what had happened; but on assuring her that no harm should be done to those with whom she was living, she told us that she was the daughter of a clerk in the Commissioner's office at Sitapur; that all her family had been killed when the rising took place at that station, and she had been carried off by a sowar to his home. We asked her if she wished to come away with us. After some hesitation, she declined, saying the sowar had married her (after the Mahomedan fashion) and was kind to her, and she had no friends and relations to go to. When asking her why she had sent to let us know she was there, she replied that she would like to join the British force, which she had heard was in the neighbourhood, but on further reflection she had come to the conclusion it was best for her to remain where she was. After talking to her for some time, and making sure she was not likely to change her mind, we rode away, leaving her to her sowar, with whom she was apparently quite content. I need hardly say we got unmercifully chaffed on our return to camp, when the results of our expedition leaked out." (Roberts noted in a footnote in his 1897 book that a few years later she got in touch with the civil authorities with a pitiful story of ill-treatment by her husband; she was sent to Calcutta, "where some ladies were good enough to look after her.")[8]

A few days later, at another small fortified town, Aligarh, the column once more ran against resistance. Lang's group was deputed to take the direct route forward, with two artillery units to circle around the outside. Soon Lang's own immediate superior came up to the line and, "sagely remarking that it was not safe to run one's head against stone walls, actually insisted that this column should turn and follow the other left column, in fact, that we should turn our backs on one gun. Even the European infantry were amazed . . . I was so ashamed of seeing such a column march back, that I could take no more pleasure or interest in the affair. We were halted, and sat in inglorious activity . . . while we envied the left column which, of course, unrestrained, was doing good work . . . at last returned Major Ouvry and Roberts who had all the fun."

Roberts reported his "fun": "After an hour's scrimmaging, they took to their heels. Luckily we hit upon the right road and followed them up. I had just mounted a fresh horse when the pursuit commenced, so none could get ahead of me . . . I looked round for the 9th Lancers, but after the long march, their horses could not stand the pace, and I found only some 20 Sikhs near me. At them we went, and I don't think one got away."

All of these smaller skirmishes, costly as they were in wounded and dead, still were preliminary to the main objective, the relief of the enormous fort at Agra. This bastion had been serving as a sanctuary for a large group of European civilians and British troops that had swelled to a size taxing all its logistic and sanitary facilities. While the fort was not under direct siege from the mutineers, Agra itself was in enemy hands. The defenders, feeling increasingly threatened, began sending "epistles, imploring aid in every language, both dead and living, and in cypher" (as Bourchier put it). The tempo of urgency in the messages increased by the day, and Greathed drove his column faster and faster; the cavalry and Horse Artillery covered the last sixty-four miles in less than thirty-six hours.

Fred Roberts, in his new role as Greathed's intelligence officer, had gone ahead to mark out ground for encamping and to learn of possible enemy concentrations: "All the Civil and Military Authorities in the Fort assured me that from the latest intelligence they had received that the Pandies had fled, hearing of our approach and recrossed a stream about 10 miles off on the Gwalior road. With this information, I returned to camp, determining not to reconnoitre the country until the evening, as I imagined such swells must have proper intelligence."

When they arrived, Agra indeed did seem amazingly placid. The weary troops were disgusted. They had pushed themselves to the limit in order to save Agra, only to find that the fort itself had been impregnable enough to keep the six-thousand-odd people inside

safe at least from actual attack. Bourchier deprecatingly commented, "Ladies were riding and driving about in all directions;
yeomanry cavalry were careering in full equestrian pride, while
from every hole and corner loomed the ugly muzzle of an iron
monster, ready to annihilate any amount of Pandies." Roberts, too,
felt considerable irritation: "We presented, I am afraid, but a sorry
appearance, as compared to the neatly-dressed ladies and the spic-
and-span troops who greeted us, for one of the fair sex was overheard to remark, 'Was ever such a dirty-looking lot seen?' Our
clothes were, indeed, worn and soiled, and our faces so bronzed
that the White soldiers were hardly to be distinguished from their
Native comrades." A contemporary observer heard much the same
reaction among a group of ladies he accompanied that day: "We
went to the royal bastion this morning, to see Col. Greathed's
moveable column cross the bridge . . . The Queen's 8th passed
within three yards of us. 'These dreadful-looking men must be Afghans,' said a lady to me, as they slowly and wearily marched by. I
did not discover they were Englishmen until I saw a short clay pipe
in the mouth of nearly the last man. My heart bled to see these
jaded miserable objects, and to think of all they must have suffered
since May last, to reduce such fine Englishmen to such worn sun-
dried skeletons." Lang even detected some racism in the Agrans'
comments: "Some . . . seemed delighted and said 'good Sikhs'
when the wild Punjabis passed . . . others could not believe the 8th
and 75th could be European regiments, and wondered at the martial
cut-throats of Green's and Wilde's."

Accepting the intelligence report of Roberts, Greathed unwisely
let down his guard and began bivouacking his troops. Suddenly, a
group of natives dressed in the same red as the troops came dancing
up to the sergeant of the guard, the lead man playing the nagara, a
native kettledrum. The drummer, pretending to be mad, danced
around the sergeant, and then whipped out a sword and cut down
the sentry. Instantly, out of the innocent-appearing high crops in
the fields around, a horde of mutineers stormed down on the camp.
The enemy cavalry were upon Greathed's artillery almost before the
men could recover from their shock. Blunt's (and Cracklow's)
troop took the brunt of the attack. The gun of the other subaltern, Lieutenant Jones, was disabled and Jones himself severely
wounded. Bourchier and Cracklow were in the center of the cauld-

ron, caught in a maelstrom of civilian visitors to the camp trying to get back inside the walls and soldiers inside the walls trying to get back out. So frantic were the former, reported Bourchier, "that an officer of the Dragoons in attempting [to pass] was fairly carried off his legs and borne back with the crowd." Some of the terrified people even seized the gun horses and rode them blindly back into the fort, thus disabling the very instruments of their own protection.

Lang had gone to the fort, to its "coffee shop," when a distracted officer came in to say that the camp was under attack. "On emerging on the open parade grounds, I saw a camp partially pitched, smoke in various directions, and heard guns banging away, but I couldn't make out affairs at all . . . A great number of the 1st light cavalry and the red-coated irregular regiment [units of mutineers] charged from left to right of our camp in rear, killing numbers of camp followers and some fighting men. They, for a moment, took one of Blunt's guns, but were driven off by the Lancers (they cut down six Artillery men at that gun)."

Despite the imminent potential for disaster, the British soldiers were up to the task; weary from their previous march and caught with their guard down, nevertheless the forces rallied, and most of the mutineers were soon in flight. Roberts, though, ran into trouble: "A few stragglers remained, and with these some very pretty single combats took place. In the confusion at first my horses had been led away and I only found a pony to ride. Mounted on this, I did not feel quite sure about tackling an Irregular Cavalryman. However, one came dancing about me, so I thought I would try my revolver. Altho' one of Deane & Adams' very best, it misfired at each barrel and I had barely time to draw my sword when we closed. I fortunately managed to get on my friend's wrong side and rolled him with a knock on his head ere he could do me any damage." Roberts echoed the feelings often expressed by Cracklow and Bourchier concerning their horses: "The great thing I have found in all cases of this sort, is a horse over which you have perfect control. My two chargers are first-rate, fiery, swift and brave, but I can manage them completely and mounted on either of them I dread no Sowar. A pony is a different affair, and the treacherous pistol nearly cost me my life." This helps us to understand Cracklow's earlier decision to remain mounted at Bulandshahr: it likely was not an act of indecision or fear but rather the well-reasoned judgment of a seasoned fighter.

Greathed's forces followed the fleeing mutineers for miles and captured many guns and baggage. Lang was among the horsemen: "I galloped on the Gwalior road and found the 3rd Europeans [the Agra troops] in gorgeous scarlet, marching out, rather late if they really wanted any fire eating. I passed them and found infantry and guns halted, because some enclosures ahead were said to be full of 'Pandies' . . . a clear reason for halting!" Lang himself rode up, and found the mutineers escaping away. Only then would the Agra troops advance. The escaping mutineers "were so panic struck that they let a few officers and (I suppose) Agra volunteers ride through them like sheep. It was absurd; excited as we were, we rode through them, slashing and thrusting, and leaving them behind . . . They didn't perceive how few we were, but of course thought numbers were at our back. Fresh Cavalry, if up then, would have killed thousands, whereas a few independent amateurs were doing butcher's work, for doing which privates are paid."

In this chase Lang, like Roberts, had a close call: "In the excitement I got quite foolhardy and when three of us were far ahead, with the fugitives behind and on both sides of us, I still further detached myself to catch three red-coated sowars who with many others had made a turn to the left to reach a village. I dashed off to intercept them and (as they did) saw too late my position. I was out of hail of anyone and the view at my back was of armed men in flight: the three sowars looked at me, exchanged glances and, still flying, drew together. I gathered my horse for a rush and, as it were, threw myself on the nearest and before he thought I could be on him I cut him down, and instantly turning on another saw him about ten paces off, firm as a rock and his carbine barrel steady and straight on me. I gave myself up for dead, but, instinctively ducking my head, with my spurs in, I spun my horse round and round like a teetotum, the fiend still steady waiting for a sure shot; my horse stumbled and fell forward, and I too, and the sowar fired simultaneously and he had missed me and was off again. Oddly enough these armed men, so intent on flying, all gave me in my difficulties a wide berth, and neither cut at nor fired at me, or they would have killed me easily, for no one saw me and I had a man-eating horse, luckily muzzled, whom I can only get one syce to hold; however, he was pretty well done (having ridden him without change from Hathras) and I managed to mount him and regain the road, and, some of our side coming up, I was all right again."

There was yet another case of cowardice, and Lang once more vented his spleen: "The 75th behaved so much as usual that Gordon, who commands, actually said to me that they were so unsteady that he was beyond words disgusted with them, and that they broke Brookes and his heart!"

Once again, men had been lost, including a respected captain in the 9th Lancers. The weary force returned to camp at about seven o'clock that evening, having over the previous thirty-nine hours marched sixty-six miles, fought a general action, and pursued the escaping enemy over nine additional miles.

Roberts understandably was embarrassed about his faulty intelligence report, albeit caused by the complacency of the Agra garrison. His own career seemed to him very much on the line. "In writing my report about the business," he told his father, "I took care to mention how it occurred, otherwise great blame might have been attached to me." Countess Roberts, in editing the Roberts letters, included this report as an appendix to the volume—the only appendix item she felt necessary. Roberts was quite matter-of-fact in this report, cleverly (but honestly) putting the finger on the Agra contingent: "The several civil and military authorities in the Fort informed me that . . . there was no doubt but what the rebel Troops having heard of our arrival were in full retreat."

This comprehensive report, expeditiously submitted, must have done the trick, for there is no further mention of blame about the incident. Nevertheless, it must have been a chastening experience for the young, egocentric officer. None of his ambition was dimmed, however, for in the same letter to his father he continued: "I want to hear about the Medals. We should have one for Delhi alone, but the government in this country affect to treat the matter lightly, and until the other day have never issued one single order of thanks, neither have any dispatches been Medals!"

After this unnecessary battle at Agra, the Greathed forces were, if anything, even more contemptuous of the garrison's contingent. "Scenes the most ludicrous passed before our eyes as we returned to camp," wrote Bourchier. "First came a fat old gentleman, on a fat and old horse, who requested Major Ouvry to give him a certificate to the effect that he had been under fire, he being the Commandant of some volunteers of whose whereabouts he was in total ignorance; next came a truly perspiring hero, jogging along with his bridle and drawn sword in one hand, while in the other was a fan of enormous size, which he managed with dexterous address; while further on might be seen a corpulent clerk, brandishing his stock over a fallen Pandy, ever and anon starting at his temerity."

Roberts was a bit more charitable, commenting that "many have become most terribly selfish, and fancy Agra is the one place in India," but "there are a few nice people still left . . . some old Peshawar friends who gave us *two picnics*!! at the Taj." Roberts's natural ebullience again comes through: "What a lovely place the Taj is. I have never seen anything like it, perfect in every way. We had it lighted up. The more you look at it, the better pleased you are. How glorious the designer must have felt when the means for bringing into reality what his wonderful imagination had conjured up were placed at his disposal. I could have spent days and days there . . . Heroes from Delhi are thought something of, and the poor creatures in the Fort were only glad of the opportunity of getting a little fresh air."

Bourchier, Lang, and Cracklow were also along on this outing, and Bourchier, noting that the ladies were "fluttering about in all the weakness of 'the last new muslin,'" concluded that "to see their happiness was ample reward for the fatigue we had undergone on their behalf." Lang's articulate prose captured the ambience of the evening: ". . . went to a most jolly picnic at the Taj. Mrs. Machell sang 'Mira! O Norma' under the dome, but I think the echoes are too distracting . . . dined on the floor of one of the side mosques, and danced on the smooth marble platform of the Taj to the music of Green's (2nd Punjab) band. The Taj was lighted after dark with blue lights."[9]

*   *   *

Much, very much, has happened since we left Thomas Watson and his mother, together again on his leave in Simla. Cracklow, Roberts, and Lang had been through the traumatic Battle of Delhi and onward with the column to Bulandshahr, Malagarh, and Agra before Thomas Watson was settled in his next post—at Delhi. Still in the headquarters component, he continued to report a quiet life within the maelstrom about him. "There is nothing to tell you from this dull place," he wrote in mid-October, and then launched into a long discussion of how he had discovered a new way of making tea. His duties in this period must not have been taxing, for there are numbers of references to long hours of sleeping: "I think it must have been rather late when I got up to go out to walk"; "I have again allowed the morning to pass by and it is now nearly one o'clock."

His sedentary life was affecting his appearance: "I have grown much stouter, my face especially appears much fatter." He had been somewhat sick in October (he mentioned trouble with his groin), and he bemoaned his inaction: "I am not suffering any pain but feel I must again lay up. How sick I am of the sight of this room! To leave it would gladly take double duty."

His mother queried him in early October about his friends: "I want to know the names of your companions—are any of them nice people?" "There are some rather nice men in the Regt.," he wrote back, but "I only see them at dinnertime . . . I have no wish to mix in society much." Several of Watson's expressions in this period seem almost to imply an incipient depression: "I am always trying to escape from my sad thoughts and am perpetually on the move, excepting when I am writing you or reading the books you gave me." Both Watson and his mother continued to be preoccupied with what was happening to Watson's brother and his wife and child, still in the Lucknow garrison.

In early October Sarah Watson moved from Simla to Kupowlie, another nearby hill station. The reason for the move is unclear from the extant correspondence. She had been very introverted at the Simla location, and at Kupowlie she continued her withdrawal, in this case exacerbated by tensions with her hostess, a wife of one of the British officers. When she first arrived she seemed reasonably happy: "I am so sorry you are fretting lest I am not comfortable. I ought not to have said a word to lead you to think so. At first I felt a little disheartened but I am really now as comfortable as I need wish and every day I feel I prefer being here to being at Mrs. ———. Mrs. ——— is so really kind and thoughtful and she is cheerful and pleasant mannered . . . I have everything I really want and go where I please about the house without any feeling of restraint

. . . everything is on a likeward scale, nothing penurious. Altogether I feel the relief of not being under that Mrs. ———'s roof."

Within weeks, though, she was feeling isolated again. "I feel *most alone* with them—I could not now feel companionable with anyone but my children." Soon her relations with her hostess turned sour; she wrote in early November: "Do not distress yourself with the fact that the ———s are not kind—they are uniformly just but [there is] no more intimacy—they are . . . in the *habit* of having people to live with them."

Watson worried about his mother's anomie: "You talk of being a 'stranger amongst strangers' . . . I thought Mrs. ——— a very different kind of person, religious and too charitable to talk slanderously of people . . . how I wish you were with people more congenial to you."

Watson's mother wanted to return to Sialkot, and particularly wanted her son out of Delhi: "To get away from such a place as Delhi even in cool weather would be an object. Oh, I know not what to advise." Watson, however, began to like Delhi and saw some opportunities: "The city is now being sold in proportions to rich Hindus . . . what will eventually be done with the whole place it is impossible to say. Many say it will be leveled. There are some capital houses here. If the Regt. is not sent from this, you might perhaps, dear mother, come and live here. I think in a very short time a great many people will be living here."

There were other signs in the lives of the mother and son that linkages with friends were not in good shape. Sarah Watson wrote in mid-October, rather enigmatically: "I have no letter from Mr. ———. If a Christian man and a father and an affectionate son takes offence at what he ought to appreciate and admire it will be yet another instance of the wisdom of the command not to lean on man and yet I think that I did not do so in this instance, though I thought more highly of Mr. ——— than of almost anyone I knew in India. But in God is our hope, and help me my darling son I humbly believe he will order all for the best for you. Let us trust in him with all our hearts."

She remained worried about her son's physical surroundings in Delhi. "I hope you have a warm enough bed at night, for now the nights must be cold . . . Do wear these bands & your woolen nightgowns at night." During the days, it was the sun: "One thing in your letter distressed me, my darling son. You speak of yourself taking your letters to the post and then taking a walk. Surely this must expose you to the sun while it is high and must be at this season terribly hot. Oh my darling son, do not do so. I feel so persuaded of the danger and injurious effects of such exposure, especially on foot."

Sarah Watson continued her religious proselytizing, both with her son and with others: "I walked and took two of the Jaunpouries with me and after a good distance sat down on a stone and talked to them. I told them God made man, that he sinned and that to save us from the punishment due for sin the Son of God came down from heaven and bore our punishment that we might by believing and trusting in him escape. I wondered to see how the poor men seemed to understand me and how greatly interested they seemed. I told them of the thief on the Cross, of some of the miracles—the raising from the dead of the widow's son, the miracle of the loaves and fishes. They seemed affected at hearing of the Saviour's suffering . . . I told them the ten commandments and explained the same and they fully agreed to it and expressed approval of all. I thought of the years in which I have had so many similar opportunities and have done so little to inform them. Would that all the calamities that Christians have met in the last seven months might stimulate us all to endeavour to teach the heathens that are continuously around us . . . many may take warning and be missionaries in their own households and to all they come in contact with."

Life at the Delhi cantonment, now just a headquarters operation, was generally rather dull. In early November, though, word came of further disturbances in the Jodhpur area: mutineers from that station were moving east toward Delhi. A column under Colonel Gerrard was sent out in early November, into the Rewari district. At Narnul, on November 16, the Jodhpur mutineers were met and defeated. In pursuing them, however, Gerrard was killed, and the column returned to Delhi. New columns now were to be formed to pacify some of central India. Watson's mother heard of this and wrote: "How fervently I hope my darling son that you will not follow the column. The execution would most likely bring on a return of that lump and still greater suppuration . . . on a march with no comfort at your command" (we have no further documentation to explain what "that lump" was). She even worried about his traveling outside the post: "Darling, darling son, the thought haunts me of your going after the regiment, travelling through those distances." She tried to raise a practical matter, that Watson did not have enough camp equipage. It was true that he had no horse of his own; he was only using a horse that he was keeping for someone else. When the Gerrard column left, Watson reported to his mother, "If Dr. Brougham had only lent me a doolie, I should have been there." This seems a surprising reason, for the dooly, a chairlike arrangement for travel, to be carried by native runners, generally was used only for carrying wounded (they had to be carried with a moving column, as there was no base hospital to send them back to). The notion of Watson commandeering a dooly seems incongruous.[10]

* * *

The Cracklow/Roberts/Lang column now headed from Agra down the Gangetic Plain from Rohilkhand to the next province to the east, Oudh. There were four key cities in this important province—Cawnpore, Lucknow, Allahabad, and Benares, the great river cities lying along the main routes of communication between Delhi in the northwest and Calcutta on the east coast. The railroad ran only about a hundred miles out from Calcutta, so the great river Ganges and its tributaries, the Jumna coming down from Delhi and the Gumti coming from Lucknow, were the transportation lifelines that had to be preserved at any cost.

At Cawnpore and at Lucknow events occurred that would symbolize in later years what most people remembered about the mutiny. When the column, now commanded by Brig. Hope Grant, arrived at the former on October 26, the unholy act that made the name "Cawnpore" notorious for all time had already happened. A look backward to this story is critically important for our understanding.

When the mutiny struck, in May, the commander at Cawnpore was Maj. Gen. Sir Hugh Wheeler, an old man who had already served fifty-four years in India. This was a large and important cantonment, but in the months prior to the mutiny many of its troops had been siphoned off to the Punjab and other areas of the northwest. After the hostilities began in May, Cawnpore was further weakened when Sir Henry Lawrence (brother of John Lawrence), the chief commissioner in Oudh, took military command of all the troops in the territory and ordered additional men from Cawnpore to Lucknow, forty-eight miles to the north.

Wheeler was left with an undermanned garrison to defend a cantonment area spread along six miles of the Ganges. As there were many Europeans and Eurasians near Cawnpore, Wheeler's preparations for defense had to include the possibility of a significant influx of refugees into whatever area he designated as the garrison. He made the first of what were a number of questionable judgments when he picked two large barracks buildings near the river, rather than the better-fortified magazine several miles to the north.

The titular head of the mutineers at Cawnpore, the Nana Sahib, was a wealthy descendant (by adoption) of the last great peshwa of this area. The post of peshwa, a faded symbol of Maratha power, had been neutralized by the East India Company, particularly by the actions of the governor-general, the marquess of Dalhousie. The Nana was left with the wealth of his father but no kingdom to rule. Wheeler's wife, an Indian said to be of the same caste as the Nana, was his close friend, as was the general.

At the start of the mutiny the Nana remained friendly with the Wheelers, even sending troops to help strengthen the garrison. By June, though, several of the native units had mutinied, and though no Europeans were killed, they did join with the Nana's men in seizing the Treasury. Quickly the situation deteriorated. Nana Sahib now sent word to Wheeler that he and his men were going to attack, and on June 6 the Cawnpore garrison was put under siege.

Wheeler had poorly prepared for such an eventuality, for the two barracks buildings afforded very little protection. The mutineers put the defenders under heavy artillery fire; a week later one of the barracks buildings was burned down. Even the path to the one usable well within the area was under direct fire during the daylight hours. On June 13, the anniversary of the Battle of Plassey, the mutineers mounted a tremendous attack. Although it was beaten off, the little garrison lost more men and was also becoming dangerously short of food and water supplies. Two days later the Nana sent a letter to Wheeler offering safe passage down the river to

Allahabad for, so his letter was reputed to say, at least "all those who are in no way connected with the acts of Lord Dalhousie and are willing to lay down their arms."[11] Wheeler met with representatives of the Nana and agreed to the terms: the British had to surrender their guns and treasure but could keep their hand arms and sixty rounds of ammunition for each man. The Nana promised transport for the women and children and the sick. Boats with supplies would be waiting for the British contingent at the edge of the river, at Sati Chaura Ghat.

The date was June 27. This was the day for the beginning of the "safe passage"—but it aborted, terribly. Early that morning the remains of the garrison marched down to the river and began piling into the boats on a helter-skelter basis. The boats were the common eight-oared "budgerows" of the local area, top-heavy structures with thatched roofs, looking at a distance like floating haystacks. Just as the last of the boats was filled, shots unexpectedly rang out. Within seconds the enormous crowds of mutineers lining the banks of both sides of the river began pouring a murderous fire down on the boats. General Wheeler was one of the first to fall. The forces of the Nana waded into the waters, killing all those who tried to escape. Of the forty boats, thirty-nine were destroyed at the ghat; one escaped, only to be captured further down the river. After many minutes of slaughter, the action suddenly stopped. The remaining British survivors, about 125, were then brought back to the mutineers' camps. The approximately 60 remaining men were killed immediately by the Nana's troops and the women and children imprisoned in a large house at the edge of the cantonment. In a few days they were moved to a small house called the Bibighur—the "Lady's House"—a bungalow built by an English officer for his native mistress.

The massacre at the ghat has been debated perhaps more than any other of the many murky incidents in the mutiny. It was unequivocal negation of the agreement itself. Whether it was a conscious decision by the Nana, or someone else, or, as one of the most respected historians of the mutiny put it, "one of those ghastly incidents that scatter the pages of history and on which any interpretation suitable to the needs of the occasion can be imposed," will never be fully ascertained. This historian continues, "Probably a musket-shot was heard and the British, fearful of treachery and with nerves tattered by three weeks of constant siege, immediately opened fire."[12]

Our concern here is not an attempt to add further analysis to these "facts" but to see how this dumbfounding event would have been seen by Cracklow, Roberts, Lang, and the rest of the British soldiers. One further event at Cawnpore needs to be entered on the record to understand the full effect on these men.

Something under one hundred women and children survived the Ganges killings. At the Bibighur they were soon joined by additional captured women and children from Fatehgarh. Miraculously, four men had made an incredible escape down the river during the shooting. By the time Cracklow, Lang, and Roberts reached Cawnpore, these four men were the only survivors. For on July 15, when news reached the Nana that a large rescue force under General Havelock was approaching the city, all of the women and children in Bibighur were murdered. After the mutiny was over, British authorities interviewed hundreds of native followers to try to get at the precise details. This later investigation was probably a futile one, as it was long after the fact and produced many conflicting versions.[13] More important to us is the existing story that summer and fall of 1857 as it was perceived by British soldiers then. It was sensationalism in the extreme.

When Havelock's forces broke into the city two days later, Bibighur was there to assail them. In a well near the Lady's House, they found many dozens of the bodies of women and children, all horribly hacked by sabre or sword blades. (A British officer later explained: "The receptacle was far too small for all, and there can be little doubt that bodies were dragged against the open space to the river, which was at no great distance. Indeed, we were told as much at the time.") In the post-mutiny hearings it was finally determined that the Nana's troops had been ordered to shoot all of the captives but had fired into the ceiling in refusal. Then, on July 15, five men with swords—butchers and hangers-on from the local market— were sent in. These five killed or mortally wounded most of the captives; a few children were left alive. The following morning the dead and wounded began to be thrown into the well. At least one child ran around the well, crazed with fear, until caught and thrown in, alive. All were dead when Havelock's men arrived. One officer, there that first day of discovery, cried: "Who could look upon that little enclosed yard, reeking with blood as if 100 bullocks had been killed there—see the long tresses of some once fair ladies' hair lying in handfuls—and above the small mark of the little children's feet, printed with their mother's blood on the floor—and then look down *that* well upon the naked bodies of our poor countrywomen, evidently only rendered lifeless the day before, and not feel that he would never forget it."[14]

There were other reputedly eyewitness accounts of the Bibighur that were outright fabrications. This inflammatory report was re-told widely, yet had no basis in fact: "In one apartment was a row of women's shoes and boots, with *bleeding amputated feet* in them! On the opposite side of the room, the devilish ingenuity of the mocking fiends was shown in a row of children's shoes, filled in a similar way!"[15]

"The Well" inflamed British ferocity and retribution as no other event, before or after. Since the very beginning days of the mutiny, the British had reacted to mutineer action with extremely harsh measures. There was a ruthlessness about these British acts of "justice" that left the English reputation for fair play in considerable shambles. After Cawnpore there was a veritable bath of British outrage about the Nana's treachery and blood lust. In retrospect, one is struck by the matching of atrocity by atrocity; surely ill motive and blame must be liberally distributed on both sides.

The massacre of the women and children at Cawnpore became an instant *cause célèbre*, a focus for all of the worst of the racist and bloodthirsty thinking. This was the same lust for revenge that had prompted John Nicholson, after the fall of Delhi and its atrocities, to advocate a bill "for the flaying alive, impalement or burning of the murderers of the women and children . . . the idea of simply hanging the perpetrators of such atrocities is maddening."[16] Nicholson then had firmly believed that the women had been—to use the euphemism of the day—"dishonoured."

The belief that the Englishwomen had been sexually molested became, after Cawnpore, one of the dominant rallying points; in the later hearings, after the mutiny was over, there were countless questions about the condition of the clothing of the women and whether any were carried off by the rebels. One story given great currency at this time supposedly involved one of General Wheeler's daughters. The account ran something like this: "One deed of heroism that has been recorded deserves mention here. A daughter of General Wheeler's was taken off by a sowar and put into his house along with his wife, near the church. This girl remained till nightfall; and when he came home drunk and fell asleep, she took a sword and cut off his head, his mother's head, two children's heads, and his wife's head, and then walked out into the air; and when she saw other sowars she said, 'Go inside and see how nicely I have rubbed the rissaldar's feet.' They went inside and found them all dead. She then jumped into a well and was killed."

After the mutiny there were some who swore to this story as "the essential facts," but real evidence was never forthcoming. It became one of the many apocryphal stories of the mutiny. Apparently there was one well-documented case of abduction (perhaps the young woman that Roberts found), but no evidence was ever adduced of rape or other molestations. Col. G. W. Williams, who conducted the hearings, concluded: "The most searching and earnest enquiries totally disprove the unfounded assertion that at first was so frequently made and so currently believed that personal indignity & dishonour were offered to our poor suffering countrywomen. The evidence also proves that the sepoy guard placed over the prisoners refused to murder them. The foul crime was perpetrated by five ruffians of the Nana's guard at the instigation of a courtesan. It is as ungenerous as it is untrue to charge upon a nation that cruel deed." George Malleson agreed that "this was the mistake of the day—there had been no dishonouring of our women, in the sense intended."[17] Yet the belief had wide acceptance at the time.

What had led to such extremes on both sides? The more inflammatory British writers of the period held the view, as one put it, that the rebels were "not human beings, but fiends, or at best wild beasts deserving the death of dogs." John William Kaye reports, "Englishmen did not hesitate to boast, or to record their boastings in writing, that they had 'spared no one,' and that 'peppering away at niggers' was a very pleasant pastime . . . enjoyed amazingly."[18] But, as the British historian Michael Edwardes put it recently, "Just as reasonable an explanation was given in a contemporary statement—that the savagery of the British 'left their foe without inducement to show mercy, since he received none, and made even women valueless as hostages.'"[19]

Cracklow, Roberts, and Lang all three visited the site where Wheeler's group defended itself—and also went to the well. Their reactions were different. Cracklow spoke in an analytic and dispassionate tone of the former: "I have just been to see the place where the unfortunate Cawnpore people defended themselves against these terrible miscreants. I was fortunate enough to go over the place with Lt. Thompson, one of the three survivors and he gave me a good account of the whole affair. What the poor ladies must have gone through is hardly conceivable. They were all in a couple of open barracks each about 80 yards long by 20 broad with guns playing on them from 3 sides. In this position the party amounting to some 350 men, women and children defended themselves for 22 !!! days against some thousands of assailants who had some 20 guns." He then continued with a strange comment, again mirroring his dominant preoccupation with the courage, or lack thereof, of the mutineers: "If the Sepoys had the most minute particle of pluck they ought to have carried the place in an hour." The well seemed less important to him; he referred to it only in his last sentences: "I saw the well (now filled up) where all who died or were killed were buried . . . One's blood runs cold to think of the atrocities which must have been committed."

Roberts, reporting more completely, appeared more compassionate about the plight of the women and children: "The place where Sir H. Wheeler defended himself is the most perfect ruin from round shot that I have ever seen—2 small barracks with an apology of a ditch, not eno' to keep a bullet out—such lamentable infatuation. They say poor Wheeler was afraid to build himself a strong position for fear of exciting suspicion amongst the natives and in this wretched place, our poor women were exposed for 3 weeks to the fearful sun of June at Cawnpore, and the shot of the enemy whose batteries were erected about 200 yards off. Many ladies were killed, others wounded. The survivors were kept in a miserable house, not fit for dogs, until the evening before our troops reached Cawnpore, when they were all murdered. God only knows how. The natives say that the children were hanged before their mothers, and that when all had been wounded by shots from the Sepoys, butchers were sent in to finish the bloody mess . . . oh, mother, looking at these horrible sights makes one feel very, very sad. No wonder we all feel glad to kill these Sepoys."

Roberts seemed drawn to the two sites and went back several times. He reported further on the entrenchment: "I went over Wheeler's entrenchment again this morning . . . there is scarcely a foot left on the walls where cannon shot has not struck—One Officer who escaped showed me spots where Officers and ladies had been killed while leaning against the walls . . . you see places where mothers have scraped away the floors to make hollows for their babes to sleep in. No words can express one's feelings while going over these horrid places."

Lang also visited twice. In describing Wheeler's defense, he could not resist again taking a swipe at the central authorities: "The fact is Wheeler never believed he would have to defend it; he summoned all the Europeans, so as to have them together; he never believed that the Sepoys would attack him, and he believed Lord Canning's *promise* that if he only held out, he should be relieved on a certain date; that certain date was a *fortnight* before the date on which Wheeler capitulated. Wheeler, trusting in *Lord Canning's word*, would not let the officers send the ladies away when they could have done so!"

Lang, ever the engineer and highly critical of the fortifications themselves, drew a detailed sketch of its sections and proceeded to analyze them: "The line round, p.p.p., represents the trench!!—see the section. What a mockery to call it an entrenchment; were you to ride over it in the dark you would not perceive it!"

After this long diatribe on the lack of engineering expertise, he continued more personally: "Fancy poor delicate ladies and little children lying out, day and night, in that trench in June, with those curs barking around them, not daring to charge that little devoted band." Lang was particularly moved by the well and wrote a highly descriptive section on what he saw: "There is a little house, near the Assembly Rooms and the old Hotel, on the road between them, a low tiled-roof house, built in Pompeian style, round an open central courtyard. In that courtyard stood a tree, where English ladies were hanging when Neill's troops marched in; it is cut down now. In every room of that little house, on floor and walls, are stains of blood, and on the walls hundreds of bullet marks; even now remain stray socks, slippers and bits of clothing. When Neill's soldiers entered, the place was heaped with clothing of women and children. In the compound stands a tree, marked with bullet holes and sword gashes; in the latter is still long hair; amongst the grass and bushes of the compound, between the house and well, are still strips of clothing and locks of long hairs; into that well upwards of 200 bodies of women and children were thrown, many still alive. The floors are still covered with mementoes of the defenders, a sock, a child's shoe, letters, leaves of books, pieces of music, papers, &c. One officer picked up Wheeler's last pay certificate; another a few leaves of a book bearing the name of a lady whom he well knew; another letters of a great friend of his, &c., and so on; it was very sad work looking at all this, and more than sad. I felt that I could vow my life to revenge, to take blood from that race every day; had I a relation at that massacre, I certainly would have."

He concluded with strong feelings of revenge: "No one who has seen that spot can ever feel anything but deep hatred to the Nana and his fellow fiends and all his fellow race. No officer standing in those rooms spoke to another, tho' each knew his neighbour's feelings. I know I could not have spoken. I felt as if my heart was stone and my brain fire, and that the spot was enough to drive one mad. Neill made his high-caste Brahmin and Musalman Sepoy prisoners lick the stains on floor and wall before he hung them. The gallows on which he hung them is the only pleasant thing in the Compound on which to rest the eye. All these fiends will never be repaid one tenth of what they deserve; many a man will cringe before us and serve us well and faithfully! (the brutes), who will secretly chuckle in his black heart in having abetted in these scenes. Every man across the river whom I meet shall suffer for my visit to Cawnpore. I will never again, as I used to at Delhi, let off men, whom I catch in houses or elsewhere. I thought when I had killed twelve men outright and wounded or knocked over as many more at the battle of Agra, that I had done enough: I think now I shall never stop, if I get a chance again."

George Bourchier seemed genuinely disturbed by his own primitive feelings: "Twice I passed the ruins, and the same feelings on both occasions seemed to rise involuntarily. I resolved never again to enter its precincts, and although on a subsequent occasion my tent abutted for six days on a corner of the entrenchment, I religiously kept my word." But Bourchier had no illusions about what would be the feeling of most: "The soldiers needed no hounding on to excite them to revenge: the difficulty was to prevent them from considering everyone with a black face as an enemy."[20]

Immediately upon the well's discovery by Havelock's forces, vindictive retribution began anew. Unbending vengeance was personified in Brig. Gen. J. G. S. Neill, the commander of the First Madras Fusiliers, who began a sweep from Calcutta toward Cawnpore. Even before "the Well" he had, in the eyes of one Indian scholar, "earned undying notoriety for the inhuman cruelties which marked the progress of his army all along the way. It would be too hideous to describe the details, and a general account must suffice."[21] (The general account described summary hangings of military and civilian alike, without any pretense of trial.) Neill, who took charge of Cawnpore shortly after Havelock's forces arrived, ordered a diabolical punishment, which he himself described: "Whenever a rebel is caught he is immediately tried, and, unless he can prove a defense, he is sentenced to hang at once. But the chief rebels or ring leaders, I make first clean up a certain portion of the pool of blood, still two inches deep, in the shed where the fearful murder and mutilation of women and children took place. To touch blood is most abhorrent to the high-caste natives; they think, by doing so, they doom their souls to perdition. Let them think so. My object is to inflict a fearful punishment for a revolting, cowardly, barbarous deed, and to strike terror into these rebels. The first I caught was a subahdar, or native officer—a high-caste Brahman, who tried to resist my order to clean up the very blood he had helped to shed; but I made the provost-marshall to do his duty; and a few lashes soon made a miscreant accomplish his task. When done, he was taken out and immediately hanged and after death, buried in a ditch at the roadside. No one who has witnessed the scenes of murder, mutilation, and massacre can ever listen to the word 'mercy' as applicable to these fiends."[22]

Historians over the years have disputed just how many times this order was actually carried through; perhaps it was as few as only two or three times. Still, it was the essence of the order that was so satisfying to the British officers and men at that time in 1857. Another contemporary observer, commenting on the reaction of one of the doctors in his regiment, recalled that "when I saw him he was examining the hook covered with dried blood and the hand

and footprints of the child on the wall, with the tears streaming down his cheeks. He was a most kind-hearted man, and I remember when he came out of the house, that he cast a look of pity on the three wretches about to be hanged, and I overheard him say to another officer who was with him: 'This is horrible and unChristian to look at; but I do hope those are the same wretches who tortured the little child on the hook inside that room.'"[23] The same observer did note that after Sir Colin Campbell arrived in Cawnpore in early November to take charge, he promptly put a stop to the Neill order as "unworthy of the English name and a Christian Government." But there was a profound intransigence in the bitterness of the British soldier, and there were to be many more chances to apply the same Bloody Assize.

The eventful month since the column had left Delhi—Buland-shahr, Malagarh, Agra, Cawnpore—had affected the three lieutenants each somewhat differently. Roberts seemed to take the atrocities and deaths in stride, though he did appear genuinely moved: "These last few months have made me feel 10 years older, not from bad health, for I have never been so well, but from all that I have seen and undergone. One can't help thinking and reflecting on these unparalleled massacres. Soldiers know what their fate may be, but one can scarcely understand why delicate women and helpless children have been made to undergo such tortures. God bless them. It makes me quite sad writing about them."

His driving ambition once more came through strongly in this same letter: "The Commander-in-Chief has telegraphed that he will be here by the 1st or 2nd, and will overtake us. Here is my good luck, being with his part of the force, and with which, if possible, I will remain. Norman will do his best to keep me, and if I succeed, I shall be all right. They took it into their hands that it was hard work, so offered me an assistant, and I have got a very nice fellow of my own Regiment, and an old friend of mine, named Mayne. He is far above me, being 12 years' service, but very glad indeed, he says, to serve under me. Rather fun is it not?" And a few days later: "Am I not a fortunate fellow to be Quartermaster-General to a force destined for such a glorious object. All the Intelligence Department is in my hands. In my wildest dreams I never thought of what was so soon to happen, and when next I write I hope to tell you that I am in the department permanently."

Lang also expressed genuine enthusiasm about his campaign life, despite (or maybe because of) its dangers. His focus was more on self-fulfillment than organizational prestige, more on "manliness" and courage than military acumen: "I am very glad that you think I only did my duty in volunteering for Delhi: it *was* my duty, and, except that you will have been doubly anxious on my account, I have every possible reason to rejoice that I was sent: I should have mourned all my life inaction at that crisis: now, if I am spared throughout, I shall look with delight and satisfaction at my *service* . . . I have really been very happy under the sad circumstances, I could not be happy in peace and quiet in England; I could not remain even at Lahore, under partial danger: I should, of course, have been burning to be employed as a man and a soldier in these stirring times, and I have enjoyed this new life which I have tried. I have found that I really chose aright when I thought a soldier's life was the life for me—exposure and fatigue; the music of ball and bullet, marching and roughing it, and all that makes up a soldier's life, I enjoy, and am as happy as possible and very thankful I ought to be that I have the disposition to bear an 'equal mind' in these sorts of scenes, as well as for the preservation amongst so many great dangers; may I be spared yet to see all your dear faces again some day."

Lang did have an unsettling brush with death in late October: "The sun again completely floored me and I lay in great pain in my tent all day. I thought I had sunstroke and should go delirious. I had a lot of leeches on my head in the evening and they greatly relieved me and I fell asleep." Fortunately, he was one of those whom fate allowed to recover.

Cracklow was more detached, more antiseptic, more fatalistic; his letters continued to harp on the "cowardliness of the Pandies." He described an engagement in early November: "They turned out as usual the most errant cowards, for although they held a very good position, a few round shots sent them scuttling away across the fields at a tremendous rate." At another engagement, "They opened upon us with a gun when we were at a great distance off, and seemed to think that we should follow their . . . game of long bowls. We just galloped straight at them . . . before we could put our good intentions to practice they bolted as hard as they could." Cracklow, too, wanted action; on picket, he reported that it was "dull work. I have got tired of the concertina, or rather of the old music. As there is not a book procurable in camp, find it difficult to get through the day." He wanted to "smash these brutes" while the good weather lasted, but "with the delays that are taking place, I much fear we shall have to pass another hot weather under canvass. If so, the effect on these new troops from England will be something fearful." He continued to feel he was overworked and being put upon: "We have only some 50 men fit for duty instead of 120 . . . yet just as much work is expected from us and as well done as if we had our full number."[24]

All three were intensely conscious of the upcoming attempt to relieve the embattled garrison at Lucknow. The column members seemed unanimous in their belief that, along with Delhi, this would be a climactic—indeed, watershed—engagement. They were correct.

Chapter 6
Lucknow: The First Battle

"We resume our march . . . to relieve General Havelock, who left this place with a force some short time ago to relieve the garrison that has been in Lucknow since the commencement of the disturbances and to bring away the women and children." Cracklow's letter to his mother about this matter is laconic: "He, however, forwards that he was not strong enough to effect his object and has been himself attacked and is unable to get away." These two sentences understate the five-month saga that had occurred in Lucknow over the months from May through October; we need perspective on it to comprehend the task that Cracklow, Roberts, Lang, and their colleagues faced.

The trauma at Lucknow was played out in close concert with the macabre denouement in nearby Cawnpore. Henry Lawrence, brother of John, was in charge of the Province of Oudh, with his headquarters in Lucknow. As soon as the mutiny began, Lawrence began fortifying Lucknow, concentrating on strengthening the residency and on leveling the buildings and other impediments immediately around it. Late in May the first attack by the mutineers was beaten off by resolute action, with Lawrence himself taking a giant's role. Outlying groups of troops and noncombatants soon were drawn into the residency, not an easily defended structure since it continued to be overlooked by higher buildings that allowed sharpshooters to fire into the compound almost at will.

At the end of June, Lawrence made a serious error by leading a force, with himself at the head, to engage a reportedly small group of the enemy at nearby Chinhat. Unfortunately, the latter turned out to be a strong, superior force and dealt a crippling blow to the

Lucknow troops, sending them scurrying back to the city after a grisly loss of men. A full-scale siege now was put in place by the mutineers. On July 2 a random happenstance dealt the beleaguered garrison another cruel blow: a solitary shell from one of the enemy's artillery pieces winged its way into a room in the residency and burst; Lawrence himself was in the room and was mortally wounded, dying two days later. With the shelling, disease, and malnutrition taking their toll, the decimated defenders continued on under the bitter siege.

Meanwhile, a potential savior had been coming from the eastern part of India, Maj. Gen. Henry Havelock, a seasoned soldier with much prior service in India. At the outbreak of the mutiny he was recalled from Persia, and by early July he was marching from Calcutta toward Oudh. Fighting his way across eastern India, he closed upon Cawnpore by late June, engaged the enemy in a major battle on July 16 outside Cawnpore, and soundly defeated them. Upon entering the town the next day, Havelock's soldiers discovered the ghoulish aftermath of the July 15 bloodbath. Maddened and sickened by the awful truth of the well, and having also come across great amounts of European liquor, they went on an orgy of drinking. As Wilson had done in Delhi, Havelock ordered all the spirits destroyed, for, as he said in a telegram that day, "It would require half my force to keep it from being drunk up by the other half."

Havelock next set off toward Lucknow, fighting pitched battles all along the way. The casualty list of dead and wounded mounted; rampant cholera among the forces was, if anything, even more deadly a foe. In mid-August Havelock mounted a major attempt to storm and relieve Lucknow but was forced back. On August 23 he received word from Lt. Col. John Ingles, now commander at Lucknow, that the situation was desperate: ". . . 120 dead and wounded . . . at least 200 women and children daily being attacked . . . their mines have already weakened our post . . . Our Native force having been assured of your approach some twenty-five days ago, are naturally losing confidence . . . if they leave us, I do not see how the defences are to be manned."

After arrival of reinforcements in mid-September, Havelock and his new superior, Gen. James Outram, once more vowed to relieve the Lucknow contingent, still prisoners of the siege. On September

25 the two generals and their main forces fought their way right through to the beleaguered garrison. But their triumph was short-lived, for they immediately found themselves cut off from behind, with their reserves outside the city. The masses of mutineers that they had slashed through had succeeded in closing the momentary breach, and the rescuers became prisoners, too. Both sides settled in for a renewed battle of attrition, with all the accoutrements of shooting and shelling and, in this instance, a particular use of mines. There were ways of getting messages in from the outside and back out. But despite this link, the simple fact was that all of them, saviors as well as the besieged, were once again prisoners of a siege. "There he has been ever since," wrote Cracklow. "Now we are on the way to relieve him & I hope we shall make a better job of it."

By the second week in November, the Hope Grant column (with Cracklow and the rest) had arrived at a designated assembly spot a few miles outside Lucknow, where a proposed new assault was to be initiated. The column was met there by a major force under the salty soldier now designated to be commander in chief, Sir Colin Campbell, a soldier with proved achievements over a forty-nine-year service that included the Peninsular Campaign, the war with the United States in 1812, China, the Sikh War on the North West Frontier, and finally the Crimean War. Lang's view of him at the start was mixed: "Sir C.C. seems a most jolly, good-hearted but impetuous, impulsive, hot man." He did indeed have a reputation for a ferocious temper and for being "a tough old buck," but he was also widely seen as cautious to a fault (sometimes he was even called "Sir Crawling Camel").[1]

Campbell brought with him his kilt-clad Scottish troop, the Ninety-third Highlanders, "who form a subject of intense delight and astonishment to the Sikhs, who have never seen anything of the sort before," Cracklow told his mother. "They say that bagpipes are the true Sungee-Raga (that is, war music) and at once applied to their commanding officer to be supplied with them as also with Highland bonnets which divide their admiration with the Pipes." Lang called them "*the* boys: such glorious thoro' Hielanders . . . the pipes are delicious, so thoroughly British." The Sikhs truly liked the outgoing Scots. Lang told of their first night's meeting: "I found knots of mingled Hielanders and Sikhs and Afghans, each

Fugitive officers, with their families, concealing themselves in the jungle

Fugitive British officers and their families attacked by mutineers

Repulse of a sortie from Delhi

Assault of Delhi—capture of the Kashmir Gate

Blowing up of the Kashmir Gate at Delhi

Capture of the king of Delhi by Captain Hodson

View of Lucknow

The relief of Lucknow by General Havelock

Charge of the Highlanders before Cawnpore, under General Havelock

Capture of the guns by the Highlanders before Cawnpore

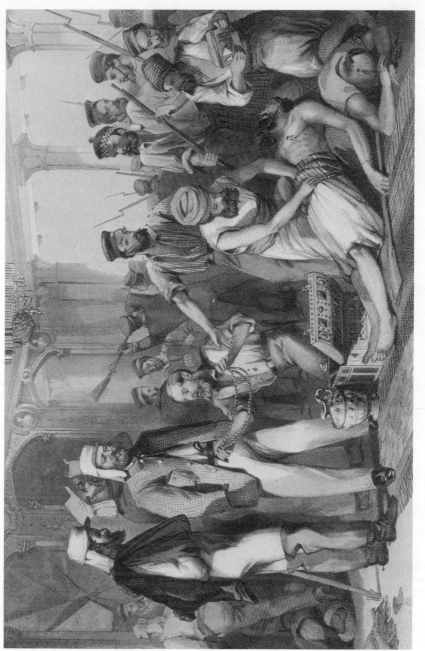

The Times correspondent looking on at the sacking of the Kaiserbagh

Outlying picket of the Highland brigade

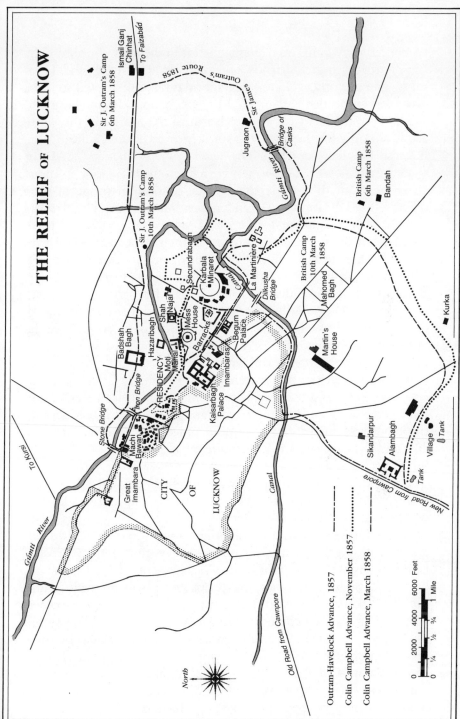

British attack routes for the first and second battles of Lucknow.

jabbering away in his own language, not in the least understood by one another, but great friends, one going on 'weel, weel', and 'Hoot mon', and the other 'Hamne Matadeenko khub mara' and so on: a great shaven-headed Pathan would be trying on a Hieland bonnet!"

The Highlanders gave a sharp boost to the morale of the entire army, not only for their fighting spirit (proved in the Crimean War) but also for their very élan. The *gogra-wallahs*—that is, the "Petti-coated-men"—soon were to acquire a fearsome reputation in India, again tinged with considerable racism; according to one of their officers, Lt. W. Gordon-Alexander, servants said the Highlanders had "a particular liking for curried black babies, especially if we could catch them ourselves, and break their backs across our bare knees!"[2] One suspects more than a bit of myth building and self-congratulation in some of the contemporary Highlander writings. Both Gordon-Alexander and a Highlander sergeant, William Forbes-Mitchell, published highly opinionated, tendentious books on the role of the Highlanders in the mutiny. Both books have the unfortunate characteristic of so many of the memoirs of the mutiny: they were written many years later, much after the fact. But both men were close by Lieutenants C. H. Blunt, Cracklow, Roberts, and Lang at a number of tense moments in later weeks, and their descriptions of life among the attacking British forces evocatively buttress the direct, at-the-moment letters of our three lieutenants and the closer-to-the-fact reminiscences of Bourchier (he published his book in 1858).

The Sikh's astonishment with the Highlanders had hardly subsided when a second Campbell unit arrived, a naval brigade. The unit was under the command of Capt. William Peel and was made up of sailors and marines from the Royal Navy ship *Shannon*, armed with eight twenty-four-pound heavy guns and two rocket launchers mounted on light carts. Cracklow commented, "The tall hairy old Sikhs could not make out these square made oddly dressed little men and said they must be the spirits of the women who were murdered come back to avenge themselves." The sailors did tend to be squat, and this tendency was accentuated by their dress. One of the naval officers, Capt. Oliver Jones, told of some special features of Peel's convoy. "The number of pets which the sailors had was marvellous—monkeys, parrots, pigs, guinea-pigs, dogs, cats, mongooses or mongeese, which you like, and lots of other creatures. Some of the monkeys were as tame and affectionate, and would follow their masters like dogs. Peel often said 'The Shannon would be a regular menagerie when they got back to her.'"[3]

It was obvious that the arrivals of Campbell, Peel, and the Highlanders had raised everyone's spirits. There even began to be a bit of horseplay and highjinks at the camp; Bourchier described a fiasco involving the Highlanders: "All things seemed quiet, when I witnessed, with several others, what appeared to be a dire disaster. From the direction of the advanced piquet, a cloud of dust at first was seen, then a few horsemen and loose horses, after them the troop of dragoons and my two guns, and last of all the Highlanders, running towards the main body of the convoy in the maddest confusion; yet no enemy was in view, and no firing was heard: still that the detachment was flying from some imminent danger there was no doubt, and with our glasses we could see the remainder of the party getting under arms. Not a moment was to be lost; and a few minutes brought us to the scene of action. There a scene the most ridiculous conceivable was being enacted; peal after peal of uncontrollable laughter greeted us, as with anxious faces we rode into the bivouac; and it was some time ere we could discover what was the cause of the apparent disaster and subsequent mirth . . . While idly dozing on the ground, two officers had espied in a tree an immense bees' nest. Possessed by the demon of mischief, they commenced pelting it with clods; and this not answering their purpose, a lance was thrown, with deadly aim, into the centre of it. The disgraceful flight we had witnessed was now easily accounted for; one of the perpetrators of the mischief was dangerously ill from the effects; but, as a body, the kilted Highlanders suffered most, and they bolted, taking with them more bees than they carried in their bonnets. The result proved the truth of the old adage, that 'idleness is the root of all evil.'"

The Highlanders indignantly defended their bare-legged attire. "The facts were," said one of their officers, "that none of our men, as far as I could learn from inquiry at our hospital that evening, had been treated for stings on their bare legs." Beyond this, "the swarm were hornets, and *East Indian hornets* . . . about four times the size of our wasp."[4] Protestations to the contrary, the Highlanders garnered much ribbing for their first "battle" in India!

Comic diversions quickly wore thin, though, and the war's grinding experience continued to tell on the weary soldiers. The enemy were all around them, probing all the time. Roberts soon ran into trouble on one of his reconnaissance trips. Lang saw it from a distance: "As usual, Roberts and Mayne (our Assistant. Qr. Mr. Generals) . . . galloped ahead; they spoke to one or two villagers asking for information, but got but few rough answers and suddenly a rush of musket and matchlock men was made from the village: off they galloped for their lines, having to take a circuitous route through the fields round the village, to rejoin the advanced guard. Roberts's horse was hit and fell over him (Roberts getting his thumb cut), but luckily he was unhurt, remounted and got safely back." Roberts told his mother: "I never felt so rejoiced in my life as when I found myself clear of the rascals and near our own men. For some minutes I gave up all hope, but my little grey carried me most beautifully, and I just managed to get round their flank in time. My horse got a nasty cut in his leg, and I one on my left hand. However, both are doing well." His optimism about the horse was premature, for he wrote a few days later, "I am in great trouble about my horses. The two wounded ones won't get well, and the third is very C.D. No money will buy horses now—none are to be had, and I must ride, so it is as bad as a Chinese puzzle."

Colin Campbell himself arrived in the camp on November 9. Wasting no time, the whole force pushed off on the tenth for the Alambagh, the vast, walled pleasure garden built for the kings of Oudh, located about four miles south of Lucknow. With the recent arrivals of reinforcements, Campbell had some five thousand men and about fifty guns.

Though this force was a large one, a great many of the camp followers disconcertingly had deserted at this point. A Cracklow letter recorded the flight of the *kitmutgar,* his personal servant. Forbes-Mitchell confirmed a wholesale disengagement: "The natives fully believed that our column was doomed to extermination; there is no doubt that they knew of the powerful force collecting in our rear, consisting of the Gwalior Contingent, which had never yet been beaten and it was supposed to be invincible . . . the *bheesties* and the dooly-bearers (the latter were under the hospital guard) were the only camp-followers who did not desert us when we crossed into Oudh . . . The *bheesties,* or water-carriers, have been noted for bravery and fidelity in every Indian campaign." Lang reported on November 2 of the retribution now being visited on the latter: "A bhisti went just now to a village to draw water and had his nose, ears and hands cut off."[5]

November 11 was a day of intensive reconnoitering, planning, adjusting. It was particularly a day for the crusty general, Campbell, to review his troops and to attempt on short notice to weld them into a cohesive fighting force. The entire army was drawn for review; as an eyewitness described it: "The scene was striking. The small army was drawn in quarter-distance columns in the centre of a vast plain, surrounded by woods. On the edge of these the piquets were posted. A mere handful it seemed. The guns of the troops and batteries who came down from Delhi looked blackened and service-worn, but the horses were in good condition, the harness in perfect repair, the men swarthy and evidently in perfect fighting trim. The 9th Lancers, with their blue uniforms and white turbans twisted round their forage caps, their flagless lances, lean but hardy horses, and gallant bearing, looked the perfection of a cavalry regiment on active service. Wild and bold was the carriage of the Sikh Cavalry, riding untamed-looking steeds, clad in loose faun-coloured robes, with long boots, blue or red turbans and sashes, and armed with carbine and sabre.

"Next to them were the worn and wasted remains of the 8th and 75th, clad entirely in slate-coloured cloth. With a wearied air, they stood grouped around their standards—war stripped of its display, in all its nakedness. Then the 2nd and 4th Punjab Infantry, tall of stature with eager eyes overhung by large twisted turbans, clad in short, sand-coloured tunics—men swift to march and forward in the fight—ambitious both of glory and of loot."[6]

The last of the units to be reviewed was the 93rd Highlanders; Forbes-Mitchell, one of the men in that troop, reached into his memory for what he believed were the general's actual words: "Ninety-Third! When I took leave of you in Portsmouth, I never thought I should see you again. I expected the bugle or maybe the bagpipes to sound a call for me to go somewhere else long before you would be likely to return to our dearly-beloved home. But another commander has decreed it otherwise, and here I am prepared to lead you through another campaign . . . The eyes of the people at home—I may say the eyes of Europe and of the whole of

Christendom are upon us, and we must relieve our countrymen, women, and children now shut up in the Residency of Lucknow. The lives at stake are not merely those of soldiers, who might well be expected to cut themselves out or to die sword in hand. We have to rescue helpless women and children from the fate worse than death. When you meet the enemy, you must remember that he is well-armed and well provided with ammunition, and that he can play at long bowls as well as you can, especially from behind loop-holed walls. So when we make an attack you must come to close quarters as quickly as possible; keep well together and use the bayonet. Remember that the cowardly Sepoys, who are eager to murder women and children, cannot look a European soldier in the face when it is accompanied with cold steel. Ninety-Third! You are my own lads, I rely on you to do the work!"[7]

The main attack began on November 14. The advance guards set off to the right of the Alambagh, across some fields and roads and on into the Dilkusha park. Forbes-Mitchell, Bourchier, Blunt, and Cracklow were all in one group together. They paused for a moment on one side of the park and found themselves in a field of carrots, which the men began pulling up and eating raw. The enclosure was swarming with deer, and as Roberts galloped ahead to reconnoiter, they bounded away on all sides. "Some of our men fired at what they thought were Pandies in the trees," Lang reported, "but what turned out to be monkeys!" Lang's strange ability to wax lyric at a moment of great danger again surfaced: "It was such a pretty scene, a very picturesque site for a battle."[8]

Bourchier's, Blunt's, and Cracklow's artillery guns covered the way for the infantry. As the attack started, Cracklow complained once again of 'Pandy cowardice': "We were for about 20 minutes, during which time the infantry were coming up and forming, under a most desperately heavy musketry fire from the front and both flanks. All this time not a nigger was seen, they being, as is always the way with the brutes, under cover and firing from behind walls out through loopholes." All now moved over the crest of a hill, taking La Martinière, a large schoolhouse used in the brighter days of the past for instruction of young European children. Lang was deputed as observer and sent to the tower of the Martinière, seven stories up.

One of the scenes he witnessed, seeing but impotent to act, involved Capt. Augustus Otway Mayne, a colleague of Roberts. For most of that first day of battle Roberts and Mayne had been together, but late in the day they had separated. When Roberts got back to headquarters that evening, several soldiers told him that they had seen Mayne shot and felled. Forbes-Mitchell later described what had happened: "About the centre of the village another short halt was made. Here we saw a naked wretch, of a strong muscular build, with his head closely shaven except for the tuft on his crown, and his face all streaked in a hideous manner with white and red paint, his body smeared with ashes. He was sitting on a leopard's skin counting a rosary of beads. A young staff-officer, Captain A. O. Mayne, Deputy Assistant Quartermaster-General, was making his way to the front, when a man of my company, named James Wilson, pointed to this painted wretch saying, 'I would like to try my bayonet on the hide of that painted scoundrel, who looks a murderer.' Captain Mayne replied, 'Oh don't touch him; these fellows are harmless Hindoo *jogees,* and won't hurt us. It is the Mahommedans that are to blame for the horrors of this Mutiny.' The words had scarcely been uttered when the painted scoundrel stopped counting the beads, slipped his hand under the leopard skin, and as quick as lightning brought out a short, brass, bell-mouthed blunderbuss and fired the contents of it into Captain Mayne's chest at a distance of only a few feet. His action was as quick as it was unexpected, and Captain Mayne was unable to avoid the shot, or the men to prevent it. Immediately our men were upon the assassin; there was no means of escape for him, and he was quickly bayoneted. Since then I have never seen a painted Hindoo, but I involuntarily raise my hand to knock him down. From that hour I formed the opinion (which I have never had cause to alter since) that the pampered high-caste Hindoo sepoys had far more to do with the Mutiny and the cowardly murders of women and children than the Mahommedans, although the latter still bear most of the blame."[9]

Roberts was terribly upset: "No one was able to tell me where his body had been taken, and I looked for it myself all that evening in vain . . . at daybreak the next morning, accompanied by Arthur Bunny, the cheery adjutant of Horse Artillery, I began my search afresh, and at length we discovered the body inside a doolie under the wall of the Martiniere. As there was no knowing how soon our services might be required, we decided to bury the poor fellow at once. I chose a spot close by for his grave, which was dug with the help of some gunners, and then Bunny and I aided by two or three brother officers, laid our friend in it just as he was, in his blue frock, coat and long boots, his eyeglass in his eye, as he always carried it. The only thing I took away was his sword which I eventually made over to his family. It was a sad little ceremony. Overhanging the grave was a young tree upon which I cut the initials, A.O.M.—not very deep, for there was little time: they were quite distinct, however, and remained so long enough for the grave to be traced by Mayne's friends, who erected the stone now to be seen."

The killing of Mayne seems to have had the same effect on Roberts as the Home death at Malagarh Fort had had on Lang. Roberts wrote his mother: "It makes one very sad seeing all these fine fellows knocked over. I have lost so many friends during the last 6 months, and at times can't help feeling very very miserable. The constant excitement we have had prevents one thinking, but a quiet day now and then brings back vividly all the horrors that have taken place." In the same letter he reported further on his career: "The C in chief brought a Colonel Biddulph with him from Calcutta as head of the Intelligence Department. He was killed, poor fellow . . . and I was appointed to succeed him, so am a great swell." [10]

November 15 was spent consolidating the lines, preparatory to moving forward to what the terrain would dictate as a dangerous battle. Blunt's Horse Artillery with George Cracklow had been shepherding the supply train forward, with the enemy constantly harrassing it from all sides. Blunt and Cracklow had had almost incessant action on the fourteenth and fifteenth, and thus little rest for the expected main assault the next day.

The focal point for the battle was clearly going to be the Secundrabagh. This was a massive, high-walled enclosure abut 120 yards square, with carefully constructed narrow loopholes all around it. Inside waited an enormous body of mutineers. To make matters worse, the mutineers also controlled a village directly across from the Secundrabagh, with well-protected cover and, again, the loopholed windows. The way forward for Campbell's forces was directly down this "defile of death." As the head of the column moved into the narrow area on the sixteenth, the mutineers opened fire from both sides. The cavalry were prevented from going forward by a jumble of abbatis and barricades in front. Gough, their leader, put the matter succinctly: "We were in a most inconvenient spot—we could neither advance nor retire . . . the narrow lane was speedily blocked by infantry and artillery hurrying up to the scene of action. It was indeed a scene of turmoil!" One British officer was heard to say to his companion, "If these fellows allow one of us to get out of this *cul de sac* alive, they deserve to be hanged."[11]

Artillery support seemed to be the only hope, but here an alien feature of the terrain seemed destined to block the rescue. There were high banks on each side of the defile, forming what appeared to be an impassable barrier to artillery.

But it was not. Blunt's troop, including Cracklow, saved the day and perhaps even the army. A well-known mutiny historian, W. H. Fitchett, told the ensuing story: "Blunt, an officer of great daring, with an enthusiastic belief that British guns could go anywhere and do anything, cut the knot of the difficulty. The bank of the lane was so steep that it seemed impossible that horses and guns could climb it, but Blunt, with cool decision, put the guns in motion, flung the horses' heads sharply round and, with whip and spur and shout, his gunners drove the snorting, panting horses up the bank into the open space under the fire of the Secundrabagh. Travers, with two of his 18-pounders, came stumbling and struggling up the steep bank after Blunt." Gordon-Alexander, one of the Highlander officers caught in the jam, witnessed the remarkable feat: "Of this I am certain, that no commander of any troop of Horse Artillery of any other country of the world would, under any circumstances, have even attempted to negotiate such a bank."[12]

Roberts, a witness, described the situation in which Blunt and Cracklow found themselves: ". . . under a heavy fire from three different directions—on the right from the Sikandarbagh; on the left and left front from the barracks, some huts (not 20 yards off), and a serai; and in front from the mess-house, Kaiserbagh, and other buildings. In these three directions he pointed his guns, regardless of deadly fire, especially from the huts on the left." Roberts wrote his mother, "How our Artillery escaped I can't imagine."[13]

G. W. Forrest continues the story: "Colin Campbell also faced the steep bank; his charger with two or three strides carried him to the summit, and following Blunt at full speed he placed himself near one of the guns. Blunt had to turn them in three directions, to the right to keep down the heavy musketry fire from the Secundrabagh, to the left and left front to reply to the cannonade which the enemy had opened from the Kaiserbagh. Men and horses were knocked over right and left." Roberts, too, had climbed up the bank and was standing directly behind Campbell when "I heard the Commander-in-Chief exclaim, 'I am hit.' Luckily it was only by a spent bullet, which had passed through a gunner (killing him on the spot) before it struck Sir Colin on the thigh, causing a severe contusion . . . it was a moment of acute anxiety until it was ascertained that no damage had been done."[14]

Forrest concludes the story: "But though the bullets flew thicker and closer, Blunt held his ground, and then the 93rd who had been supporting the 53rd in clearing the enclosure came forth from the winding lane and rushed at the huts to the left from which the most severe fire came. A dead wall stopped them. 'In at the roof, tear off the tiles and go in through the roof,' . . . shouted the old Chief. In an instant the Highlanders sprang on the roof, tore them open, and drove the rebels out. Then supported by two of Blunt's guns they pursued them across the plain."[15]

Thus concluded a moment of terrible suspense for Blunt and Cracklow, an action of high heroism by the two young officers and their men, and a critical sortie in the entire Battle of Lucknow. Had Campbell and his crack troops been decimated in this defile, the attack probably would have been fatally stalled. Now, breaking through the defile, the troops were able to bring up the heavy guns. Mortar fire fell all around these pieces; the captain of the battery was killed, a lieutenant wounded, and Blunt's horse shot from under him. But the guns continued to fire, and soon the combination of the light and heavy pieces breached the wall of the Secundrabagh.

Then came the storming of the great fortress, the Secundrabagh itself. "It was a magnificent sight," reported Roberts, "a sight never to be forgotten—that glorious struggle to be the first to enter the deadly breach, the prize to the winner of the race being certain death!" The bugle sounded and the Highlanders and the Punjab Rifles, assisted by several support units, dashed forward. "It was," wrote an eyewitness, "a glorious rush. On went, in generous rivalry, the turban of the Sikh and the dark plume of the Highlander. A Native officer of the Sikhs, Subahdar Gokal Singh, waving his talwar above his head, dashed on a full five yards in front of his men. The Highlanders, determined not to be left behind, strained nerve and limb in the race. Their officers led like gallant gentlemen, shaking their broad swords in the air. Two young ensigns springing over a low mud wall gave the colours of the regiment to the breeze."[16]

All were running toward the one hole, a small opening in a bricked-up doorway about three feet square and about the same distance from the ground. The first man, a Sikh, was shot dead as he jumped through. A similar fate awaited the second man, a Highlander. A young officer of the 93rd was luckier. Blunt was nearby and described it: "His jump into it reminded me of the headlong leap which Harlequin in a pantomine makes through a shop window, and I thought at the time that if he was not rushing to a certain death life would be very uncertain to those first making entrance by that ugly blind hole."[17] Roberts was one of the group coming through the hole and noted the situation at the inner entrance: "A drummer-boy of the 93rd must have been one of the first to pass that grim boundary between life and death, for when I got in I found him just inside the breach, lying on his back quite dead— a pretty, innocent-looking, fair-haired lad, not more than 14 years of age." Cracklow was too busy outside to see the breaching: "I had no time to look about me, so did not see who was first in, but in they all went like so many tigers, every man thirsting for nigger blood."[18]

The crush to get through the small opening became so great that there was a traffic jam of eager men on the outside. Further down the wall the enemy were in the process of trying to close the heavy doors when one of the Punjabis, Mukarrab Khan, rushed up and pushed his left arm, on which he had been carrying a shield, into the closing door, thus preventing it from being shut. When his hand was badly wounded by a sword cut he drew it out and instantly thrust in his other arm, which was all but severed from the wrist. But his gallant act accomplished the object: the doors were not able to be closed and were soon forced open altogether, allowing large numbers of the attacking troops to pour into the bastion.

The fight for possession of the Secundrabagh was bloody and desperate. The rebels fought with all of the energy of despair. "Every room, every staircase, every corner of the towers were contested. Quarter was neither given nor asked for." Lang was one of the first in, deputed to take one of the towers: "At each little corner tower a few desperate men were holding out, and lives were being thrown away in attempting to force little narrow winding staircases where men were determined to hold out as long as possible. I had a muzzle at my chest, the hand which held the stock even I couldn't see, and back I sprang, you may be certain. That same man held out for two hours up his staircase, and when his ammunition was done, appeared on the roof at the top, and with fury, hurled his tulwar down amongst us, and fell amongst a volley of bullets . . . I was hit, for the first time, by a bullet but was unwounded most fortunately: I was sent spinning by a stinging crack on the shoulder and thought I was killed, but I was highly delighted when I found I didn't drop, when a man called out that the bullet had hit the wall beyond me. It was a sharp glance off my pouch-belt, and the only effect was to make my shoulder and arm bruised and stiff for a couple of days."

The gruesome battle downstairs lasted just about one half hour, when all at once "there was perfect silence around us, the enemy evidently not being aware of how the tide of victory had rolled inside this Secundrabagh, for not a soul escaped from it to tell the tale. The silence was so great that we could hear the pipers of the Seventy-eighth playing inside the Residency as a welcome to cheer us all."[19]

As the British looked around them in the aftermath they discovered a veritable charnel house. The estimates of the number of mutineers killed ranged in later chronicles from two thousand upwards. Bourchier stated: "I was subsequently informed that upwards of 2700 bodies were buried, and numbers more were burnt. The probability is that the enemy's loss was some 3000 men." Roberts told his mother: "I never saw such a sight. They were literally in heaps, and when I went in were a heaving mass, some dead, but most wounded and unable to get up from the crush. How so many got crowded together I can't understand. You had to *walk over them* to cross the court. They showed their hatred even while dying, cursed us and said, 'if we could only stand we would kill you.'"[20]

Ahead lay other deadly obstacles along the twelve hundred yards separating Campbell's forces from Havelock's beleaguered garrison in the residency. Even while the Highlanders, the Punjab Rifles, and the other units were concluding their grisly bayonet battle,

Campbell sent some other infantry and Blunt's and Cracklow's guns forward through the opening and out beyond on the plain southward for almost half a mile, to a large building called "the Barracks." This was a longer way around from the Secundrabagh to the enemy-held Kaiserbagh.

The shorter road from the Secundrabagh to the Kaiserbagh and on to the residency ran directly westward. About three hundred yards along this road there was a small village with garden enclosures around it. In the village's center, on the right side of the road, stood the Shah Najaf, a large mosque enclosed by thick masonry walls. The intervening ground was covered with undergrowth, so that it was difficult to see. The enemy occupied the mosque in force, pouring incessant fire from the top of the structure.

Campbell decided that the mosque had to be taken that very day, and again chose the Highlanders for the assault team. Now, though, they were aided by a new weapon—Peel's heavy artillery. In their few short days with the army, the members of the naval brigade had already ingratiated themselves with everyone. The "little men four heet high, and four feet in the beam, always laughing and dragging about their own guns," had infiltrated the camp with their fun and good temper. Normally the enormous guns were fired from far back in the rear echelons, where Peel had shown his mastery of precise, hairline sighting (he was quoted as saying, proudly, "It should not be said of these guns that one can shoot with them as well as with a rifle, but rather that one can shoot with a rifle as well as with them"). Now these troops were to show their mettle as front-line attacking artillerymen. As they approached the Shah Najaf, Peel "led up his guns with extraordinary gallantry within a few yards of the building, to batter the massive stone walls," according to Campbell in his later report. "The withering fire of the Highlanders effectually covered the naval brigade from great loss but it was an action almost unexampled in war; Captain Peel behaved himself very much as he had been laying the *Shannon* alongside an enemy's frigate."[21]

Forbes-Mitchell told of another strange aspect of the Shah Najaf battle. In addition to the regular army of the mutineers, there was a large body of enemy archers on the walls. When one of the Highlanders raised his feather bonnet above the low wall behind which he was crouching, an arrow passed into it, catching in the folds of the forage cap. Forbes-Mitchell recalled the man's response: "Bows and arrows! Have we got Robin Hood and Little John again?" Forbes-Mitchell continues: "Just then one poor fellow of the Ninety-Third named Penny, raising his head for an instant a little above the wall, got an arrow right through his brain, the shaft projecting more than a foot out at the back of his head. As the poor lad fell dead at our feet, Sergeant White remarked, 'Boys, this is no joke; we must pay them off!' We all loaded and capped, and pushing up our feather bonnets again a whole shower of arrows went past or through them. Up we sprang and returned a well-aimed volley from our rifles at point-blank distance, and more than a half-a-dozen of the enemy went down. But one unfortunate man of the regiment, named Montgomery, exposed himself a little too long to watch the effect of our volley, and before he could get down into shelter again an arrow was sent right through his heart, passing clean through his body and falling on the ground a few yards behind him. He leaped about six feet straight up in the air, and fell stone dead."[22]

The enemy counterattacked strongly, aided by an artillery piece from the opposite bank of the river, and the British artillery was forced back. For a moment it seemed as if the tide of the battle would really change. At this point, Campbell had Peel send a volley of rockets into the enclosure. When the first of the Highlanders scaled the wall they saw only the retreating heels of the defenders, apparently scared away by the accuracy and destructive power of the rockets.

In a sense the rocket was the ultimate weapon. As Bourchier put it: "There is something undeniably horrible in the bang of a roundshot; its very whiz at a distance makes you feel uncomfortable: nothing in reality is more destructive, and one thing only worse in sound; and that is one of Peel's rockets. Though on your side, the very sight of the little car, with the mast slipt in its centre makes your hair stand on end. Reader, if you ever see it coming near you . . . and you are trying to snooze off the effects of a hard day's work, quietly move off as far as possible: your rest is gone. A more diabolical apparatus for rousing an army from its repose never was invented; but, abominable as is the disturbance they make, their effect, as Peel used them, must have been terrific in a crowded city."

Lang was also at this hot spot, and reported: "Sir Colin led us himself for some way across the open, and we went over the plain and into a cluster of mud huts which lie almost under the outer walls of the place. Here, within some 20 or 30 yards of the wall, Peel's gun opened to make a breach, and our poor fellows were being knocked about dreadfully; the sun was setting; what with the 'sulphurous canopy' and the failing daylight, we couldn't see where we were, and it was crouching, undecided work, reminding me of the first advance on the Lahore Gate at Delhi. An hour of this work had cost us no end of lives and all light had gone, but that from burning thatch, when it was decided that Peel's breach was no good (for the outer wall breached, revealed only an inner one intact) and the gun was withdrawn and the troops were being moved back, when, by luck, another breach was found, which had been made by the previous battering and in went the 93rd and the place was ours; into the garden went the glorious kilted boys and with the piper playing ahead made the circuit of the garden."

Thus ended a climactic day. The toll on both sides in killed and wounded was devastating. Cracklow's troop had lost almost half its men: "Our poor troops suffered the worst of any in proportion." The men slept uneasily that night, arms by their sides, to be awakened by the pealing of bells and the sound of enemy drums early on the seventeenth. In the first moments of wakefulness, it sounded to the men like an enemy call to attack. But no such effort came, and Campbell was able to complete the fight this day on his own terms. He first secured his left flank to prevent an encirclement from the Kaiserbagh around to his rear; then he shelled the next obstacle, the mess hall, storming it with little opposition. Next came the Moti Mahal, breached by sappers and taken by the infantry. Now only several hundred yards separated Campbell from Outram and Havelock.

The latter two, together with six other officers and a civilian, made a dash through the open space, amid a rain of bullets, to confer with Campbell. Then they again made their way back through the whistling lead around them. Four of the nine were slightly injured in the effort, but the final plans for the link were now set. The forces inside fought their way toward the rescuers, and finally the two forces became one. A British colonel described the scene (and in the process telegraphed his class bias): "In the ragged summer clothing in which they had entered, these men looked worn and hungry, and in one corner was seen the curious spectacle—I suppose common enough in the garrison—of a British soldier making chappaties (unleavened cakes) for himself out of his scanty allowance of flour. Entering a battery which was trying to silence some of the enemy's guns across the river, these officers saw a few men grimed with smoke and without coat or waistcoat, all so alike in costume and appearance, that it was only by asking which was the officer, that they ascertained they were standing close to one they well knew—one of the bravest officers in the Bengal Artillery."[23]

But the newly combined forces were still pitifully small in the face of the thirty thousand rebels yet lurking around the town. The following day several more skirmishes occurred, and Cracklow's fellow officer H. E. Harrington contributed yet another feat of artillery valor by dashing out under "a very hot fire" and rescuing an enlisted man who had lain wounded in a garden for an hour and a half, pinned down by constant musketry shots.

The position of the British remained precarious, because now they had to manage not only the troops but the substantial contingent of women and children, together with a distressingly large number of sick and wounded soldiers. To Campbell, there was no question of trying to hold onto Lucknow in the face of overwhelmingly superior forces. But the thought of giving it up, after the siege and the two great battles, grated harshly for many. Cracklow wrote: "We soon found out what it was all about. We are all going to evacuate . . . in fact, to make a regular bolt of it, a thing the British Army does not like to do often." Lang reiterated the dislike: "I think we all feel the shame of marching away, as if beaten."

The evacuation would have to be done cleverly if further lives were not to be lost. Lang was sent ostentatiously to the Gumti with a detachment of men to begin making a "demonstration" bridge, as he called it, the whole operation a feint for a secret plan. That night, Campbell executed a midnight evacuation in the opposite direction. The British went down a narrow winding lane, almost single file, with the troops spread precariously thin along the line of march. One of the civilians in the residency described the march: "Most of them were conveyed in carriages closely packed, every description of vehicle being pressed into service on the occasion.

Many were seated on native carts, and not a few walked . . . They entered and passed through the court of the Moti Munzil, on the further side of which they gained the high road leading to the Secundrabagh. Here, and near Martin's House, they were exposed to the fire of the enemy's guns placed on the farther side of the river. Screens formed of the canvas walls of tents, or doors placed on each side of the way they traversed, as far as the Moti Munzil, concealed the march of the fugitives from the enemy, and on one side of this a ditch or traverse had been dug, along which, dismounting from their carriages, they walked past all the exposed places."

One of the complications that first day was the condition of the horses from inside the residency, "They had been so long on siege fare that they had forgotten the use of their legs and had no strength and so came to a standstill every five minutes, invariably choosing the most dangerous parts of the road for their halt. At one place we were under so hot a fire that we got out and ran for our lives, leaving the vehicles to fate; and two natives who were helping to push behind were shot."

Maria Germon, one of the women who had gone through the entire siege (and whose *Journal of the Siege of Lucknow* became a classic book) found that it was not just the ponies that were weak; when she tried to mount hers, she nearly fell off. She, too, had to dismount early in the evacuation because of the hostile fire, and she had considerable difficulty remounting. "On I went steadily," she wrote later that night, "till I came to another dangerous part when a soldier told me I had bettter dismount but I thought of my former difficulties, so I made Herar Singh double the pony across— the balls whistling over our heads." Lang seemed to capture the essence of the moment: "We glided out one by one like ghosts."[24]

A few men had the very uneasy role of staying on guard until all were out and far enough away to be reasonably judged out of danger. Cracklow was one of these, and he wrote movingly about his experience: "I think the most unpleasant night I have spent since the whole affair commenced was this one—waiting, waiting, waiting for the guns to come out. We were drawn up on one side of the road and on the other a troop of artillery, in our rear some infantry, about a regiment. The garrison were to come out about 12. About 11 the enemy made an attack, which lasted about an hour. At last all the firing ceased and everything got quiet again. Old Sir Colin was walking up and down the road by the guns in a dreadfully fidgety state. At last, about 2 o'clock, they began to pass, regiment after regiment. We had been on the lookout since sunset and you may imagine were pretty tired ot it. About 3 all had passed. Then our own picquets began to come in, the most distant ones first, all after the other until nearly the whole force had passed in view before us.

"Then came the most anxious time when all had passed and we had to wait an hour to give them a good start on the road. Had anything gone wrong at this time and the enemy discovered that all our advanced posts were deserted, we should have had them down on us in thousands and had hard work of it. All luckily went well and about half past 4 I got the order to retire my guns, and never gave the order 'limber up' with more hearty good will. We all got safely back to Dilkushar."[25]

It was decided that the safest place for the first night's stop was the Secundrabagh itself. It still looked like a charnel house, so Gordon-Alexander volunteered a troop of Highlanders to put it in order: "With an extra ration of rum to fortify them against the fearful stench of the operation, we could get all the men of No. 6 not on sentry duty to volunteer to clear out the Sepoy dead from a corner of the enclosure and its approaches . . . We then swept and washed out the rooms, ready for the reception of the women and children. The men worked most cheerfully, although many of us were very sick, and felt we had well earned Sir Colin's extra 'tot' of rum. We carried out into the trench a little over 500 dead Pandies and Oudh Irregulars."

Roberts told of their arrival that night: "Not a very agreeable resting-place, for though the 2000 dead mutineers had been got out of sight, they were merely slightly covered over in a ditch which they themselves had recently dug outside the North wall to strengthen the defenses. The survivors of the siege, however, had become too inured to horrors of all kinds, and were too thankful for their deliverance from the fate for which months had constantly threatened them, to be oversensitive . . . It was a sad little assemblage; all were more or less broken down and out of health, for many were widows or orphans, having left their nearest and dearest in the Residency burial-ground."

During the retreat an enormous artillery barrage was directed at the Kaiserbagh to cover the evacuation, and by early on the twenty-third the garrison had completed the move further on to the safer Dilkusha. Havelock, already weakened by the long defense of Lucknow, had a sudden severe attack of dysentery and died on that day. By the end of the day, they reached the Alambagh, with Havelock's dream of the successful relief of Lucknow accomplished on the very day of his death.

Here most of the dependents had to be bedded outside. Lang was almost nonplussed: "We encamped south of Alam Bagh, with ladies and children interspersed, in extraordinary fashion, amongst us. One lady got admission, as well, in Stevenson's tent, and completely turned him out, and at daybreak she got her mother and sisters also installed."[26]

The whole contingent stayed at the Alambagh; for two more days, and Lang continued to be amazed at the experience of women in a field encampment: "It is extraordinary to see how the ladies are 'gypsying' it everywhere, and anywhere about the Camp. Mrs. Barlow was living beneath a durree [native carpet] spread about four feet from the ground." Cracklow was considerably more acid about the women and children: "Sir Colin making arrangements for safety of women (who were just encumbrance to us, taking nearly half our men to guard them)."

Once the initial euphoria of the rescue wore off, recriminations began to surface about the handling by Havelock and Outram of the first "rescue," debates that continued for many years. Immediately after the evacuation, Roberts wrote his mother: "Sir. C. Napier's opinion of Outram was true in every item. He is no soldier, and I should say no politician. The whole business from Cawnpore to Lucknow, for which he and poor Havelock got so much praise, was simply disgraceful. Nearly all their wounded were left behind in the streets and cut up. Those that reached the Residency were in a state of disorderly flight, and as they brought no provisions were but an encumbrance to the garrison, who could have subsisted till the end of the year, added to which, we received letters as I may have told you, day after day, urging our rapid advance for fear of their being starved, and our whole force is actually living on the grain we brought out of their camp."

Countess Roberts, probably feeling it not diplomatic for her father, as Lord Roberts, commander in chief, to be so critical of a high-ranking officer, appended a footnote to this comment from

Roberts as a young lieutenant: "The writer's connection with General Hunter, who took Sir Charles Napier's part in the well-known controversy between Napier and Outram, . . . probably accounts for this boyish criticism. Lord Roberts's admiration for General Outram was very real, and it is interesting to compare this letter with the chapter in *Forty-One Years in India,* in which, with a fuller knowledge of the difficulties encountered by their small force, he speaks of the 'Bayard of India' and Havelock, the 'hero of a hundred fights.'" To the great credit of the Countess, she nonetheless let Roberts's early statement stand.[27]

Campbell left Outram at the Alambagh with a sizable force of men, charging him to develop plans for retaking Lucknow, and then set off with his force of three thousand, convoying with them another two thousand women, children, sick, and wounded. After a day of marching, the reunited column was jarred anew with the startling information that Cawnpore was again under attack. Fearful that the "bridge of boats" across the Ganges might fall, cutting off his retreat route, Campbell initiated a forced march back to Cawnpore. Cracklow described it: "During our absence at Lucknow, Cawnpore was attacked by the Gwalior force and we had to come back as hard as we could to relieve the garrison which is on an entrenched position on the bank of the river. We just arrived in time, making a march of 30 miles in 10 hours. The regiments have been by all accounts behaving very badly and it was nearly impossible to hold out against the overwhelming force of the enemy who have some 10,000 men whilst ours only amounted to 2,000. They might have done much better but somehow or other I believe our side got very nearly licked three different days and were obliged to retreat into the entrenchment where the enemy were shelling them when we arrived. Since our arrival on the 30th we have not been doing much as we cannot advance until we get rid of the 500 women and children, who are a great encumbrance. Arrangements are being made for them and we shall then go into the black guards and I hope fix them well." Cracklow's caustic comment that the British forces had been "behaving very badly" was, if anything, an understatement. Windham, the officer in charge at Cawnpore, had foolishly gone out to chase the mutineers, been forced to retreat, and lost all his stores. Meanwhile, the town itself had been occupied by the Gwalior rebels.

At this point Campbell arrived and, after securing the bridge, rescued Windham's forces. Campbell must have been quite exasperated with Windham, but nevertheless he phrased his telegram back to Calcutta diplomatically: "In consequence of the force under Major General Windham leaving here so much pressed at Cawnpore, prior to my arrival, I regret to say that very large portions of the camp equipage abandoned on this occasion of his retreating from outside the city and the storerooms containing all the clothing of some of the eight or ten of his regiments here and in Lucknow have been burnt by the enemy. I would entreat your Lordship to give the most urgent orders for the transferrence of clothing, greatcoats from below to make up the deficiency which has occurred in consequence of this lamentable circumstance."[28]

As Cracklow succinctly noted, the five hundred women and children were "a great encumbrance," so Campbell, eschewing the temptation to have at the town itself, first evacuated the noncombatants down the road to Allahabad. This delicate task accomplished, he turned to the attack. Good tactician as he was, Campbell sensed that if he could split the rebels and control the Ganges, and thus open up the key communications link back to the Punjab, the British would truly be "in the ascendant." If he failed, pacification of Oudh (and thus all of central India) would be set back many months, might perhaps not even be accomplished.

The Gwalior mutineers had an immense force under the wily rebel general Tantia Topi (who had so outmaneuvered Windham the week before). The total rebel forces numbered about twenty-five thousand, with forty guns, although Malleson downgraded its potency: "At the outside, fourteen thousand were trained soldiers." Still, when one had only five thousand infantry, six hundred cavalry, and thirty-five guns, the task appeared in a more serious light. Windham's rout had left the rebels in a formidable position. Forrest, the official historian, described it: "Their left occupied the whole cantonment from which General Windham's posts had been principally assailed. The ground is high, studded with trees and much intersected with ravines; it was also then covered with ruined bungalows and public buildings which afforded admirable shelter. Their centre was in the city itself, and they lined the houses and bazaars overhanging the canal which separated it from Brigadier Greathed's position. The narrow winding streets were singularly

susceptible of defense, and the principal thoroughfares were afterwards discovered to be barricaded. Their right stretched away behind the canal some distance beyond where the Grand Trunk Road
crosses it. The bridge over it and some lime kilns and some mounds
of brick in its front were held by them."[29]

To Campbell, the left seemed difficult because of the terrain, the
center almost impregnable. The right had the dangerous crossing
at the bridge but offered considerable open ground. However,
given the enemy strength, Campbell opted for an unexpected
move, a dangerous one but offering surprise and boldness—the
very qualities that seemed decisive throughout the mutiny. The tac-
tic was the time-honored one of the fake attack from the position
of apparent strength, coupled with a real attack on the flank.

On the morning of the sixth, Windham was ordered to open a
heavy bombardment while Greathed was to make every appearance
of starting a major attack from his position in the center. In actual-
ity, the Greathed forces had been pirated to build up the flank attack force. Only a skeleton crew held the center. It was a bold
gamble, but Malleson was probably right in his patently chauvinistic analysis of the move: "Sir Colin did leave an opening of which
a Napoleon or a Frederick would have taken advantage. But the
great thing for a general is to know when to dare. Sir Colin knew
that the opponents' general was neither a Napoleon nor a Frederick
and that the soldiers he commanded were neither Frenchmen nor
Prussians. He felt that with his actual opponents he would take
liberties which they would not resent."[30] (Hindsight is useful:
Windham, of course, might have been less patronizing after his
smarting defeat by Tantia Topi a few days before.)

The obvious funnel point for the real attack was the bridge. What
happened there became one of the favorite stories of the war, much
embroidered over the years. Forrest again: "The Sikhs and 53rd
quitting the cover made a spring for the bridge. But the enemy
were ranked again in many lines and they swept it with musketry
and grape. The skirmishers were baffled: they could advance no
farther. The moments were running out, and unless help came
quickly they must fall back. Then a rumbling sound was heard. Peel
and his sailors, dragging their heavy 24-pounder as if it were a light
field piece, came up; passing through the skirmishers and through
the murderous fire, they ran it across the bridge, Peel, accompanied

by a soldier of Her Majesty's 53rd, named Hannaford, leading the way, and quickly brought it into action."[31]

The incredible sight of a twenty-four-pound gun in the front line of skirmishers was electric. With a tremendous shout the British poured across the bridge. The mutineers, only a moment before confident of their defenses, were totally demoralized and fled pell-mell back and out of the town.

At this point, "the gallant Bourchier, always in the front" (Malleson's words), rushed forward. Not to be outdone by Peel's artillery rivals, the troop swept past the infantry and took out after the mutineers. "For two miles without a check the pursuit was carried on by the battery alone accompanied by Sir Hope Grant and his staff," recounted Bourchier. "Four times in the distance did we come into action, to clear out front and flanks, until General Frank, thinking wisely we were too far from our supports, determined to wait until the Cavalry arrived. A halt was called; not until it was required, for the horses, though in the condition of racers, had felt the pace."

Cracklow, having been deputed, none too happily, back to Bourchier's heavy guns, was alongside him on this lightning chase: "I was in great luck in being with Bourchier's battery on the 6th as the troop I belong to was left in the rear and did not fire a shot . . . We were then ordered to advance again and after a gallop of about a mile suddenly came on their camp. Into there we fired grape at a distance of about 200 yards, killing I am afraid more cattle than men, and then limbered up and started in pursuit . . . One great mistake occurred. The Cavalry and two troops of Horse Artillery were misled and taken round by a road a long way to our left. This greatly delayed them and the consequence was the battery got ahead and kept ahead during the whole of the pursuit, the H.A. only arriving just at the last and not firing a shot. The Cavalry men caught up with us at about the 4th mile and cut up a good many but had they been with us when we came upon the camp they would have slaughtered an immense number."

Once the cavalry did catch up they "spread like lightning over the plain, with Colin Campbell himself in the lead." Cracklow described this, and in the process movingly captured the troops' adulation of the crusty general: "He galloped up to our battery . . . to know if we did not want the Infantry in advance, and then it quite did one's heart good to see the old fellow take off his hat and cheer on the Sikhs 'Chulo Sikh log Chulo' ('Come on, Sikhs, come on') and away he went at their heads with the shells bursting over his head and the round shot whistling round him. With such a jolly old fellow, who wouldn't join."

The pursuit continued with gusto, "assuming all the character of fox-hunt," Bourchier commented exultantly. Campbell continued with them for part of the chase, reportedly calling it the "very best run" he had ever had.[32] Cracklow added the finale: "We pursued the brutes up to the 14 mile stone on the road and killed a great number of them. Took 17 pieces of ordnance, 12 ammunition wagons and immense quantities of ammunition and stores of all kinds. For 12 miles the road was strewn with their baggage and carts. We took everything they had but the clothes on their backs . . . Altogether the affair was well managed and the Pandies well thrashed."

Apparently, though, Campbell did not give Bourchier and Cracklow full credit for their central role at this skirmish, for Cracklow later wrote: "Old Sir Colin did not, I see in dispatch of the affair at Cawnpore of the 6th Dec., mention a word about Bourchier's battery. This is very unfair. With the exception of 3 guns of Peels which were ordered up before the battery all that was done by Artillery on that day was done by the battery. We did all the pursuit, being joined by the Cavalry about 3 miles from Cawnpore and the H.A. only came up when we had to stop at the 14th mile and were watering our horses preparatory to returning. The fact is the Chief made a mistake in sending the Cavalry and H.A. the way he did and has just said nothing about the matter in order to conceal the mistake."

The euphoria of the troop, so evident in Bouchier's and Cracklow's description of this chase, was dampened by the seemingly inexorable attrition of men. Cracklow's own troop was down to a pitiful thirty-eight, having lost ten men just in a small skirmish the day before the major Cawnpore battle. The artillery had been truly heroic in the many battles, but, as Cracklow succinctly put it, "Artillery officers are now so scarece that it is hardly to be expected that they will allow me to go quietly off to cantonment."

Cracklow was plainly discouraged: "The Chief was delighted with the battery and has given Bourchier the command of the troop H.A. worth about 120 £ a month clear. Bourchier will also get his majority and Brevet Lt. Colonelcy. See what a nice thing it is to be

Captain commanding instead of a subaltern officer who does all the hard work. I am now back again with the troops, as another subaltern, one Hawkins, has been caught to do Harrington's duty in the battery."

The future looked bleak: "I do not fancy another hot weather under canvas and have quite enough of fighting . . . I fully expect to be nailed to do duty with some fresh troop which will be sent down to join the avenging army proceeding into order. Should this be the case I shall be awfully disgusted as I think that by the time we have fought our way back to Meerut again through Rohilkhand, we shall have had quite enough knocking about and the rest may be left to the Royal Artillery to do. Bourchier has promised to apply for me to be posted to his troop at Lahore. This would be the first thing I should like. But a good deal of time must pass before this can be carried out."

The outlook appeared considerably brighter to Roberts, as he noted in a letter to his sister on December 31: "I do so long to leave India for a while, and have some quiet days at Suir View. That, however, cannot be yet. If I could keep in health, I would not leave for anything. There must be Service for months and months, and your brother Fred, Harriet darling, has no end of ambition. Besides, soldiers should make up their minds to work with their life's best blood at such a crisis to restore peace and order, and show these rascally Musalmans that, with God's help, Englishmen will still be masters of India." Roberts continued to have an optimistic outlook about his own personal life, too: "It will be doubly sweet going home when all is over. You must look out for some nice girl with 'blue eyes and yellow hair' (such as MacKinnon raves about) for me, Harriet dearest, who will console me for having to return to the gorgeous East."

Lang now had a change in command, too; in describing it, he gave some clues about his attitude toward the European Corps, particularly the "Royals": "The 4th Company of Royal Engineers has joined us, and Major Nicholson commanding it (a young fellow only regimentally a 2nd Captain) is Chief Engineer: he brings four subalterns to strengthen our roster . . . Nicholson has evidently always done regimental duty and is more like a strict little Adjutant than an Engineer officer, fond of smart drills, pipeclay, *et hoc genus omne*. I fancy the 'Delhi' style of the Bengal and Punjab

Sappers 'perplexes' him, our scorn of appearances and drill, our absolute sway over our men. I expect he will soon ask me to doff my peacock feather plume for my helmet! Perhaps, too, he may ask me to doff also my loose khaki tunic and jack boots, and my black pouches and belts, &c., and request me to wear red and russia leather, and gold lace, and other pomps, a more glittering, but not one half so soldierly looking a set of harness. However, I hope he will let us 'gang our ain gait' and rub pipeclay into the Royals."

Lang at this point seemed ambivalent about his dual roles as fighting man and professional engineer; the former now appeared more attractive: "I have had a fear of being sent to Benares, or of being kept at Cawnpore, as Ex. Engineer, to build Barracks, both hateful *in prospectu,* especially the latter. However, I trust I may get safe away with Grant's division; if I do not, I must try and submit patiently, tho' it will be a good lesson in self denial: in these days one ought to be ready to sacrifice 'self' in every possible way, *pro bono publico,* and be even glad to be called upon to make some sacrifices in the good cause." Just what this self-denial was is not clear. What was it that appealed so much to Lang in these battles?

There was considerable excitement among the men when a rumor reached them that the Nana Sahib had thrown his family treasures down one of the wells at his Bithoor palace. Hope Grant investigated on December 11 and found the well in question full of water. One of the officers described the salvage effort: "It was a very difficult operation, for the water stood at 30 feet depth, its surface being 20 or 25 feet below the mouth of the well; and all that water had to be drawn out before the people could work at the bottom; nor could they, with all their exertions reduce it more than within two feet of the bottom. They had four buckets, of bullock's hides, each holding eight or ten pails full, constantly at work, with about forty men upon each pulley. At night when the work was perfomed by bullocks, the water gained upon them to about 13 feet deep, and it took from daylight until eleven or twelve o'clock before the level of the water was sufficiently reduced to work at the bottom." The first item hooked in the not-very-shallow water was only a log of wood. "Nowise disheartened," related Grant, "we renewed our efforts, and this time we discovered a number of gold and silver articles . . . there were some curious gurrahs or pots, lamps which seemed of Jewish manufacture, and spoons of a barbaric weight.

All were of the purest metal, and all bore an appearance of antique magnificance."[33]

But Cracklow was dubious of any of them sharing in the treasure: "They say we are to get 6 months *batta* instead of prize money for Delhi. It will be a great shame—prize money of a subaltern would be about 200 £ whereas *batta* is only about 70. Not enough to pay our mess bills."

* * *

And Thomas Watson during these critical battles at Lucknow and Cawnpore? He was still doing garrison duty in Delhi.

Chapter 7
Skirmishes, Banners, and Crosses

"It is very dull here, now and then a sepoy hung or blown away, a cricket match or two, and a little quail shooting," reported one of Colin Campbell's officers in mid-December.[1] Campbell now began a debate with his Calcutta superiors about the forces' next moves. The December 6 battle at Cawnpore may well have marked the turning point in the mutiny, but Campbell and all his troops knew that until Lucknow was retaken, the possibility of a turnaround in fortunes was always present. Indeed, Outram's position in the Alambagh was under almost constant threat, attacked six times between the moment in November when Campbell left with the women and children and the February date when the two generals again linked up. Campbell now put himself on record that he preferred to pursue the enemy into Rohilkhand and attempt to surround the province of Oudh, rather than move through the latter directly. However, political considerations apparently outweighed Campbell's military strategies: the governor-general insisted that Oudh be reconquered immediately, before hot weather made a summer campaign necessary. So the forces turned back toward Cawnpore for a rendezvous with new troops coming from Delhi and Calcutta, in order to build the necessary strength for the second attack on Lucknow.

For a while, General Walpole's column (with Cracklow and Lang) had a blessed respite from any hostilities. Cracklow exulted: "We have had a very jolly march from Cawnpore through a beautiful country. The weather delightful, short easy marches, and plenty of shooting . . . halted on Christmas day and had a grand dinner, peacocks and venison supplying the place of turkeys and roast beef." Lang told more about Christmas Day: "After service (at 9:00) . . . Cracklow and I went out on foot with a gun and rifle and horses led behind us. We were out till about 4 p.m. . . . had dinner again all sociably together, in a big tent." A few days earlier, there had been one of those cricket matches. Lang played, and bemoaned the quality of the effort: ". . . one inning each . . . very bad, but none of us had played since last January."

Cracklow had a special passion for hunting and just a few days after Christmas was out in the countryside again, by himself. It was a foolhardy act (and not his first, either); Lang reported unsettling news that Cracklow had been shot at by a number of rebels and chased back to camp. The area was still bristling with enemy; the British really had only a salient, driven into a packed mass of mutineers and sympathetic civilians. Cracklow cautioned his mother, in a letter on December 30: "I will write you a longer letter when we get to Mainpuri or at some safer place for sending letters from. There is but little chance of this ever reaching; as a rule all the daks are stopped . . . a man is going off with a donkey whose saddle is to be stuffed with letters and this will be one of them. As these infernal Sepoys catch almost all the people we send and cut off their hands and noses, it has been rather a hard matter to find a man who will venture, however great the reward, to take any letters."

Campbell still wanted to harass the rebels at every opportunity and soon sent Walpole on an expedition (with Cracklow and Lang) to check out the wrecked town of Etawah. "We expected to have had a fight, as some 2 or 3 thousand men were collected here with 7 guns," reported Cracklow. "However, they thought better of it and took themselves off and we only had a mild affair with a few who remained behind (having apparently overslept themselves) in which about 10 were killed and two small guns taken."

Cracklow had skipped over some ugly details, though. Bourchier gave the particulars. "A few desperadoes were still hemmed into a walled enclosure, a stronghold under one of the bastions which flanked each corner. For three hours they kept the whole brigade at bay, wounding several men with their muskets. Their position might have been stormed, but only with the loss of several men.

We tried every expedient to dislodge them—hand grenades, burning straw &c.—with no avail; at last nothing was left but to blow in the whole bastion. For this purpose, with Scatchley, of the Engineers, I made a mine in the roof from a number of my gun cartridges; its explosion was most successful: it buried our friends below. About twenty were taken out of the ruins, with unfortunately two or three women and children." Lang, a witness to the whole episode, told more about the latter: "Some poor women and children were with them when they died, and they cut them with their tulwars." Killing their own women and children to prevent capture was a not uncommon policy among the mutineers.[2]

Suddenly, now, the war also became personal for Thomas Watson. He wrote his mother on December 7: "We marched this morning from Delhi at about 2 o'clock." Col. P. Seaton was his commander; the column was to bring an immense amount of grain and stores required for Campbell's forces. A precious material this, and fighting forces necessarily came along—a troop of carabineers, Hodson's Horse, a Sikh regiment, a group of Horse Artillery, and the 1st Bengal Fusiliers. Watson was assigned to the latter, in charge of some of the stores and acting as finanical officer.

It was foregone that his departure would upset his mother: "You say how much you wish I might remain in Delhi. Dear Mother, on your account I should have been happy to remain there, tired as I was of the place. Could I only feel that you were not anxious on my account, I would enjoy this marching very much." Anticipating his mother's perpetual remonstrances about his physical comfort, he continued: "You asked if I have not yet two tents. I had two, but recollecting that in time of war one cannot send on their second tent, I allowed Boyle to have it for what I paid . . . I could have sold it but I did not feel I had much right to make profit on what in the first place I had no right to appropriate. Besides, Boyle has no tent and is hard up."

She wrote back immediately: "I was cheered by your dear letter, especially as it gave me hope that please God your regiment will not go farther than Alighar." His mother not only was *trembling* lest you should be in danger" but also reverted back to her long-standing preoccupation with sunstroke: "How reckless of you to squander your dear strength walking all night 20 miles, at least without a rest or sleep, then going out in the sun for hours to shoot—my darling son, every act that produces an *over amount* of *fatigue* is *injurious* to the constitution; you make a great mistake in supposing it strengthens."

Seaton's lush cargo, terribly tempting to the rebels, brought a sharp skirmish within days near that very town of Aligarh which Sarah Watson had hoped would be a safe refuge. Surprisingly, given what we already know about this mother and son, Watson frankly reported the details to her. "Just as our camp was pitched and we were all resting after our march, a force advanced upon us. In a minute we were all out. The Cavalry went on and were immediately opened upon from the enemy's guns. On the arrival of our Artillery a few shots were exchanged and then the guns (I hear 5 in number) were taken . . . Captain Wardlow and another Captain were killed, Captain Head and Lieutenant Vic were wounded . . . the Infantry did not as much as see the enemy once except those who were dead in the plain when we got up." As if to further reassure his mother he ended, "There is now little chance of their ever again showing us a front."

Of course this was wishful thinking, and it took only three more days for another pitched encounter to take place. This time a charge by the infantry put the mutineers to flight, and a six-mile chase ensued. Watson was left in the rear guard, only to hear about the battle after it was over. Nevertheless, he did end up with his own battle assignment, and once more he told his mother the whole story: "After breakfast this morning a party of us went out into the sugar cane field and killed a large number of the rascals who were hiding all round us. I came across no one, though I was up just at the death of several." The British had only light casualties in this second battle; the mutineers suffered severe losses that included a commander in chief of the nawab of Farukhabad, killed while trying to escape on his elephant.[3]

Both mother and son continued their introverted way of living; being on march seemed to alter nothing. Sarah Watson was increasingly unhappy at the Kupowlie house—"I kept in my room for two days," she wrote in January—and began making plans to go back to Simla, perhaps to live with Mrs. Bourchier. Her son wrote, "I am glad that you will return to Simla, for even Mrs. Scott with her stingy ways is better than where you are." In turn, Watson now opted to leave the group mess, ostensibly to save money: "I have determined on leaving the mess on the 1st of next month. I did not know till yesterday that I could do so . . . it will not be nearly so pleasant. I like the officers of the regt. They are very sociable and civil. I do not see a great deal of them except at mess and during the march." Having been granted his request to pull out of the mess, he wrote a few days later: "I do not much dislike living alone. I see quite as much as I wish of the officers of and with the regt."[4]

Campbell's columns still were acutely short of transport, as most of it had been sent down with the convoy of the women and children from the Lucknow residency (the units were also woefully short of boots and shoes, according to Lang). Fresh troops, however, were beginning to arrive from other British colonies outside India—from Burma, Ceylon, Persia, Mauritius. Even an expedition that had been on the way to China was drafted. The seasoned fighters were alternately disdainful of the abilities of these newcomers and irritated at the possibility that they might usurp promotions and commands. Cracklow at this time was a bit more charitable than he became later: "The Royals have not had at all a fair chance as they were new to the country and had equipments they were unaccustomed to. They have all been left behind at Cawnpore or sent down country." Lang assumed once more his mantle of skepticism: "Most of our new regiments are Crimean ones, and we hear that the 'Crimea was nothing to this,' 'by Jove, this *is* fighting, this is service'. By writing to you sober sense and true accounts of what happens, what we think, you have a true idea . . . of what is going on, but we cease to be heroes; the unvarnished tale of our doings looks mild beside the usual style of narration of past battles and wars . . . To compare our campaign with others, read the newspapers and historical accounts; but to know the truth of these and of Crimean &c., accounts, believe mine."

During this pause in hostilities, Roberts, too, wrote of his feelings. Ever ebullient, he rambled on to his mother: "I have seen battles now in every shape and shall not be sorry to have a rest. Losing so many dear friends and knowing what misery each fight entails is eno' to make one soon satisfied, for a time at any rate. I always longed for service and would not have missed being thro' these past six months for all I hope ever to possess. Few have been lucky eno' to get off so easily as I have. One slight wound. Now, unless we have to return to Oudh, our work may be said to be over.

I hope to remain at Meerut all the hot weather. The C. in C. will probably be there with a large force."

His enthusiasm about the tangible rewards of campaigning showed through once more: "We are very anxious about *Medals*. One should be given for Delhi alone, and another for other parts in India. The Governor-General does not seem inclined to reward the army himself, so I hope Parliament will. Fancy having 2!!" A few days later, he wrote again: "I could not be happier or better than I am now. Garden, of the Quartermaster-General's Department, left for England a few days ago on medical certificate. Sir Colin was going to put me in his place at once, but Norman very properly suggested it would be better to wait for Becher's arrival, who was with Seaton's Column, before deciding upon anything. It will only occasion a short delay and no one will be annoyed, for, once I am in the Department permanently, of course they can do as they like. I am greatly pleased at having given Sir Colin satisfaction, for he is rather a particular old gentleman."[5]

Cracklow was properly prideful about his exploits at Lucknow and told his mother: "You will by this time most probably have seen all the Lucknow dispatches, so mind Blunt's is the troop of H.A. I am with. Sir Colin has given the Bengal Artillery as much praise as we could possibly wish for." Despite Cracklow's pleasure at being noticed, he continued to hope for relief: "We proceed to Fatehgarh where we shall meet another column under Brigadier Hope and take Fatehgarh, after which I hope the troop will be sent with one of the columns proceeding up country and be sent to cantonment either at Agra or Umballa."

Fatehgarh had been a rebel bastion, and a hard battle was expected. But the supposed great battle turned into a quick rout. Cracklow reported: "We have, I am sorry to say, been disappointed in our hope of having another crack at the Pandies as although we came in a double march of 25 miles, the affair was over before our arrival. On the 3rd the Commander-in-Chief with Hope's and Windham's Brigades reached within 4 miles of Fatehgarh and intended to have waited there until we arrived from the opposite direction, when all three columns were to have attacked together. The Pandies, it appears, were misinformed as to the C. in C.'s strength, and hearing that he had only a small force with him turned out and attacked him. They made a grievous mistake, for

old Sir Colin went at them and gave them a great licking, taking all
their guns. The Pandies ran so fast and had so little time left them
by our people who pursued them into the cantonment of Fatehgarh, that they could not even destroy the bridge or burn the gun
carriage factory which is established in the Fort, and by this means
property belonging to Government was saved to a vast amount, the
machinery, steam engines, and wood being valued at about half a
million. The mutineers had destroyed nothing, evidently intending
to keep the place for themselves."

The Fatehgarh capture was indeed a fortuitous one, for it gained
a position of no small advantage, effectively barring the way for any
threatened reentry of the mutineers from their strongholds further
north. This time Cracklow missed the action, despite the "double
march" of twenty-five miles. His fellow subaltern, Roberts, *was* on
hand, though, and became yet another of Cracklow's close acquaintances to earn the Victoria Cross. Forrest described the circumstances: "At that moment he spied a Sikh sowar [cavalryman]
and a rebel sepoy standing at bay with musket and bayonet. The
horseman with his sword was no match for the foot soldier with
the 'Queen of Weapons.' Roberts rode straight at the Sepoy, and
with one stroke of his sword killed him on the spot. Then he saw
two Sepoys making off with a standard. He galloped after them,
overtook them 'and while wrenching the staff out of the hands of
one of them, whom I cut down, the other put his musket close to
my body and fired; fortunately for me it missed fire, and I carried
off the standard.'"

Here Forrest was quoting Roberts from his 1897 memoirs. However, in the letter that Roberts wrote his father at the time, it appeared to be less of an exploit: "I accompanied the first line, and in
the scrimmage captured a very pretty Standard! which I will send
home to adorn Suir View the first opportunity. A great piece of
luck my getting it, was it not?" A few weeks later he was surprised
to learn that the "scrimmage" had indeed earned him a recommendation for the coveted award. He excitedly wrote: "My own
mother, I have such a piece of news for you. I have been recommended for the '*Victoria Cross*' . . . is this not glorious . . . *such a
medal to wear* with '*For Valour*' scrolled on it. How proud I shall
be, darling mother when I show it to you—better than all the other

Medals put together. All get Medals when given for a campaign, but few, very few, this glorious Cross."⁶

Several standards were captured that day, and when the men rode triumphantly back to camp, an eyewitness described the scene: "Their return was a stirring sight of war. In front came the 9th Lancers, with three captured standards at their head; the wild-looking Sikh horsemen rode in the rear. As they passed the Commander-in-Chief, he took off his hat to them with some words of praise and thanks. The Lancers shook their lances in the air and cheered; the Sikhs took up the cry, waving their sabres above their heads, the men carrying the standards gave them to the wind; the Highland Brigade . . . ran down and cheered both the victorious cavalry and the veteran Chief, waving their bonnets in the air. It was a fair sight and reminded one of the old days of chivalry."⁷

Why was it, then, that Roberts garnered such special mention? Many years later, Rudyard Kipling recounted the story as told to him by another officer who had seen the event; this version will help to explain why Roberts apparently was singled out: "One morning, when they were all shaving or washing, a rumor ran round that a young Gunner of the name of Roberts had 'done something good' in the way of cutting down a mounted Pandy and bringing in a standard, and that he was riding down the lines at the moment. So all the officers ran out, some of them 'with the lather still on their faces' and saw 'young Roberts' with his mounted orderly behind him who was carrying the captured standard. They were not much interested in the fact that he had also saved the life of an Irregular Horseman in the skirmish. What impressed them was the boy's splendid riding and the look of happiness on his face, and the swagger of his orderly with the trophy. They cheered him and went back and 'went on with our shaving' . . . Colonel Fielding [*sic*] dwelt often on the youth and trimness of the figure riding through, and the graceful horsemanship."⁸

It seems clear that it was the dash and the daring of Roberts, more than anything else, that stood out and that especially impressed Campbell, who made the recommendation for the award. There is always some difficulty in putting in perspective the earlier life of a later-famous figure, such as Roberts. In most of the memoirs written years after the mutiny (and there were many around the turn of the century, as the participants came to old age), there seems to have been a temptation to "dress up" some of Roberts's mutiny exploits, and sometimes in the process to exaggerate the writer's personal relationship with Roberts. This particular instance, involving the Victoria Cross, was a natural for such a puffing.

Yet it also seems clear from contemporary writings that there was something about the "style" of Roberts that did stand out. Oliver Jones, one of his fellow officers, wrote his book in 1858, long before Roberts attained exalted status, and said this about him: "Lieutenant Roberts, of the Bengal Artillery, General Grant's Assistant Quartermaster-General, also made himself conspicuous by his gallantry in the Cavalry pursuit, and earned the much-coveted declaration of the Victoria Cross. He is one of those rare men, who, to uncommon and daring bravery in the field, and unflinching, hardworking discharge of duty in the camp, adds the charm of cheering and unaffected kindness and hospitality in the tent, and his acquaintance and friendship are high prizes to those who obtain them."

A local rebel leader who was "deeply implicated in the barbarities practiced upon our women and children," as Oliver Jones put it, was captured in this battle at Fatehgarh and sentenced to execution. Jones described the result, another favorite story for retelling in memoirs, though not this time involving Roberts: "One would have thought that, on so serious an occasion as that of an execution, especially of a person of rank, there would have been some decorum and decency of behaviour; but on the contrary, most people seemed to think very lightly of it, and were cutting their gibes and cracking their jokes. Some country people came up with some poultry, which was seized and sold by a mock auction, by an officer acting as auctioneer; in the middle of which *good fun* the guard with the convict arrived.

"He was tied down on a charpoy—a sort of native bedstead—and carried under the fatal tree, upon which he cast an anxious look when he saw the noose suspended therefrom. He was then stripped, flogged, and hanged. He had on a handsome shawl, which an officer took possession of on the spot—an action which requires no comment. The man behaved with great firmness. While the rope was being adjusted, a soldier struck him on the face; upon which he turned round with great fierceness, and said—'Had I had a sword in my hand, you dared not have struck that blow:' his last words before he was launched into eternity.

"As Peel and I rode home to the camp, we agreed that it would have been much better to have conducted the execution with more decorum; and that such a display of jesting and greediness, and the careless off-hand way with which it was done, were more likely to make the natives hate and despise us, than to inspire them with a salutary dread of our justice."[9]

There were subsequently many embellishments of these "last words," to suit whatever purposes the speaker might want to develop. Vivian Majendie, another officer in the column, writing many months later, called it "the taunting boast ... that he died happy in a consciousness of having himself assisted and taken part in the killing of English children, and the dishonouring of—as he expressed it—'your wives, your mothers, and your daughters.'"[10]

British retribution during this interim period between the two Lucknow battles did continue harsh. A few days after the hanging of the rebel chief, Harcourt Anson rode out to one of the nearby enclaves: "Going through the village, I saw one of the most remarkable sights I ever in my life beheld; no less than twenty men all hanging naked to one tree, beside three or four others hanging to different trees close by. I thought for a moment I was in Madam Tussaud's Wax Exhibition in Baker Street. I cannot describe to you what a queer sight it was, seeing 20 fat and lean fellows all hanging pendulous on one tree. War certainly familiarizes one with horrors."[11]

Roberts mirrored the majority opinion among the soldiers that these hangings were necessary, but even he began to waver at this point: "Going a little farther, I came on three women watching the dead bodies of their husbands, none of them Sepoys I believe. It was such a sad sight, however, that I felt quite unhappy and wished most sincerely this horrid war was at an end. You must not think, darling Harriet, that I pity the Sepoys or black guards who are rebelling against us. On the contrary, few are more unrelenting than I am. When a prisoner is brought in, I am the first to call out to have him hanged, knowing that unless the severest measures are adopted we shall have no end to our war. But it does make one melancholy to come across such accidents as I have related. They cannot be expected to distinguish between the guilty and the innocent in the heat of the moment, yet such scenes make one wish that it was all settled. Like everything else, one can have eno' of fighting, I suppose."

Oliver Jones witnessed another incident involving Roberts a few weeks later, where again the latter personally had granted clemency: "Roberts, the Assistant Quartermaster-General, was giving directions about burning a part of the town when an old, infirm man, who was sitting at the door of the house, entreated him to spare it, saying 'yesterday morning he was a happy father of five sons; three of them lie there, (pointing to three corpses); where the other two are, God only knows, that he was old and a cripple and if his house was burned he would have nothing left but to lie down and die.' Roberts, who is as good as he is brave, gave directions for sparing the old man's house; and I hope that the two missing sons have escaped, and have returned to comfort his few remaining days." [12]

Cracklow, on the other hand, had seemed to sour, the natural optimism that he had carried through battle after battle overpowered by a hatred that now broke into an overt physical act: "The inhabitants have returned to the villages and everything looks much as it used to. All the chaprassies and blackguards who were formerly in the Government Service and who have been cutting European throats in the meanwhile are again in the service and the despicable brutes come sneaking and cringing about as of old. We meet daily gangs of the dear faithful 'Sepoys' whom Government can't make up its mind to hang from going up with passes to rejoin their regiments. These fellows are men who have been away at their homes on furlough and who have been assisting in the outfringes. Now that the affair is nearly quashed and they see that we were not all wiped out as they at first supposed we were, they go to the nearest [authorities] and as nothing of course can be proved of them, they are granted passes and allowed to return.

"We met a party of them today all with a kind of sneaking grin on their black faces at the way they were bamboozling us. I could hardly restrain myself from driving my sword through the man I spoke to. However, as he looked rather impertinent, I consoled myself with punching his Brahminical head until he hardly knew whether he stood on it or his heels. I do hate these fellows, they have dishonoured the women, murdered the children and men, knocked down the churches, and you'll hardly believe it, gone so far in their hatred as to dig up the graves, positively. I saw the entire burial ground dug up. All the coffins pulled out . . . government are taking them back again, paying them wages and *pensions* and almost patting them on the back . . . Delhi has not been destroyed but is again peopled with the same scoundrels who inhabited it before and who have all been allowed to return unquestioned . . . what fools we are for treating them so mildly. They don't understand it and despise us for our leniency. I heard a native say the other day in the city of Fatehgarh that the natives thought we behaved mildly for fear 1857 should occur again. I only hope they will stand at Lucknow and then they will get a lesson they will remember for many a day."

* * *

Cracklow articulated the view now held widely among the troops, that the final stand would be made at Lucknow: "I do not expect they will ever stand again except perhaps in Oudh—they are thoroughly broken and disheartened. They have lost nearly all their guns and have been licked so often that they only seem to think of getting out of the way whenever we come across them. They are gradually being driven into Oudh where we expect a sort of final stand will be made. They are making a strong fortification round the Kaiserbagh in Lucknow and are provisioning the place. If they will only not run away, this will be a capital arrangement and will save a deal of trouble in following them about the country."

The adulation that Cracklow and so many others felt for their leader, Campbell, came through again in this letter: "Sir Colin is a brick and manages these fellows capitally. The other day when we were in Lucknow where none of us had tents and had to bivouac every night, although there were plenty of places he could have slept in and made himself comfortable, he never would sleep anywhere but in the open air, and generally selected the most windy, uncomfortable place he could find, much to the disgust of his staff who had to remain with him. He's always in the thickest of the fight."

The realities of the military situation dashed any hopes that the young lieutenants might have had for personal leave. Cracklow wrote his mother: "I am sorry to say, dear, that there is no chance of my coming home until entitled to my furlough in /62 unless I get sick or badly wounded. I feel very much your kind offers of assistance but I hope to be able to pay my own way (as indeed I ought now) and not be a burden to you . . . As we have not in force recruited, I do not think we shall go up country yet. Sir Colin will not spare a single Bengal Artilleryman until all is over. The Royals from their ignorance of the language and of how to manage in this country are not of much use and get left behind a good deal."[13]

Fred Roberts expressed the same opinion about the new troops in a letter to his mother that same week: "I am sorry for the Royal gunners, who are all nice gentlemanly fellows. As Artillerymen, I do not think we need be in any alarm of their surpassing us, but unless our field officers are increased and a certain number of 2nd Captains given, they will ever command us." (Roberts's sublime self-confidence shows through again, nonetheless: "Men of my service are all Captains, so I hope for the best, and expect to be one myself ere long, and then Brevet Major!!")[14]

The spartan camp life was at least easing the financial plights of the young lieutenants. Cracklow commented: "The H.A. is a very pleasant service and one I should prefer had I my choice. The pay is good, about 35 a month clear and I shall now be able to save some money to pay my passage home some day or other. Camp life is not very expensive and I have put by sufficient to buy my new kit—required, and shall not require to borrow any money. What with prize money and compensation for losses I shall, should I get safe through this business, be better off than before. I think it will be a hard thing if they do not give us prize money for Delhi. They have given us only 6 months *batta* worth about 70. Prize money of a subaltern would have been about 200."

The prize money was on Roberts's mind, too: "This Order about prize money renders me quite independent . . . at least 400 £ or 500 £, it may be a great deal more, so that I shall have something to spend on furlo' . . . This just be a commencement to show the dear General that there is still some hope for me."

Cracklow continued: "I have heard of the arrival of the pistol you so kindly sent me, dear mother, at Allahabad. There will be some delay in getting it sent up but it will I hope arrive soon and will be a most useful acquisition. I had intended several times buying one but they fetch such enormous prices in Cawnpore—£25 each—that I contented myself with a pair of Government pistols. The revolver I brought out got out of order some 3 years ago and I could not get it repaired. I got rid of it. My little dog Meg who you also ask about is quite well and a great favourite with all the men. I think she ought to have medals for all the fights she has been at."

Cracklow here mentioned his dog Meg for the first time, and "all the fights she has been at." It seems amazing that a dog actually went with him through all those terrible campaigns—the assault on Delhi, the Bulandshahr engagement, Agra, Cawnpore, Lucknow. Even if Meg had always stayed with the supply wagon (Roberts had a dog named Faust who did this), it would have been quite a trip. More likely, Cracklow put her right into one of his own ammunition carriages.[15]

*   *   *

The pace of the column now slowed inexplicably, much to the puzzlement of the troops; Cracklow discussed Campbell's strategy at length in three long letters to his mother (on January 25 and February 10 and 14): "We have secured boats and can cross and give the brutes a licking whenever we like and were to have done so on the 17th, but Sir Colin came out to have a look at the state of affairs and decided that nothing should be done for the present, as if we crossed we should most probably have an engagement which would precipitate matters which he wished to retard for the present. So here we are doing nothing. I am heartily tired of it. I am so accustomed to marching every day and hard work that this halting does not suit me at all . . . nothing to do but to take piquet every third day at the bridge. Here we get an occasional shot at the Pandies and now and then one in return. The Enfield rifles astonish their weak nerves considerably and they keep at a very respectful distance. It seems such a pity to be losing all this nice cold weather, halting and doing nothing. Everything is kept so close that no one but Sir Colin and the Chief of the staff know anything of the plans for the campaign . . . Sir Colin has no doubt good reason for this delay and although it's tiresome work waiting, it will no doubt be attended with good results . . . everyone is lost in astonishment at the tremendous delay which has occurred since Fatehgarh was taken. For 6 weeks of the finest weather in the year, the whole Army has been lying idle."

Lang was considerably more acerbic about Campbell, writing on February 21: "Sir Colin dawdled a month at Fatehgarh, then like a flash of lightning, at a few hours' notice, went off for Cawnpore, leaving the Ramgunga force unbeaten and Fatehgarh weakly garrisoned: he went off thus, as all thought, to strike one of his rapid, sudden blows and has dawdled a fortnight at Cawnpore. The most wary *Fabius* was a joke to him in the 'delaying' policy. Since Sir Colin came out, Havelock or Neill or Nicholson (or even Greathed or Grant, blundering gallantly in their happy-go-lucky style) would have done fifty times as well. Any of those Generals would have had their troops in summer quarters by this time and all India ours."

For Roberts, the view of the commander was from a different perspective, now that the latter had recommended him for a Victoria Cross. He wrote his mother in mid-February: "The papers go before Sir Colin today, so ere I close this I shall know for certain whether I am to get it or not. My name has also gone in for a Brevet Majority on promotion to a Company. Major Fred Roberts, V.C.! will sound well, will it not . . . all has prospered with me as yet. A few young fellows in the Army have been so lucky, and I always look forward to everything turning out well." A few days later he penned a shorter letter, and this time there was some uncertainty: "I had hoped that by today I should have been able to give you some certain information about the V.C. but it seems that the business cannot be decided just yet. Norman writes: 'the Chief will, I think, give you the Victoria Cross, but the papers will have to be submitted again with some others. However, I think you may be quite easy as to obtaining it, tho' not for some little time.' This looks as if it were all right—only delayed by official routine. However, I shall be very anxious until I see my name in General Orders."

To his sister, a few days later, he wrote, "I think of nothing else but going home, and am saving as fast as I can so as to have a little money to go about with, for Major Fred Roberts, V.C. must cut a dash you know, Harriet." He confided in his sister at this point what seemed a tentative plan for coming home: "I can always get prize money advanced at a slight discount so that if I get in the least sick, I'll be off this year." Yet any plan for opting out because of sickness might leave some stones unturned; he continued, in the same letter: "I am vain eno' to hope that if a force is sent anywhere, I may be selected for it. After all my preaching about the war being over, Harriet, you will laugh at my wishing to go on. I do wish the war over, but at the same time, I hope I may be actively employed until it is finished, hot weather or cold."[16]

Now, what of Thomas Watson? He, too, was with Colin Campbell's fighting force, preparing with the others for the great assault on Lucknow. What preoccupied him?

Certainly he evidenced no concern for grand strategy, seemingly had no interest in the larger forces that swirled around him. He mentioned Colin Campbell seldom, and then only with brief unconcern. The battles around him—and there were some even in this period of relative inaction in January and February 1858—were only briefly noted as though by what appears to be a disinterested bystander. Bystander he was during all of this period, for his role as headquarters duty officer kept him back at the protected headquarters post when anything substantial ensued. The battles seemed always fought by "they," rather than "we." Perhaps some of this detachment was feigned, written self-consciously to a worried, indeed neurotic, mother, residing just out of the battle zone. Still, this thoroughgoing concern for petty family details and the abiding preoccupation with personal safety and personal comfort permeated all of his letters.

Watson worried often about his own appointment: "Now is the time to push one's way; those who fail now may fail forever." He had a chance to chat with Gen. Hope Grant in mid-January—it was Grant who had helped his brother John obtain a good appointment as interpreter—but nothing much came of this momentary opportunity. Later in the month he heard of two appointments that he thought he might be able to get, one as interpreter to the Fifty-third Queen's, "a very nice regt.," the other as an irregular cavalry officer. Were either to work out he would have a salary of one hundred pounds per month. Still, he seemed to have no personal conviction whatsoever about any of this: "I desire to do that which you would best like, but it is hard to see men all around getting appointments and to stand still one's self . . . an interpretership is an appt. I could throw up at anytime and I should be very much my own master whilst holding it. I wish dear John or Edward were here to advise or you yourself, dearest Mother, which would be still better." Neither of these jobs materialized.

A complication, perhaps, was Watson's continued diffidence toward his fellow officers. His letters are replete with "loner" behavior: "I spend the day now very much in my own tent reading" (January 11); "I am going to read a great deal in my own tent today" (January 17). His isolation finally began to bother him, for late in the month he wrote, "I am heartily sick of dining alone and if I do not leave the regt. must rejoin the mess." At the first, right after joining the fighting forces, he had found George Bourchier quite friendly and had advocated that his mother consider the possibility of joining Mrs. Bourchier in Simla. By the end of January, though, he wrote: "I do not wish you to go to Mrs. Bourchier, for really I think there is but little sincerity in the Bourchiers. Captain Bourchier was very cold and distant in his manner. I went to see him twice but though he was in our camp very often he never came near me nor was he more than civil when we did meet. FitzGerald, too, treats me in much the same way. I have called on him but he takes no notice of me when he comes into our camp." His final comment about these experiences was defiant: "I do not care much about this, for I have quite as much society as I care about in the regiment."

His brother John, too, seemed despondent—about harsh treatment by a superior, apparently relating back to something that happened during the siege of Lucknow. Watson commented: "I am sure the whole case is seen through much better than John supposes. Young Havelock told me John is thoroughly appreciated by all in the Lucknow garrison. He said he was never away from his post for a moment and was always to the front in anything." Was there once more a question being raised about attention to duty, as had happened with Thomas after the Sialkot mutiny? In this same letter, incidentally, Watson made one of his few comments about the overall situation, like the others a chiding remark about Colin Campbell: "We still know nothing at all of the Chief's intentions. His remaining here so long does certainly seem a great waste of time."

By early February Thomas Watson's brother-in-law, Lieutenant Edward Atlay, came to the huge camp, and the two had several evenings together. Almost immediately, though, Watson's unit broke camp to begin a move toward Lucknow. He at once wrote his mother: "We were most suddenly unexpectedly ordered to march on the evening of the day before yesterday. For your sake, dearest Mother, I would give anything that I were marching in your direction for well I know how sad and anxious you will be when you know that we have marched one march into Oudh. In reality, dearest Mother, there are no grounds for anxieties, for the Chief is taking each step with the utmost care." Incidentally, he ended this letter, "I propose reading in my tent for the greater part of the remainder of the day."[17]

By mid-January Sarah Watson was making increasingly invidious comments about her landlady: "I spent last evening with Mrs. Dickens . . . The evening before I dined with the Beechams. It is a relief to be with the kindly people in one's own class of life." Then, in early February, she had yet another quarrel with her landlady, and this time a split ensued. She moved in with another woman in Kupowlie, and Watson wrote back: "I am so glad, darling Mother, that you are more comfortable. May Mrs. Dickens continue to treat you with consideration and kindness." Soon she was complaining about this arrangement, too: "Mrs. Dickens breakfasts very late. It is nearly twelve o'clock today before we were given breakfast."

This new living situation turned out to be only temporary, and by the middle of February she had moved further north, to Simla: "I am to pay by the month Rs. 80. This will leave me at liberty to go with you, please God, or to take a house there. I think Mrs. Gachett is pleased to have me with her, especially if her sister does not come to her. If she does, there will still be room for me unless Colonel Downes comes, but for the present I am settled, please God, and glad not to be obliged to go into a house by myself. Mrs. Gachett is very kind & attentive to me & I think is glad to have me and in a pecuniary point of view it is a convenience to her. I dare say, I think she is a good woman." She began taking walks by a road that she and Watson had taken when he was home with her on leave: "Our sad hearted walks there, your trembling lest you should be ordered from me, as alas you were. How I thought as I came along that road which I had watched you along from the door of my room that 23rd Sept. Oh, that by the good mercy of our gracious God you and I may walk along that road together and oh may we both be ever found in that better road, even the road that leads to everlasting life through the blood and righteousness of our dear Saviour."

Watson's house in Sialkot was also on her mind; the tenant, she felt, was not at all cooperative: "There is a note from Capt. Dunbar. Of course you will not hear of going to any expense for his convenience when he pays so small a rent. Capt. Ness says a monthly tenant has no right to expect it. The very circumstances of the garden—leaving yours to ruin—is reason for keeping a mali who I hope will get it back into order. I have requested Capt. Ness to look a little after the mali to see that he does so. Of course Capt. D. would rather not keep one, as I recollect he is to pay his wages. I think you ought to advertise your house at Sialkot ere long. It is said that at least 2 European regiments will be sent there. My darling son, how it pleases me to have helped you purchase that house. I hope it will be a nice little sum at your command ere long. You will deserve to have it. You have been so willing to practice self denial and then so unselfish always in your expenditures."

She continued to intrude into Watson's financial decisions; for example, she wrote in early January: "I do not like to advise about the black pony. You ought to get a good large price for him, he is so good in draught and a safe description of pony. The one you got at Delhi is I think a mare. You never told me her size or colour. Please do. By all means sell old Guyind if you can. Perhaps get Rs. 30 or 35 or even my price Rs. 40 might be got for him. If you do sell him, I will be glad, for I am in want of what his price would get me . . . would advise your not selling the gold embroidered shawl for less than its weight and a good sum for the workmanship, but do try and sell it."[18] Sarah Watson continued to embed herself deeply in her son's life.

* * *

Inaction, waiting, the suspense of anticipating a terrible battle agonizingly slow to come—all these doubts and fears were running through the troops, exacerbating the already-raw feelings of hostility toward the enemy. Particularly galling to the soldiers, who had seen so much and borne so much, were the increasing applications of amnesty. Decisions here were, fortunately, civil rather than military; if the choices had been left to the George Cracklows there would not have been a mutineer left alive. Mercy, forgiveness, amnesty—these were swallowed up by the bloodthirsty drive for revenge. Were the British being "fools for treating them so mildly," as Cracklow bitterly put it? For those preaching a hard line, it was much too early for any show of softness. When the Lucknow die was finally cast, when the enemy's will and way were truly broken, then compassion—perhaps.

The grist of the soldier's life went on through all this: promotions, transfers, awards. Bourchier left to join his troop at Lahore, and Cracklow's commander, Lt. C. H. Blunt, succeeded to the command of the Foot Artillery Battery No. 17. A new officer, Capt. W. A. MacKinnon, took charge of Cracklow's troop; he was a close friend of Roberts, just out from England. Two other lieutenants from Bourchier's battery also moved over to join Cracklow in the Horse Artillery troop, one of whom was H. E. Harrington, recommended along with Roberts for the Victoria Cross. Then, in early February, a great honor came to both troops. Cracklow included it verbatim in his letter of February 14:

No. 206/Adjutant General's Office,
Camp: Cawnpore   Feb. 7th/58
Sir,
The Commander in Chief being of opinion that the Bengal Horse and Foot Artillery noted below (viz., 1st Troop 1st Brigade, 2nd Troop, 3rd Brigade, and No. 17 Light Field Battery) were eminently distinguished during the operations at Lucknow in November last under His Excellency's personal command, has determined to confer the "Victoria Cross" under the 13th clause of the Royal Warrant of 29th June/56 upon one Officer, one non-commissioned Officer, and three gunners of the detachment by election.
                              (signed) H. W. Norman, Major
                                        D.A.E. Army.

Cracklow's comments on the award are revealing: "I have enclosed a copy of a portion of a letter from the Adjutant General of the army (see last page) by which you will see that Sir Colin appreciates the services of the Bengal Artillery. The honour paid us is very great and I think more than deserved, as it has not been as far as I know conferred on the Royal Artillery or on the Naval Brigade who did quite as much as we did. The latter I think more. I really do not know who to give my vote for among the Officers as all did their duty equally well and I did not see one distinguish himself more than another. The award seems to be not at all the most advisable one, as it will be productive of some jealousy and ill feeling among the men, two or three having received a nearly equal number of votes. I should have infinitely preferred to have had some distinguishing name given to the troop, some mild unassuming title such as 'The Pandy Smasher,' equally honourable, applying to all."

The Victoria Crosses were awarded to the three stellar artillery units under a provision of the original Royal Warrant of 1856 establishing the award that "in the event of a gallant and daring act" of a unit not under fifty in number, with "all equally brave and distinguished," the men had the privilege of democratically selecting individual recipients (the proviso had wide usage in the mutiny but died out almost altogether later).[19]

Campbell's awards could not have been more deserved, as we know well by the chronicle of events to this point. Cracklow's concern about the method of "electing a hero" seems well founded, however, given the wide slate of candidates that deserved consideration. It is clear that Cracklow himself was not one of those collecting votes. For want of a syce to hold his horse at Bulandshahr, he had not been able to join Diamond and FitzGerald in their Cross-awarded exploit. He was with Blunt on the famous charge at Lucknow for which Blunt got many commendations (though no Victoria Cross); Cracklow was not even mentioned. Often acting with valor, he still did not quite make the grade to warrant a "with Valour" on the back of a Victoria Cross.

Cracklow's modest suggestion for a medal gives us new insights into his character. There seemed to be no envy that others were getting awards, that he was being "passed by." Lacking also were his earlier cynical remarks about higher officers always reaping the glory. Cracklow had keenly coveted the kind of public recognition that the Victoria Cross and its lesser counterparts gave, but nine months of almost continuous battle, marked by a most devastating loss of personal friends, officers, and men right in his troop, had matured him greatly.

Others, too, were beginning to feel that the "race after the Victoria Cross" had become too important. William Howard Russell, a field correspondent for the London *Times,* had just at this point joined the column, fresh from a widely reported assignment in the Crimean War. He quoted General Mansfield as holding the view that the striving after the Cross "is destructive to discipline, and is determined to discountenance it." One of the officers in the Campbell force seconded this view: "There were rather a lot of V.C.s. for these operations. It was a new award, and there was no other than a company's 'Order of Merit.' Thus it came more easily in those early days than it was intended to. There cannot be any doubt, I fancy, as to Maude's award under any circumstances, but, when all behaved like heroes, this supreme decoration at this period sometimes went to those who had only done their duty as had their comrades. Later, as we know, it attained the pinnacle from which it has not fallen."[20]

Gordon-Alexander, for one, alleged that Colin Campbell himself was less than enthusiastic about the award: "He never liked the Victoria Cross, and, instead of waiting for the recommendations of commanding officers, in accordance with the regulations for its distribution, had a rough-and-ready way of directing that so many and no more or no less were to be given to each rank of the battalions or corps which had pleased him, without any regard to the circumstances under which these different corps had worked, so that on one occasion, when His Excellency had thus directed a V.C. to be given to the 9th Lancers, where no one of the troopers had had any opportunity of distinguishing himself, the men voted it to one of their native water-carriers, the 'Gunga din,' in short, of their splendid regiment, and I believe he was permitted to wear it." (The story of this award to the water carrier is clearly apocryphal—no native soldier was even eligible.)

Gen. Hope Grant, on the other hand, felt that the Cross had a positive effect; he commented on its impact in his "V.C." recommendation for Roberts: "The Victoria Cross has been a grand thing for making men and officers fight like Turks. They seem more anxious to obtain this distinction than any mark of honour which has yet been given to them for the same distinction, and I trust H.M. will bestow it upon [him] . . . I am sorry I should not be able to get it for ———. His conduct was very brave and excellent, but there was no particular deed of valour that I can return his name for. Besides which, those recommendations do not come well from relations."[21]

* * *

Nana Sahib, the rebel commander at Cawnpore when the women and children were killed, was reported to be still in the area, and Cracklow chronicled another effort at trying to capture him: "At the last moment we were ordered back up the Grand Trunk Road with a couple of regiments and some cavalry, the object of the expedition being kept a strict secret. We halted at Chobeepore last night and the secret leaked out. We have been sent out after the Nana Sahib, who is supposed to be trying to escape from Oudh to cross the Ganges somewhere near this and get thence to Kalpi. We started again this morning at 3 o'clock and came into this place expecting to have a fight and every one of us having privately made up his mind to catch the Nana himself, but as yet bad luck to the miscreant, we have seen nothing of him or his followers. He's supposed to have received intelligence of our being on the lookout for him and has not crossed yet.

"I do not think we have the slightest chance of catching him as the country is so covered with clumps of trees and high crops that a mounted man can disappear in a few minutes. What I am greatly afraid of is that we shall be kept here looking after this wretch and so miss the Lucknow business. This would be a dreadful piece of bad luck and most provoking if it so happens, as Lucknow will not be an everyday affair, but such a one that we may not have the opportunity of assisting at again.

"The Nana is in rather a desperate way. He's about 5 miles from us, but on the opposite side of the river. All the ghats and places where the river can be crossed are watched and we have lots of troops in the vicinity on the look out for him. The only thing wanted is for him to cross. Sir Colin's force is on the opposite side of the river and I can't think why he does not attack him and either catch him himself or drive him over to us. The intelligence brought by our spies was that he intended coming over today, but our arrival has made him alter his plans. We have tolerably good information regarding him. He keeps a horse saddled night and day ready to fly.

A 5000 £ reward is on his head and altogether I think his life must
be a burden to him."

Lucknow was on everyone's mind now; Cracklow laid out the
task: "The Pandies have given out that they intend to make a fight
of it and that they mean to meet us outside Lucknow. It is most
devoutly to be hoped that they will do so and that their hearts will
not fail them at the last moment. If they will only stand they will
get a most fearful lesson. They always come out with the best intentions, bring all their guns, tents and plunder and are sometimes
even the first to attack, but as soon as ever we go at them their only
idea seems to be who can go the hardest. Nothing but the Cavalry
and Horse Artillery ever get at them. The Infantry stand no chance
with the exception of that at the Secundrabagh. I have never yet
seen a good slaughter made of them, not even in Delhi. It will be a
great thing for us if they come out to meet us, as if we have to
attack the city we shall lose a fearful number of men. The Sepoys
fight well behind walls, but never stand a minute in the open. Lucknow is a tremendous city—17 miles round resting on the river
Gumti. The Pandies number some 60,000 men, and the fighting in
the little narrow streets and lanes of the city will be hard work. We
shall have a tolerable force to take into Oudh, some 15 or 16,000
men. This is an immense army of Europeans for this country but
even this is not half enough. I feel perfectly convinced that the
brutes will escape us as they have always done hitherto. We always
take all their guns and baggage, but the men are such good hands
at running that we hardly ever make a good bag of them."[22]

Now Colin Campbell was ready. Ahead lay the Lucknow described by Cracklow.

Chapter 8

The Final Battle for Lucknow

Though excitement was imminent, the first step was away from Lucknow. On March 3 Cracklow and Lang were sent back to the "rear serai" to pick up the siege train of heavy equipment and guns. "We have to drive along all day in the sun in the rear of the line of guns and carts, progress being from 1 to 1½ miles an hour. The train consists of 86 pieces of ordnance and some thousands of carts laden with ammunition," bemoaned Cracklow. Lang added: "I had dreadful work to get through the choked up roads of Jalalabad . . . baggage choked every inlet and outlet. As day broke, I got a few guns through Jalalabad and on we marched, slowly overtaking the 1st Fusiliers, Engineers and Sappers, Hodson's Horse, &c. We en-camped behind Dilkusha Park . . . a capital ground, retired, shady, abounding in lungoors (the great white-bearded ape)."

Cracklow did not fare as well with his quarters: "We are camped in a most horribly dusty plain, the sort so sandy that the tent pegs will hardly hold and with a hot wind blowing which drives the dust in clouds. Everything in consequence is in a most disgustable state. On in front our heavy guns are pounding away at the enemy's guns which are in battery by the Martiniere and the round shot every now and then come rolling into camp. In all respects except the increasing heat we are now very well off. I have a capital tent and have managed to get some light clothing made in Cawnpore and some new shirts—so shall get on very well. Our poor gunners look fearfully sloppy and cut but a sorry figure alongside the Royal H.A. who had come out spick and span new. This does not matter much though, and they find some difficulty in holding their own when we go to work alongside them. Old Sir Colin is a great friend to our Regt. and we have never come out so strong as since he has held the chief command."

Even on attack, the soldier would be lost without his refreshments. In this regard, Cracklow had just pulled a coup: "It is utterly impossible to get on in the hot weather without beer and this is a luxury which has been almost unattainable lately. By great luck I managed to get three 64 gallon casks of porter from the commercial officer at Cawnpore who is a friend of mine, and this has been a perfect godsend to us. You would be amused to see us every day anxiously looking out for the arrival of the hackery on which the beer is carried. When it arrives there is a fervent rush at it. A large tin pot which services for milk jug, tea, coffee or porter indiscriminantly is filled and everyone has a long pull. It does one's heart good to hear the sigh of satisfaction every man gives after his draught. Of course there are lots of outsiders who see what is going on and are invited to come and have a pull. Our three casks which were to have lasted us three months will I fear, barely hold out till the fall of Lucknow."

Camp life thus went on as it had for eons with the time-honored ritual of foraging along the route for anything that would make life more comfortable—animals, food, whatever was movable and momentarily useful. Cracklow continued: "We have our old leucebit which was captured at Aligarh, drawn by a couple of bullocks. This always follows in back of the troop, and contains all the requisites for turning out breakfast at half an hour notice. Then I have a little poor grey pony which trots along with us carrying a small tent, and 4 black milk goats, who have a man specially to look after them and always march with the troop. We manage to get on pretty comfortably on the whole and in a manner which excites great astonishment in the Queen's Officers who have lately arrived and who have very little experience in Indian arrangements." His newsy letter concluded rather suddenly: "I have to go and get a horse of ours out of a well into which he has managed to tumble."[1]

Thomas Watson, meanwhile, had watched the troops move into action beyond the Dilkusha from his headquarters at the Alambagh. "This morning the chief arrived with a large force which went straight towards Lucknow. I galloped out to Jalalabad fort to watch the distant fight but even with a glass could not see more than the mere masses of infantry and cavalry as they moved along. The firing at first was very hot but soon subsided. Now it is only occasional. We have not heard anything of the results." The inaction seemed to be bothering Watson, for he continued: "Dr. Brougham the surgeon of the regt. said to me the other day that he thought he could get me appointed to Hodson's Horse. I should like nothing better, but I fear to do anything that might in any way distress you."[2]

Even with this momentary desire for action he continued mainly to be concerned about the minutiae of his own personal life; this letter was filled with details about listing his lost possessions in order to claim compensation for them. By March 5 Watson, too, had had his headquarters unit moved up to the Dilkusha, and he and some troops were sent to one of the pickets. They were backed up against a long, high wall: "Pandy continued to send his shot into the huge enclosure which our wall formed one side of . . . almost all the shot that came were nothing else but pieces of iron hammered into a roundish shape. The amount of scrap in these shells cannot be less than 6 or 7 Rupees worth, so Pandy will find using them rather expensive." The picket duty lasted only a few hours, and soon he was relieved and sent back once more to head-quarters camp.

A major reinforcement now arrived in camp, and this time it was an especially exotic group, the Nepalese Gurkhas, led by the renowned Jang Bahadur. "I was anxious to see this famous Nepalese chief," wrote Hope Grant, "and Sir Colin kindly permitted me to be present. His large tent, with a semianah—a large canvas awning upon poles to keep off the sun—was already pitched, and a strong guard of the 42d Highlanders, kilted, guarded the entrance, with the regimental pipers in attendance. Shortly after, Jang Bahadur arrived, followed by his two brothers and about twenty of his staff. He was magnificently dressed, and his turban was ornamented with a splendid tiara of diamonds and emeralds. His countenance was remarkably intelligent, and though he had the flat Nepalese features, he was dignified in his bearing and manner. There was, however, a suspicious glance in his eye, so characteristic of the Eastern disposition; and during his conversation with Sir Colin and Colonel McGregor, political agent, between whom he was seated, though he gave utterance to a good deal of soft-sawder, he had a restless wandering look, as though he mistrusted everybody . . . The effect was very remarkable and quite theatrical. My fighting turn-out was, however, very indifferent, so I got behind the crowd in the durbar tent, and conversed with a stoutish gentleman in Hessian boots and frock-coat, who was a stranger to me. I talked with him for some time, for his remarks were very clever and much to the point. On riding home, I learned to my surprise that my acquaintance was Dr. Russell, correspondent to the 'Times' newspaper."[3]

As Campbell approached Lucknow for the second time, he faced once more the patchwork of gardens, huts, mosques, and buildings that the troops had bulled their way through back in November. Here were the same names—Dilkusha, La Martinière, Secundrabagh, Kaiserbagh, the residency—still holding within them the whispers of the previous clash that had raged through them. Russell, with a well-honed ability to draw word pictures, described the scene: "The site selected by the Chief was in a series of magnificently-wooded parks, attached to several palaces, or country houses, of the royal family of Oudh, South of the Dilkusha. The trees were of great age and extreme beauty, affording us a fine shade and cover to innumerable langures, or black-faced long-tailed monkeys with white hair and whiskers. Some deer which were captured also lived here. When we arrived, the tents were just being pitched. We were pitched in the part of the Bibiapore, and just outside that wall is the Dilkusha. It is occupied by men who also hold some walls in front of it, within musketry-fire of the trenches and rifle-pits of the enemy in front of the Martiniere.

"Stewart, who is on duty, for he is to work up the telegraph to the Dilkusha, starts with me. We walk under an avenue of mighty trees, bordering a drive which leads to a gateway in the wall, arched over, ornamented by pilasters. There is a slight irregular fire of musketry going on outside. On emerging from the gateway there extends a wide, broad plain, right, front, and left, which contains some remarkable objects; on our right, at the end of the park which we have just emerged, is a walled garden filled with cypresses, summer-houses, plaster statues, with kiosks, and pleasant walks 'mid orange-trees. Beneath it flows the Gumti, about 500 yards from us, coming down with many a curve from the city of Lucknow. Beyond it, on the right, there's an expanse of meadow and corn-fields, bounded, as usual, by wood. One small hamlet and a few cottages are all the signs of habitation we can see here, but in a break in the trees far away we can make out an arched bridge, which is the viaduct of the road from Lucknow to Fizabad, over the Kak-raal stream nullah.

"Directly in front of us is about 1200 yards of broken ground, intersected by two ruinous old walls, which run down to the river, and seem to have been part of an outer enclosure of the Bibiapore. Above these walls there rises the most curious structure I ever saw. At first glance one exclaims, 'How beautiful! What a splendid building!' At the second, 'Why it must have been built by a mad-man!' At the distance of more than half a mile we can make out the eccentric array of statues, the huge lions' heads, the incongruous columns, arches, pillars, windows, and flights of stairs leading to nothing, which are the distinguishing features of the Martiniere. The centre of the building is the most grotesque; the wide sweep of the wings and their curve in width from the triad stairs leading to the entrance have a fine effect. But the statues! They are perched on every angle, drawn up as close as they can stand all along the roof, fixed on the pinnacles, and pillars, in all directions. In front of the whole building (rising from a sheet of water in shape of a letter T) there is a tall pillar, not unlike the monument to the Duke of York." (Another contemporary account was less complimentary: "It is a handsome effect at a distance from a lofty tower in the centre . . . but on a nearer approach the wretched taste of the ornaments only excites contempt.")

Russell continued: "At the top of the left corner of the Marti-niere, there is just visible the embrasure of a low earthwork. On the top of the left of the Martiniere, there are a few one-storied white houses, a wall which stretches a long way to the right, inside which there is a park full of dense trees, which completely screens the city in the line of the enemy's works from where we stand. Following the landscape, about 400 yards away, on our left, is the Dilkusha, which is nothing more or less than a good specimen of a French Chateau of the beginning of the last century, improved by an Italian artist. Where is the city of Lucknow? Somewhere over there be-yond the Dilkusha, and stretching behind the park of the Marti-niere."[4]

Although the physical appearance of the area was approximately the same as in that perilous week just three months back, there were other significant differences. First, the forces on each side were vastly augmented. Campbell's fighting men now numbered about twenty thousand, four times as many as in his undermanned force in November. In addition, a vast group of camp followers—transport drivers, blacksmiths, artisans, and so on, and, of course, their families—had joined Campbell's troops (whereas before the earlier Lucknow assault many had deserted). Supply and transport were handled separately by each unit, and the confusion made for an incoherent logistic base. As Michael Edwardes put it, "With the number of draft animals required to pull everything, the army had the appearance of some vast menagerie which ate up the land as it went, like a plague of locusts."

The rebels' situation had changed, too. The number of fighting men, estimated to be approximately thirty thousand in November, was guessed by Outram to be ninety-six thousand by the beginning of February. "This computation did not include artillerymen, the number of whom was unknown, nor the armed followers of the talukdars, estimated at 20,000; altogether, there could not have been less than 120,000 armed men in Lucknow on that date," added Malleson in his later history. These figures may well be inflated; after all, Outram was bottled up in the Alambagh and not in much of a position to count noses, except those thousands that were constantly attacking him there. Nevertheless, it is undisputed that the mutineers had vastly larger forces than the British.

Another major difference from November was that the rebels had been feverishly strengthening their fortifications, "exhibiting prodigious labour." Herein lies a story, and to unravel it we need to know Campbell's final attack plan.

In broad outline, it applied straightforward military tactics. The city was to be attacked from the east (as in November), blockaded from the south, and enveloped from the north. (The west was to be left open; a second important story will eventually develop from this detail.) The main attack was to be made by Campbell himself, with three salients commanded by James Outram, Edward Lugard, and R. Walpole.

The rebels had three main defensive lines. The outermost ran along the canal on the west side; here new bastions had been built, and the banks of the canal had been scarped to render them almost impassable. The second and third lines, heavily bastioned with artillery, were located in the many large, highly defensible main buildings in the town.

But the mutineers had made a stupifying error of assumption: they apparently believed that Campbell would take the route he had followed in November, crossing the canal and attacking the Secundrabagh directly. No troops at that earlier time had taken the long circle around the big oxbow of the Gumti to the north. Apparently the mutineers thought that no one would this time, either. It seems inconceivable that they would follow up this reasoning by a decision not to fortify the flank side to the north, but that was precisely what they did. Outram's salient did go north, right around the flank, and almost from the start was staring straight down into the exposed rear of a great many of the intricate fortifications so laboriously constructed over the three months. An Achilles' heel of monumental importance was lain bare, and the course of the battle was probably decided even before the first shot.

How could such an incredible misjudgment have happened? Malleson, in his usual patronizing way, said that it was "the absence of original thinking . . . the natives of India are essentially creatures of habit, of custom. When set to repeat a task already once accomplished, they follow implicitly the lines previously trodden." Vivian Majendie, always ready to denigrate the rebel mentality, added: "Alas for Pandy, he had quite overlooked one thing; the side of the city along which the little river Goomtee runs (a side against which no hostile demonstrations had been made on former occasions—a fact which, according to Pandy's reasoning, inferred that none ever would be made) was left bare, naked, and comparatively unguarded. True, there was the river, and was not that a defense in itself? *Nous verrons.* And, in the meantime, my black friends with the black hearts, child-killers and murderers of women, lie calm and happy within your fortified palaces; set your sly traps, and blaze away with matchlock and booming gun, and heap fresh insults upon those two English ladies whom you hold captive within your walls." Majendie, equally willing to insult the two religions of the rebels, continued: "Be merry, my friends, over the coming fall of the 'Feringhees,' for have not your *fakirs* and *gooroos* told you that the sun of the infidels is set, and that they shall be confounded and put to shame? And is not Allah great, and Brahma good and powerful?" The superior intelligence of the British would, of course, hold sway: "It was a pity, to be sure, for your sakes, that Sir Colin should have had a head upon his shoulders at all, or that any of our generals should have been capable of logically putting *this and that* together, and that it should have occurred to us to make a demonstration on that particular side of the city where the Goomtee is the sole defence."[5]

The engineer major, Nicholson, when he and Outram looked out over those vast impotent fortifications, took a more professional stance, almost sympathetic: "Poor creatures! They have not a grain of sense. They have thrown up the most tremendous works, and they are absolutely useless." Roberts exhibited considerable relief: "We have been able to enfilade the line of works the rebels had erected on the line of the Canal—a most formidable position and one that would have cost many valuable lives but for the great error they made in not erecting a flanking defence on this bank. With a little trouble, we were able to see completely in rear of their batteries, and thus prevented their firing a shot—from a fortification which must have taken them weeks to make—perfect in every way but for this one grand mistake."[6]

Let us now put together the entire attack. First, we follow Outram in exploiting the fortuitous soft spot around the Gumti. George Cracklow was with him. At 2:00 A.M. on the sixth, they crossed the river and marched off rapidly to the north; the final battle had begun. By dawn they had sighted enemy forces on the left flank. The cavalry and Horse Artillery dashed way out ahead of the rest of the troops and rapidly became engaged with various small pickets in the area, quickly decimating each one. "We gave them a licking and drove them in towards the city," Cracklow tersely reported.

As the infantrymen moved forward they, too, encountered resistance, and soon men were being downed. Maj. Percy Smith of the cavalry was killed far out toward the front by a round, and his body had to be left in the field (despite the courageous efforts of two enlisted men to bring it back). Another officer was able to retrieve Smith's helmet, medals, and watch, but not until the next day was that particular area under enough control for any of the British to be able to approach the body. The worst fears of Smith's men soon were confirmed. Majendie described it: "Even respect for the dead is unknown to our barbarous enemies, and the body was found, as we feared it would be, with the head and legs severed from it and the trunk otherwise horribly mutilated . . . The Sepoys gave out, by way of advancing their interests, that it was the Commander-in-Chief who had been killed, and that this was his body."

After encamping at Ismailgunge that night, the British troops attacked once again at dawn. The terrain was very rough, with groves and ravines crisscrossing it, and this made it very difficult for the Punjab Cavalry to operate. At this point Cracklow and his fellow Horse Artillery troops were again brought forward, in a move that had become familiar in past battles. J. R. J. Jocelyn, one of the military historians of the mutiny, described their tactics: "Dashing to the front by alternate half troops, they searched out with case fire the rough ground . . . and it was by case fire alone that the rebels were driven back across the Korkral."[7]

"On the 9th," continued Cracklow, "a general advance having been arranged on, I was sent with my 2 guns to join the 1st Fusiliers who were ordered to storm a position held by the enemy and called by us the Yellow House. We managed the affair with very little trouble and drove the enemy out. The Fusiliers were left to hold the house and I with some Highlanders pursued them along the bank of the river, where we got some beautiful shots at them with grape, killing a great number. On examining their buttons afterwards, I found them to be chiefly 56th N.I. men. This was one of the Cawnpore Regts. and we were very glad to have had this opportunity of punishing some of them."

The Yellow House, officially the Chakar Kothi, was the linchpin, for it was the position that looked back down the exposed enemy flank directly behind the Martinière. Cracklow described this to his mother with a hand-scrawled map: "We advanced on our side up to the position marked 'mortar battery' thus taking the poor Pandies' beautiful line of entrenchments in rear. This was a move they never contemplated and he seems to be perfectly dumbfounded [*sic*]. All his works he has been making for the last 3 months are rendered useless."

The Yellow House was an odd-looking building that had been the grandstand of the king of Oudh's racecourse. The attack was well planned, and though the rebels were there in large numbers,

Outram's forces quickly were the possessors of the main floor and a small room on the second floor that was to provide the critical observation post for the artillery barrage on the camp fortification. However, not all of the Yellow House was secure. Cracklow described the situation: "Most unfortunately about 12 of the Pandies remained in a kind of cellar. Out of this they could not be got. 2 Officers and several men of the Fusiliers were killed in repeated attempts to dislodge them. At length they were blown out. No quarter is shown nowadays; as I passed the house on my way back to camp, I saw about 100 of the Fusiliers standing around the door of the cellar with their rifles ready to tumble them over when they rushed out."

A brave infantry captain named St. George had rushed down into the dark, honeycombed chambers and quickly shot several of the rebels, only to be shot and rendered insensible himself. Two other officers and nine men followed, all being killed or seriously wounded. At this point the British pulled back to the main floor and tried to burn the defenders out with flaming thatch from the nearby cantonment area. Finally, they decided to cut holes in the floor. It was at this point, with dozens of the fusiliers standing around the entrance with fixed bayonets, that Cracklow had ridden by. Soon the holes were opened, and live shells were dropped into the cellar. The remaining mutineer rushed out, trying to run the gauntlet to the river. Majendie was there to see the final grisly act: "Infuriated beyond measure by the death of their officer, the Sikhs (assisted, I regret to say, by some Englishmen) proceeded to take their revenge on this one wretched man. Seizing him by the two legs, *they attempted to tear him in two!* Failing in this, they dragged him along by the legs, stabbing him in the face with their bayonets as they went. I could see the poor wretch writhing as the blows fell upon him, and could hear his moans as his captors dug the sharp bayonets into his lacerated and trampled body, while his blood, trickling down, dyed the white sand over which he was being dragged.

"But the worst was yet to come: while still alive, though faint and feeble from his many wounds, he was deliberately placed upon a small fire of dry sticks, which had been improvised for the purpose, and there held down, in spite of his dying struggles, which, becoming weaker and more feeble every moment, were, from their very faintness and futile desperation, cruel to behold. Once during the frightful operation, the wretched victim, maddened by pain, managed to break away from his tormentors, and, already horribly burnt, fled a short distance, but he was immediately brought back and placed upon the fire, and there held till life was extinct. It was his last despairing effort, and very sad to see; but I thought it sadder still, that those hoarse, choking cries for mercy should have been disregarded as they were; his shrieks, his agonized convulsions, his bitter anguish alike unheeded; that those upturned eyes, searching for pity in the swarthy faces which gazed with savage pleasure on the frightful scene, should have searched in vain . . .

"So in this 19th Century, with its boasted civilization and humanity, a human being should lie roasting and consuming to death, while Englishmen and Sikhs, gathered in little knots around, looked calmly on. No one will deny, I think, that this man at least adequately expiated by his frightful and cruel death, any crimes of which he may have been guilty. Such was the state of excitement and rage that the Sikhs were in from the loss of their officer, that I firmly believe that it would have been quite impossible to prevent this act of torture . . . the whole business was done so quickly, and with such noise and confusion, that, to me who beheld it from a short distance . . . it seemed almost like a dream, till I rode up afterwards and saw the black trunk burned down to a stumpy, almost unrecognizable cinder."

Russell was told the story that evening and expressed great moral outrage. "His cries, and the dreadful scene, said my friend, 'will haunt me to my dying hour.' 'Why didn't you interfere?' 'I dared not, the Sikhs were furious. They had lost Anderson, our own men encouraged them, and I could do nothing.'"

Nonetheless, in his diary just the day before, Russell had prophetically spoken of barbarism in war with somewhat less judgmental words: "War can never be purged of a dross of cruelty and barbarism. It is all very well to talk of moderation in the hour of victory, but men's passions do not cool in a moment, and in every army there must be ruffians who rejoice in a moment of licence when killing is no murder. Soldiers do not always spare a wounded foe. Indeed, I have been struck by the prominence given to the conduct of those who have done so. You have all heard of the French officer at Waterloo, who, perceiving that the antagonist at whom he rode in a charge had lost the use of his sword arm, threw up his saber, saluted, and rode on. It is not the grace of his act so much as the act itself that has made it so well-known. It would have been reckoned cowardly if the Frenchman had passed a sword through his enemy's body, could he have made the latter a prisoner; but if the Englishman with his bridle-arm had shot the Frenchman dead, you would esteem it as a gallant act; just as some of our officers did who got away from their Russian captors at Inkerman by shooting them with their revolvers. Conduct warfare on the most chivalrous principles, there must ever be a touch of murder about it, and the assassin will lurk under fine phrases. The most civilized troops will commit excesses and cruelties, which must go unpunished, as they did at Badajoz. With all its chivalry, the field of Crecy or of Agincourt must have been fearful in its cruelty, when, not to mention the slaughter of prisoners, the kermes and churls with their sharp knives went searching out the chinks in the armour of the fallen knights and nobles, and pierced them to death as they lay helpless on the field."[8]

George Cracklow must either have seen the Yellow House incident himself or have learned of it immediately afterward. Letters home seldom tell of the realities of a conflict, and Cracklow's terse "no quarter is shown nowadays" glossed over the specific act—and, indeed, it would have been almost incomprehensible to someone back in England.

We must now catch up with the other main salient, the "left attack." This force had remained at the Dilkusha park, but Peel had once more done the unusual with the great, heavy twenty-four-pound guns by bringing them again right up to the front, barely six hundred yards from the enemy's nearest works. An officer described the process: "Our elephants being harnessed to the guns, the convoy slowly and silently moved along, aided by a bright, clear moon, . . . it had been anticipated that some resistance would be offered; but not withstanding that the elephants, in disobedience of the orders of their mahouts, occasionally trumpeted, and the noise consequent on getting the guns in position was considerable, the enemy did not interfere."[9]

On the tenth, the day the Yellow House was secured, Campbell attacked the Martinière and easily took it; the enormous artillery barrage had forced most of the mutineers out earlier. In the process, though, Peel, the naval captain who had been responsible for the heavy guns' being used so well, was seriously wounded. (He began to recover later but was suddenly stricken with smallpox and died a month after the fall of Lucknow.)

Just a day after the loss of life at the Yellow House a shockingly similar shooting took the life of the swashbuckling, controversial William Hodson, leader of the famous Hodson's Horse and the murderer of the three princes at the storming of Delhi. The Begum Kothi, a block of palaces with many inner chambers, was attacked by Campbell's salient—"the sternest struggle of this siege," said Campbell afterward. In one of the rooms a group of the Ninety-third had cornered a few of the mutineers. Determined not to be needlessly killed, they waited at each side of the door, poised to kill anyone coming out. At this point Hodson came up and said, "Where are the rebels?" One of the sergeants pointed at the door, but as Hodson yelled, "Come on," the sergeant grabbed the impetuous captain by the arm. Hodson took one step forward and was shot, point-blank, in the chest.

Lang, who was following a few hundred yards behind with a group of engineer sappers, commented on Hodson's shooting: "He had no right to be at the Begum Kothi, and the State runs the chance of losing the finest Cavalry and 'Intelligence' officer in the army." Thomas Watson, back at a headquarters picket, also learned of the incident; the story there was more garbled: Hodson had been "shot when foolishly riding almost unattended through places where there were still some of the enemy lying hidden. " A day later Hodson died, and Roberts wrote his father: "Amongst the [killed] was Hodson whom you must remember at Peshawar, a gallant soldier. He died this morning and is a sad loss. His death was entirely owing to himself. He should have been at the time miles away with his own Regiment, but a strange fatality urged him on, I suppose." This enigmatic comment can be read a number of ways, but it is clear that Roberts was trying to call attention to some aberration. Countess Roberts, in editing his letters, footnoted this sentence and referred to Roberts's later book for "the correct account." In this 1897 work, Roberts wrote a footnote that began, "It was current in camp, and the story has often been repeated, that Hodson was killed in the act of looting." He went on to explain at length

why he did not believe Hodson was guil⸣
seems a bit lame.

These mean little skirmishes like the
were terribly costly of life. Men who we⸣
in huts, or in rooms of the cavernous palaces ⸜
had the momentary advantage (though, of cou⸣
long run; usually there was no escape route, and th⸣
eventually forced out in the open to die). The natural incl⸣
the British soldier for dashing ahead, forcing the action to
enemy, was superb overall performance. But, oh the cost.

The storming of the Begum Kothi was certainly the "sternest struggle" if one measures by the enemy slain. There were perhaps as many as five thousand men in the palaces at the start, and the fierce fighting that resulted left over six hundred mutineer bodies littering the inside. Russell's assiduous reporting brought him to the spot early the next day, and he duly noted the scene: "Here the traces of the fight were frequent. Patches of blackened blood, parts of soldiers' uniforms, arms, and accoutrements. The ditch itself was filled with the bodies of sepoys, which the coolies were dragging from the inside and throwing topsy-turvy, by command of the soldiers; stiffened by death, with outstretched legs and arms, burning slowly in their cotton tunics, those rent and shattered figures seemed as if they were about to begin a dance of death. We crossed literally a ramp of dead bodies loosely covered with earth . . . from court to court, and building to building, the sepoys were driven, leaving in each hundreds of men bayonetted and shot. The scene was horrible. The rooms in which the sepoys lay burning slowly in their cotton clothing, with their skin crackling and their flesh roasting literally in its own fat, whilst a light-bluish vapoury smoke, of disgusting odour, formed a veil through which the dreadful sight could be dimly seen, were indeed chambers of horrors ineffable." Forbes-Mitchell, the Highlander sergeant, saw Russell poking around the Begum Kothi that morning, taking notes, and overheard General Lugard telling him to "take care and not to attempt to go into any dark rooms for fear of being 'potted' by concealed Pandies." Several such were found during that day, and, noted Forbes-Mitchell, "as there was no quarter for them, they fought desperately."[10]

ussell had stayed back that day with the artillery battery estab-
hed outside the Martinière park, watching the incessant inter-
hange of shells flying in both directions: "Many of our shells burst
short. Just as I was turning to go away, I heard an exclamation of
alarm from one of the men at the mortars. As the smoke of the gun
cleared away I saw the headless trunk of a Naval officer on the
ground. It was a horrid sight. He had been killed by the shell which
was discharged just as he rode before the muzzle. He will be buried
this evening, forgotten tomorrow." Lang saw something similar
happen that day: "Our own shells from some of Outram's batteries
passed uncomfortably close over us, and at last one came into the
garden and took off the arm of one of the 53rd."

Unaccountably, there were many difficulties with armament at
this point; Oliver Jones, who had charge of the heavy guns, explained the problems: "The Naval Brigade had some eight or ten
rocket-tubes, 24 and 12-pounders, and some were on the right of
our battery. In the relief of Lucknow, Sir William Peel told me, out
of 140 rockets (I think is the number), only one did not go truly to
its destination. On this occasion they did not behave so well. The
sticks had got too dry, and caught fire, and away went the rocket
anywhere but where it was wanted; and the composition had also
got too dry, and burnt so quickly, as, in many cases, to fall or explode far short of their proper range. Whether it was an older batch
of rockets, or whether their having been exposed to the sun for
some months was the cause of their misdoings, I do not know, but
they were a great failure . . .

"While the guns were upon hard ground—which it was in the
Dilkooshah Park—they were worked with great ease; but afterwards, when we had possession of Banks' House and the first line
of defence in Lucknow, the soil of the batteries was so soft and
sandy that it took immense labour to run up and work the guns.
All manner of expedients had to be adopted—sandbags placed
under the wheels; planks, doors, shutters under the trails; and as
these had to be renewed or altered each round, considerable time
was wasted; and from the wheels often not being quite level, the
balls did not go as truly as they ought.

"We had a good deal of trouble, also, with some of the shells;
especially those supplied for our 8-inch howitzers; they were joined
in the wooden disk, which prevents their turning in ramming

home, by a tin cylinder, which embraced the disk and half the shell. A great many got loose, and turning in ramming home, the fusee got inwards, and gave us great trouble in getting them out and ramming home again; in some cases it was impossible, and they had to be fired as they were, and burst in or close to the muzzle of the gun . . .

"It would be a wise precaution if all fusees made beyond a certain date were burnt, and none issued which had been long enough in store to be deteriorated. The wooden fusee is not an expensive article, and the metal ones could be refilled; and though a certain expense would be incurred, yet, as a pounds, shillings, and pence question, it is only sacrificing a penny to save a pound; for every faulty fusee used causes a shell to be thrown away. The waste of ammunition in the field, where it often cannot be replaced, the confidence the comparative harmlessness of the fire gives the enemy, and the tendency the want of success in firing has to render the artilleryman unsteady and careless in laying and aiming his gun, are serious evils."[11]

Cracklow continued his account of the battle: "On the 11th we advanced to the Iron Bridge and the Chief took the Kaddam Rasual and Shah Najaf. Today we advance to the Stone Bridge and the Chief has taken a position called the Motee Mahal. Everything is going on swimmingly. Nothing could be better than the Chief's plans."

Majendie, who was with Cracklow on March 11, vividly reported this next attack. "We had not advanced very far before we found ourselves on a narrow road leading into a thick wood; here operations commenced, for, hidden in the jungle, or in the small cottages, which, snugly embosomed among the trees, formed excellent temporary fortresses, were parties of the enemy, who opened a smart fire on us as we advanced. Skirmishers were pushed forward, and two guns brought into action abreast, on the road, to riddle the woods with case-shot, and so drive out our hidden foes . . . What noise and wild confusion and excitement then prevailed, what a smell of gunpowder, and what hurrying about of skirmishers, and bursting of shells, and the like . . . some of the enemy had crept into a dry drain which ran underneath and across the road, and there, crouched in abject terror, mingled probably with the hope that we might pass them unseen, huddled up, one getting behind the other for shelter, they were discovered by our men, and a volley of bullets sent in among them. It was horrible to see, through the semi-darkness, these poor wretches trying to screen themselves behind the corpses of their comrades, but trying in vain, for pitilessly did bullet after bullet whistle in among them, striking to death those in this doomed and dying mass of humanity who still lived; while their groans and shrieks seemed, reverberated as they were by the echoing, sonorous, arched roofs of their under-ground retreat, to acquire a strangely deep and awful tone. There was no escape, no pity; there, in their self-chosen grave, they all died, and there, for many a day after, they lay, a horrid heap of rottenness, and worm-eaten abomination.

"I do not mean to say we did wrong in shooting down, in *open fight,* any man, Sepoy, budmash, villager, be he whom he might, that used arms against us; but I do mean to say that it would have been more satisfactory, if for the people of Oudh—Sepoys ex-cepted—there had been some mercy and quarter, that they at least should be treated as fair enemies, and that unless proved to have participated in or connived at the murder of Englishmen, captives of this class should not necessarily be put to death, but treated as prisoners of war usually are. At the time of the capture of Luck-now—a season of indiscriminate massacre—such distinction was not made, and the unfortunate who fell into the hands of our troops was made short work of—Sepoy or Oudh villager, it mat-tered not—no questions were asked, his skin was black, and did not that suffice? A piece of rope and the branch of a tree, or a rifle bullet through his brain, soon terminated the poor devil's existence. Short shrift was his, and but little time given him to make his peace and pray, and close his soul's accounts, ere he was hurried off to die the death of a dog."

So rapidly were the British troops rushing forward that day that they soon pushed into a rebel rear-guard camp—and surprised the enemy while the latter were engaged in cooking their dinners under the trees. Panic-stricken at the unexpected appearance, the rebels fled precipitately. The order was given to push on quickly, while parts of the companies were detached from the main body to chase the fleeing rebels. An observer described the resulting chaos: "How vividly do I remember this moment, perhaps the most exciting in my life!—how clearly do I see the regiments running forward to join in the work of slaughter—how clearly hear the deafening din, the shouts now of terror, now of triumph—how clearly see the Sepoys, as they fled in wild affright, throwing away arms, clothing, cooking pots, and all or aught soever that might tend to hamper their movements; while, ever high above the tumult rose the cheers of our men, as they drove the enemy before them like so many hares . . . 'Kill! Kill! Kill!' was still the burden of the cry . . . who were *unable to kill fast enough,* so numerous were the foe! . . . At last to the great relief of 'pumped' horses and bumped gunners, we were ordered to 'halt—action front!'. We then let fly shell among the fugitives, apparently to some success."

Frequently, the buildings in which the battles were raging were themselves ignited by the musket fire ranging through them. Majendie described such an instance when the so-called Engine House was taken: "The scene of horror at last began to draw to a close; the shots becoming less frequent, told that the work of death was nearly over, while our men exhausted and sated with carnage were firing a few last shots down the pipes, and among the machinery, to put an end to the small number of Sepoys remaining, who were attempting to hide therein. Just then, as though to magnify this overwhelming accumulation of horrors, a fire broke out in the building, the beams and door posts of the room having become ignited from the constant discharge of fire-arms, and the flames communicating with the clothes of the dead and dying Sepoys who lay piled on one another on the floor, and spreading rapidly, owing to these clothes being in great part cotton, soon reduced the whole . . . to a sickening, smoldering mass of disfigured corpses . . . Mixed up with, and among these corpses were several *living* Sepoys, who had hidden themselves underneath the dead bodies of their comrades, in the hopes of so escaping the general slaughter, and that these wretched creatures thus roasted alive, my readers will agree with me that it would be scarcely possible to imagine a more terrible and ghastly scene."

The day finally ended, and the troops settled down for the night near the Iron Bridge, "much of our time being passed in shooting or hanging prisoners taken during the day," records Majendie. "Many a poor wretch breathed his last at this spot, dying, for the most part, with a calmness and courage worthy of a better cause. I am sorry to say that, in one instance, an officer took upon himself the office of executioner, and shot with his revolver two prisoners whom we had brought up to him in a cold-blooded, deliberate way, which was most repulsive. I do not mean to infer that the men were unjustly put to death, for independently of this being a time when no quarter was given, there was the additional argument that we were then occupying a very exposed and important post, sur-rounded by the enemy, and it was but justice to ourselves to exert the utmost vigilance, and adopt the extremest precautions, treating as spies any whom we might find prowling about near our position. That these two men were spies I have not the slightest doubt, so that it was not their fate which surprised or distressed me, but that an *officer* should choose to take upon himself the unpleasant duty of an executioner, and so far lower himself as to stain his hands with those miserable beings' blood. It was not as though an ex-ample of severity was needed—the men were ready enough, God knows, to shut their eyes to prayers for mercy, to kill and destroy whoever they might catch—perhaps too ready; and it was scarcely necessary for an officer to come forward as fugleman, and foster this taste for blood among his men."

The two bridges, Iron and Stone, were the twin avenues to the city from the north. Just across them lay the residency and, more important, command of the escape routes to the south. Outram easily controlled the approaches to the Iron Bridge, but a probe at the Stone Bridge showed that the enemy had it well enfiladed. On orders, they held steady for two days. The delay frustrated the troops terribly. Majendie reports: "The heat is really becoming tre-mendous, number of flies terrific, amount of mosquitoes at night unbearable, and the whole affair generally unpleasant. The stench from the dead bodies is also terrible, there are some hundreds of them buried about the village everyday; but under ground or above ground is all the same; the stench of a dead Sepoy would baffle the most strenuous sanitary measures."[12]

The frustration soon led to new excesses: "After we had occupied the Iron Bridge for some days, and when we supposed that the houses immediately in the neighbourhood were quite clear of the enemy, we were astonished one evening by hearing a shot in one of the buildings which we occupied. And directly after, some of the soldiers rushing in, dragged out a decrepit old man, severely wounded in the thigh. It seems that the sentry had heard somebody moving about the house, had challenged, and receiving no answer, fired, and shot the poor old wretch in question in the leg. He was brought out, and soon surrounded by a noisy, gaping crowd of soldiers, who clamoured loudly for his immediate execution; expressing themselves in language more remarkable by its vigour than either its elegance or its humanity. 'Ave his 'nut' off,' cried one; 'hang the brute,' cried another; 'put him out of mess,' said a third; 'give him a Cawnpore dinner',' (i.e., six inches of steel) shouted a fourth; but the burthen of all these cries was the same, and they meant 'death.' The only person of the group who appeared unmoved, and indifferent to what was going on, was he who certainly had every right to be the most interested: I mean the old man himself whose stoicism one could not but admire. He must have read his fate, a hundred times over, in the angry gestures and looks of his captors . . . His was a case which hardly demanded a long or elaborate trial. He was a native—he could give no account of himself—he had been found prowling about our position at night; stealthily moving among houses everyone of which contained a quantity of gunpowder . . . In this time of stern and summary justice such evidence was more than ample; he was given over to two men, who received orders to 'destroy him.' (The expression usually employed on these occasions, and implying in itself how dreadfully common such executions had become.) And they led him away. This point being settled, the soldiers returned to their games of cards and their pipes, and seemed to feel no further interest in the matter, except when the two executioners returned and one of their comrades carelessly asked, 'Well, Bill, what did yer do to him?' 'Oh,' said the man as he wiped the blood off an old tulwar, with an air of cool and horrible indifference which no words can convey, 'Oh! Sliced his 'ed off.'"

Majendie still was able to defend the act: "My object in selecting this instance has been, not to vilify the British soldier, or to show that *ordinarily* he is cruel, bloodthirsty, or callous to human suffering, for I am sure he is not so . . . It would scarcely be reasonable to expect a man whose wife had been put to death with every atrocity and indignity conceivable—whose children perhaps had been crucified, and whose home made bare and desolate, to retain in his breast any merciful feelings toward those who had thus wronged him, or to forget and forgive, when his day of triumph came, the cruel deeds of his enemy while *he* had the upper hand."

The troops' concern about stray civilians was rooted in reality, for many of the people were acting as saboteurs. Just the day after the old man was summarily executed, the troops found an elaborate mechanism and a long gunpowder train set through one of the buildings, leading to a large store of gunpowder. An old woman who had been working in the neighborhood over the past several days was suspected of laying this trap, fortunately discovered before it was set off.

The ferocity of the entire Lucknow battle was astounding. A bystander told of one graphic incident exemplifying the British attitude: "At one house in particular, I remember, close to the Iron Bridge, six Sepoys made a determined stand; our men at last got in, killed three, and dragging the others into the street, placed them in a row against the outside of the building, and fired at them. One man, hit in the chest, sank down in a half sitting posture against the wall, and when I saw him life was not quite extinct; his dull eyes were wide open, and stared horribly into vacancy, and his head turned in a slow and ghastly manner from side to side (much like those waxwork figures with movable heads, which my reader may have seen) as though he were mourning over his comrades, whose bodies, pierced with several bullets, lay at his feet . . . We got a soldier who was passing by to send a bullet through the poor wretch's head, and so put him out of his misery."[13]

By March 14 the other column (Campbell's) had advanced rapidly, capturing in quick succession the Little Imambara, the King's Brother's House, the Kurshid Mangal, and finally the prize itself—the Kaiserbagh. Lang went right along with the first troops; they moved so fast that "before we could realise the fact we were in the Kaiserbagh. Few as our troops were, on they pushed, 'Pandy' never being allowed to turn and reform." Later in that day, Lang and a group of four Sikhs became separated from their unit in the myriad of passageways: "We forgot how we had entered and went out on the wrong side and wandered in courts of which we could not find the way. Presently came a volley of bullets, with shouts of 'Maro Feringhee Soor' and I thought I should be caught, for I was in 'Pandy' quarters, knew no way out and even if I was only wounded,

I must be captured. We rushed desperately at every door attempting to smash it open, and tho' urged by desperation, fired at, bullets smashing on the walls about us, we could not get through; at last I sprang up at a Venetian window with all my force; it gave way and I fell into a room and saw light beyond; the four Sikhs followed me, and we got through the building into another court, and through a gateway, and saw some of our men." A few minutes went by, and then, as Lang continued his account: "Wandering, we discovered some enemy sulking about in a garden: this garden proved a Cul de Sac from which they could not escape. We left a few men at the windows overlooking it (after having shot some 4 or 5 in the garden) and went in to kill the rest: while beating carefully through the garden, one of our watchers came to say that the remainder were killing one another, and so we found 14 lying in a heap dying in one corner."[14]

Thousands of rebels were being pushed back to the rear, and Outram was beside himself with the desire to rush behind them and close the trap. At this point one of the most incredible battle orders of the war was issued by Campbell. This wily general had outfought the enemy at every turn. His personal courage was beyond question; his fearless action during the Blunt-Cracklow bravery near the Secundrabagh three months earlier was only one of many examples of personal valor. But he was a cautious soldier who sought to protect his men, thus passing by chances for aggressive action that might be more decisive. This protectiveness asserted itself here. Outram begged for the authority to cross the Iron Bridge. Campbell came back with an order so ambiguous and unusual that military historians are still debating it today. Campbell told Outram "that he was not to do so if he thought he would lose a single man."

Outram thought he had no choice but to wait. In retrospect, this order has been seen as a terrible blunder on Campbell's part. The rebels had a clear escape route to the south, and they used it with alacrity and in large numbers. Michael Edwardes, the respected contemporary historian of the mutiny, simply could not explain it: "Of all the extraordinary orders given by commanders during the Mutiny—and there were many—this most surely ranks high on the list. Why, in fact, Outram accepted such an outrageously unwarlike prohibition is not known. When asked by his officers for orders to cross the bridge, Outram replied, 'I am afraid, gentlemen, you will be disappointed when I tell you that I am not going to attack today.'!"

Roberts, writing his memoirs many years later, was harsh on Campbell: "The campaign, which should have then come to an end, was protracted for nearly a year by the fugitives spreading themselves over Oudh and occupying forts and other strong positions, from which they were able to offer resistance to our troops until towards the end of May, 1859, thus causing the needless loss of thousands of British soldiers." Roberts was probably right, but one needs to look at the situation from Campbell's view that day to gain a full perspective. As P. R. Innes pungently put it: "India was reeking with British blood, and the capture of the City of Lucknow must be accomplished without needless loss of life. Sir Colin's policy was irrevocable."[15] The next day the Stone Bridge fell to Outram, and he crossed over to the West Bank. But it was too late.

Cracklow, reporting the fall of the Kaiserbagh in his letter of March 15, also included a surprise: "Some 60 heavy guns and 50 old Begums [queens, princesses, and other ladies of high rank] belonging to the court captured and I am happy to say, some of our own countrywomen rescued. Amongst others I hear the names of the Miss Jacksons who have been on their hands since May last."

The rescue of the "Miss Jacksons" deserves mention, as it is one of the most bizarre stories of all the mutiny. Cracklow was partially wrong: it was not two Miss Jacksons but two women, one Miss Jackson, the other Mrs. Orr. These two were the sole survivors of a band of beleaguered British from one of the outstations on the frontier of Rohilkhand. They had gone through an incredible nine-month saga of privation and despair, much of it spent hidden away in the jungles (Malleson, in his usual florid style, commented: "By this term, jungles, the reader must not understand an ordinary forest, the noble trees of which would have afforded a grateful and necessary shade; he must picture to himself a vast and dreary extent of land, covered with thorny brushwood, and where it was necessary to light fires at night to scare away tigers, wolves, and other wild animals"). After all of the other members of their party had been murdered, they were spirited away to Lucknow by a sympathetic Indian. Malleson chronicled the rescue: "On the 20th March, two British officers attached to the Nepal troops, Captain McNeill and Lieutenant Bogle, when exploring some deserted streets near the Kaiserbagh, were informed by a friendly Native of the place the two ladies were confined. They at once procured the aid of a party of 50 Nepalese, and after walking through narrow streets—about half a mile—they reached a house occupied by one Wajid Ali, an officer of the old Court. In a room within the house, they found the two ladies, dressed in oriental costumes. They at once procured a palanquin and notwithstanding the opposition by a body of ruffians, who would have prevented the rescue, they conveyed the ladies in safety to the camp of Jang Bahadur."[16]

There were no such heroics for Thomas Watson. He stayed back at the headquarters picket for the entire battle at Lucknow, hearing of the historic skirmishes and feats only from afar. "I think the 1st Fusiliers are not destined to hold a gun and fire in the capture of Lucknow," he wrote on March 14. The next day he complained once more about being stuck at the one picket, apparently not so much because he was missing the fighting as because of his own discomfort: "When we are able to return to camp I shall be heartily glad, for this place is very far from comfortable . . . I am again seated as yesterday writing on my desk supported on my knees and in the shade of the Musjid. A high wind is blowing my paper which makes it more difficult to write . . . You can fancy the life anything but an agreeable one. It is just like close imprisonment in a very uncomfortable prison."

On March 18 he reported, "Lucknow is taken—we have had some days of very disagreeable work but no fighting." Now he was stationed in the city proper, "still in a wretched state of discomfort, occupying a large building." They remained there another four days, and he again griped: "I commence a letter to you from these, our wretched quarters. Most truly sick am I of this life of discomfort we are leading." Realizing that he might have sounded a bit cavalier in the face of others' efforts, he penned a note at the end of this letter: "You must not fancy from what I say regarding our quarters that they are worse than others in the city. Indeed they are not so bad as most of the places where regiments are on piquet. The Musjid we occupy is on the highest ground to be seen anywhere and further from the dirty streets of the city than any of our other positions."

Watson also mentioned to his mother that "looting has been put a stop to." In the next breath, he admitted that he, too, had been immersed in this pervasive practice: "Before the prize agents were appointed, I found and sent into camp a very handsome buggy. I have also got a pair of magnificent bullocks and a pony, all of which I hope I shall be able to get away when we march."[17] Cracklow had reported on this stripping of Lucknow in detail: "I can give you no idea of the destruction that has taken place. The beautiful buldings are very much battered with our shot. The palaces which were all furnished in the most sumptuous and costly manner with enormous mirrors, chandeliers, pictures, and splendid furniture have been ransacked by our troops. Not a thing remains entire. What the men could not carry away, they smashed and the floors are covered inches deep with the payment. Property worth it is said, a million has been destroyed here alone. The Sikhs and Ghurkhas were allowed to take what they liked and this is the result, not that the Europeans were at all behind hand, as they quite equalled the other savages in the work of destruction. The whole city presents a most melancholy appearance. The roofs of the houses are nearly burnt off and it has suffered severely from the incessant shelling to which it has been subjected."[18]

The looting of the Kaiserbagh so vividly described by Cracklow was probably one of the vintage plunderings of all time. Russell, the *Times* correspondent, gave a journalist's fillip to the story: "Discipline may hold soldiers together till the fight is won; but it assuredly does not exist for a moment after an assault has been delivered, or a storm has been taken. Imagine Courts as large as the Temple Gardens . . . through all these, hither and thither, with loud cries, dart European and Native soldiery . . . at every door there is an eager crowd, smashing the panels with the stocks of their firelocks, or breaking the fastenings by discharges of their weapons . . . here and there the invaders have forced their way into the large corridors, and you hear the musketry rattling inside; the crash of glass, the shouts and yells of the combatants, and little jets of smoke curl out the closed lattices. Lying amid orange groves are dead and dying sepoys, and the white statues are reddened with blood. Leaning against a smiling Venus is a British soldier shot through the neck, gasping, and at every gasp bleeding to death! Here and there officers are running to and fro after their men, persuading or threatening in vain. From the broken portals issue soldiers laden with loot or plunder. Shawls, rich tapestry, gold and silver brocade, caskets of jewels, arms, splendid dresses. The men are wild with fury and lust for gold—literally drunk with plunder. Some come out with china vases or mirrors, dash them to pieces on the ground, and return to seek more valuable booty. Others are busy gouging out the precious stones from the stems of pipes, from saddle cloths, or the hilts of swords, or butts of pistols and other fire-arms. Some swathe their bodies in stuffs crusted with precious metals and gems; others carry off useless lumber, brass pots, pictures, or vases of jade and china . . . the scene of plunder was indescribable. The soldiers had broken up several of the storerooms, and pitched the contents into the court which was lumbered with cases, with embroidered clothes, gold and silver brocades, silver vessels, arms, banners, drums, shawls, scarves, musical instruments, mirrors, pictures, books, accounts, medicine bottles, gorgeous standards, shields, spears, and a heap of things the enumeration of which would make this sheet of paper like a catalogue of a broker's sale . . . Oh, the toll of that day! Never had I felt such exhaustion. It was hard enough to have to stumble through endless courts which were like vapour baths, amid dead bodies, through sites worthy of the Inferno, by blazing walls which might be pregnant with mines, over breaches, in and out smouldering embrasures, across frail ladders, suffocated by the deadly smells of rotting corpses, of rotten ghee, or vile native scents; but the seething crowd of camp followers into which we emerged in Hazratgunj were something worse. As ravenous, and almost as foul as vultures, they were packed in a dense mass in the street, afraid or unable to go into the palaces, and like the birds they resembled, waiting till the fight was done to prey on their plunder."[19]

Forbes-Mitchell gave a more self-righteous tone to the sack on Lucknow: "The Sikhs and Goorkhas were by far the most proficient plunderers because they instinctively knew where to look for the most valuable loot. The European soldiers did not understand the business, and articles that might have proved a fortune to many were readily parted with for a few Rupees in cash and a bottle of grog . . . with few exceptions the men of the Ninety-Third got very little."[20]

Majendie corroborated the British soldier's lack of discrimination: "If I recollect right, fowls were great favourites, likewise pi-

geons and green parrots; some men positively smothering themselves with these feathered captives . . . Others, again, bore along
in triumph a chaotic mass of tobacco, grass, lamp-shades, books,
bits of silk, scent bottles, plates, brass pots and utensils of all descriptions; of which, if the quality was inferior, the quantity amply
compensated."

"Among the prizes taken at the Kaiserbagh by the 53rd," added
Jones, "was a rather curious one—a tame rhinoceros, who was reputed to be a hundred years old; it certainly was nearly blind, and
quite stupid, but very good-natured, and would let one pull him
by the horn or rub his scaly coat of mail without showing the
slightest displeasure. He was taken up to their camp, and when I
left them, he was there in safety, and, if not in clover, certainly in
the midst of plenty."[21]

It took Herculean efforts to bring the looting under some semblance of control. Prize agents were appointed and guards placed
at intersections of thoroughfares to intercept plunderers and, if
possible, to force them to disgorge their booty. But Forbes-
Mitchell probably spoke for many another soldier when he expressed skepticism at the system: "It was shrewdly suspected by the
troops that certain small caskets in battered cases, which contained
the redemption of mortgaged estates in Scotland, England, and
Ireland, and snug fishing and shooting-boxes in every game-
haunted and salmon-frequented angle of the world, found their
way inside the uniform-cases of even the prize-agents. I could myself name one deeply-encumbered estate which was cleared of mort-
gage to the tune of £180,000 within two years of the plunder of
Lucknow. But to what good? . . . Before we left Lucknow the plunder accumulated by the prize-agents was estimated at over
£600,000 (according to *The Times* of 31st of May, 1858), and within
a week it had reached a million and a quarter sterling. What became
of it all?"[22]

Neither Cracklow nor Roberts ever mentioned again the "prize
money" (both had exulted about the possibility in letters to their
mothers in early 1858, before Lucknow), and it seems likely that the
amounts were not very large. Gordon-Alexander was quite embit-
tered about the actions of the government in regard to the booty:
"I have previously animadverted on the refusal of the Supreme
Government at Calcutta to grant us either salvage or prize-money

for saving the treasure of the Oudh Royal Family from the Lucknow mob at the Relief of Lucknow, and the meanness of the same Government in ignoring our claims for the recovery of the Nana Sahib's treasure, after the hard labour of many days and nights, from the well at Bithur; but both these acts of injustice were eclipsed by the mismanagement, to use the mildest expression, by the military authorities of the collection and sale of the loot of Lucknow itself, our right to which the Supreme Government at Calcutta did not venture to dispute, but took no trouble to look after in any way. Before the end of June the accumulated plunder amounted, according to successive estimates in the *Times,* to more than one million and a half pounds sterling. A private soldier, who had served at both the relief and capture of Lucknow, eventually received, in four or five instalments, spread over a year or eighteen months, the equivalent in rupees of about one pound fifteen shillings as his share! I, as a Lieutenant, received the equally munificent share of about £18 sterling! The question was universally put in the army, 'What became of the rest?'!"[23]

If there was no booty to extract, the British soldier fell back on random graffiti: "Everywhere, on every side, appeared symptoms also of that monomania for scribbling names and drawing faces, so peculiar to us English—no place was spared the infliction, the humble outhouse and the lofty council chamber, the king's stable and the innermost and most mysterious recesses of the love-breathing Zenanah, alike bore on their walls the British soldier '*hys marke*' done in the blackest charcoal and biggest characters, or scratched with the point of his bayonet, with a startling prodigality of capitals."[24]

Arthur Lang had no stomach for any of this. On March 17 he lost his dear and best friend, Elliot Brownlow. They had been cadets together at Addiscombe, graduating next to each other on the Bengal Engineers' list. It had been one of Lang's delights that he had linked up with Brownlow through most of the mutiny campaigns. Indeed, the Lang letters are full of references to days and evenings spent with him.

By March 17 most of the heavy fighting was finished. Lang and Brownlow were coming back through the town, near the Jamuniabagh. Lang told the chain of events: "A street was nearly choked with gharees full of dubbas of powder, apparently Pandy ammunition deserted in rapid flight. I was ordered to bring up men to remove and drench it. Passing, I saw Clerke and some of his company and I told him my errand; he moved up to commence work (Elliot was with him). I rode further to the rear and got some men at last, but had difficulty, providentially for me, in getting them up to the front. Before I got back, I heard the rumbling of powder and saw a black column rise up." H. P. Pearson, another young officer in the unit, hypothesized a deliberate enemy act: "In one street the niggers put three or four hackeries laden with powder and covered them over with silks and shawls, etc. When the men saw it they thought it was loot and rushed to it, when a nigger left for the purpose fired the train and 31 men were blown up, amongst whom were two officers." Lang continued, "I rushed on to see, and there were charred and burning carts, burst dubbas, scorched bodies of men; some bodies were almost inaccessible from the fire. With horror and despair I hunted for half an hour fruitlessly for Clerke and Elliot, longing yet dreading to find them. At last a man brought Elliot's sword and said that he had been carried away."

James Aberigh-Mackay, the unit's chaplain, was one of the first to reach Brownlow: "Never did I witness a more awful spectacle. Lieutenant Brownlow lay in a doolie on the floor naked, and burned most frightfully. His face was black, and his eyes were scarcely visible through the blistered eyelids. The skin of his arms and legs were peeling off. Patches of scarlet, perhaps a foot square, covered his back and legs. His chest and stomach were hopelessly scorched. The sufferer was almost mad with pain."

Lang rushed among the doolies searching for Brownlow. "At last heard my name: Poor fellow, he was so scorched I should not have known him; his face was black and I thought he was blind but he said he could see with one eye. He said he knew he should die but was quite prepared and did not fear. Poor fellow, he was, of course, in dreadful pain, and very nearly sank before the long road to the Kaiserbagh was traversed. I fed him with water all the way, and when he got in he was given a little brandy and water which revived him. Poor Clerke had been brought in before, speechless and unconscious, and he died in an hour or so." Brownlow lingered on for hours, with Lang at his side. "For a long time he would take no opiatives, for fear of dying insensible, but at last we persuaded him to take laudanum, and that at last had effect and quieted the pain and he gradually fell asleep and at last sank and died."

Lang wrote his mother a few days later, "He was a friend such as I can never find again in this world, more than a brother to me. He would have sacrificed himself in any way to have benefited me. He was such a splendid fellow, a man destined, anyone would have said, to win the highest renown and to carve a great name for himself." Lang felt this loss so deeply as to question his own living, for he ended his letter, "I cannot help feeling how strange it is that I live, am untouched and unharmed, while I see daily so many better and nobler struck down before me." It was a terrible loss, executed in a terrible way, and reminiscent of the death of his close friend Duncan Home, who had been blown up at the fort at Malagarh.[25]

Cracklow, too, seemed to be in a state of deep depression once the Battle of Lucknow was over. He wrote at length to his mother on March 28: "The weather is becoming desperately hot, and the Commander in Chief does not seem at all in a hurry about making arrangements for the disposal of the army. One would really think that it was just the commencement of the cold instead of the hot weather from the very deliberate manner in which the authorities are proceeding. Lucknow has been in our hands about 10 days now, and not a step has been taken or a move made. I am beginning to look upon another hot weather under canvas as almost certain. There is some talk of our troop being sent into cantonment at Umballa but as that station is some 30 odd marches from here and the proposed route through Bareilly and Shahjahanpur is still unopened, both places being held by the enemy in force, we should have some more fighting to do and most probably not get in till late in the season.

"There really seems to be no end to this business and I am heartily sick of it, there is nothing to be gained for a subaltern. The Generals, Brigadiers, Colonels, Majors, Captains all come in for honours, distinctions and rewards—even the Sergeants get commissions—everyone gets rewards but the subaltern officers who do all the hard work. I am sure this year's hard work and exposure have taken 10 years out of my life, and all I have got for it is a wretched 6 months *batta,* some 70 £ and this is I believe to be cut down to 50 as my promotion did not appear in orders until after Delhi fell, although in fact I was promoted from the 15th June. A

gunner's *batta* amounts to the magnificent sum of thirty-eight rupees, eight annas. A splendid reward for all the poor devils have
gone through . . . Delhi taken and India saved for Rs. 38.8.0. This
troop was the first in the field in May last, it has suffered more than
any other in men and horses and has been through everything and
I really ought to be sent into cantonment for we are regularly
worked to the bone. The authorities don't seem to think so a bit.
We are recruited again up to strength, have a new Captain just
arrived fresh from England red hot for honour and glory and rampant to distinguish himself and get his Brevet Majority and altogether I expect we have a deal more before us yet. I see no end to
this business.

"The rebels have escaped from Lucknow with little loss, and be-
taken themselves to Bareilly. They were allowed to get off almost
without molestation through the incompetence and stupidity of
some wretched old man, who has command of the Alambagh Brigade, and now the work has all to be done over again. We are
inundated with Generals, Colonels, and Field Officers of the Royal
Army who have the greater part never seen service at all and are
great martinets and disciplinarians, who harass their men and cattle
to the last extremity. The remaining portion who have seen service
insist upon doing everything exactly as it was done in the Crimea
which system, although I have no doubt very good there, does not
suit in this country. All the old Officers of our service (I mean the
Artillery) are superseded by men much their juniors and perfect
Griffs at work in this country, and altogether we are quite sick of
the business.

"It is very sad the number of fine, dashing go-ahead fellows we
lost in these little despicable fights, men who have been in a hundred battles and killed scores of these brutes single handed get
picked off in this miserable street fighting. Of the old Delhi column
now few remain. A great many have been killed or have died of
their wounds. A great many have gone home sick or are going. I
see no chance of anything of the sort for myself. I wouldn't mind,
however it's very certain all can't go and I am not one of the lucky
ones. 120 guns of various calibres have been taken. The enemy have
certainly been beaten but they have lost so few that very little good
has been effected. The old Chief goes so awfully cautiously to work

and so slowly that all the dash and prestige of the thing is lost. He maneuvers them out of their positions and batters them out with heavy guns but kills few and the matter remains much as it was with regard to the Sepoys.

"Really letter writing is such an undertaking on account of the heat, dust and flies that I can hardly ever make up my mind to write a letter. Certainly everyone who is compelled to waste the best years of his life in this country was born under an unlucky star."

In contrast, the three letters Roberts wrote in this period were enthusiastic, almost euphoric. His perceptions were quite different from Cracklow's at the war's end. In his letter of March 12 he, too, showed the pervasive battle fatigue: "A Column will have to follow up Rohilkhand direction and see the last under any circumstances. I fancy I shall go with it, tho' I am nearly tired of fighting and shall not be sorry to be quiet." Yet in this same letter he continued: "Tired as I am of fighting now, I would not be in any other profession for a Kingdom, whether as Infantry, Cavalry, Artillery or Engineers. I have seen all and tried all, and I scarcely know which branch to choose. The Artillery perhaps is my favourite. It is indeed a noble service. So, you have the satisfaction to think that whatever has happened, I am in the very berth I like best."

The glory and the rewards of battle still centrally preoccupied Roberts, and his imminent Victoria Cross lay at the top of his mind: "My own Mother, if I could only get home now to see you, how truly happy I should be, more especially if I get the Brevet Majority. Norman seems to think that a few Subalterns will be made, and that I have as good a chance as any. I shall be indeed a lucky fellow—a Major at 25, with the 'Victoria Cross,' and sure of a good appointment, it would perhaps be better to remain for a few months longer just to get something before things settle down, strike while the iron's hot, and then try for a Medical Certificate and spend 15 months with you dear ones. Were I to leave now they might forget Fred Roberts. Not likely, however, to be so as long as I am with them."

The incessant killing obviously troubled Roberts, and he mentioned the death of his friend MacDonnell in his letter of March 27: "Such a fine gallant fellow, killed by a bullet thro' his head . . . I picked him up almost immediately after he fell. He was quite insensible and died in a few seconds. I could scarcely check a tear when I saw the poor fellow I had been laughing with a few moments before lying dead. It makes one horribly tired of fighting, these sad sights, Mother."

Roberts, too, was prepared for further chase of the rebels: "It is rather a nuisance starting off in such a hurry, without even seeing the inside of the place, but I suppose it can't be helped. The Infantry all remain behind, so you will have an account from Hamilton about the Palaces, captured ladies, etc. The war may now be fairly fought over. Occasional scrimmages will probably take place, but there is no fear of any number collecting together again. Just finished in very good time. It is getting too hot for pleasure knocking about all day."

Promotions—and the competition from the newly arrived troops from England—were very much on Roberts's mind: "This last *Gazette* promoting all the Delhi heroes bothers some of us Subalterns amazingly. I am the only man in the Quartermaster-General's Department who has had the good fortune to be thro' all, and I am the only one who has not got a Brevet. It can't be helped, I know, under the present rule, but it seems rather absurd. Dear old Norman is in the same fix, and as they cannot possibly pass him over until he becomes a Captain I hope they will make one or two more exceptions. It would be a great thing for me, getting a Majority now, and really of little use 6 or 7 years hence. Few young fellows have had the luck to see so much hard service as I have, and I can't help thinking the reward will come ere long . . . Sir Colin, I know, wishes me well. Talking to me the other day rather warmly about Staff Officers rushing on ahead, he said, seeing a smile on my face: 'I am in earnest. Were it my best friend, or one of the best Staff Officers in India (and as such I consider you, my dear Roberts) I would send him back to his Regiment, if I caught him out of his place.' I happened to answer him properly, and left him in high favour. So, my dear old Father, your idle son after all the trouble he has cost you may yet do you honour, and prove that all the money and trouble you have spent on him has not been thrown away."

Roberts first mentioned in his letter of March 28 that his side had been bothering him and that he had "ordered 40 leeches." Just a few days later, on April 2, he wrote his mother that his medical leave to England had already been approved, and he would be disengaging from the troop immediately to leave for Calcutta and the steamer. In his 1897 book Roberts explained this sudden change as follows: "For some time I had been feeling the ill effects of exposure to the climate and hard work, and the doctor, Campbell Browne, had been urging me to go on the sick list . . . I placed myself in Browne's hands, hoping that a change to the hills was all that was needed to set me up; but the doctors insisted on a trip to England. It was a heavy blow to me to have to leave while there was still work to be done." Still, one is left to wonder just a bit whether this leave was in part a put-up job, remembering Roberts's offhand remark to his sister Harriet a few weeks earlier, in which he proposed almost exactly what happened here. Roberts thus parted company with his fellow lieutenants at this point, to return to his family in England.[26]

The big battle was over, but the small mop-up operations were destined to continue, seemingly interminably because of Campbell's indecision at key moments. Cracklow blamed the "wretched old man who has command of the Alambagh Brigade." This was probably Brigadier Franklyn, who if anything was to be commended for his clever tactics with the fleeing mutineers. It appears in retrospect that Campbell, despite his superior military knowledge and experience, made some foolish blunders here at the tail end of the war. "All the dash and prestige is lost," bemoaned Cracklow. What a far cry from that exultant day in January when he had adoringly said of Campbell, "With such a jolly old fellow, who wouldn't join."

Chapter 9
Small, Nasty Mop-ups

"We have been marching about this disgusting country," wrote Cracklow a few weeks after the Lucknow battle, "destroying forts, burning villages, etc., etc., in fact trying to settle it. This, however, turns out to be a rather more difficult matter than was at first imagined. The country swarms with armed men whom it is impossible with the small force we have available to catch. The way affairs are managed is most ridiculous—something in this style. We hear perhaps that at some large village about 10 miles ahead there is an army assembled who mean to dispute the road with us. Everything that can possibly insure secrecy as to our movements is put in force. No orders for marching are issued until about an hour before the time for starting and any possible precaution is taken to prevent the enemy knowing of our intended attack. Off we go to this blessed place.

"Before we have started an hour they manage to get information and decamp. On our arrival not a soul is to be seen in the shape of a fighting man, but some dozens of old men, women and children come out to look at us, never having seen an European before. Well, we halt a day at the place and get a few of the people together, who say they are awfully glad to see us, that now we have come there will be justice for them, that they have been plundered by the soldiers until they have nothing left and that the only thing they hope is for the re-establishment of the Company's rule. Well, the Commissioner tells them to be good people and asks if they have any revenue ready to pay. This, of course, bears absurdity on the face of it. How can we expect any revenue?

"Well, we leave half a dozen policemen and away we march to

the next place and before our baggage is well off the ground, back comes the Army!!! who had occupied the place before our arrival and settles itself down again in perfect security. Then they have a good laugh over the way in which those who were left behind gammoned the Commissioner. They get the policemen and cut their throats and then everything goes on exactly the same as before.

"Of this delightful country of Oudh we hold just as much as we stand on and usually about a mile all round from our camp. Beyond this the enemy's cavalry are always to be seen at the watch and ready to pounce down on any straggler. I can't see how this business is to end. Every man in Oudh is a soldier and until we make it worth their while to serve us, they will always be ready and willing to fight us, for they hate us bitterly."[1]

So now it was guerilla war, all over Oudh and Rohilkhand. Campbell had split the army that had conquered Lucknow into three separate divisions, each with its own tasks and objectives in this huge area. Cracklow and Thomas Watson accompanied the division under Gen. Sir Hope Grant, a force in all of about three thousand men, who had been given a series of targets in the area of Oudh east of Lucknow.

(By this time, Roberts had left Calcutta aboard the Peninsula and Orient steamer *Nubia,* on his way to England, and Lang had settled into the cantonment at Lucknow, being now detached from the fighting forces and back to duty in the Public Works Department.)

Malleson's disparaging remarks about the tactical judgments of the mutineers in their fortifications at Lucknow were probably valid. But any generalization that "the Pandies were poor soldiers" simply does not stand up if we consider the experiences the British forces now had to face. It was hide and seek, sally and fall back. Soldiers immemorial have hated guerilla fighting, with its ambush and pervading sense of suspense, never knowing what will be next. The "Pandies" were indeed very often as Cracklow had described them; one can readily conjure up the vision of the huge Campbell army ranging about Oudh, a large, moving bubble, with the troops in the center and the one mile of control extending out around them. If they moved a mile forward, the rear boundaries silently moved the same distance.

But the contacts with the enemy assuredly were not confined to phantom brushes. All through the spring pitched battles were fought, and hundreds of men died, including several more of the great, heroic figures who had led so decisively. For example, Adrian Hope, the fearless colonel of Lucknow fame, was instantly killed in a disastrous battle at Ruiya Fort in April. Cracklow, learning of Hope's death, raged: "As was expected, Walpole has made a trump of himself. How they ever trusted such an old idiot with a column is difficult to understand. He has command of about 10,000 men in all . . . and he has been driven back from a little mud fort garrison by 2000 men. His loss is 119 men killed and wounded, and the wounded he left behind and they were cut up by the enemy . . . Brigadier Hope, one of the finest fellows in the service, worth 50 of old Walpole, has been killed. Sir Colin will be in a tremendous rage when he hears of it and we all hope that Walpole will be removed out of this command. It is the most absurd thing the way the home papers write up some of the Generals who are serving out here . . . the greatest imposter that ever breathed, this man Walpole, who has never done anything yet except that he got licked at Cawnpore."

Many of the rebel leaders were excellent tacticians in this hit-and-run, cat-and-mouse game. One leader in particular was ruefully respected by everyone: the maulvi of Faizabad, Ahmed Ahmadullah Shah. Reputed to be one of the original instigators of the rebellion, he was a key leader at the defenses of Cawnpore and Lucknow. Now he was ranging about the countryside of Oudh, defying and confounding Grant's forces. A salient of the latter, with George Cracklow, soon had an encounter with the maulvi that was almost disastrous to the Horse Artillery. It happened on April 12, near Bari, twenty-nine miles from Lucknow.

Grant's forces came on the maulvi at a location eminently suited for the latter's plan of defense (and attack). The small village site had a stream running all along its front, with high, honeycombed banks. The wily rebel chief's plan was to hold this strong position long enough for his cavalry to encircle Grant's flank and cut up the ammunition trains and supplies. Grant did, indeed, march forward at daybreak, unsuspicious of danger. The maulvi's cavalry sneaked all the way round the flank undetected; the bolt was ready to thrust home.

At this point the rebel cavalry succumbed to an unfortunate

temptation. Seeing Hunter's two guns from Cracklow's own troop cantering along the flank, they could not resist the temptation to fall upon them. They attacked Hunter and in the process gave themselves away. There were a few tense moments for the Hunter gun crew, before Cracklow and some cavalry of the 7th Hussars came to their rescue and drove the rebel horsemen off. Instantly the British were alerted to the threat on their flank. The maulvi attacked twice more but then, seeing that his initial advantage had dissolved, faded into the countryside. (Less than two months later he was deliberately ambushed by one of the local rebel chieftains, who cut off his head and delivered it in a sack to the British officers at Shahjahanpur. The latter conspicuously showed it around the town the next day and reportedly paid the murderer five thousand pounds for killing the number-one British nemesis.)[2]

The pessimistic view held by Cracklow and others that the war was nowhere near termination apparently was not enough to persuade Jang Bahadur and his Nepalese troops to stay in Oudh and continue the chase. The entire Nepalese contingent had left Lucknow shortly after its conquest and sacking, and the eight thousand men were already on their way north. Hope Grant had orders to link up with them briefly to make sure that they had safe-conduct through the alien territory. He found them at Masauli, midway between Ramnagar and Nawabganj. The British officer who was accompanying Bahadur expressed considerable concern to Grant that the Nepalese force was not really able to protect itself moving through the hostile territory. Apparently only about two thousand of the eight thousand were actual fighting troops. Not only were there two thousand sick in the troop, but there was an enormous line of four thousand carts, each with a separate man to guard it, filled with loot from Lucknow. Grant had orders, however, to move thence southward, and the Nepalese continued on north, finally arriving safely back in their own country in early June.

Cracklow soon had another pitched battle: "We had a grand fight on the 12th [May] with a Chief named Beni-Madou. This gentleman said that it was all nonsense letting us win every battle in this way and that he intended to commence a new era and rout us out, bag and baggage. He and his army, some 7000 men, performed their funeral obsequities and gave out that they were going to fight us to the death. Well, we started on the night of the 11th and

marched 10 miles, put our baggage into a village, and halted under
some trees until 3 in the afternoon of the 12th. We then left a strong
guard over the village and marched to meet them at a place about 5
miles distant. We succeeded in giving them a thrashing, but it was
all we could do, owing to the wretchedly bad arrangements of our
General. We were very nearly being licked ourselves. The enemy
outnumbered us about 5 to 1. They are most extraordinary people
and have no idea of standing and making a good fight as we would
do. They generally appear in a long line varying from one to two
miles not formed up but straggling all over the country, usually
holding some bad ground which it is impossible to get our guns
over.

"Old Grant went in, in his usual idiotic manner, tearing ahead
with the H.A. and Cavalry. The Infantry were done up with their
march in the sun and could not get on very quickly, and the enemy
got round our right flank. It became rather a critical business towards evening. The old general was skying about somewhere to the
left and there was no one to give orders. Our troop had to work
double tides and we managed to keep the brutes back. When it
became dark they ceased firing and we lay down on the ground
with the enemy all round us, our people scattered all over the field
and no one knowing where to find anything. Old Grant then made
up his mind to retire to the place where our baggage had been left,
as he was apprehensive of their making a dash at it. This would
have been fatal, and it would have been a regular retreat—however,
MacKinnon persuaded him out of it and we remained on the
ground all night."

This was the battle at Simri, a small town about midway between
Lucknow and Allahabad. In Cracklow's list of his battle engage-
ments, it is noted only as an "affair." But to Cracklow at the time,
as the troops "lay down on the ground with the enemy all round,"
it was something else again. Not only were men being killed in
battle, the sun was wreaking additional havoc. Cracklow commented on the day of the Simri battle: "The heat is tremendous.
On the day of the fight upward of 100 men were knocked over with
sunstroke. The heat and sun is killing these new regiments off at a
tremendous rate. We bring about a dozen every night. It is useless
attempting to march in this weather. The sun kills a great many
more than the enemy."

Though Bourchier, Roberts, Jones, and many others of Crack-low's fellow officers were no longer with the column—off at rest stations or on their way back to England—Lieutenant Majendie was still along. He graphically reported on the implacable sun at Simri: "Few who belong to this column will ever forget that day—how the scorching rays of the sun beat through helmet, cap, and turban, and struck down by dozens the healthiest and strongest among us; how, still cheered by the prospect of a fight, the men kept gallantly on, stepping out with 'pluck' and determination which cannot be too highly praised . . . one after another, however, the doolies filled with wretched men in all the convulsions of sun-stroke; one after another, sergeants came up and reported some fresh victim. With some, the attack was only temporary; and in a few hours or days or weeks they recovered; others lingered perhaps till evening, or the next morning and then sank into their last long sleep; but many fell, almost as if they had been shot, and in five or three minutes were no more. Never before had we seen sunstroke in all its horrors, and a more appalling spectacle it is difficult to imagine than beholding not one, or two, but dozens of strong men lying speechless and insensible, gasping and jerking with a convul-sive tetanic action; while bhistees standing over them, vainly strive, by saturating their heads with cold water, to arrest the sands of life that are running out so fast—to see the person with whom you are talking, suddenly turn pale and sick, fall reeling to the earth, like a man in a fit, and to hear a quarter of an hour afterwards that he is no more. Who could have blamed our men if sights such as these had unnerved them, and daunted their spirits?"[3]

As to the battle itself, Majendie could not resist yet another den-igrating slap at "the Natives": "As regards the fight (Simri), much need not be said, as there was nothing remarkable about it. It was the old story of Europeans versus Asiatics: White versus Black . . . at about 6 p.m. Pandy fled in 'admired disorder' . . . had we only had to combat a mortal foe, we might perhaps have found reason to congratulate ourselves . . . but alas! it was far otherwise, the sun fought on the side of the enemy, a more potent ally than shot or steel . . . it is difficult, in fact, to see what we gained by this victory: the slaughter of three or four hundred Sepoys at the expense of between 70 and 100 British soldiers . . . by sickness and sunstroke."

That night, as they lay down on the ground for their uneasy rest, the darkness and the unseen threats all around them brought a tension that soon erupted unexpectedly. Cracklow described it: "During the night a panic took place. Nobody knows exactly how it occurred but I believe a horse got loose and ran over someone, who thinking the enemy was coming, raised a hullaballou, and the whole line was up in a moment. Such a scene as it must have been. I was out on piquet about a quarter of a mile in front and only heard the noise. It was a very dark night and the men could not see what they were doing. They began to run in every direction, firing their rifles and using the butt ends freely. Rather a good story is told of the officer commanding the Artillery, a Royal! He first got knocked down in the general rush. However, he managed to scramble on his heels and commenced using his revolver freely. First, he shot a camel, then a dhoolie bearer and then he fired a round through his leg. He was then fortunately prevented from doing further damage by being knocked down with the butt of a musket by a soldier who took him for a Pandy."

Hope Grant himself added a few details: "The Rifles also set to work in grim earnest, everyone fighting his neighbour, and breaking each other's heads with the butt-ends of the rifles. Fortunately, at the time, none happened to be loaded, or the loss would have been serious. As it turned out, ten or twelve men were sent to hospital. The alarm had been caused by a snake creeping over the face of a Madras sepoy, who, terror-stricken, started up with a scream. The confusion was then increased by several of our horses breaking loose and galloping about."[4]

The incident of the nighttime "attack" that the British forces inflicted on themselves illustrates very well the raw nerves and the uneasy tensions infecting the forces in this ugly guerilla war. The poor artillery captain fresh out of England thoroughly disgraced himself, of course, by shooting the bullock driver and then himself; he was relieved of command and sent to the rear. But Cracklow, removed from the stupid antics by virtue of picket duty, must have felt only relief that he had not been shot at once again.

It was not just the heat alone that was responsible. It was everything about a spring campaign in the hottest period of the Gangetic Plain. There were, for example, flies. Forbes-Mitchell, who was with Cracklow, elaborated: "All around Lucknow for miles, the country was covered with dead carcasses of every kind—human beings, horses, camels, bullocks, and donkeys—and for miles the atmosphere was tainted and the swarms of flies were horrible, a positive torment and a nuisance . . . at mealtimes they were indescribable, and it was impossible to keep them out of our food; our plates of rice would be perfectly black with flies."[5]

Majendie, too, hated the flies: "As one lies wearily tossing about on one's bed, so hot as to doubt the possibility of ever getting cool again, these evil spirits keep one in a continual paroxysm of rage; as the old lady in *Punch* says: 'They settles on your noses, and they whizzes in your eyes, And they buz-wuz-wuzzes in your ears; Oh! drat them nasty flies' and you smother yourself by covering your face with a pocket-handkerchief in an attempt to escape them, and throw yourself into a yet more profuse perspiration by endeavouring to capture or kill them, it is needless to add, without the least success."[6]

A few days later, as Grant's troops spread out again over the same area, they passed by the little village called Poorwah, where they had stopped briefly after the Battle of Simri to bury several of the men overcome by sunstroke. "When the column paid this second visit to the place, it was discovered that during their absence the enemy had opened the graves, defiled them in a most disgusting manner, torn up the bodies, and after scattering the bones all around the place, had carried off the heads for trophies! This little anecdote speaks volumes for the *animus* of our vile, barbarous foes, and yet all the while pseudo-philanthropists at home were crying for mercy for the poor Sepoy and trying with that *laudable* spirit of perseverance and benevolence which would seek to wash the Ethiopian white, to palliate, almost to vindicate his deeds of cruelty and mutiny. With no little astonishment, as we read speeches and leading articles, did we behold the respected positions of Sepoys and Englishmen reversed, the former being the martyrs now, the latter the persecutors. Misguided officers and soldiers who had been inwardly congratulating themselves that they had established a sort of claim upon the gratitude of their country, by their services in India . . . suddenly discovered, on reading the record of proceedings at Exeter Hall, and elsewhere, that it was all a mistake; and that they were, by certain sets in England, looked upon, individually, as something between a cannibal and a grand inquisitor. One unfortunate who, not anticipating this revulsion of public feeling, and who, when the cry of 'no quarter' was echoing far and wide through England, had written a little letter home, stating much satisfaction that he had killed several Sepoys, was astonished to find by return of mail that he was a monster, and not the least bit of a hero."[7]

It was a depressing and discouraging life, and Cracklow ended his letter about Simri at a low ebb: "We are now on our way back to Lucknow which is threatened, the rebels having collected in force at about 15 miles distant and have given out that they are going to retake the place. So we are likely to have plenty more fighting on our hands. In fact it appears as if it were just about to commence instead of being nearly over. Our life is terrible. Not a book to read or even a newspaper. Nothing for it, day after day, when we get in from our march at about 8 in the morning, but to lie with one's head wrapped in a wet towel and long for sunset. Hunter is away on sick leave and McLeod has been on the sick list ever since we left Lucknow so I have had plenty of duty and piquet nearly every day. McLeod is mugging up for a sick certificate I think. A delightful state of affairs, isn't it . . . I expect by the time we get into Lucknow the road in our rear will be shut up, as the Pandies are hanging about our rear in thousands."

By this point, Cracklow's views of his superior officers had truly soured: "We have a Royal Artillery officer in command of the artillery with this force and he has been grinding us preciously. He does not allow the battery which is with us to take any duty and the consequence is that our troop has had to do it all." He elaborated on his accusations of preferential treatment for the Royals in his next letter: "We are all heartily tired of this kind of work, and want to see the Royal Artillery used a little more than they have been. The whole brunt of the work has fallen on our regiment . . . there is a Royal troop here which has hardly seen a shot fired, which has 240 men, whilst we have only 74 or 80 . . . they will not use them, but keep us grinding away as if we were fresh from cantonment . . . we consider it a very dirty trick of the old chief, this leaving us here to do all the dirty work."[8]

By early June the troop was back in Lucknow, in temporary cantonment. This break gave Cracklow, Watson, and the other men of the unit a chance to catch up on some of the simpler things of daily life—clothing, letters, news from home, and instructions back to family. Cracklow's gentle concern for his mother again is evident: "I am glad to hear, Dearest, that you are not going on this journey to Dusseldorf. It would have been too much for you alone. I am much distressed to hear such a bad account of your poor eyes. You must suffer dreadfully, dear Mother. I hope you are taking the best advice. I have become or am becoming quite a rich man and hope that you will not let economical motives stand in the way of your having the best attendance, as it would be a great pleasure to me to defray the cost of it."

Thomas Watson's duties at headquarters in this immediate post-Lucknow period remained humdrum, away from the action. In addition to his responsibilities as financial officer in charge of the treasure chest, he was now formally assigned the title "Provost Marshal." He wrote his mother, "You will, I know, be glad to hear that I am on the staff. The appointment I hold is not a very nice one but one thing leads to another . . . I am Provost Marshal to the division, and have to flog and punish all who misbehave, that is, I have to see it done." He clearly felt unsure about this post; he wrote his mother the next day, "I long to hear whether you approve of my having taken this appointment and whether you think I am able to perform the duties."

His mother's response was lukewarm: "You hold an appointment with such a high sounding name. I fear the duties are irksome and fatiguing and may God preserve you through them and order everything for you." Watson's reply was revealing of his feelings of personal inadequacy: "I fear you will blame me for leaving the Fusiliers . . . I cannot but feel sorry for myself at times that I have left the regiment, for I feel nervous lest I should prove incompetent to hold the appointment I have been given." Nevertheless, he still seemed unwilling to put his energies into his work; he wrote two weeks later: "This hot weather makes me very disinclined for any occupation . . . I read a good deal and I am ashamed to say sleep a good deal."

Watson's interpersonal links remained skimpy during this time in the field. "I club with Mr. Lang, the clergyman of the column," he wrote on May 1; "we mess together and generally manage to pitch under nice trees." Watson could not resist a few digs: "Mr. Lang, as far as I know, is more inclined to low than high church views, but he is not at all given to talking on religious subjects and takes things in general rather too easily for my liking. He is certainly not clever, though thoroughly gentlemanly and therefore not an unpleasant companion." Watson seems to have had more than a bit of social snobbery in him; for example, he wrote in late April: "Alfred Wallace is the largest little fellow I ever saw in my life. He sleeps all day and night and never writes or reads. His great want of polish almost amounts to vulgarity and is even worse off for ideas than I am myself. How thankful I feel, darling Mother, that I was not brought up in Ireland."

Watson, too, reported frequently on the ghastly effects of the sun. This nonbattle threat seemed to terrify his mother more than anything; her letters to Watson were filled in this period with remonstrances about staying out of the sun. For example, she wrote in late April: "The cloudy weather of the past two days have been such a comfort to me, for I trust it is equally cloudy with you. [they were several hundred miles apart!]. Oh, how I fear the thought of your being in tents, marching at this season." Watson replied: "To me, it seems a most shameful thing to send Europeans out in this weather, for they cannot stand marching and sentry duty under such a sun. There is no immediate need of their going out now— we can well afford to wait till next cold season."

Except for finding a cobra in his tent in mid-May, Watson had a quiet life during this busy period. Late in May he split up with the minister for mess but stayed with him in the tent. Watson could well live alone at this time—he chronicled to his mother his eleven servants: "A kitmutgar [server], a cook, a bearer [in charge of clothes and furniture], a hillman, a punka coolie, a syce, a grasscutter, a dhobee [a laundryman], a goat herd, a camel man, and a matee [an assistant to the bearer]." "I am not able to get much in the way of comforts," he added, "but I am as well off as most people in camp who have not a mess to go to."

His mother was not getting along well in her house. She continued to rail at Mrs. Scott, calling her a "hard creature." "It is really a shame to see the fare she orders for me generally, when she is not to partake of it herself. I do not really care a straw, but she is intensely mean and it disgusts one." In early June Sarah Watson changed her residence in Simla, moving to the home of Mrs. E. K. Money, the wife of the artillery captain in Cracklow's troop. This must have been a surprising move to Thomas Watson, for he had briefly bunked with Money early in the year and had written his mother at that time, "Wallace has left this guard—it is now commanded by Money, a man that I do not like at all; he is sharing the tent, so I have no privacy." Watson probably felt better, though, when his mother wrote that Mrs. Money was "very kind."[9]

Cracklow had just one more major battle to endure, and it was an important one. His letter of June 22 covered the essential facts: "We have been out on another expedition and have had a very satisfactory fight with the Pandies. The poor old troop has as usual suffered a good deal, not so much from the Pandies, who only wounded 2 but from the sun which killed 6 of our fine old soldiers. There will I think soon be few of us left to lead the troop. Losing so many men is very dispiriting at the time but we are pretty well accustomed to it now and soon get tolerably jolly again."

This "very satisfactory fight," at Nawabgunge-Barabanki, was an important one, for it finally drove the rebels from the vicinity of Lucknow. Once more it was a well-fortified spot, with the inevitable stream bank this time covering three sides and a jungle protecting the fourth. Grant completely surprised the enemy at daybreak, but despite the rebels' confusion they fought back viciously. Their first target again was in Cracklow's own troop, Lieutenant Percival's two guns. They were rescued in time, but the rebels regrouped, deciding to take a stand. Grant himself described the sequence of events: "A large body of fine, daring zemindari men brought two guns into the open and attacked us in the rear. I have seen many battles in India, and many brave fellows fighting with a determination to conquer or die, but I never witnessed anything more magnificent than the conduct of these zemandaris. In the first instance they attacked Hodson's Horse, who would not face them, and by their unsteadiness placed in great jeopardy two guns which had been attached to the regiment. Fearing that they might be captured, I ordered up the 7th Hussars, and the other four guns, belonging to the battery [including Cracklow] within a distance of five hundred yards from the enemy, opened a fire of grape, which mowed them down with a terrible effect, like thistles before the scythe.

"Their Chief, a big fellow with a goitre on his neck, nothing daunted, caused two green standards to be planted close to the guns, and used them as a rallying point; but our grape-shot was so destructive, that whenever they attempted to serve the piece, they were struck down . . . the gallant 7th Hussars charged through them twice, and killed the greater part of them. Around the two guns alone there were 125 corpses."[10]

The enemy lost 600 men and six guns, and the British had 67 actual battle casualties. But 33 died of sunstroke, and 250 were hospitalized for the same reason. Of these sunstroke dead 6 were Cracklow's own men (most of whom expired in the night, falling asleep never to awaken, felled by apoplexy).

At this point the exhausted troops, many of whom, like Cracklow, had been in the field without letup for over one full year of battle upon battle, were now put into reserve at the Lucknow cantonment. Grant took fresh troops out over Oudh throughout the summer and fall to engage in additional small skirmishes and campaigns, but at last Cracklow was reading about the war in dispatches, rather than being the constant subject of them.

Cracklow and his colleagues had just settled their tents on platforms, with some thatching for sides, when orders came again to move out in the field, not into battle but as a replacement outpost at a small village called Nawabpuje, on the road to Faizabad. "Nawabpuje is a wretched place . . . folly, isn't it—this being turned out again after making up our minds for a little rest." But this time Cracklow was almost apathetic: "I have become perfectly indifferent to what they do with me. We are all looking rather seedy and desperately thin, pale and washed out. We have lost a good many men within the last 3 months and can now only turn out 4 guns and have been reported unfit for service. But this the authorities do not care about a bit!" His bile toward the Royals again surfaced: "It's shameful the way our regiment is treated. Those miserable directors have now got 4 new European cavalry regiments sent to this place. You will hardly believe it, but notwithstanding our small numbers, they have sent a requisition for our troop for 6 sergeants to teach these fellows to ride! Yet they expect us to do our duty as well . . . They don't care a bit how they use our regiment, which has saved India for them." Cracklow's pride in his own unit still welled up: "I don't care about the work a bit for myself; with us one man always has to do the work of three. But it's impossible to keep up the credit of the regiment. You need not be surprised if you see them begin to pull us to bits in the papers—the fault's not our own, but the system."

By late August Cracklow's recurring rheumatism was troubling him again. This malady, combined with the inaction and the incessant rains, seemed to depress him profoundly: "I have been very homesick lately but I might as well be moonsick for all the likelihood there is of my obtaining my desire. As for getting home on sick leave, the committee never pass any but those just on the point of death and then they generally have not strength to get down country. Even leave for a month or two to the hills is quite out of the question in our regiment, where there are so few officers that one always has to do the work of three. At present I am the only subaltern with the troop." For the first time he talked of getting out of the service altogether: "I do not think I will stand another hot weather out, I'd rather cut the service altogether and try my luck elsewhere. I am thoroughly sick of this business and would give something to get out of it. It's a melancholy thing, having to spend the best years of one's life in this beastly country, but the life we are leading now is perfectly fearful—no pleasure of any sort, no amusements, not even eatable food to be got. The only object is to get through the time. I generally try to sleep it out, but can't manage more than 12 hours out of the 24."

Cracklow's troop was situated in a vulnerable spot, as he pointed out in a letter in early September: "We are in a rather unpleasant position here, as the whole Pandy force south of us will be sure to retreat before the Chief's advance and must pass between us and Lucknow . . . Unless we be reinforced, we should hardly be able to manage them." Yet his zest for battle again surfaced: "I am rather looking forward to this cold weather campaign, as although I would of course rather be on my way back to some quiet station, yet anything is preferable to this monotonous life in a standing camp." He continued to rail at higher officerdom: "The only thing I am particularly anxious about is the man by whom we are to be commanded. These Brigadiers are usually such wretched old muffs and bad managers that I have got quite sick of being under them, they make such mistakes, get into such scrapes and worry everyone under their command to death. I should like to be under the Chief again. He seems to me to be the only man worth his saber or that knows whether he is standing on his head or his heels."

A brief action—a "slight skirmish," according to Cracklow—in mid-October brought back his rheumatism, this time a rather severe attack. "The doctor talks of a medical certificate next hot weather, but I shall not avail myself of it unless positively necessary. Much as I should like to come home, it would not suit my book at all. I shall, if possible, hold out until my furlough is due in /62." The contrast to Roberts's machinations about sick leave, just a few months earlier, is striking.

In late October the decimation of the officer ranks in Cracklow's troop led to his being put in charge. But before he could lead the unit into any kind of an engagement, a senior officer returned to the troop, "much to my disgust, as such an opportunity does not offer often." At this point Money replaced MacKinnon as head of the troop, and Cracklow's opinion was much the same as Watson's had been earlier: "Money is rather a brute. Everybody abuses him up hill and down dale. I do not yet know much about him for although I was in his battery at Dang, I was then a griff and did not know any difference between one commanding officer and another. He is a slack, slovenly-looking man, rather stout and not at all a horse-artillery-like looking fellow. What we want just now is a smart, sharp, active fellow who knows his duty and can teach the men theirs. Money is anything but this. He is a great pudgy fat man of about 5 and 40—27 years in this country has made him a perfect nigger in thought and habits. He has got a wife and large family, and thinks nothing but scraping together money, eating and smoking. He won't delegate any authority, keeps everything in his own hands to the smallest trifles. He is slack in duty matters and slovenly in dress. So much for our beloved commanding officer." Yet Cracklow still seemed somewhat ambivalent about Money: "I hope we shall get on well."[11]

To the central authorities, it now seemed time to hold some carrots forward toward a peaceful conclusion of the hostilities. The question of amnesty had been a sensitive one all through the mutiny. Some of the British officers were remarkably humane in their views; for example, Hope Grant wrote in March 1858, just after the fall of Lucknow: "The day before the Kaiser Bagh fell, there must have been some 2000 or 3000 killed and wounded (on the part of the mutineers). It really sickens one to think of slaughtering any more of the poor wretched creatures. If it goes on, it will cause the death of many a noble soldier in H.M.'s service, and, after all, will do little good. If we were to put to death 10,000 more, we should not nearly have come to the end of them; and should we once come to guerilla warfare, farewell to peace and comfort in the country for years. The Governor-General, if he has strength of mind . . . ought to issue a proclamation declaring an amnesty to these wretched creatures, of whom three-fourths were forced into the Mutiny, and having once entered in, could not get out of it. Of course, certain individuals, and especially those who have committed murders, must not escape; but they would certainly be given up were leniency shown to the mass."[12]

However, the fighting men generally found any form of amnesty very distasteful; better "to have licked them well all around first," as Cracklow had put it. But it was past time to try to bring the country back to some semblance of normalcy. The process that had been earlier accomplished back at Delhi and at Cawnpore had to be applied to Lucknow—persuading the terrified citizenry to return to the city and making that city a safe and attractive place to be.

J. D. Forsyth, the secretary to the chief commissioner of Oudh, penned a long letter to G. F. Edmonstone, the secretary to the governor-general, in late May 1858, a letter that put the problems in focus: "On the arrival of the Chief Commissioner upon the city of Lucknow he found it entirely in military occupation and the inhabitants, though invited to return to their homes, were still nearly all outside the city. The Governor General's proclamations to the Talooqdars and Zamindars of Oudh have been extensively circulated but no landholder of any rank or from any distance save a few petty men in the immediate neighborhood of Lucknow had come in. Feeling that the first duty was to convey the order and offer of the government to the people of Oudh . . . the Chief Commissioner took into his own hands the task of singling out certain Talooqdars such as Raja Hashi Pershasis and others whom he summoned to his presence, explained fully the views and intentions of government. Having treated them with proper consideration, he dismissed the Talooqdars to spread the intelligence amongst their neighbors and friends.

"Having made this small commencement, it was necessary to select some deputy of tact and local experience who could summon the chief Zamindars and Talooqdars from a distance. Major Barrow . . . was strongly recommended to the Chief Commissioner as a man of sound program and local knowledge and to him was entrusted the duty of negotiation and settlement with the landholders . . . Simultaneously with these political arrangements, the Chief Commissioner's attention was turned urgently to the city which was all in a state of ruin and desolation, consequent on a very traumatic siege. General Outram had issued a proclamation calling on the peaceable inhabitants to return but fear and the rude treatment experienced at the hands of the soldiers kept the majority away. By degrees, however, they crept in and as the military authorities exercised a strict control the people found themselves comparatively unmolested and gradually flocked in.

"For ordinary protection and conservancy purposes a large staff of police was organized under Major Carnegie. The task of leveling the fortifications, filling in ditches and repairing the breaches consequent on the war has evolved partly on the military and partly on the civil department and by the united exertions the streets which were intersected with trenches, blocked up by barricades and filled with filth are now clear, clean and passable for traffic. To render the military posts properly defensible and to secure their approaches extensive demolition of surrounding buildings is being carried on and wide roads from end to end of the city are being made."[13]

However, the beginning of pacification and amelioration in the cities left many of the smaller towns and villages in the countryside less protected. Forsyth continued: "After defeating the rebels at Simri, General Grant found himself obliged to return to Lucknow partly owing to the fearful sickness of his men, twenty of whom died in one day and nearly two hundred went into hospitals. This withdrawal of the troops entirely upset all our fiscal arrangements in these parts, as though there are numerous Zamindars and Talooqdars most favorable to our cause, yet unless they are supported by the presence of British troops they are unable to stand before the attacks of rebel landholders. Many who come to Lucknow are assailed and plundered by the rebels on their return . . . As regard treasuries, the Chief Commissioner considers it would be unwise to keep large sums in any of our outposts, and dangerous to send the money in to Lucknow. Reference has been made above to the police kept up by the Talooqdars and the returns show that 5,531 men are in the various Thannahs and Tehseels. Major Bruce has been raising 2000 recruits, men selected with regard to physical fitness and without care for caste. In addition to these, the Aloowala Rajah is now on his way from Cullamder with a contingent of 2000 men and three guns. From Umballah, 1000 men have been dispatched and are near Cawnpore and more will follow from Agra. The Chief Commissioner had heard that 500 men are being enlisted for service in the Oudh police battalion. With the country but very partially under our control, it cannot but be that crime flourishes almost unchecked, and those who are at all forward to show their loyalty become special objects of vengeance to their fellow countrymen. Indeed until the whole province has been thoroughly subdued and strong military posts are planted all over the country it will be in vain to expect order and quiet."

Queen Victoria took the first major step toward putting the empire's house in order on August 2, 1858, by placing the entire government of India in the hands of the British Crown. No longer was there to be a semiautonomous East India Company, with its own soldiers (e.g., Cracklow, Roberts, Lang, and Watson) and with its own government, acting as an enormous fiefdom. The Queen did not ask the soldiers involved whether they would prefer working for the Crown; a great many did not, and there were rumblings of discontent bordering on mutiny (inasmuch as the decision did not allow them a bounty for reenlisting). The so-called White Mutiny (a term left from a previous case in 1809) never amounted to much, but many of the company's Indian Mutiny veterans chose to retire. Cracklow wrote his mother, not very tolerantly, about a rebellious instance in Meerut: "I have no doubt some of them will be shot, and it will serve them right for going about it in the manner they have . . . The only danger is that the Natives seeing us quarrelling among ourselves, may take it in their heads to rise again."

The proclamation transferring the government to the British Crown and offering amnesty to the mutineers was promulgated three months later, in November 1858. Both in its wording and in its intent, the offer was genuine and positive. Full amnesty would go to all who participated in the mutiny except for those actually found guilty (presumably now by post-mutiny British standards of justice) of taking direct part in the murder of British subjects. All leaders, "instigators," would have their lives spared but would be subject to punishment.

In a letter written later in November, Cracklow reported on the first weeks after the queen's edict: "Then we had the Proclamation and expected something would be done. Never was there a greater mistake. After collecting an enormous army (without which he never moves) he [Campbell] advances on a little miserable Raja in a mudhut with two other columns, one under Grant and the other under Weatherall, either of which was large enough to march from one end of Oudh to the other alone. Well, he sends forward the Proclamation and gives the brutes 10 days!!! to think of it. Mind, 10 days when we have only 2½ months more cold weather left, to do everything in. The man refuses to have anything to do with us and after more delay and being told two or three times that the time for going in was past, the Chief at length makes up his mind to attack, pointing to attack, and then the man says he will knock under and is allowed to come in, after holding us at defiance some 10 or 12 days. Anyone else would at his first refusal have just battered the fort down about his ears and then taken him out, given him a good flogging and hung him. As it is, in virtue of his having given himself up under the Proclamation he will have all his estates given back to him, and be ready to hatch treason against us on the first opportunity.

"I forgot to mention that while the Raja was coming in himself the Chief having carefully left a road open the whole of his followers with their guns and arms got away and were not pursued!!! After the triumphant settlement of the affair the Army! advances on the next fort about 5 miles off and after about equal delay the same farce is repeated. In about another month he will have worked up to our position. I suppose I will be dragged along in the train to act a part in the farce. It's most laughable, he treats these miserable Rajas with their thousands all ready to bolt at the first shot, with the same caution and management as he would a like number of French or Russians."[14]

It was concluded, finally, that in order to have the proclamation carry its full effect, a major and impressive ceremony was needed, the time-honored practice of the durbar. One of these ceremonies, that held at Sialkot (Cracklow's and Watson's old station) illustrates well the flamboyance of the day: "A plain to the East of the Sudder Bazaar was selected so as not to be too far for the people to come to from the town. On three sides, a railing was put up with triumphal arches here and there on which the illuminations were to be shown and the fourth side was left to be occupied by the Durbar tents. On Saturday, I took counsel with the Brigadier commanding the station and Proclamations were issued summoning the loyal Jagheerdars, Chowdrees, Punches, Agricultural Chieftains and all well-disposed subjects to attend on the great day. On Monday morning, crowds were seen assembling on the plain. The loyal Chieftains pitched their tents so as to give greater attraction to coming events. Every measure was set on foot to secure a sufficiency of supplies and prevent disturbances. After due consultation with the Military Authorities, 5:00 o'clock in the afternoon was decided as the most convenient time for the reading of the Proclamation.

"I went down town with my assistant at 10:00 o'clock to see that seats and accommodations were provided for the upper classes, the Official, and the Commercial and Agricultural Classes. The Durbar tents were then arranged so as to cover the greatest space possible. Three large tents were placed in a row, and in the center a 'beehola' tent made, which raised in a dais and covered with a handsome shawl, carpet was placed, and a chair enrobed with cloth-of-gold, across which again was laid a sword, wrapped up in a shawl. By the chair were two more shawls suspended in loose curtain fashion with a crown and a VR worked upon them in letters of gilt-covered silk. On either side of the Chair of State, intended to represent royalty, two rows of seats were arranged in a semi-circle with one corner seat apart for the ladies. Beyond these, again on one side, accommodation was provided in a tent at the end for the women and children of British soldiers, on the other, for native gentlemen and for the residents of the city and cantonments, both official and otherwise.

"Owing to the afternoon being fixed upon, a little difficulty was contemplated in keeping the assembled masses amused and supplied with provisions. For that purpose then, a massive bazaar was extemporized and shopkeepers of the city were active in taking up stalls arranged in streets under the cordial superintendent of the city Punches. Jugglers and wrestlers too of known fame had been invited and ground was assigned to them for their games and feats of strength, the whole control of which was made over to the Kotwal.

"At 4:00 o'clock, the troops arrived and under the order of the Brigadier Major, Captain Rolfs took up their position. The infantry consisting of Her Majesty's 52nd Regiment under the command of Colonel Vickers, then the Sialkot Cavalry under Captain Caulfield and the disarmed 29th under Colonel McDonald in a line on one side, etc. . . . By the arrival of Brigadier Stisted C.B. the arrangements were complete. The Brigadier moved down the line of troops, Officers fell out, dismounted, and we then all walked up the procession to the seats, arranged in Durbar. Silence was proclaimed and at 5:20 I proceeded to the table in front of the dais which held the Queen's message, and bowing to royalty, read out in English her Majesty's Proclamation announcing from this day her assumption of the Indian territories. A signal was then given and vernacular copies were simultaneously read out by Mr. Assiott to the Residents of the city and cantonments and by the four Tahseeldars to their respective cantonments. Further copies which were hurriedly lithographed in a jail were distributed as handbills to the people, and a large placard was hoisted up at the well, announcing the message of the day. The royal salute was fired, bands struck up the National Anthem, and then a *fen de jois* was given by her Majesty's 52nd to the surprise of the new lieges and the pride of every British heart present.

"The crowd was immense and kept increasing. It swayed to and fro at each movement in the program, stilled with the aid of the police and a few dragoons. Perfect order was maintained. The square was kept open, the military moved to their places when the Brigadier very properly ordered the troops to march by in slow time and salute. Bands playing as company after company passed in front of the Chair of State. This movement seemed to make a great impression on the people. It was successfully and soon achieved. The crowds swayed back and the troops returned to places in squares. I called upon all who were loyal subjects to walk up to the Chair and make obeisance to their Queen. It was a pleasing testimony to me to see the interest and orderly demeanor with which this was done, Sudder Mungul Singh and even Mehta H. Singh, a man of pride and unusual reserve taking a prominent part in showing they appreciated the honour conferred upon them. Some of the Agricultural Chieftains were not satisfied until they were allowed to touch the dais on which the chair was placed. Some, I remarked, in bended position touched the crown with their right hand then raised it to their heads, while one man of more simplicity perhaps, perhaps decorum, threw himself with his head on the ground as though he were bowing to his God.

"It is a pleasure to be able to report this and the fact that with the active homage rendered, rough men with rough hearts were heard to exclaim 'Iyemulka, Iyemulka' in a true old feudal style. On the completion of these ceremonies it was rapidly becoming dark, so order being proclaimed, the fireworks were displayed, and on all the squares the illuminations set out glowing light. I am happy to say everything passed off very rapidly. The European community were satisfied. The people seemed pleased. There were no accidents, though there must have been at least, at the lowest computation upwards of 20,000 people, while rumour would add to this number. They all moved off in the night without a single theft or affray or scuffle having been reported . . . I take every opportunity to make known, both personally and through my subordinates, the nature and meaning of the Proclamation, and as usual I found the most absurd reports afloat. One which seemed to be most alive and most keenly relished by a public so thoroughly agrestic as was here assembled, was that Her Majesty had been pleased this day to announce reduction of land revenue. Possibly this might account for so very large a number attending."[15]

Most of the rebels, including many of the leaders, took advantage of the amnesty. Some would not (or could not, being implicated too deeply to expect any mercy) and continued to fight and/or flee up into 1859. Still, the proclamation signaled the real termination of the awful war.

Through all this period of high moments of political and military tension, Thomas Watson was overwhelmingly preoccupied with his own narrow concerns. First, there was the matter of "the appointment" (just about every one of his letters for the second half of 1858 contained one or more allusions to this dominating concern). Watson sensed that his post as head of the military chest was going to disappear, once the unit settled into cantonment and the bulk of the treasure was forwarded to higher command. What would he then do? There were a number of police posts becoming available in Oudh, but these had one fatal flaw for Watson—they were not near his mother. His overriding concern was to get back to her.

The two, mother and son, now began a convoluted campaign to obtain him an appointment closer to her. So assiduous were both in pressing this claim that they succeeded in antagonizing some of the key players. Watson's highest contact was his commander, Hope Grant, and he wrote his mother in early July: "I shall, of course, make it a point to see the General. I will ask him to try and get me some appointment up country. I will tell him how much I long to be with you again." He reported this maneuvering in the next letter: "I called on the General in the morning with Alfred. He did not receive us at all cordially. In the evening, at the band, I was very glad at his coming up to us asking us to share with him at dinner. He was as friendly as usual. He gave me no hopes of being able to get away. He says there are so few officers in this part of the country altogether. I came away in the morning from the General's feeling very low spirited. It is now very certain the Genl. will not assist me unless I get away through other contact."

It was soon clear that he had actually antagonized Grant: "General Grant, I know, would do nothing to help me. His answer when I asked him was most decided, and I think he was vexed at my hinting at such a thing." Apparently this encounter brought back Watson's old feelings of inadequacy, for he closed: "I could never write a good letter. Indeed, I can do nothing well." In this same letter he told his mother of participating in a small "society for athletic exercise of an evening," with a few others. Still, his next sentence went on, "I am, as you know, not very fond of society and I see quite as much now as I care for." He admitted that "my life is as lonely almost as yours, though I live in such a crowd. Everyone is civil in manner to me, but none cultivate my acquaintance. My own fault, I dare say." Interestingly, his mother had written him in the same vein; she had just had a stroll with Mrs. Money's dog: "I took a long walk today and feel the better for it, thank God. I go out alone with Jake, the only living thing at Simla that wishes to be with me!"

Hints of Sarah Watson's irritation with her new landlady also surfaced in this letter: "Mrs. Money had liked to walk with me, but she dawdles so & gets up late." Sure enough, early in the next month her son learned of further trouble: "I fear, dearest Mother, from all you say of Mrs. Money, you are not comfortable with her. If she should make herself disagreeable, where will you go?"

By early September, Sarah Watson's relations with Mrs. Money had apparently turned quite sour. Thomas Watson wrote, "I should like to hear how Mrs. Money has been behaving. I have long thought from your silence regarding her that she has not been making herself agreeable. How much you have been troubled and annoyed by disagreeable people since we parted, dearest Mother. I think nice people are very scarce, especially in India."

Early in October Sarah Watson left Simla to join her daughter Annie in Meerut, where Annie's husband, Captain Edward Atlay, had just been reassigned. Thomas Watson often seemed less than enthusiastic about his brother-in-law. Watson had sent the buggy he had "liberated" in Lucknow back to his mother in Simla. A few weeks later she unilaterally decided to give the buggy to Edward, and Watson wrote right back: "I am sorry that you seemed to have quite made up your mind that Edward is to have the buggy, which I got at Lucknow. For more than one reason, I should like to keep it and give Edward the other. It is almost the only momento of the day we entered Lucknow. The place that it occupied was but one minute before in the hands of the enemy. It was in the same yard with that loaded gun which was pointing down the street. I ran up, and many many bullets passed me as I did so." Yet he felt that he could not buck his mother: "Still, dearest Mother, I should like you to please yourself."

The issue continued to rankle, and he wrote a few weeks later: "Edward says the buggy will be at Meerut soon and thanks me for giving it to him. If he would refer to my letters, he would see that I have distinctly said from the first that you were to take your choice. I might safely have given him our old one at once, for though I have never considered it mine, I might have felt sure you would like the other better. I must run the risk of Edward being a little annoyed and tell him that I still wish you to take your choice when you go to Meerut. You might yourself, I think, write the same." We know from earlier letters that Watson was now overdramatizing the incident in Lucknow; his mother apparently wrote Edward about these comments, and Watson was most upset: "I am very sorry, darling Mother, that you wrote to Edward about the buggy, especially if you mentioned what I said of the danger . . . I may tell you of far narrower escapes some day, but I should not like to have it supposed that I made them a topic in writing to you. Besides, I fear Edward thinks I persuaded you to write him and may fancy I have not behaved handsomely about it." He took other little digs at his brother-in-law in the succeeding weeks—"Edward is not a careful man about small things." The buggy went to Edward, nonetheless.

Watson continued to live well in cantonment. He confided to his mother in late June that he now had the best tent in camp: "It is assuming quite a respectable appearance . . . far more advanced than almost any habitation in camp—far larger than any are likely to be." A few days later he elaborated: "My house is in every way the best and most comfortable in camp. It is situated on the extreme flank on a high mound by the roadside. It faces away from the camp and in front there is really a very pretty view of trees and undulating ground in the distance, whilst nearer, the ground is broken and raviny, with patches of trees all about." He admitted, though, that "one gets very selfish living by oneself in the jungles."

All during this period, his mother continued her religious remonstrances with him, particularly urging him to proselyte: "Do talk to your people, my darling son—you have acquired the tongue, *use* it to tell of the Saviour & the law of God. I am persuaded that the Christians in India should do this. I often feel grieved with myself for not trying to do so to the few poor creatures about me oftener than I do." She seemed to feel that Watson was a backslider, for she wrote a few weeks later: "I have been thinking much of these injunctions of our blessed Lord. Oh that you, my darling son, may think of them and obey them . . . we must receive the kingdom of heaven as a little child. What volumes that speaks—implicit faith, unquestioning, undoubting as a little child has in its kind Father's words. Satan would prompt questioning doubts, wanting finite man to reason with omnipotence. Christ says receive these glad tidings with faith, the faith of a little child."

Despite this apparent concern for the natives' religious persuasions, she was still a thoroughgoing racist. Edward had had difficulty with some of his younger officers, and there had been a court of inquiry, with a native jeweler as the complaining party. The latter was exhibiting some of his goods to the young men, and they had played tricks and pretended to hide them and snatch them away. He vowed that he had lost five hundred rupees' worth of his goods. Sarah Watson's response, as she wrote her son, was that "it is very wrong to take native evidence against European gentlemen."

Despite all of the string-pulling on the appointment by both mother and son, the chances continued to look poor. In mid-August he wrote, "I have now nearly given up all hope of anyone troubling themselves to assist me." His recalcitrance on some of his earlier appointment opportunities now came back to haunt him: "Anything in the Punjab as long as Sir Lawrence is there is not to be thought of. He evidently recollects my having refused the appointment he gave me." By mid-September he was becoming a bit paranoiac about the job search: "I have felt very disinclined to work and have generally ridden instead. The anxiety I feel about an appointment makes me shun society." By the end of September he wrote: "I sometimes think there may be some secret cause for my not hearing. I do not think anyone who knows me would think me capable of holding an appointment. I find it more difficult every day to bear the suspense patiently and often feel very low spirited." He now began to doubt his every move: "I received a line from the Mly. Secy. in answer to my letter. He merely says that the levy at Meerut are not police and that appointments in it are the gift of the C-in-C only. I am nervous lest my letter to Major Williams should have done harm."

In mid-October Watson suddenly had his assignment in Oudh changed. He was given command of a unit of 130 men in Hodson's Horse. It was not a regular unit but rather an assortment of artillery, cavalry, and infantry. He seemed pleased: "The men I am commanding are a queer lot . . . some of them very noisy characters. But the sergeants are good men. I think I shall get along very well."[16]

There still were substantial hostilities in these waning weeks of 1858. The unit Watson had joined was headed by Brigadier Wetherall, with instructions from Hope Grant to take a fort at Rampore, some ninety miles south and east of Lucknow. Wetherall was under orders from Grant to wait until the latter's forces arrived to join him before attacking the fort. Rashly, though, Wetherall decided to attack on his own (he had been given information by a spy that there was a momentary weakness on one side of the fort, and so made the decision to strike quickly). Fortunately for Wetherall's reputation, the fort's weak point allowed a breach, and the British were quickly successful (albeit with a loss of some seventy-eight killed and wounded). Forrest, reporting on this incident in his *History,* was uncomplimentary: "The taking of the fort and entrenchments was a gallant affair, but it was a mistake on the part of the commander. By not doing what the Commander-in-Chief had planned he allowed a large body of rebels to escape . . . the Chief's anger was great when he heard of Wetherall's disregard of the instructions." When Grant joined Wetherall, the combined forces then moved to attack the fort of the rajah of Amethee. This time the rebel leader decided not to make a fight of it and surrendered without hostilities.[17]

Watson's involvement in the skirmish at Rampore turned out to be his only substantial battle experience in the whole of his mutiny service. Apparently he did well enough in the engagement to be mentioned in dispatches for having commanded "in an efficient manner and as having been of service in obtaining information." Nevertheless, something had gone wrong in his handling of the unit, for in late November he had his command taken away from him. He wrote his mother, "I do not grieve at all at the loss of my command of the 138 irregulars, for I have seen quite enough of their fighting never to wish to be in action with them again." His sensitivity to criticism led him to add, "Do not say that I say this for it would not do to give Hodson's Horse a bad name."

Watson now reverted to his job as treasurer and interpreter. In early December he was sent back with his unit to cantonment in Lucknow. It was a safe post, but still his mother continued to press for his return. She wrote in early 1859: "Perhaps I too much desire the comfort in the evenings of my oft troubled day to have you with me. I do not doubt the love of my other precious children but I believe no earthly being now loves and understands me as you do, my darling, good kind son."[18] Then, after the months of scheming and planning by mother and son, to their mutual amazement Thomas Watson *did* obtain a temporary post as adjutant in the Meerut Levy and once more was reunited with his mother.

It remains now only to see the last of our four, George Cracklow, into relief. Finally, he, too, was given leave from the fighting forces.

In February 1859 his unit headed north toward Umballa, and he wrote his mother, "By the time we come to the end of our journey I shall have marched nearly 3,000 miles since I started in May 1857, and with the exception of a month, just before the mutiny I have not lived in a house for nearly 3 years . . . I feel in a very restless, discontented state and have done so for a long time. Nothing but a year or so in England will set me all right, but I see little chance of it until 1862."

Upon arriving in Umballa, he was given leave to go to the hill station of Simla, and his spirits rose. He put up with friends at "the Club" and wrote: "The quarters are comfortable. There are a nice set of fellows in the house. Table is good and everything very expensive . . . the hills are at this time looking lovely and the climate cannot be surpassed. It is so cold that I am wearing all my warmest clothing and we have fires in our rooms. Out-of-doors bright sunshine and the most delicious air. It is a blessed thing, a little enjoyment of this sort after the hot season under canvas . . . at present, few people here and not much gaiety going on, but in a short time when people have shaken down a little there will be lots of fun." Apparently his mother had asked him in an earlier letter whether he had "liberated" any treasures during his many battles. "About the loot," he replied, "I got 1 dozen of beer and 2 loaves of sugar at the fort of Malagarh, and at the assault of Delhi I got a horse . . . riderless horses had galloped in and as there was no one to own him, he was made over to me. This is the brute I was riding that day at Bulandshahr, so I did not get much good out of him. My third piece of loot was the cloak of a trooper I shot at Gordaspore . . . I have a number of battery medals I've taken off men I have had the pleasure of putting an end to but they hardly count as loot." It was, indeed, not much for all that time.

Cracklow complained of constant headaches and now wanted to go home: "It would do me all the good in the world to get home for a year or so but as I am not thin and weak looking and have a little colour in my face (which is rather scarce here) the doctors all laugh at me even if I mention the subject of Sick Certificate. 7 years is quite long enough to be out here at a time. It's an infamous thing, keeping us here." He still felt unenthusiastic about matrimony: "I don't at all fancy the idea of toiling away in this country whilst my wife is kicking her heels in the hills or at home in which it always ends, as after 3 or 4 years out here if the woman does not become sick herself she has to take home the children . . . I dread the idea of getting married."[19] No one could blame him for these negative thoughts amid Simla's beauties, given the twenty-two months of tension.

Chapter 10
A Mutiny's Legacy

We have followed four young men, each going through the same great drama. What were the effects of the mutiny on them? What eventually happened to them (and to Sarah Watson)?

Fred Roberts is the easiest to trace. Indeed, the scope of accomplishment in his subsequent career makes summarizing it succinctly somewhat difficult. We left Roberts on board the Peninsula and Orient steamer *Nubia,* heading away from the hostilities and toward a long leave in England. He arrived in late June 1858 and found his father, the general, "hale and hearty at seventy-four," his mother "almost as young and quite as beautiful." Roberts wintered in Ireland, hunting often with the Waterford Hounds. He had told his sister Harriet the previous Christmas, at the height of the mutiny, to "look out for some nice girl with 'blue eyes and yellow hair' for me, Harriet dearest, who will console me for having to return to the gorgeous East." A romance soon blossomed (history has lost whether Harriet helped), and in May Roberts married Nora Bews, tenth and youngest child of a retired officer. She became his lifelong mate. In early June he and Nora were summoned to Buckingham Palace, where Her Majesty decorated him with the Victoria Cross. Three weeks later they were aboard ship to India.[1]

Roberts continued in his outstanding army career. He was a captain in 1860 and a major general at the end of 1878, just in time for the Second Afghan War (1878–1880). The first war of this name, in 1839–1842, had witnessed a popular uprising that led to the murder of the incumbent British resident and the destruction of the British army in the country (with only one survivor in a ghastly evacuation from Kabul). The second war began in 1878 with a mutiny by soldiers of the Afghan regular army stationed in Kabul, who then joined with a local mob to sack the British residency. The resident and all his escort were massacred. British troops were sent to the country to avenge the murders but, as invaders, soon found themselves with a full-scale war on their hands. Amid mixed feelings about the whole campaign back in England, the British finally held sway and eastern Afghanistan became quiet.

Unfortunately, though, southern and western Afghanistan were not subdued. A British force at Kandahar soon was almost overwhelmed, and memories surfaced of the debacle in 1842. At this point, in August 1880, the besieged, decimated British forces were relieved and saved by a column under Roberts, who led one of the most famous military exploits of all British Indian history. He put together a highly mobile column, and in twenty days, with only one day's rest, he and his men covered 280 miles. It was an endeavor made to order to be noticed. Upon arrival, Roberts's forces took on the besiegers, and the latter were routed and most of the Afghan camp captured. This episode ended the Second Afghan War, and the remaining troops of the Indian army were withdrawn from Afghanistan the following May.

Though sober military analysis later reassessed his military exploits, bringing them down from their first Olympian heights to the level of a good, smart campaign, Roberts's reputation remained bigger than life. By 1885 he was commander in chief in India; he held this post until 1893.

Roberts came back to England in 1893 in retirement, to the adulation of the British public. They loved the "lithe, soldierly little figure with his extraordinary directness and simplicity," as one biographer put it.[2] At this point a singular literary event pushed him into even greater prominence. Rudyard Kipling published in this year his doggerel poem "Bobs," set to a popular tune of the day, "Samuel Hall." The ode is important enough for us to take the space here for its entirety:

> There's a little red-faced man,
>   Which is Bobs,
> Rides the tallest 'orse 'e can—
>   *Our* Bobs,
> If it bucks or kicks or rears,

'E can sit for twenty years
With a smile round both 'is ears—
   Can't yer, Bobs?

Then 'ere's to Bobs Bahadur—little Bobs, Bobs, Bobs!
'E's our pukka Kandaharder—
Fightin' Bobs, Bobs, Bobs!
'E's the Dook of "Aggy Chel";
'E's the man that done us well,
An' we'll follow 'im to 'ell—
   Won't we, Bobs?

If a limber's slipped a trace,
   'Ook on Bobs.
If a marker's lost 'is place,
   Dress by Bobs.
For 'e's eyes all up 'is coat,
An' a bugle in 'is throat,
An' you will not play the goat
   Under Bobs.

'E's a little down on drink,
   Chaplain Bobs;
But it keeps us outer Clink—
   Don't it, Bobs?
So we will not complain
Tho' 'e's water on the brain,
If 'e leads us straight again—
   Blue-light Bobs.

If you stood 'im on 'his head,
   Father Bobs,
You could spill a quart of lead
   Outer Bobs.
'E's been at it thirty years,
An-amassin' souveneers
In the way o' slugs an' spears—
   Ain't yer, Bobs?

What 'e does not know o' war,
   Gen'ral Bobs,
You can arst the shop next door—
   Can't they, Bobs?
O, 'e's little but he's wise,

'E's a terror for 'is size,
An'—'e—*does*—*not*—*advertise*—
    Do yer, Bobs?

Now they've made a bloomin' Lord
    Outer Bobs,
Which was but 'is fair reward—
    Weren't it, Bobs?
So 'e'll wear a coronet
Where 'is 'elmet used to set;
But we know you won't forget—
    Will yer, Bobs?

Then 'ere's to Bobs Bahadur—little Bobs, Bobs, Bobs,
Pocket-Wellinton 'an arder—
Fightin' Bobs, Bobs, Bobs!
This ain't no bloomin' ode,
But you've 'elped the soldier's load,
An' for benefits bestowed,
    Bless yer, Bobs![3]

Kipling meant to send some telegrams here, and by the time one is finished with "Bobs," a word picture of Roberts the general has emerged. To start with, there was his horse, Vonolel (named after a legendary native chieftain in Assam); Roberts obtained this steed in 1871 and rode him to glory at Kandahar and for countless subsequent ceremonial parades the length and breadth of India. It was a small horse (the first stanza of the poem to the contrary), a grey Arab; "this grand horse," said one of Roberts's biographers, "ranks with Bucephalus, Copenhagen and Marengo among famous chargers . . . almost the last famous war charger the world would see." Vonolel was brought back to England when Roberts retired and was decorated by the queen; his "good looks and high spirits were quite enough to endear him to an English crowd." The great horse died in 1899, at the age of twenty-seven-plus.

It was not just the horse and the other trappings that endeared Roberts. Here was a genuine soldier, many times wounded in battle, one who was strict but always sticking by the enlisted man; a teetotaler, "Blue-light Bobs," but always watching out for his troops' perquisites and necessities; a strategist, a real leader, yet still giving the appearance of being modest (". . . 'e does not advertise"). So it was, as the *Madras Times* put it, "'Bobs, Bobs, Bobs' on the hoarding at the music halls, everywhere it is 'Bobs, Bobs, Bobs,' just as it used to be 'ta-ra' and 'Bow-Wow.'" England had a hero, the genuine article.

Roberts had been tendered a peerage in 1892; now he took his seat in the House of Lords. He spoke widely, but always apolitically, on all manner of issues relating to the armed forces. Given the honorary title of Commander of the Forces in Ireland in 1895, the old soldier seemed to fit easily into his role as senior statesman of military matters.

But there remained another chapter in the Roberts story, an amazing one. The Boer War had begun in South Africa in 1899. The early stages went poorly for the British, and the setbacks soon brought personal tragedy to Roberts. In one of the losing battles of that first year of the war, Roberts's son, Lieutenant Fred Roberts, was mortally wounded; he died a day later. The very next day after this tragic news, Roberts himself was appointed commander in chief of the British forces in South Africa and, at age sixty-seven, left for there forthwith.

The Boer War was very complicated, and I will attempt no summary. The simple fact was that the fortunes of the British turned around under the leadership of Roberts. By the end of 1900 the British forces under Roberts and his chief of staff, Herbert Kitchener, had defeated the Boer armies. There followed an eighteen-month guerilla war, but finally this resistance, too, was overwhelmed, the Boer leaders Louis Botha and Jan Smuts agreed to negotiations, and a peace treaty resulted.

The Boer War visibly enhanced the Roberts reputation. He was knighted as Lord Roberts of Kandahar, Pretoria, and Waterford and returned to his honorific posts in England.

Roberts was to see still another armed conflict. Right at the start of the Great War in 1914, an Indian division landed at Marseilles, along with many other troops whom Roberts knew from firsthand leadership. He was manifestly too old to step back into a leadership post, but it seemed eminently right that he should visit the front. So he and his elder daughter, Aileen, were brought over by the government in early November 1914 for a moving, highly personal visit to a number of units, right at their battle stations. Tragically, Roberts caught pneumonia while at the front and died just a day or so later, right there. It was tragic, yes, but it also seemed right: he had gone to France to see the Indian Army he loved, had met just about all of his old friends, and had died, as his biographer put it, "in the midst of the Army he had served for sixty-three years."[4]

Our other three lieutenants combined did not have nearly the excitement of the Roberts post-mutiny saga. George Cracklow was, after all, allowed the leave to England that he had forsworn; in early 1860 he was sent back in charge of a contingent of discharged men. He was there just two months. Writing his mother from Aden in May, on the return trip, he was already awaiting with trepidation another summer in India: "I am gradually becoming a barbarian again. My two months in England has polished me up a very little, but I am gradually sinking back into the old Indian habits . . . I have been rather miserable since the intense heat has come on and begin to regret that I did not take good advice and get an extension."

He continued in a more pessimistic vein: "I am also beginning to find out that I am a deal too long-headed. This looking to the future is, I am inclined to think, a mistake. I have always done so and do not seem to have half the fun that other fellows do who never look beyond the present." There were a number of good-looking young ladies aboard the boat, many of them probably members of the matrimonially minded "Fishing Fleet." As a matter of fact, said Cracklow, the young women on the boat were "exceedingly larky." Still, he continued his near-misogynist ways: "However, I do not feel much inclined to join in the fun, and not having spoken to one of them yet, in consequence am considered rather a brute. They have generally the most distinguishedly high spirits, are perpetually shrieking with laughter, making a horrid noise and are a perfect nuisance." As the ship approached Ceylon a few weeks later, he reported a new stage: "The passengers as usual from having been awfully fond of each other have all quarreled. The rows the women have are something quite astonishing."

Cracklow had been ordered to an outstation, Jubblapore, far down in the central provinces, but after he had left Calcutta on the way to the station, a telegram came shifting him to a better post, Muttra, about thirty miles from Agra. Even this good news failed to revive his spirits, and he wrote in late June from Agra: "The days spent alone in the dak bungalows with nothing to do but lie and think of home and curse one's fate. Unable to sleep and forget one's existence, uneatable food and perpetual thirst." He continued, overtly suicidal: "I have frequently felt inclined to end it all with a shot from my revolver. It is only looking forward to 1862 that has prevented me, I believe. I wish now I had never been home at all."

When he arrived in Muttra in July, he found a destroyed station, one of the worst hit in the mutiny. Housing was scarce and he wrote: "Can't get everything for the mere asking as formerly. It is rather lucky I did not get married, eh?" He described his life: "The weather has been intensely hot, not getting out of the house after 8:00 this morning. I don't know whether this is much of a deprivation, as there is nothing to do, no amusement of any sort in this weather. The whole place is a sort of howling desert at present, just a plain of sand over which you can't see 50 yards for the dust." He ended again on a low note: "10,000 pounds a year would not recompense one for such a life . . . What is to be the end of it?" He did not write again for several weeks, and then apologized: "I was so taken aback by the intense dreariness of the whole thing that I regularly collapsed and hardly spoke for a week. I am now gradually subsiding and find myself sometimes positively laughing at the abject misery of the whole thing. I think I shall become cracked some day."

His mother apparently had had an accident; Cracklow wrote feelingly about it and then continued: "I have had a bit of mishap myself coming home one very dark night . . . my horse shied at a man going along with a lantern. I was mooning along stupidly not thinking of what I was doing and got a bad fall, right on my head. I was insensible for a short time but the doctor soon set me to rights."

By October his spirits had sagged further: "The men are low spirited and down on their luck. I am regularly sick of the whole thing, country, service and prospects. I take no interest in anything connected with my duty—one cannot with the grumbling, insubordinate set of brutes we have to deal with."

Then, in November, personal disaster struck: "I had been rather unwell and in low spirits for some time, previously to the 13th of last month, when as I was sitting alone in the bungalow on the evening of that day I suddenly began to feel very ill. I had just time to get to my bed when I had a paralytic fit. I just managed to make the servant understand that he was to fetch the doctor, but before he came I had another fit and after this I found that my left leg and arm were quite paralysed." This letter was written several weeks later, and by this time he was able to use his leg some, with the aid of a crutch, but still had no movement whatsoever in his arm (nor did it ever return). The doctors felt that there was a link between the earlier fall and the paralytic seizure; Cracklow had a more personal view of the cause: "This illness will have some good for me after all, dear mommy. It seems a sort of judgment on me for the bad life I have led. I hope if I recover my strength, to lead a better one for the future." This is a puzzling comment. He *was* unhappy, likely even clinically depressed, but, judging at least by the letters, moral and generally good in what he did.

He apparently had left England with a serious romantic attachment, but now he wrote: "I think you had better write and tell Minnie that she had better not trouble her head any more about me . . . it would have been a deal better to have been killed in action than to have been crippled for life." Perhaps he was rationalizing to himself as he continued about the young woman: "I am pretty much of your opinion now about that affair, having got over the feeling nearly. I do not think it would be a very advantageous arrangement. I hope she will not be very much disappointed. She has no one to blame but herself. The matter would never have gone so far had she not forced it."

Cracklow returned to England soon after and went on medical leave; the record becomes skimpy from here on. The Bengal Military Fund Ledger records that he retired on January 13, 1864. On February 14, 1867, he married Harriet Agnew. In his will, written in October 1874, he mentioned two sons, Reginald William, "to whom I give my gold watch and chain," and Charles Reginot, "my gold signet ring." Another son was born in 1878; Cracklow himself died on February 17 of that year at Cheltenham, England. He was forty-six years old.[5]

Arthur Lang had the longest life of the four, dying in retirement in Guildford, England, in August 1916, in his eighty-fourth year. When he returned to the Public Works Department in 1858 he was given various posts in Oudh and the Punjab, concentrating primarily on road building. One of his most exciting jobs in that period was the construction of the road into Tibet: it was an incredible engineering feat to carve a narrow roadway from almost inaccessible rocky scarps, overlooking vertical cliffs into gorges thousands of feet deep.

In 1871, still a captain, Lang was appointed principal of the Thomason Civil Engineering College at Roorkee, in central Oudh. He stayed at Thomason until 1878, in the process helping to train a group of young engineers who later became quite famous in India. He also rewrote the treatise on civil engineering. Lang still loved sports and played rugby with the young students as their equal (he was in his forties by this time). One of the students commented: "We played a very rough Rugby game, and he was the neatest 'hacker' I ever saw. In those days I was a heavy forward, weighing over 13 stone, and fast, but Lang would back me off my legs with the greatest ease and precision."

After leaving Thomason College, as a lieutenant colonel, Lang took several major posts in engineering, both in Oudh and the North West Provinces and also in Burma. He retired in 1887. We noted earlier a quotation from his obituary about this work: "As an engineer he made no particular mark in India . . . Colonel Lang, in most of his service, was in the buildings and roads branch, which lent itself less to the distribution of honours and distinction."

If, indeed, the work itself was prosaic, Lang became greatly beloved as a human being. He was married three times—he lost two wives from sickness in India, an all-too-common experience. He left a widow and nine children; the three sons were all in the army. His twenty-nine years of retirement were apparently happy but uneventful. His obituaries mention his "bright, unspoilt temperament" and his "unfailing tact." He was considered to have charming but frank manners and to be "an earnest and sincere Christian." One of his friends said of him, "He was one of those men who could not be gloomy and dismal if he tried." The final epitaph perhaps put it best: he was "a true gentleman."[6]

Thomas Watson has always been the most elusive of our four lieutenants. We are fortunate to have extensive correspondence from both him and his mother for the mutiny period; there is no extant correspondence beyond this time. We do know that his mother died in 1874, at age seventy-six; his sister, Annie Atlay, died much earlier, in 1859, at age twenty-five. Watson's military records give us the bare outlines of his subsequent career. We had left him in his temporary post as adjutant in Meerut, a spot he coveted in order to get back to his mother. He went from there to the 17th Bengal Cavalry, and he stayed for the rest of his career with various units of the Bengal Cavalry. He retired with a "colonel's allowance" in 1883, having attained the rank of lieutenant colonel; in 1892 he was tendered the honorary rank of major general. The skimpy records for this whole period show only that he had participated in the "Bhootan expedition" (a minor skirmish in 1865) and had served on the eastern front in the Second Afghan War, but had seen little action there. He was married in 1861 at age twenty-nine, to Mary Green, who was seventeen. Interestingly, George Bourchier was one of the witnesses—apparently the tiff between Mrs. Bourchier and Mrs. Watson had been ameliorated! Watson had four children; his only son went into the service in India, and in 1897, as a lieutenant, won the Victoria Cross in a skirmish at Bilot, on the North West Frontier. Watson himself retired to Tasmania and died there in 1905. He was sixty-nine years old.[7]

* * *

Despite a paucity of documentation for everyone except Roberts in these later years, the record from their mutiny letters is indeed comprehensive. We know these five people well. What observations, hypotheses, and lessons might we derive from this rich source of human interactions?

It is tempting to paint with a broad brush. The decade of these letters was one of the heights of Victorianism—"Victoria's heyday," as J. B. Priestley put it. The queen's adored consort, Albert, was still living, and her dominion seemed at its apogee. Victorianism as we think of it today had many roots in this drama-filled decade. Victoria began her reign in 1837, when the four lieutenants were all five years old. She died in 1901, by which time Cracklow was dead, Roberts was still playing out his final great act in the Boer War, and Lang and Watson had been retired for a number of years. So the period of Victoria dominated their lives.

We start with certain commonalities, some of which have come up earlier. All four came from families rooted in India; three of the fathers were army officers in India, the fourth a civil servant there. Roberts was separated from his father from age two, having been sent back to England to school. This was often the pattern in Victorian Britain: children separated from both their parents at a very early age. If a family resided in England, at least the young man could get home at holiday; if the parents were in India, the physical separation often stretched into years. Roberts's father was a general, both a Knight Commander of the Bath and a Knight Grand Cross of the Bath in retirement; he lived to his ninetieth year. Cracklow's father, a captain, died in Cracklow's infancy. Lang's letters during the mutiny were written back to his mother in England; it is not clear whether he was sent back to England from India in his early school days. The early school days of Thomas Watson, too, are unclear; his father, a lieutenant colonel, was dead by the time Watson became an officer in 1851; his mother at that time resided at Simla, so Watson had probably been sent back to England alone to school.

An important thread is that all four went to English public schools in the 1840s, and two of them, Roberts and Lang, to top-ranked institutions. These school experiences must have had profound influence on the four lieutenants, as they did on just about all of their contemporaries. As noted in chapter 2, public schools came under sharp attack with the investigations of the Clarendon Commission in 1861. This became a thoroughgoing search, looking into both administration and finance as well as methods of instruction and other student-related aspects. It was not the first reform effort directed at the public schools in this period, but it turned out to be a watershed. Indeed, it mirrored a profound change in life and society in England that had begun to happen about the time of Victoria's accession and that now became much heightened. As John Chandos put it in his excellent *Boys Together: English Public Schools, 1800–1864,* "The intemperate licence and wild escapades that had characterized public-school life began to become an anachronism in a world of increasing orderliness and standardized public propriety."[8] The reform movement had picked up steam in the 1840s, and the 1850s had witnessed a reining in of juvenile liberty within the public schools. Our four lieutenants, who were in these schools in the 1840s, were undoubtably subject to aspects of both the earlier and the later styles—on the one hand, the extremes of student self-government (fagging, birching, etc.), and on the other, the tighter constraint that resulted from the heightened "Victorianism" (if that loose phrase can be used here) characterizing the period from the 1850s on. David Roberts's *Paternalism in Early Victorian England* called it "that prosperity and ordered life which dominated Victorian England from 1848 to 1900."[9]

The evocative, seminal book *Tom Brown's Schooldays* came out in 1857 to enormous public acclaim as a true characterization of public school life. It captured the essence of the public school, albeit with the edges rounded and the surfaces sandpapered. The friendship between the younger boy, Tom, and the upperclassman, Brooke, was idealized, the bully Flashman pictured in stark detail. Cracklow had obtained a copy of the book almost as soon as it was published and was reading it all through the battle period in the spring of 1858. He wrote his mother, "There's a book called *Tom Brown's Schooldays* which somebody lent me the other day to amuse myself with on piquet, which would be just the thing for Georgy. Get it for him and give it to him in my name."

In truth, the public school realities of the first half of the nineteenth century were considerably more primitive than pictured by Thomas Hughes in the Tom Brown book. I discussed flogging earlier in this book as a frequent event in the army, a practice in turn mirroring the widespread birching in the public schools. The fagging system (a younger minion serving an upperclass boy) was widely considered a mechanism for bringing order through self-administration by the students and for preventing the excesses of bullies like Flashman. Yet, as Chandos points out, more than infrequently it led to homosexual relationships, a subject of greatly heightened concern to the reformist mentality of the 1850s: "The kind of Dickensian suppression used in *Oliver Twist* to disguise the real nocturnal activities of Nancy was used in *Tom Brown's Schooldays* to conceal some of the real activities of Flashman and his like at Rugby but the author well knew of their existence and, thirty years later, when the emotional pressure had risen, we find him publishing anonymously a pamphlet addressed to boys on the subject of depravity." There seemed to be a pervasive avoidance of any discussion of sex among the English public by the mid-nineteenth century, a "see no evil, tell no evil" approach that today has come to define, simplistically, "Victorianism."[10]

As noted earlier, after Roberts, Cracklow, and Lang left public school they moved on to Addiscombe, the military seminary that prepared young officers for service in India. Thomas Watson did not; his commission was a direct one, obtained by a process of quasi-political patronage. This special aspect of Watson's career may, indeed, have had a unique influence on his subsequent behavior—his lack of professional commitment, his lesser military acumen.

One final common experience linking the four lieutenants needs to be noted, namely, that all four were officers in the Indian Army, under almost exactly the same conditions, during the mutiny itself. All four as young officers were operating under the rubric of the East India Company (as distinguished from the queen's troops, the "Royals"). We noted earlier the strong negative features of low pay, lack of decent quarters, and constraints on marriage as profoundly important influences on the thinking of the young officers in India at that time. Boredom and frustration were endemic; the dangers of "Demon Rum" and gambling fever taking hold were always lurking. We have recounted chapter and verse from all four of these men about these complicating special features of service life in India.

Armchair hypothesizing in any depth about our four lieutenants (and the one mother) on the basis only of their letters written in their mid-twenties, with no corroborative material from any of the four from their schoolboy days, legitimately would be considered arrant nonsense. While it is widely assumed by laypersons and psychologists alike that cognitive expressions of behavior reflect underlying psychological characteristics or traits, yet the process of drawing accurate inferences about such characteristics is fraught with difficulty. To interpret the behavior of an individual in a given situation, we need to know how the individual acts in similar and in dissimilar situations, how others react in similar situations, and how the individual has acted *in the past* in the same situation. In other words, we need to see the world through the person's eyes as well as through our own. We need to be able to distinguish situational from personal causes of behavior and to separate stable personal causes like traits from unstable moods. Much of this background detail is not available for the four lieutenants and the mother: there is too little information, and there are too few with whom to compare, to be firm in our generalizations.

Even were a great deal more be known about these five, the question remains whether a historian can competently do a psychohistorical analysis of a person or people not living and therefore not available for personal query. Indeed, the professional establishment of historians has attacked the field of psychohistory with a vengeance. Peter Gay, the eminent Yale historian, has put it well: "The syllabus of errors rehearsing the offenses of psychohistory looks devastating and seems irrefutable: crimes against the English language, crimes against scientific procedures, crimes against commonsense itself . . . to summarize these objections, psychohistory is Utopian, vulgar and trivial." David Stannard, in his angry book *Shrinking History,* is even blunter: "Psychohistory does not work and cannot work. The time has come to face the fact that, behind all its rhetorical posturing, the psychoanalytic approach to history is—irremediably—one of logical perversity, scientific unsoundness, and cultural naïveté." Nonetheless, Gay concludes that although "the historian intent on mapping the course of mind in the past needs a fine pen and a powerful eraser . . . however difficult his work and problematic his discoveries, the historian can only profit from acting as though Clio is analyzable after all."[11]

I must eschew joining this debate, for my data are not wide-ranging enough for any one of the five correspondents to be a choice for psychohistory. But I should note once again that I did have a special helper in trying to assess the five—the computer.

The quantitative, computer-driven analysis initiated for this book proved to be useful, and the reader is urged to look at the Appendixes for specific details. My colleagues and I generated a number of interesting new methods in this effort, and I feel comfortable with the quality of the findings. The computer analysis did produce significant additions, for it made me rethink and restate a number of earlier subjective judgments about the letters. However, I continued to warn myself throughout this statistical effort that I was dealing with five people about whom I knew far too little. Indeed, my colleagues in the computer work, professors of psychiatry at Dartmouth Medical School using the same computer-based content analysis to study modern-day schizophrenia, have warned me to be most cautious in generalizing about personal, psychological traits among the correspondents.

Yet while the story recounts a vivid composite picture of the place and events, it remains the sharply drawn differences among these five people that stand out in their letters. Let us take each one of the five and, without psychoanalyzing, let them speak for themselves about their own feelings.

First, Frederick Roberts. Here, always, is a man on the move. There is a verve, a sense of excitement, a real *joie de vivre* permeating the Roberts letters. He had a lip-smacking excitement about battle, a self-conscious, extremely confident view about moving through the ghastly events he encountered. There seems no doubt whatsoever of his courage. Early in the war, in the skirmish before Delhi, he recounted to his mother and father in a frank way some of the atrocities and harsh retributions, yet in the next breath he continued: "Don't think I am in low spirits, darling Mother, writing as I do, very far from it. I could not be jollier." Right from the start he expressed the soldier's fatalism about battle: "One does not mind Officers being killed so much, it is more or less expected to be the fate of soldiers."

When he first arrived at Delhi in June of 1857, he soon was wounded in a skirmish, hit in the back but saved from a fatal shot by the bullet's deflection into a pouch on his belt. "Am I not a lucky fellow, my own mother, and has not God been merciful to me, I can never be sufficiently thankful." He wrote later that the wound took many weeks to heal and he was frustrated, for he could not ride his horse: "However, I am very jolly and happy and appreciate my luck and feel thankful to God when I see so many poor fellows around me infinitely worse off."

It was courage for a purpose, though, for Roberts saw clearly the great opportunity for his career in these exploits. He wanted to be in every battle, not for the joy of combat and the thrill of killing but for the opportunity to be "ubiquitous"—to be noticeably out in front everywhere, with dash. Indeed, he used that word in describing some of his cavalry colleagues: "I've seen enough to convince me that they are all show, as far as actual fighting . . . on the few occasions I've seen them out, they have always disappointed me, European as well as Native, not half the dash they ought to have. I can't understand the reason. Officers I know personally to be fine plucky fellows, have lost splendid chances of a good charge from merely hesitating."

Arthur Lang had much of this enthusiasm for battle, but from a very different perspective, as we shall see in a moment; he seemed not personally ambitious. Roberts, on the other hand, was almost the epitome of ambition; almost everything he did seems to have been an effort to further his career. Indeed, Roberts was relentless in his pursuit of advancement. In nearly every one of his letters there are remarks about his assignments, his promotions, and his hopes for furtherment. Particularly evident is his abiding desire to win the Victoria Cross. Back before the Battle of Delhi it was "What I want more than any other is the *Victoria Cross*. Oh! If I can only manage that, how jolly I should be." After both Delhi and Lucknow it was "We are very anxious about *Medals* . . . fancy having two!" Just after the first of the year 1858 he was nominated for the Cross and wrote: "My own mother, I have such a piece of news for you. I have been recommended for the '*Victoria Cross*' . . . Is this not glorious . . . *such a medal to wear* with '*For Valour*' scrolled on it. How proud I shall be . . . few, very few, this glorious Cross."

Yet his was not unbridled ambition; Roberts had more to him than just a raw desire for personal advancement. He unerringly picked the quartermaster job, among several openings available to him, as the best spot to participate in and learn about military tactics and strategies. He had a feeling for tactics in both his own personal combat experiences and those of his whole unit. He evidenced a keen sense of "place"—it was not just that he wanted himself to be seen in the right places (though he certainly did), but he was able to place the whole unit in its context. Moreover, he had also an embryonic sense of overall, longer-term strategic concerns. Others in that small contingent of British soldiers at Delhi's gates were raging for attack and criticizing the leadership for timidity. He commented in August 1857: "Even in this Country several cry out to take Delhi, without any more delay, as if we were not one and all anxious to do so, but the fate of all India depends on our success. Were a failure to be the result, God only knows what would take place." Like Lang and Cracklow, he could be critical of superior officers, but he appears to have liked soldiering primarily for what it was and could get for him, less for the excitement it provided.

Roberts was not infallible in his military judgments; there was the embarrassing gaffe at Agra in October 1857, where he took others' words about enemy strength around the town and thus left the force open to an enemy sneak attack that almost became extremely serious. In this case, Roberts probably was eager to visit inside the big fort and renew old acquaintances (he *was* there when the surprise assault took place). Yet there was no self-recrimination; he was able to spread the blame around by his detailed report to his commander; the Roberts instinct for organizational gamesmanship included an ability to cover himself. We can infer another questionable move, though there is no way to prove it: that Roberts manipulated his own leave just after the second Battle of Lucknow—he seems to have planned it right on paper in a letter to his sister a few weeks earlier.

Slips aside, Roberts had a keen sense of self-discipline and expected it in others. When higher command ordered the "blowing from guns" as an especially devastating form of summary execution Roberts wrote, "It is rather a horrible sight, but in these times we cannot be particular. Drum-Head Courts-Marshal are the order of the day in every station, and had they begun this regime a little earlier, one-half of the destruction and mutiny would have been saved." He was terribly shocked by the Cawnpore well, stuffed with Englishwomen and children, and wrote very harshly: "For a year or two, I would like to have charge of some very bad district to see if I could not break them in. Our civilians have ruined India by not punishing natives sufficiently, and by allowing all the rascals in the country to hold high offices in their Kutcherries."

At the same time, Roberts seemed always to take the side of the soldier. Others, for example, Lang and Cracklow, wrote scathingly about British cowardice and drunkenness. Roberts referred to these things only in passing and never disparagingly. I posited in an early chapter that this restraint might have been imposed because he was writing to a father who was a general and who would have been embarrassed by these events.

In these mutiny letters, at several points, Roberts recited in a matter-of-fact way his extending of compassion to the Indian civilians. He wrote his sister on one occasion: "I came on three women watching the dead bodies of their husbands, none of them Sepoys I believe. It was such a sad sight, however, that I felt quite unhappy . . . You must not think, darling Harriet, that I pity the Sepoys or black guards who are rebelling against us. On the contrary, few are more unrelenting than I am . . . But it does make one melancholy to come across such accidents as I have related. They cannot be expected to distinguish between the guilty and the innocent in the heat of the moment, yet such scenes make one wish that it was all settled." One of Roberts's fellow officers wrote of another incident just about this same time, in which Roberts had spared a civilian's house: "Roberts, who is as good as he is brave, gave directions for sparing the old man's house." There were several more of these at-the-time judgments about Roberts from his fellow officers, and they were uniformly complimentary, not only about Roberts's courage but also about his compassion.

Roberts seems to have had a romantic view of the opposite sex, though the few exhortations to his sister Harriet to "find him a blue-eyed blond girl" do not give us much of a clue about his real feelings. It certainly is not surprising that he found a young woman as soon as he returned to England. It is quite in keeping with what we know of him that he stayed happily married to her throughout his lifetime. (It is also not a surprise that George Cracklow did *not* marry until quite a few years later.)

Thus Roberts comes through with the appearance of a model young officer, just the mix of dash and caution, personal ambition and refined sense of organizational realities, that would make for a good professional soldier, a leader. A less charitable view might consider him overly manipulative. In either case, we can say that his meteoric, star-studded subsequent career must have had its roots right here in the mutiny; indeed, one might well have predicted that this was "a young man to watch." He as much as told us so!

The second lieutenant, George Cracklow, stands sharply in contrast to Roberts. His pre-mutiny letters give early clues about his perseverative behavior, his rigidness in adapting to changed circumstances. For example, in the high Himalayas, on leave, he encountered a raging storm with swollen rivers and streams, yet insisted on riding alone at night to his self-appointed rest stop. In the process he almost lost his horse, put himself in jeopardy, and was lucky to survive. Similarly, he went out game shooting in enemy territory around Christmas 1857, without any protection. Driven back by sharp enemy attack, he again almost lost his life senselessly.

During battle, there was no doubt about this young officer's courage. He was chauvinistic about England, speaking at several points about "British pluck"—"it will I have no doubt carry the day as it has hundreds of others against equal odds." He seemed pre-occupied almost to the point of distraction by what he saw as the lack of similar qualities in the enemy. He railed against "Pandy cow-ardice," though he defined it quite narrowly. Indeed, his own testi-mony chronicled many cases of enemy military abilities; what troubled him was that the enemy would not fight "in the open," would not "stand and fight." On the Delhi ridge he described the terrain as covered with trees and old walled gardens and ruined houses, adding, "This affords excellent shelter to the Pandies, who fight very well behind a wall but never think of coming out into the open." A few days later, the same theme recurred: "They never advance in line, charge or do anything boldly, but content them-selves with creeping around walls and trees and sniping our men from a distance." Before the second Battle of Lucknow he wrote: "It is most *devoutly* to be hoped that they will stand and that their hearts will not fail them at the last moment . . . The Sepoys fight well behind the walls but never stand a moment in the open." Cracklow had a very incomplete sense of guerrilla warfare and was vehement in his denigration of it (he seems particularly out-of-date here, for the British had had good lessons about this form of battle as early as the French and Indian War in America in the early 1760s).

Similarly, he pulled no punches in his castigation of cowardice in his men, fellow officers, or anyone else who seemed to be faltering in any way. He himself was a good soldier, followed orders, reacted well under pressure, and remained dispassionate about the horrors he experienced. He could not stomach weaknesses in others. When Nicholson fell at Delhi, Cracklow attributed his death to "some unaccountable backwardness of our Eighth and Seventy-fifth, who could not be persuaded to advance, though Lieutenant Briscoe sac-rificed himself . . . in a vain endeavour to arouse them. Nicholson's Europeans had the same recreancy when ordered to storm the Burn Bastion." He wrote his mother a few days later: "You will probably see them crowing in the papers about the gallant conduct of the British soldiers, so don't believe a word of it. Even when they were sober, they behaved some of them with the most rank cowardice . . . they on several occasions bolted from less than their own num-ber of niggers."

This latter word is another clue to Cracklow's mind-set, for his writings are laced throughout with racist accusations against the enemy. He seems vengeful and callous on many occasions; he ad-mitted as much to his mother in mid-1857: "I myself have become a regular Jack Vetch and think no more of stringing up or blowing away half a dozen mutineers before breakfast than I do of eating the same meal." He was harsh, too, with his superiors, a thread that seems to surface all through his letters. He was jealous of the Royals, fearful that they were going to take assignments from him and his fellow officers. The war seemed to sour him about British army leadership. He almost idolized Campbell at the start, but even the crusty old general came under his attack at the end. He felt that he himself was overworked (evidence seems to corroborate this perception) and commented scathingly upon some of his fellow officers for what he saw as favor seeking: "McLeod has been on the sick list ever since we left Lucknow . . . mugging up for a sick certificate, I think. A delightful state of affairs, isn't it." His description of his immediate superior, Money, is a classic: ". . . slack, slovenly-looking man . . . not at all a horse-artillery-like looking fellow . . . a great, pudgy, fat man of about five and forty—twenty-seven years in this country has made him a perfect nigger in thoughts and habits . . . slack in duty matters and slovenly in dress."

Yet even here Cracklow concluded his comments with the remark "I hope we shall get on well." He seems to have had a strong sense of pride in his unit and self-discipline about the job to be done.

Cracklow was prone in the later stages of the war to personal discouragement. He was pessimistic about his own chances to advance: "See what a nice thing it is to be Captain commanding instead of a subaltern officer who does all the hard work." He was cynical about the motives of the native populace, especially as the British began to extend clemency. He wanted revenge; often he would examine the bodies of enemy dead to see if any of them were from units he knew. He wanted the personal satisfaction of punishing individual people. Late in the war, in the period of clemency, he met a group of natives who had probably just given up their uniforms and become villagers: "We met a party of them today all with a kind of sneaking grin on their black faces at the way they were bamboozling us. I could hardly restrain myself from driving my sword through the man I spoke to. However, as he looked rather impertinent, I consoled myself with punching his Brahminical head until he hardly knew whether he stood on it or his heels. I do hate these fellows."

As the war went on, beyond the period of the glorious battles to

the petty skirmishes, Cracklow became more discouraged and discontented, more depressed and battle-fatigued: "I have become
perfectly indifferent to what they do with me." A few weeks later,
as the war wound down and he was moved to cantonment, he
talked of getting out of the service altogether: "I am thoroughly
sick of this business and would give something to get out of it. It's
a melancholy thing, having to spend the best years of one's life in
this beastly country . . . the life we are leading now is perfectly
fearful—no pleasure of any sort, no amusements, not even eatable
food."

Cracklow expressed an ambivalence toward women all through
his writings. He was vindictively bitter about their "dishonouring,"
yet when the contingent that had been beseiged in Lucknow was
rescued, he made several disparaging remarks about the women in
the group, and he considered them a hindrance: ". . . just incum-
brance to us, taking nearly half our men to guard them." He had
some sort of a romantic attachment with a woman whose name we
have only as Minnie; he saw her on his short leave in England in
1860. On his return to India he mentioned the young women on
the boat with him as "exceedingly larky," but he admitted acting
"rather a brute" toward them. When he got to his post at Muttra,
he reported on the bad housing conditions and continued, "It is
rather lucky that I did not get married, eh?" Then, when his seizure
came in November of that year, he was blunt in his rejection of the
young woman back home: "Write Minnie that she had better not
trouble her head anymore about me." His further gratuitous comment—"she has no one to blame but herself. The matter would
never have gone so far had she not forced it"—also seems surprisingly patronizing.

Of course, his seizure was a devastating blow to him; he had been
extremely active, dependent on his physical exercise to keep himself
on relatively even keel. Now this was gone. He expressed a curious
resignation about his paralysis, almost as in expiation: "It seems a
sort of judgement on me for the bad life I have led. I hope if I
recover my strength, to lead a better one for the future." It is not at
all clear from his letters just what was so "bad," but at least he felt
that something was.

Cracklow's letters in total portray an enigmatic man. There are
curious anomalies in his attitudes and actions: vindictive, harsh,

and judgmental at times, gentle and kind on other occasions (especially with his mother). His personal code of ethics, at least in his role as soldier, seems to have been very high. Yet *he* did not think so. He was excited by battle on many occasions, but he had a generally pessimistic view of life. Indeed, one might infer from his words a clinical depression at several stages, culminating in the blunt and overt threat of suicide after his return to India from the first leave: "I have frequently felt inclined to end it all with a shot from my revolver." This seems to have been an unhappy man, overly prone to worry and always thinking so far ahead that the present moment seemed insignificant and negative.

The medical reports on his seizure are very superficial; one cannot infer much from them. The ostensible cause was the fall from the horse and the subsequent concussion; the rheumatism he had often complained about could even have been an incipient case of rheumatic fever. If one adds up all of the signals throughout these letters, one can readily build a case that this was a person of extremely high inner tension, a prototypical example of someone suffering from what we today call stress. George Cracklow lived the shortest life of the four, and at least from what we can read here, the most unhappy.

The third lieutenant, Arthur Lang, fits believably into his own separate box; indeed, he seems the quintessential engineer. In the main he was detached about the battles and his role in them (though he did get carried away just before the assault on Delhi, when he signed his letter, "your most affectionate son, A.M. Lang who tomorrow will be field engineer 'avenging army,' camped before Dehli, the doomed city of the Moghuls, etc., etc."). He had a singular ability to be evocative about his physical surroundings, more than once describing a pitched battle and then in the next sentence waxing lyrical about the physical world he saw. He exhibited a keen descriptive ability all the way through, always cautioning his family about the excesses of hyperbole that others were sending forth about the mutiny and exhorting them to accept his more dispassionate view.

Lang was not only top in his class academically at Addiscombe, shortly before going out to India, but also a sports hero, both there and earlier at Rugby. References throughout his letters tell of playing one or another game right in the middle of the mutiny; the testimonial about him when he became head of Thomason College, in his forties, is one more example of his thoroughgoing enthusiasm for the "manly sports." Surprisingly, given this almost role-model position as a sports hero, he also had the intellectual's ability to wonder about things, rather than simply to assume them. He seems to have been preoccupied right from the start with whether his own personal courage would be up to the challenge. While Cracklow disparaged out-and-out cowardice, Lang was more sweeping in his denunciation of "Croakers" and others who exhibited in any way some fear. When some of the Europeans in his cantonment at the very start of the mutiny rushed to the fort for safety, Lang complimented those who remained in their own homes: "The Montgomeries alone stand firm in their isolated place and quite right they are too, I think." (Lang was not being very realistic here; many people in such isolated situations were murdered.) He was particularly vitriolic—this seems the right word choice—about some of the higher officers, whom he thought "funked," were too timid and fearful. He seemed to wonder if he himself would have these fears; for example, he wrote at the start of the mutiny: "The state of things I am very happy to find braces me up instead of depressing me or unstringing my nerves . . . The result shows me that a campaign would suit me, a fact I was not sure of . . . I find that actual danger or expectation of it, calms and 'irons me' at once."

At the beginning of the mutiny, Lang was engaged in a serious romance with the colonel's daughter, Sarah Boileau. He was genuinely torn about wanting to stay with her "in Mme. Boileau's drawing room playing 'La Ci Darem' and such like." He continued, "This is no time for men to be idling and shirking [in] this luxurious, dawdling cantonment life." There was, of course, no doubt about Lang's courage once the battles began; his action on the glacis at Delhi is only one example of several where he exhibited great personal courage and aplomb. There was an impetuousness about his actions under fire that sometimes seems excessive, as if he could react only within his own small personal arena, "see" only a few yards in any direction from himself. In the Battle of Delhi, for example, he recklessly wanted to cut his way further into the city, despite tactical orders not to do so until the Kabul Gate was secured.

Lang was just not a military tactician. He seemed to have a view of battle much akin to the sports field. We can wonder, still, why he liked fighting so much, particularly given his lack of overt expressions of competitiveness or deep hatred for the Sepoy (it might be fair to say that he was only moderately racist). Roberts and Cracklow expressed much more desire for revenge; the latter in particular seemed to fight out of anger, whereas Lang seemed to fight for fun and challenge.

By the end of the war, Lang appeared torn between the role of a battle soldier and that of an engineer. He wrote at that time, "I have had a fear of being sent to Benares, or of being kept at Cawnpore, as Ex. Engineer, to build Barracks, both hateful *in prospectu*." One wonders how he adapted back to the dull work of building roads, a task he was quickly put to at the end of the war. He did marry Sarah soon after, and from all indications this marriage and two subsequent ones were quite happy. Indeed, Lang seems to have become over his lifetime an ideally kind, thoughtful, open man, of even disposition and a friend to his fellows. He seems not to have been personally ambitious—his subsequent career was a slow, plodding one. His hobby interests were very strong: he became an authority on Himalayan and other Indian moths and butterflies, and he delighted in cultivating flowers. He also seemed little concerned about personal recognition. His position as, in effect, a civilian engineer in military uniform fitted him very well. He was, indeed, a gentleman!

Thomas Watson and his mother Sarah were two rather less attractive people, or at least so their letters make them seem during this period. Both appear at many points to have been self-centered to a fault. Our first view of her is her attempt to manipulate Watson's appointment as an officer in the East India Company army to fit the family's own travel plans. Her machinations aborted, and then she was uneasy in retrospect that she had tried to put pressure on the directors: "I feel anxious at having not taken your advice that the appointment should immediately be on its being given in November." This pattern of trying to manipulate events behind the scenes, being found out, and then in retrospect being sorry they tried is a thread through the letters of both all through the mutiny.

Most of these efforts were designed to obtain better appointments for Watson, better in most cases being defined as located closer to his mother. Sarah Watson's relations with her various "landladies" (in reality, other service wives willing to tender her a temporary home during the mutiny) were generally acrimonious. She seemed unable to get along with any of them. Similarly, Watson himself was a real loner. There are recurring references to spending his days "in my own tent reading," and he several times left the officers' mess to eat by himself. He was self-conscious about this tendency and often expressed feelings that almost seemed to be self-loathing: "Captain Bourchier was very cold and distant in his manner . . . FitzGerald, too, treats me in much the same way . . . he takes no notice of me." In this particular set of remarks he ended in a defiant vein: "I do not much care about this, for I have quite as much society as I care about in the regiment."

As he tried to pull strings to obtain appointments closer to his mother, he antagonized many of his superior officers. His worst faux pas was with his best chance, Gen. Hope Grant: "General Grant, I know, would do nothing to help me. His answer when I asked him was most decided, and I think he was vexed by my hinting at such a thing."

Unlike his mother, Watson had pervasive self-doubts, seemingly about any position in which he was given responsibility. In the case of the antagonizing of General Grant, he closed his letter to his mother reporting the sad turn of events: "I could never write a good letter. Indeed I can do nothing well." Previously he had expressed real doubts about being up to the job of provost, a position he had been given in early 1858. As a matter of fact, he lost this job at a later point. Similarly, he had a battle command for just one engagement; it was taken away, too. There was even some murky problem of inadequacy involving him back at the start of the mutiny, when his own cantonment at Sialkot was subject to its own personal mutiny. He did something, only hinted at in the letters, that came in for reprobation at a later date. Did his mistakes here give him a bad reputation? He expressed deep suspicion and self-dissatisfaction in one letter, when he wrote: "I sometimes think that there may be some secret cause for my not hearing. I do not think anyone who knows me would think me capable of holding an appointment."

Watson and his mother both articulated a number of racist thoughts, though perhaps no more so than Cracklow. Their particular version was also interlaced with negative comments about other English people; the social snobbery in their comments often was as much of a denigration as was some of their more overtly racist language concerning the "niggers." Thomas Watson made several disparaging remarks about his Irish colleagues, and Sarah Watson talked of those "in our own social station." Perhaps this was one reason both were so concerned about perquisites. Watson recounted at several points his extensive menage of servants. There were many letters back and forth about the Watson possessions at Sialkot and the "liberated" buggy that Watson had found at the battle of Lucknow, and many more discussions about the quality of Watson's tent, what to do with the house in Sialkot, and so on. At least as one compares these two peoples' letters with those of the other three correspondents, the amount of minutiae and preoccupation with personal comfort seems overwhelming.

The four young men were all officers. Explicitly, they had been placed into a role of leadership. Superficially, it might be tempting to generalize from these four young officers to one or another global theory of leadership. The body of literature on leadership is voluminous.[12] Earlier attempts at identifying "traits" turned later to a focus on the situation, treating leadership as a process dependent upon specific settings. Recently, a more eclectic look at leadership has stressed a combination of these two, fitted together holistically as "contingency" theory. But these are vast arenas of study, laced full of contentious differences in viewpoint among the various experts. Our earlier cautions about psychoanalyzing these people apply equally here—we do not have enough information about their lives, their actions, their "traits," to be able to formulate believable theories of leadership.

Rather, a few more modest comments can be made, particularly about Roberts, who turned out to be the most prestigious military leader among the four. There *are* some special things to be said about him that might give some clues to his high eventual rank. He had a style, an élan, that gave him that almost undefinable "divine gift," charisma. He among the four seemed most aware of the historical moment they were in, and most able to recognize the importance of a crisis situation. He had more wide-ranging interests than the other three, at least at that moment (Lang, of course, exhibited breadth at a later stage). Roberts wanted, and was offered, many different posts; he weighed these one against another for their value to his career. This weighing process was not done alone from a calculated, selfish focus on promotion; he considered also the learning experiences that might be gained. Watson, on the other hand, while also considering (and even holding) several widely different jobs, seemed always to be taking them on an idiosyncratic basis, sometimes almost in desperation, with the goal always linked to extramilitary concerns (particularly being able to return to his mother). Cracklow was the most single-minded about his goals, apparently quite willing to stay in one single rut within the military structure. Roberts, more than the other three, seemed to be able to make linkages, to find elements that would lead to a "critical mass," and to use language in his letters that evidenced what linguistic analysts have called "cognitive complexity." This gift does not depend much on the level of IQ; rather, it is a characterization of a person's style or innate approach to problem solving. The hallmarks of cognitive complexity, according to one expert, include "the ability to plan strategically without being rigidly locked into one course of events; the capacity to acquire ample information for decision-making without being overwhelmed and being able to grasp relationships between rapidly changing events."[13] This seems to describe Roberts rather better than the other three. Though Lang has the best vocabulary of the four, and seems at least by his word choices to be the most educated, Roberts's vocabulary evidences the cognitive interlacing of many disparate thoughts.

Charisma has sometimes been defined as "inner directedness" as opposed to "other directedness." The latter quality typically produces a "consensus" leader. Roberts likely had an ability to produce consensus, even in those earlier days; certainly he had it in the later stages of his career. Yet he also was the most self-confident of the four, the most self-assured in an inner sense. Roberts, Cracklow, and Watson all exhibited major doses of self-interest, Lang perhaps less so. However, Watson's self-interest was laced throughout with self-doubt, and Cracklow's was focused narrowly on certain overweening themes (the courage or lack thereof of others, etc.). Roberts, alone of the four, seemed to have his self-interest pointed squarely at his overall well-being and that of his family, particularly his family's military reputation. In this same breath we need to say also that Roberts was the only one of the four to evidence positive feelings and specific actions in relation to the enlisted men of the military organization. To put it another way, Roberts alone seemed to have an instinct of "followership," as well as leadership.

As we assimilate the evocative words of these five people, we also see evidence of broader forces at work, dimensions that concerned England itself, as it looked out on its mid-nineteenth-century vista as a worldwide imperial and colonial power. The subject country, India, was the "Jewel in the Crown," with a special relationship back to Victorian England. In a recent, somewhat hyperbolic essay entitled "India: The Imperial Summer," Nicholas Wollaston commented: "No part of the Victorian empire exerted such a strong emotional pull as India—an alien sub-continent wrested from savagery and heathenism by the imposition of British order and values and organised, during the brightest heyday of the Raj, very much like an overseas branch of English suburbia, with bands playing on the lawn to elegant spectators and regimental cricket matches. The age of Victoria leaves a heavy mark on Indian life, institutions and customs."[14] While one blanches a bit at the implication that all the English viewed Indians as "heathens" and "savages," there are indeed numerous writings from this period and by earlier British missionaries and others couched in blatantly prejudicial religious terminology. Remember the 1822 missionary letter "back home" cited earlier, with its allusions to "the Crescent of the Eastern Impostor" and the "Braminical flames from the widow's pile" and its conclusion that "India is in moral night . . . superstition like the Angel of Death still spreads her raven wings over this immense territory so that darkness covers this portion of the earth."

Certainly here in the letters of our five people are chapter and verse of this convoluted relationship between Christian Britain and "heathen" India. Threads of religious proselytization run through Sarah Watson's writings as well her son's, but also extend to the other three (we must recall the exhortations of the archbishop of Canterbury at the Addiscombe graduation of Roberts and Cracklow).

The mutiny challenged what had become a master/servitor relationship as nothing had before and nothing would again, until the mid-twentieth century. There is a love-hate syndrome apparent here in varying degrees among all five of our correspondents. India was their home, yet they sent their children back to England for education, hoped and schemed for leaves to England, and finally, in most cases, retired back to the home country. The words of these five seem apt for the period, each writer in his or her own way picturing a lifetime relationship with a difficult, dangerous country halfway around the world. The words of these five people express eloquently a profoundly moving relationship between the closely entwined countries.

In the final analysis, it is the letters themselves that count. For here we are privileged to have brief glimpses inside the private, personal lives of these five quite different people. We can see the process of individual maturation as each strives in his or her own way to reach a potential—sometimes a career goal, but more often a personal dream. It *is* the letters that count, because it is these lives that count.

Appendixes

An Essay on Historical Method via Computer-driven Content Analysis

The notion of analyzing content in a rigorous, nonbiased way has had currency since before World War II. Indeed, the war itself was the trigger for much-heightened research on lexical method. For example, German radio broadcasts and writings that reached the West were subjected to intense scrutiny in an effort to detect German military strategy. While the results of this effort were spotty, the notion itself has continued to gain credibility over the succeeding years. The methodology of content analysis has been applied to such divergent fields as the attempts to discover who wrote certain ancient texts and the analysis of a product image of a major modern corporation.[1]

In the early 1960s a group from Harvard University's Department of Social Relations, under the leadership of Philip J. Stone and Dexter C. Dunphy, began a pioneering effort to investigate computer-aided content analysis as a research technique. They gave a rather sweeping title, the "General Inquirer," to their project.[2] Out of this collaboration came a practical way of analyzing written content by computer, and it is this project on which I have drawn for my work here.

The idea of the General Inquirer, in its original form, was a simple one: A dictionary would be developed, with words in several or many categories, which would be analytically representative of a particular construct (in this case it was a psychosociological dictionary). In turn, a computer program would take a text and count each time one of the words in the dictionary was used, in the process putting it into the agreed-on category. For example, in the Stone dictionary, the word "passion" is slotted under the category "arousal"; every time the word "passion" comes up in a text, a count is put into a computer file named "arousal." When the requisite number of words from a given text has been analyzed by the computer, the researcher ends up with a pattern of word counts among the various categories that gives a special profile to that writing, a profile that can be compared statistically with other such profiles.

This seemingly rudimentary version of computer content analysis, the simple word count, has proved remarkably efficacious in content analysis.

To be sure, more than a few words carry two or more meanings. We might not have any trouble with "passion" as a word most often fitting "arousal." Yet if one wanted a category called "sex," one would probably want to count passion there, too. Indeed, in the eighty-three categories in the Stone dictionary, both "arousal" and "sex" are included, and "passion" is counted in each place. (Incidentally, there is no inherent inconsistency in having a word counted in two different ways.) What is done by having two separate word counts is the beginning of what the content analysis professionals call "disambiguation": distinguishing a word by its context in a sentence—in effect, differentiating between the blind Venetian and the venetian blind. There are more complex means of disambiguation, treating nouns, verbs, adjectives, and adverbs in their contextual relationship in a sentence. These efforts very quickly become quite intricate. The Stone group, as one of its subsequent refinements, has developed its own experimental version of disambiguation.

Still, as content analysis experts a number of times have pointed out, the simple word count itself, granting that some words may be counted in the wrong way, still can be a highly useful, dependable way of analyzing text, once the number of words to be analyzed over each of the samples is large enough to have a "law of large numbers" come into play. Ithiel de Sola Pool, one of the pioneers in content analysis, made this very point back in the early days: "The assumption that the frequency of statements provides a good index of an intensity of attitude is probably reasonable for a large class of cases. By 'attitude' here, of course, we mean the attitude expressed in the body of the text, not the covert feelings of the author. Even with this limitation, the assumption baldly spelled out sounds absurd, because it is perfectly clear that the frequency is only one of a variety of devices by which feeling is expressed. But the experience of more than one analyst who has tried refinements in measuring intensity has been that nothing much is added by other measures than the frequency one."[3]

Recent research at Dartmouth College and elsewhere gives added weight to this judgment. Donald P. Spence comments in a recent article: "The choice of language in an interview will reveal many examples of non-random word selection. These hidden features constitute a kind of underground code by which many themes can be expressed, protected as they are from the scrutiny of both the listener and the speaker." Spence's own findings, as well as the recent work of my colleagues at Dartmouth, professors of psychiatry Stanley Rosenberg, Gary Tucker, and Thomas Oxman and psychologist Paula Schnurr, demonstrate the utility of word counting as a means of translating this lexical code. (The Rosenberg group, in studying the free speech of various categories of psychiatric patients, has found that patients convey important information about themselves and their experiential states that enables professional analysts to sort out clinical differences among them.[4]

Here in this book I used the simple word count with the four lieutenants and the mother. Every word from every one of the letters of all of the five—a total of some three hundred thousand words—was typed into the computer. The program that my colleagues and I employed used the eighty-three-category dictionary of Stone and Dunphy and also a fourteen-category dictionary developed by David McClelland, another member of the Harvard Department of Social Relations, to test "achievement motivation." Every word of the letters was matched against these two dictionaries, and a precise computer count of the words appearing in these two dictionaries was put into the files. To this raw material we applied sophisticated quantitative (multivariate) techniques, some of which are new, used for the first time in this study. The analysis has allowed us to tease out of the raw data a great many quantitative facts, facts that have given a stronger basis for inferences and subjective judgments.

Our methodology, explained in detail in the Statistical Note that follows this essay, can be stated simply as follows: Using a set of clustering programs we allowed the computer to construct what was statistically the best set of composite variables, based on the original ninety-seven separate variables. Its best solution collapsed the full set of variables into an eighteen-variable set. We analyzed the sets of variables that fell into these eighteen categories and then gave a name to each. The full set of original variables can be found in the Statistical Note; here I list our descriptive name for each of the eighteen, with representative lists of the words the correspondents frequently used:

1. *Family affection/communication* (mother, father, etc.; marriage, family, lesson book, flag, advise, answer, behave, feel, hear)

2. *Recognition of authority* (determine, because, duty, should, accept, obey, responsibility)

3. *Concern about well-being* (excitement, cheerful, comfortable, hope, want, understand)

4. *Power and valor* (capture, recover, steal, siege, bold, brave, honor, mercy)

5. *Male theme* (brain, foot, gun, sword, large, knife, limb, excitement, overcome, destroy, danger, enemy)

6. *Competition* (gain, overtake, risk, win, people, group, met, toward, maybe, if, problem)

7. *Aggression* (attack, conquer, defeat, fight, murderer, punish, difficulty, control, savage, kill, death)

8. *Environmental awareness* (clothing, dress, insects, snakes, cool, hot, tent, camp, road, water, dirty)

9. *Preoccupation with physical state* (food, beer, sun, expose, night, illness, move, drag, march)

10. *Avoidance* (escape, beaten, absent, cannot, failure, shrink, forget, withdrew, hopeless, detach, neglect, leave)

11. *Political sense* (appointment, campaign, rule, prisoner, occupy, company, corps, troop)

12. *Work orientation* (use, work, make, ability, service, engineer, inferior, capable)

13. *Overstatement* (altogether, capital, exceed, everyone, most, splendid, impossible)

14. *Role consciousness* (captain, colonel, official, guard, ruler, servant, royal, queen, lord, hero, leader)

15. *Striving* (appoint, command, attempt, try, plan, advance, complete)

16. *Assertiveness* (lead, must, hatred, wrath, enraged, assure, hostile)

17. *Economic concerns* (account, wagon, wealth, afford, employment, debt, supply)

18. *Compulsiveness* (desire, want, evening, day, future, time, defense, compulsive, repress)

Using these eighteen composite variables, the computer analysis clearly shows that each of the five people is a distinct, separate "prototype," if we can use that rather pretentious term. To put it simply, if we were to black out the name of the person who wrote each one of the total of 251 letters, and then put all the letters through the computer to sort into five piles, the discriminant function would sort them with almost 90 percent accuracy. Compared to statistical results in general, this is a quite impressive showing. The computer is able to both sort and compare in a rigorous, helpful way.

When we programmed the computer to give the means of the total number of tagged words for each of the five people for the eighteen categories, we then obtained statistical profiles of the people involved. Table 1, for example, shows the way this set of means pictures the four lieutenants, each against the other (our terminology ["high," "low," etc.] is derived explicitly from recognized measures of statistical significance; see the Statistical Note for explanation).

As we analyze this set of highs and lows, we see computer-generated profiles for all of the four men, profiles satisfyingly close to our earlier subjective characterizations. Roberts rates the highest on recognition of authority and on problem solving, just as both his letters indicate and his subsequent life confirms. He is low on both environmental concern and awareness of his own physical state. Cracklow is in the middle: high on compulsiveness (we have seen this manifestation), believably low on en-

Table 1   *Summary of a Multiple Discriminant Analysis of the Lieutenants' Letters*

Variable	Roberts	Cracklow	Lang	Watson
1. Family affection/ communication	Fairly high	Fairly low	Low	High
2. Recognition of authority	High		Low	
3. Concern about well-being	All approximately the same			
4. Power and valor			Low	
5. Male theme	Fairly low	Fairly high	High	Low
6. Competition	High	Fairly low	Low	Fairly low
7. Aggression			High	Low
8. Environmental awareness	Low	Low	High	Low
9. Preoccupation with physical state	Low	Fairly high	High	Low
10. Avoidance	All approximately the same			
11. Political sense	Fairly high	Fairly low	High	Low
12. Work orientation			High	Low
13. Overstatement			Low	
14. Role consciousness			High	
15. Striving			Low	High
16. Assertiveness			Fairly high	Fairly low
17. Economic concerns	All approximately the same			
18. Compulsiveness	Fairly low	High	High	

vironmental awareness (particularly during the war), and between the others on many other measures. Lang scores a number of lows and highs; his personality is in many respects most strikingly strong (again as confirmed by his own words). He is low on several of the variables that imply organizational and personal linkages—he is a bit of an iconoclast. He is high on the physical and environmental measures (perhaps because of his engineer bias, combined with his interest in butterflies and flowers), and his observational skills are high. He is also high on work orientation (once more his engineer training shows), fairly high on assertiveness (as his words confirm), and high also on aggression. He has a keen sense, too, of his role situation. Again, these characterizations are congruent with the words in Lang's mutiny letters. Thomas Watson's means, too, are consonant with his words. He scores the highest on family concerns, also highest on the striving, so apparent in his efforts to attain "the appointment." Watson is also low on six of the variables: the male theme and aggression, the environmental and physical states, political sense and work orientation. All six of these lows would appear to be confirmed by a reading of his letters to his mother during the mutiny.

In sum, the computer has reinforced in a useful way most of our subjective judgments—not exactly, to be sure, for when the antiseptic computer interfaces with the real world, it does not do so with 100 percent accuracy. But having available this totally mechanical view helps to keep us objective and drives us back to test our hypotheses again, to reformulate our generalizations.

When the totals for Sarah Watson's words are added to the comparative set of means, she comes out the highest of all five in several categories. Predictably, she is the highest in the family affection category, and she outscores even her son in the striving variable. She becomes the most assertive, too; her concern about well-being is much the highest; and her status seeking is also above all the others. Predictably, she is lowest on work orientation, on the male theme, on aggression, and on environmental awareness. Once more, the computer seems to reinforce the judgments that we have made about Sarah Watson.

We also treated all the letters to a separate analysis based on the smaller "Harvard Need-Achievement Dictionary," a set of words developed, as already noted, under the aegis of David McClelland of the Department of Social Relations at Harvard; this dictionary was designed to duplicate a previously existing hand-scoring system of content analysis for achievement motivation.[5] The dictionary's fourteen categories are as follows (the words in parentheses are again representative words from the letters):

1. *Need* (want, desire, hope, wish, need)
2. *To be* (become, to be)
3. *Compete* (win, overtake, gain, surpass, succeed)
4. *Verb—positive* (do, make, work, discover, seek)
5. *Adverb—positive* (carefully, properly, cautiously, earnestly)
6. *Adjective—positive* (great, powerful, splendid, glorious)
7. *Value—positive* (ambition, ideal, effort, reputation)
8. *Role—positive* (hero, leader, worker, surgeon)
9. *Block* (crisis, impossible, harass, restrict)
10. *Success* (fame, success, glory, honor, victory)
11. *Failure* (error, incorrect, mistake, blunder, careless)
12. *Affect—positive* (job, cheerful, happy, glad)
13. *Affect—negative* (ashamed, sad, sorry, disgusted, worried)
14. *Time* (lifetime, years, weeks, life)

The original McClelland hand-scoring techniques utilized disambiguation; in other words, they placed the individual words in the context of the sentence to determine the scoring. In turn, McClelland and his associates were able to score not only need achievement but affiliative and power motives as well. Here we have used the simple word count once more, and despite its simplicity, we are able to draw further useful insights about the five people. Their mean scores for these fourteen categories were compared by several statistical techniques; in addition, we treated our data to a grouping process suggested by the developers of the dictionary (all of these are described in the Statistical Note). Uniformly, the results show George Cracklow and Fred Roberts with substantially higher scorings than the others by all of these measures (Cracklow is consistently a bit higher than Roberts). The other three are separated somewhat, with Thomas Watson a bit ahead of his mother and Lang at the rear.

What we have here is a rather simplistic measure that detects only the existence of an expressed need for achievement. From the modest hypothesis that this analysis does reflect achievement need, we conclude that the actual words of the five correspondents seem to corroborate our earlier findings. Cracklow and Roberts both seem quite achievement oriented. The two Watsons use noticeable achievement imagery, although directed to a narrower, more personal set of purposes. Lastly, Lang does seem more willing to take things as they come, more modest in his overall goals.

We carried through two more statistical analyses, both of them rather preliminary and rudimentary in nature. The first came out of one of the questions that we frequently asked ourselves: "How do these four young lieutenants measure against other lieutenants in that Indian Mutiny situation, and how does the one mother measure against other mothers living in India at the time of the mutiny?" We can readily compare the four lieutenants qualitatively and subjectively against the many dozens of others who reported their reminiscences and experiences in the mutiny. Yet we have in our letters a narrower, more constrained set of materials— actual battlefield letters, written *at the time*. Reminiscences and other after-the-fact writings are a different genre. There are perhaps only a dozen or so extant sets of battlefield letters from British soldiers going through the Indian Mutiny that are lengthy enough (remember that our smallest set was thirty letters, for Roberts) to be comparable to our extensive data sets. Someday, perhaps, someone may take the other comparable letter sets and do the same kind of statistical analysis we have done. Even then, there would still be a question whether the set was large enough to provide normative judgments of true statistical veracity.

We have attempted a rudimentary comparison against a norm, utilizing a much simpler technique. In the past few years there has been widespread interest among linguists and other social science professionals in developing extensive word data bases that can be made available in machine-readable form for the computer. One of the best known of these is the "Brown Corpus," developed initially by a group at Brown University, with some recent additions by others at the Norwegian Research Council for Science and the Humanities.[6] The Brown Corpus contains just over one million words of present-day American English, taken from published materials during the calendar year 1961, covering fifteen categories of writing (such as newspaper reportage and editorials, reviews, religious writing, technical materials from learned journals, biographies, and various kinds of fictional prose).

As an experiment, we decided to take three of the fifteen Brown groupings and subject the writings in these three to the content analysis computer program described above. We groped for the right three to use and finally picked samples from categories called "Belles Lettres" (thirty excerpts of five hundred words each from essays and biography), "Adventure and Western Fiction" (twenty-nine, again of five hundred words each), and "Romance and Love Stories" (twenty-nine, again of five hundred words each). Then we compared the Brown sample means for each of our eighteen variables with those of our five people. A number of different comparisons now could readily be made: for example, one could group the three Brown categories into a single figure and then group the four lieutenants as an additional single figure. Individual comparisons of all sorts were possible—each of the three Brown samples compared first with the four lieutenants, then with the four lieutenants and the mother, and so on. We did all of these things and found a remarkable number of statistically significant differences in a number of the comparisons (as we describe briefly in the Statistical Note). Taking as an example just the composite of the three Brown categories and the composite of the four lieutenants, one obtains the comparison shown in Table 2.

On its face, the comparison of the four lieutenants to this "norm," if we can call it that, has some logic to it. The lieutenants are higher on communication/family affection, higher on aggression, and higher on role consciousness. It is a set of battle letters, compared to peacetime 1961 writings, and one would expect overstatement to be more prominent among the lieutenants' writing. The lieutenants do not seem to be as competitive as might the heroes of the adventure and love stories or the subjects of the

Table 2 *Comparison of the Four Lieutenants with the Brown Corpus*

The twelve categories for which there was a statistically significant difference	Where the four lieutenants stood in relation to the Brown data
Communication/family affection	Higher
Well-being	Lower
Competition	Lower
Aggression	Higher
Environmental Awareness	Lower
Physical comfort	Lower
Political	Lower
Work	Lower
Overstatement	Higher
Role consciousness	Higher
Assertiveness	Lower
Compulsiveness	Higher

belles lettres. All in all, these kinds of comparisons (and others that we made from the Brown data) are interesting artifacts, with the methodology itself useful for further exploration.

One might ask, of course, about the validity of comparing mid-nineteenth-century writing with that of the 1960s (the time period of the Brown data, as well as the decade in which the General Inquirer and Need Achievement dictionaries were developed). Linguistic colleagues thought instinctively that the letters of the lieutenants would in the main fit nicely into twentieth-century dictionaries of the types of the two we used, and we made a simple test to attempt a corroboration of this judgment. Using two thesauri of the time period of the lieutenants, Roget's *Thesaurus of English Words and Phrases* (1853) and Crabb's *English Synonymes* (1850), we searched in an organized way for all the words appearing in three of our original ninety-seven tag categories.[7] Having previously carefully read all of the letters, we were able to make a subjective comparison, and this seemed to show that few additional words would have been necessary to convert the dictionaries we used to mid-nineteenth-century ones. There is a laborious way to check this guess statistically: One could add to the dictionary all the additional words for each of the tagged categories, using Crabb and Roget, and then run all of the letters once again through the content analysis programs. If the percentage of tagged words remained essentially the same, one could expect that the results would be comparable. The magnitude of the effort discouraged us, and inasmuch as the experts thought that this extra step would be only a refinement, we eschewed the effort.

Statistical Note
Victor E. McGee and Wayne G. Broehl, Jr.

The content analysis categories of the "General Inquirer" project at the Department of Social Relations, Harvard University—the so-called

Exhibit 1   *The Harvard Third Sociological Dictionary*

FIRST-ORDER TAGS

Social realm	Cultural realm	Psychological processes	Behavioral processes
Persons	Cultural objects	Emotions	Social-emotional
SELF	FOOD	AROUSAL	actions
SELVES	CLOTHING	URGE	APPROACH
OTHER	TOOLS	AFFECTION	COMMUNICATE
ROLES	Cultural settings	PLEASURE	GUIDE
male	SOCIAL PLACE	DISTRESS	CONTROL
female	Cultural patterns	ANGER	DEFENSE
neuter	IDEAL	Thought	ATTACK
job	DEVIATION	SENSE	AVOID
Collectivities	ACTION	THINK	FOLLOW
SMALL	MESSAGE	IF	Instrumental actions
LARGE	THOUGHT	EQUAL	ATTEMPT
Natural realm	NONSPECIFIC	NOT	WORK
BODY PART	OBJECTS	CAUSE	MOVE
NATURAL OBJECT	*Qualifiers*	Evaluation	GET
NATURAL WORLD	SENSORY	GOOD	POSSESS
	TIME	BAD	EXPEL
	QUANTITY	OUGHT	
	SPACE		

SECOND-ORDER TAGS

Institutional contexts	Psychological themes	State connotations
ACADEMIC	OVERSTATE	HIGHER STATUS
ARTISTIC	UNDERSTATE	PEER STATUS
COMMUNITY	SIGN—STRONG	LOWER STATUS
ECONOMIC	SIGN—WEAK	
FAMILY	SIGN—ACCEPT	
LEGAL	SIGN—REJECT	
MEDICAL	MALE	
MILITARY	FEMALE	
POLITICAL	SEX	
RECREATIONAL	ASCEND	
RELIGIOUS	AUTHORITY	
TECHNOLOGICAL	DANGER	
	DEATH	

Harvard Third Dictionary—were grouped by the Philip Stone team as indicated in Exhibit 1.

The "Harvard Need-Achievement Dictionary" of David McClelland and his colleagues utilized the fourteen tag categories listed in Exhibit 2, not further grouped by Stone. Additional statistical refinements were made in these categories both by our team at the Amos Tuck School and by the Stanley Rosenberg/Gary Tucker/Thomas Oxman/Paula Schnurr group at the Department of Psychiatry, Dartmouth Medical School.

All our work using these two dictionaries involved simple ("naive") word count, applied to these sets of carefully developed tag classifications validated over a number of years of study by the Harvard groups. The computer-driven word-counting program allows any text to be analyzed and provides the following:

1. The counting of every word of any particular manuscript as (a) a tagged word in one or more of the 97 psychosociological and achievement motivation categories, (b) an "N" word—articles, prepositions, etc.—or (c) a "leftover" word, any word that is not in the first two categories. The program prints into a matrix the number of tags for each category in each particular letter or other form of manuscript and also calculates for each of the 97 categories the percentage of total tags, the percentage of total words, and the percentage of tagged words in each category. Thus for any given manuscript, irrespective of length, the Dartmouth program provides a 97 × 4 matrix. For the analysis reported here, the fourth of these, the percentage of tagged words, has been used.

2. A set of summary statistics showing the number of words in the text, the number of words tagged, the number of words left over, the percent of leftover to total words, the number of words tagged "N," the number of sentences, the average number of words per sentence, and the total number of tags in the text. Inasmuch as some words are tagged in two or more categories, the total number of tags in the text can exceed the total number of words tagged. (See Exhibit 3.)

3. An annotated print of the particular manuscript analyzed, with the

Exhibit 2 *Harvard Need-Achievement Dictionary Tag Categories*

Need	Role—positive
To be	Block
Compete	Success
Verb—positive	Failure
Adverb—positive	Affect—positive
Adjective—positive	Affect—negative
Value—positive	Time

Exhibit 3   *The Dartmouth Program Summary Output for One Text of a British Lieutenant (First Ten Tags Only)*

Number of words in the text	1,100
Number of words tagged	519
Number of words left over	153
Ratio of leftovers to total words	13.9091
Number of words tagged "N"	428
Number of sentences	96
Average number of words per sentence	11.4583
Number of tags in the text	834

No. and category	No of tags	% of tot. tags	% of tot. wds.	% of tagged wds.
1. SELF	22	2.6	1.9	4.2
2. SELVES	32	3.8	2.9	6.1
3. OTHER	24	2.8	2.1	4.6
4. MALE ROLE	22	2.6	1.9	4.2
5. FEMALE ROLE	0	0	0	0
6. NEUTER ROLE	2	0.2	0.1	0.3
7. JOB ROLE	1	0.1	0	0.1
8. SMALL GROUP	4	0.4	0.3	0.7
9. LARGE GROUP	5	0.5	0.4	0.9
10. BODY PART	11	1.3	0.9	2.1

number of tags and the specific tag categories printed after each line of the text. (See Exhibit 4.)

4. A listing of the tag and "N" words as they occur serially within the manuscript. For example, the list for the first five tagged words of one of the mutiny manuscripts reads as follows:

I I # 01
TO TO # N
ON ON # N
THE THE # N
GIVING GIV # 44, 73, 75

Thus the first word of the manuscript is I, and it falls in category 1 ("self"). The second, third, and fourth words are articles or prepositions and are therefore tagged as "N." The fifth word, GIVING (whose root word is GIV), is tagged in three categories: no. 44 ("approach"), no. 73 ("sign—strong") and no. 75 ("sign—except").

This fifth line illustrates one convention adopted throughout the Harvard Third Dictionary program. Six suffixes have been eliminated prior to utilization as tag words: ION, LY, ED, ING, S, and silent E. When we use this convention, a number of different words with related meanings and the same root can be picked up by the computer from a given text. Thus in line five above both the word GIVE and the word GIVING will be picked up if either one occurs in the text. Note that this process can

Exhibit 4 The Dartmouth Program Analysis of an Individual Letter (Partial Content)

19,9,9,2# THE TRUMPET SOUNDED "LIMBER UP" (WHICH WAS THE SIGNAL = 1643

10,15,8,13# AGREED ON.) I SHUT MY EYES FOR HALF A SECOND AND THE GUNS EXPLODED WITH = 47750146011019191382776373

11,8,6,7# ONE REPORT. I COULD HARDLY SEE FOR THE = 19430180731633

12,14,5,7# SMOKE FOR ABOUT 2 SECONDS WHEN DOWN CAME SOMETHING WITH A THUD ABOUT 5 = 1917184475157 2

13,16,7,9# YARDS FROM ME. THIS WAS THE HEAD AND NECK OF ONE OF THE MEN. YOU CAN'T = 206001101079190403

14,14,7,14# IMAGINE SUCH A HORRIBLE SIGHT. ON EACH SIDE OF THE GUNS ABOUT 10 YARDS = 345844133191813827763732060

15,14,7,13# LAY THE ARMS TORN OUT AT THE SHOULDERS. UNDER THE MUZZLE AND BETWEEN THE = 55747910773174831876101818

16,12,4,8# WHEELS LAY THE REMAINDER OF THE BODIES WITH THE ENTRAILS SCATTERED ABOUT. = 1367557479105376

17,16,6,12# THE HEADS HAD FLOWN UP IN THE AIR AND FALLEN IN REAR OF THE GUNS. I = 10558018801813827763 7301

18,13,8,17# COULD NEVER·HAVE IMAGINED BODIES WOULD GO TO PIECES SO EASILY. THE GUNS = 8073377134578410425576711382776373

19,9,4,8# WERE LOADED MERELY WITH A SERVICE CARTRIDGE, NO BALL. = 19197254671377765

40,12,5,11# CHAMBERLAIN WHO COMMANDS US IS A SPLENDID FELLOW AND ONE THAT DOES = 46763024071808904 6919

41,15,6,10# NOT FEAR RESPONSIBILITY AND IS NOT TO BE TRIFLED WITH, IF THEY HAD HAD A = 37317496226181373503

42,13,8,11# MAN OF HIS STAMP AT BARRACK-PORE WHERE THE MUTINIES FIRST BROKE OUT HE = 0404136420173174187604

43,13,6,8# WOULD HAVE STOPPED THE BUSINESS AT ONCE. AT PRESENT THERE IS NO SAYING = 4283255917177243

44,16,4,5# WHEN IT WILL END SINCE 22 OR 23 N.I. REGIMENTS AND TWO OR 3 CAVALRY HAVE = 1717831719

45,12,6,8# MUTINEED AND I BELIEVE ALL THE OTHERS WILL WILLINGLY JOIN THEM WHEN = (01) (34) (19) (71) (47) (75) (03) (17)

01 Self ("I")

34 Think ("believe")

19 Quantity reference ("all")

71 Overstate ("all")

47 Follow ("join")

75 Sign accept ("join")

03 Other ("others")

17 Time reference ("when")

Line number
No. of words in sentence
No. of words tagged in one or more tag categories
No. of tag categories in sentence

sometimes give misleading results; for example, in this Tuck project on the Indian Mutiny letters, the word CORPSE is a word that appears in category 84, "death wish." When the silent E is eliminated to fit this convention, any military usage of the word CORPS appears as a "death wish." This form of difficulty with suffix conventions is probably a minor one, though, and can be readily spotted by reading down the line-by-line listing of the tags to pick up inconsistencies.

5. Finally, a list of leftover words, those proper names and other, more specialized, words that do not appear in the Harvard dictionary. Again, the listing of this set of words allows a simple visual check of unique words and other special forms that lie in the text, as well as a ready method for spotting any typographical errors in words that should be tagged. (When manuscripts are prepared for running in the program, occasionally certain conventions are necessary. For example, if a colloquial word is used, or if there is an intentional misspelling, the analyst may wish to retype the word in its regular tagged-word form, in order to have it picked up as a relevant word in the analysis.)

Our analyses that led to the establishment of the eighteen composite variables utilized letters from Cracklow (58), Roberts (30), and Watson (43)—a total of 131 letters. (It was only later in the project that we were able to find additional Watson letters, to bring his total to 95; to find the letters of his mother, a total of 34; and to learn of the Lang letters, which we consolidated into 34 composites.)

The results from the content analysis program were summarized in the form of a "raw" data matrix X, containing 131 rows (for the 131 letters) and 97 columns ("% of tagged words" for each of the 97 categories). Exhibit 5 shows schematically what kind of analyses were conducted on the data matrices X and Z, and interested readers can pursue the more technical aspects by checking the endnotes. In brief, when we concentrate on separating the 131 letters into three authorship categories, it is more appropriate to deal with the X matrix. If we concentrate on reducing the 97 measures into a smaller number of composite measures, it is more appropriate to deal with the Z matrix.

Application of a "K-means clustering procedure"[1] to the raw data matrix X (or order 131 × 97) yielded the following results. When three clusters were formed, cluster 1 showed that the Cracklow and Roberts letters were readily confused, but cluster 2 showed that Watson's letters were strongly identified. There were only three authors, but three clusters did not do a good job of sorting the letters into proper authorships. When the number of clusters (K) was increased from 4 through 7 there was still a cluster that confused approximately 20 letters from Cracklow and 20

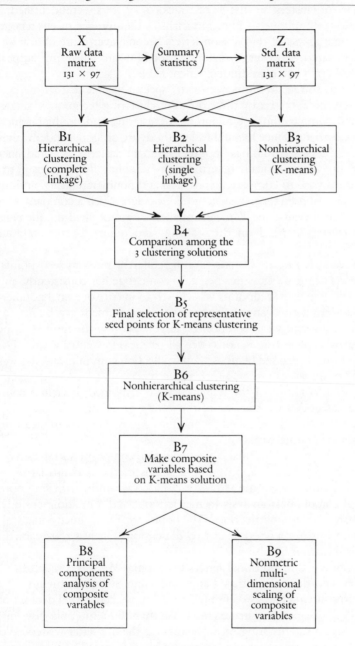

letters from Roberts. However, there was some advantage in increasing the number of clusters, in that 23 of Cracklow's letters were identified as being reasonably unique to him. Similarly, as the number of clusters increased, some 22–24 of the Watson letters become ever more clearly isolated. It appeared, however, that none of the K-means clustering outputs showed Roberts's letters as uniquely identifiable.

In order to soften the influence of the species-specific textual material we analyzed the Z matrix by three different clustering techniques, single-linkage and complete-linkage hierarchical clustering and nonhierarchical K-means clustering. Since hierarchical methods are order dependent (they never "undo" a cluster that has been formed in an earlier stage), and since this order can be whimsically determined by sampling fluctuations in the data, it seems wise to compare hierarchical and nonhierarchical solutions in the hopes of finding stable structure in the data. Such a comparison is also important because the K-means method does not yield unique clusters: the clusters depend on the starting seed points for the iterative method.[2]

After several K-means clusterings using different random seed points, some subsets of the 97 measures began to come together consistently, and a set of 18 nonrandom seedpoints was chosen to initiate one final nonhierarchical clustering run. The 18 clusters that were formed (see Exhibit 6) had both strong and weak composites, largely because the limited scope of the textual material does not cover all 97 measures equally well. For example, cluster 1 (defined by us as "family affection/communication") was comprised of measures 1, 5, 25, 29, 33, 34, 36, 37, 43, 58, 60, 66, and 75. The corresponding columns of the X matrix were combined to yield a composite tag category that was one of the strong groupings. On the other hand, cluster 17 (which we called "economic concerns") refers to measures 24 and 59 and is rather weak.

For all 18 clusters in this final cluster solution, composite variables were computed by combining appropriate columns of the X data matrix. A check on the similarity of the 18 new variables was conducted using both a principal components analysis (a metric look) and a multidimensional scaling analysis (a nonmetric look). The nonmetric multidimensional scaling solution was not a good fit in two dimensions but was reasonable in three; it is shown in Exhibit 7.

After entering the additional letters of Thomas Watson, the letters of his mother, and those of Arthur Lang, and subjecting all of them to the Dartmouth content analysis computer program, we had a total data set of 251 letters (217 for the four lieutenants). We then did a multiple discriminant analysis on the resulting mean vectors for the five letter writers, and our results were statistically significant to a high degree. The significance

Exhibit 6 *How the Variables Grouped using a Convergent-Means Clustering Program*

1. *Family affection/ communication*
   - SELF
   - FEMALE ROLE
   - MESSAGE FORM
   - *AFFECTION
   - SENSE
   - THINK
   - EQUAL
   - NOT
   - COMMUNICATE
   - COMMUNITY
   - FAMILY
   - RELIGIOUS
   - SIGN—ACCEPT

2. *Recognition of authority*
   - CAUSE
   - OUGHT
   - FOLLOW
   - *AUTHORITY THEME

3. *Concern about well-being*
   - *AROUSAL
   - PLEASURE
   - ACADEMIC
   - NEED

4. *Power and valor*
   - *IDEAL VALUE
   - GET
   - MEDICAL

5. *Male theme*
   - BODY PART
   - TOOLS
   - QUANTITY REFERENCE
   - *MALE THEME
   - ASCEND THEME
   - DANGER THEME
   - ADJECTIVE—POSITIVE

6. *Competition*
   - SMALL GROUP
   - THOUGHT FORM
   - IF
   - APPROACH
   - TO BE
   - *COMPETE

7. *Aggression*
   - SELVES
   - SPACE REFERENCE
   - *ATTACK
   - MILITARY
   - UNDERSTATE
   - SIGN—STRONG
   - SIGN—REJECT
   - DEATH THEME
   - BLOCK
   - SUCCESS

8. *Environmental awareness*
   - CLOTHING
   - NATURAL OBJECT
   - SENSORY REFERENCE
   - SOCIAL PLACE
   - EXPEL
   - RECREATIONAL
   - *FEMALE THEME
   - ADVERB—POSITIVE
   - AFFECT—POSITIVE

9. *Preoccupation with physical state*
   - FOOD
   - NATURAL WORLD
   - *DEVIATION
   - MOVE
   - PEER STATUS
   - SEX THEME

10. *Avoidance*
    - DISTRESS
    - AVOID
    - *SIGN—WEAK
    - AFFECT—NEGATIVE

11. *Political sense*
    - NEUTER ROLE
    - LARGE GROUP
    - POSSESS
    - LEGAL
    - POLITICAL
    - *LOWER STATUS

12. *Work orientation*
    - *WORK
    - ARTISTIC
    - TECHNOLOGICAL
    - FAILURE

13. *Overstatement*
    - NONSPECIFIC OBJECT
    - *OVERSTATE

14. *Role consciousness*
    - JOB ROLE
    - HIGHER STATUS
    - *ROLE—POSITIVE

15. *Striving*
    - OTHER
    - CONTROL
    - ATTEMPT
    - *VERB—POSITIVE
    - VALUE—POSITIVE

16. *Assertiveness*
    - *MALE ROLE
    - ANGER
    - GOOD
    - GUIDE

17. *Economic concerns*
    - *ECONOMIC
    - ACTION NORM

18. *Compulsiveness*
    - TIME REFERENCE
    - URGE
    - DEFENSE MECHANISM
    - BAD
    - *TIME

NOTE: Asterisks denote "seed" points developed from a hierarchical clustering program.

Exhibit 7 *Nonmetric Multidimensional Scaling Solutions for the Eighteen Composite Variables: Best-fitting Coordinates for a Three-Space Fit (Work = 3.354 at Iteration 25)*

	1	2	3	
1	1.38	-0.39	0.10	Family/communication
2	0.71	0.48	0.41	Recognition of authority
3	0.80	-0.43	0.67	Concern about well-being
4	1.12	-0.58	-0.82	Power and valor
5	-1.05	-0.39	0.09	Male theme
6	1.01	0.49	-0.48	Competition
7	-0.74	0.12	-0.41	Aggression
8	-0.71	-0.96	0.47	Environmental awareness
9	-0.65	-0.86	-0.26	Preoccupation with physical state
10	-0.21	0.13	-1.23	Avoidance
11	-0.23	0.37	0.05	Political sense
12	-1.00	0.49	0.10	Work orientation
13	-0.56	0.48	0.84	Overstatement
14	0.00	0.75	-0.68	Role consciousness
15	0.79	1.12	0.46	Striving
16	-0.56	1.04	-0.02	Assertiveness
17	-0.39	-0.56	0.99	Economic concerns
18	0.30	-1.31	-0.29	Compulsiveness

NOTE: For details of the methodology see Victor E. McGee, "The Multidimensional Scaling of 'Elastic' Distances," *British Journal of Mathematical and Statistical Psychology* 19 (1966), 181–196.

tests for the 217 letters of the four lieutenants are presented in Exhibit 8 (summarized as Table 1 in the previous Appendix).

In order to develop the highs, lows, medium highs, and medium lows for Table 1 in the preceding Appendix, we did post-hoc analyses, using the mean square error and the error degrees of freedom (Newman-Keuls test).

Next we applied a classification analysis to see how well the four sets of letters could be sorted into their respective authorships; this analysis yielded the results shown in Exhibit 9. We applied two kinds of classification procedures, Geisser's Case 8 and Eisenbeis and Avery's Rule R:5.4, which gave slightly different results.[3] However, both showed very high hit rates (over 86%). The letters of Arthur Lang and Thomas Watson were particularly well differentiated, those of Fred Roberts and George Cracklow less so.

When the mother's data were added, the classification hit rate increased—she was different from all the four lieutenants, as we might expect. Sixteen of the eighteen variables showed statistically significant differences at a probability essentially of zero, one more at .002. The two tests, Geisser's and Eisenbeis and Avery's, gave identical hit rates (Exhibit 10).

Again, post-hoc analysis, using the Newman-Keuls test, made possible

Exhibit 8   *Results of a Multiple Discriminant Analysis of the 217 Letters of the Four Lieutenants*

Variable	F ratio	Probability
1. Family/communication	116.36	.000
2. Authority	5.25	.002
3. Well-being	2.38	n.s.
4. Power	4.40	.005
5. Male theme	50.70	.000
6. Competition	11.48	.000
7. Aggression	82.50	.000
8. Environment	29.38	.000
9. Physical state	30.30	.000
10. Avoidance	0.96	n.s.
11. Political	61.63	.000
12. Work	8.14	.000
13. Overstatement	8.43	.000
14. Role consciousness	5.27	.002
15. Striving	13.11	.000
16. Assertiveness	4.97	.003
17. Economic	2.16	n.s.
18. Compulsiveness	3.59	.015

A. Test of equality of the four mean vectors (Rao's F test). F ratio is 12.47, with (54,584) df and PROB = 0.
B. Univariate F ratios with 3 and 213 df.

Exhibit 9   *Results of a Classification Analysis of the Lieutenants' Letters*

	Cracklow	Roberts	Watson	Lang	Total
		Eisenbeis and Avery's Rule R:5.4			
Cracklow	47	3	5	3	58
Roberts	6	23	1	0	30
Watson	6	2	87	0	95
Lang	1	0	0	33	34
Total	60	28	93	36	217
		Geisser's Case 8			
Cracklow	48	2	5	3	58
Roberts	8	21	1	0	30
Watson	6	2	87	0	95
Lang	2	0	0	32	34
Total	64	25	93	35	217

NOTE: For each classification procedure, hits and misses for the sample data are shown. Cell (I,J) shows the number of Group I members classified as belonging to Group J. Number of hits = 190 (87.56%) and 188 (86.64%), respectively.

Exhibit 10   *Results of a Classification Analysis of All 251 Letters*

	Cracklow	Roberts	Thomas Watson	Lang	Sarah Watson	Total
Cracklow	46	2	6	0	4	58
Roberts	7	21	2	0	0	30
Thomas Watson	6	2	87	0	0	95
Lang	0	0	4	30	0	34
Sarah Watson	1	0	0	0	33	34
Total	60	25	99	30	37	251

NOTE: Number of hits = 217 (86.45%).

Exhibit 11   *Results of Ten Random Runs*

Random run	Hit % in larger sample	Hit % in holdout sample
1	87.56	84
2	88.56	76
3	86.57	74
4	86.57	78
5	87.56	82
6	85.07	80
7	84.58	84
8	90.05	76
9	88.56	76
10	88.06	76

the description in Chapter 10 of Sarah Watson's position relative to the four lieutenants.

In order to check our results for consistency, we did ten random runs of multiple discriminant analysis with holdout samples, with 50 of the 251 taken out (10 for Cracklow; 5 each for Roberts, Lang, and Sarah Watson; and 25 for Thomas Watson—i.e., proportional to the N's for each). The results were excellent (Exhibit 11).

The means on the fourteen achievement motivation variables for the four lieutenants were as shown in Exhibit 12.

If these means are ranked and these ranks summed, the score for Cracklow is 41.5, for Roberts 37.5, for Watson 28, and for Lang 33. If the four negative measures (block, failure, affect—negative, and time) are excluded, the numbers are, respectively, 33, 28, 22.5, and 26.5.

As noted in the previous Appendix, we also did a number of experiments using the "Brown Corpus," initially developed by Henry Kucera and others at Brown University and more recently extended by the Norwegian Research Council for Science and the Humanities.[4] The Brown Corpus contains 1,014,232 words in fifteen separate categories; each of these fifteen contains a number of samples of approximately 2,000 words each, as shown in Exhibit 13.

Exhibit 12 *Means on the Fourteen Achievement Motivation Variables for the*
Lieutenants

Variable	Cracklow	Roberts	Watson	Lang	Univariate statistical significance
Need	1.03	1.28	1.30	0.70	.002
To be	0.09	0.02	0	0.03	000
Compete	0.18	0.19	0.10	0.23	.03
Verb—positive	2.93	2.60	2.84	2.34	N.S.
Adverb—positive	0.08	0.05	0.11	0.04	N.S.
Adjective—positive	1.23	0.86	0.57	0.89	000
Value—positive	0.62	0.60	0.36	0.54	.002
Role—positive	0.27	0.30	0.17	0.54	000
Block	0.27	0.29	0.18	0.18	N.S.
Success	0.13	0.17	0.08	0.21	.01
Failure	0.10	0.07	0.07	0.10	N.S.
Affect—positive	0.36	0.33	0.68	0.29	.0001
Affect—negative	0.64	0.81	0.75	0.42	.01
Time	0.48	0.32	0.28	0.28	.03
Grand mean	0.601	0.564	0.535	0.485	

NOTE: Hit percentage in the classification analysis = 64.06.

Exhibit 13 *Number of Samples in Brown Corpus*
Categories

Categories	Samples
Press: Reportage	44
Press: Editorial	27
Press: Reviews	17
Religion	17
Skills and Hobbies	36
Popular Lore	48
Belles Lettres, Biography, etc.	75
Miscellaneous	30
Learned and Scientific Writings	80
Fiction: General	29
Fiction: Mystery and Detective	24
Fiction: Science	6
Fiction: Adventure and Western	29
Fiction: Romance and Love Story	29
Humor	9
Total	500

Exhibit 14 Comparison of the Brown Corpus Sample, and the Mutiny Correspondence Sample

Categories	Brown sample	Mean of our five samples	Cracklow	Roberts	Thomas Watson	Sarah Watson	Lang
1. Family affection/communication	23.44	29.64	21.17	26.16	35.82	41.20	18.33
2. Recognition of authority	4.09	4.40	3.94	5.07	4.19	6.06	3.53
3. Concern about well-being	4.29	2.97	2.77	2.69	2.98	3.70	2.74
4. Power and valor	3.86	4.40	4.55	4.06	4.44	5.42	3.33
5. Male theme	19.35	18.56	20.90	18.62	15.94	14.17	26.28
6. Competition	4.61	3.84	4.08	5.14	3.62	3.32	3.40
7. Aggression	24.79	26.21	32.41	30.74	19.52	19.40	37.10
8. Environmental awareness	9.20	7.52	7.90	6.05	6.96	4.69	12.54
9. Preoccupation with physical state	6.81	5.23	6.12	4.59	4.27	4.47	7.74
10. Avoidance	4.68	5.01	5.09	5.31	4.88	4.82	5.14
11. Political sense	5.53	3.91	3.29	4.67	2.37	5.76	6.71
12. Work orientation	4.39	2.74	2.97	3.12	2.39	1.91	3.82
13. Overstatement	6.09	7.73	8.42	7.89	8.38	5.88	6.45
14. Role consciousness	1.91	2.57	2.03	2.51	2.26	3.63	3.38
15. Striving	8.08	8.99	8.61	8.40	9.56	10.88	6.70
16. Assertiveness	9.99	5.82	5.20	5.26	4.35	11.25	6.10
17. Economic concerns	2.85	2.63	2.84	2.41	2.65	1.93	3.14
18. Compulsiveness	9.48	11.12	12.26	10.75	11.63	8.92	10.32

We took excerpts from three of these: Belles Lettres, Biography, etc. (thirty excerpts); Adventure and Western Fiction (twenty-nine); and Romance and Love Story Fiction (twenty-nine). These were run through the Dartmouth content analysis program and then compared with our data by use of discriminant analysis. In order to find where each of our five people were placed in each of the eighteen variables, and how they compared to the combined Brown sample, a table of means for each was constructed (see Exhibit 14).

When the means of our five were compared with the composite mean of the three Brown sets, eleven areas were significant at $< .001$ and two more at $< .05$; when just the four lieutenants were compared, eight areas were significant at $< .001$, two at $< .01$, and two at $< .05$. The results of our classification (using Eisenbeis and Avery's test) were as follows:

1. For the three Brown categories, taken separately, and all five of our data sets, taken separately—79.94% hits, 17 of 18 significant $< .001$

2. For the three Brown categories, combined as one, and all five of our data sets, taken separately—94.99% hits, 10 of 18 significant $< .001$

3. For the Brown set, combined, and the four lieutenants, taken separately—85.57% hits, 14 of 18 significant $< .001$

4. For the combined Brown set and the combined four lieutenants—94.10% hits, 8 of 18 significant $< .001$

5. For the combined Brown set and the combined five in our set—94.99% hits, 11 of 18 significant $< .001$

Bibliography for the Content
Analysis Project

Anderberg, Michael R. *Cluster Analysis for Applications.* New York: Academic Press, 1973.

Broehl, Wayne G., Jr. *The Village Entrepreneur.* Cambridge: Harvard University Press, 1978.

Broehl, Wayne G., Jr., and Victor E. McGee. "Content Analysis in Psychohistory: A Study of Three Lieutenants in the Indian Mutiny, 1857–58." *Journal of Psychohistory* 8 (1981), 281–306.

Crabb, George. *English Synonymes, with Copious Illustrations and Explanations, Drawn from the Best Writers.* New York: Harper & Bros., 1850.

Dunphy, Dexter C., Cedric C. Bullard, and Elinor E. M. Crossings. "Validation of the General Inquirer Harvard IV Dictionary." Unpublished MS, University of South Wales, n.d.

Eisenbeis, R. A., and R. B. Avery. *Discriminant Analysis and Classification Procedures.* Lexington, Mass.: Heath, 1972.

Ellegard, Alvar. *The Syntactic Structure of English Texts: A Computer-Based Study of Four Kinds of Text in the Brown University Corpus.* Gothenburg Studies in English 43. Gothenburg: Acta Universitatis Gothoburgensis, 1978.

Francis, W. Nelson, Henry Kucera, and Andrew W. Mackie. *Frequency Analysis of English Usage: Lexicon and Grammar.* Boston: Houghton Mifflin, 1982.

Geisser, S. "Posterior Odds for Multivariate Normal Classifications." *Journal of the Royal Statistical Society* 26 (1964), 69–76.

Gottschalk, Louis, and G. C. Gleser. *The Measurement of Psychological States Through the Content Analysis of Verbal Behavior.* Berkeley and Los Angeles: University of California Press, 1969.

Holsti, Oli R. *Content Analysis for the Social Sciences.* Reading, Mass.: Addison-Wesley, 1969.

Iker, Howard P. "An Historical Note on the Use of Word-Frequency Contiguities in Content Analysis." *Computers and the Humanities* 8 (1974), 93–98.

Johansson, S., in collaboration with G. N. Leech and H. Goodluck. *Man-*

ual of Information to Accompany the Lancaster-Oslo/Bergen Corpus of British English for Use with Digital Computers. Oslo: University of Oslo, 1978.

Kelly, Edward F., and Philip J. Stone. *Computer Recognition of English Word Senses*. Amsterdam: North-Holland, 1975.

Krippendorff, Klaus. *Content Analysis: An Introduction to Its Methodology*. Beverly Hills, Calif.: Sage, 1980.

Kucera, Henry, and W. Nelson Francis. *Computational Analysis of Present-Day American English*. Providence: Brown University Press, 1967.

McClelland, David C. *The Achieving Society*. Princeton: Van Nostrand, 1961. 2nd ed., 1976.

McGee, Victor E. "The Multidimensional Scaling of 'Elastic' Distances." *British Journal of Mathematical and Statistical Psychology* 19 (1966), 181–196.

———. *Multivariate Package of BASIC Programs*. 3d ed. Hanover, N.H.: Dartmouth College, 1978. © Dartmouth College.

Oxman, Thomas E., Stanley D. Rosenberg, Paula P. Schnurr, and Gary J. Tucker. "The Language of Paranoia." *American Journal of Psychiatry* 139 (1982), 275–282.

———. "Linguistic Dimensions of Affect and Thought in Somatization Disorder." Paper read at a meeting of the American Psychiatric Association, Los Angeles, May 5–11, 1984.

Oxman, Thomas E., Stanley D. Rosenberg, and Gary J. Tucker. "Characteristics of Paranoid Speech." Unpublished MS, 1980, Department of Psychiatry, Dartmouth Medical School.

Pool, Ithiel de Sola. *Trends in Content Analysis: Summary*. Urbana: University of Illinois Press, 1959.

Roget, Peter Mark. *Thesaurus of English Words and Phrases, Classified and Arranged so as to Facilitate the Expression of Ideas and Assist in Literary Composition*. 2d ed. London: Longman, Brown, Green & Longmans, 1853.

Rosenberg, Stanley D., and Gary J. Tucker. "Verbal Content and the Diagnosis of Schizophrenia." *Proceedings of the 129th Annual Meeting of the American Psychiatric Association* (1976).

———. "Verbal Behavior and Schizophrenia." *Archives of General Psychiatry* 36 (1979), 1331–1337.

Rosenberg, Stanley D., Gary J. Tucker, and Bernard Bergen. "Computer Content Analysis in Psychiatric Research: Issues and Applications." Unpublished MS, 1980, Department of Psychiatry, Dartmouth Medical School.

Spence, Donald P. "Lawfulness in Lexical Choice: A Natural Experiment." *Journal of the American Psychoanalytic Association* 28 (1980), 115–132.

Stone, Philip J., Dexter C. Dunphy, Marshall S. Smith, and Daniel M. Ogilvie. *The General Inquirer: A Computer Approach to Content Analysis.* Cambridge: MIT Press, 1966.

Tucker, Gary J., and Stanley D. Rosenberg. "Computer Content Analysis of Schizophrenic Speech." *American Journal of Psychiatry* 132 (1975), 611–616.

———. "Computer Analysis of Schizophrenic Speech." In Joseph B. Sedowski (ed.), *Technology in Mental Health Care Systems.* Norwood, N.J.: Ablex, 1980.

Weintraub, Walter, and S. Michael Plant. "A Verbal Behavior Analysis of the Watergate Transcripts." Unpublished MS, 1976.

Notes

Introduction

1. George Malleson, *Kaye's and Malleson's History of the Indian Mutiny of 1857–8.* 6 vols. London: Longmans, Green, 1897, iv., 64.

2. The Diary and Letters of A. M. Lang, *Journal of the Society for Army Historical Research,* XI (1932), 25.

Chapter 1. Victoria's Heyday

1. J. B. Priestley, *Victoria's Heyday* (New York: Harper & Row, 1972), p. 11. Quotation from Young is on p. 12.

2. H. M. Vibart, *Addiscombe—Its Heroes and Men of Note* (London: Constable, 1894). W. Broadfoot, "Addiscombe: The East India Company's Military College," *Blackwood's Magazine,* May 1893. F. Clark, *East India Reporter and Army List, 1850* (London: Allen, 1850), pp. xxviii–xxxiii. [Octavius Sturger], *In the Company's Service: A Reminiscence* (London: Allen, 1883), bk. I. Samuel Steelpen [pseud.], *Frederick Green, or the Adventures of an Addiscombe Cadet during the Green Term* (London: Yates, 1851).

3. S. P. Cohen, *The Indian Army* (Berkeley: University of California Press, 1971), pp. 1–9.

4. Vibart, *Addiscombe, p. 24.*

5. Clark, *East India Reporter and Army List, 1850,* p. xxix.

6. Vibart, *Addiscombe,* pp. 107–109.

7. Ibid., p. 71.

8. Ibid., pp. 71–76.

9. Ibid., pp. 80–82.

10. Ibid., pp. 92–97.

11. Ibid., p. 238.

12. Ibid., pp. 240–242.

13. Ibid., pp. 286–289.

14. Ibid., pp. 291–293.

15. Most primary information comes from the extant military records of the two George Cracklows, father and son, in the India Office Library, India Office Records, Foreign and Commonwealth Office, London (hereinafter noted as IOL); the manuscript set used in this study is in the "Indian Mutiny" collection, Special Collections, Baker Library, Dartmouth College (cited here as IM). Basic biographical and career information for the elder Cracklow is at IOL, L/Mil/10/2; for the

son at L/Mil/10/75/29. Records on retirement and pension for George Cracklow the son are at Bengal Military Fund Ledger, L/AG/23/6/8. The officers' annual assignments are noted in Bengal Army Services, L/Mil/10, passim. The services of the elder Cracklow are noted in V. C. P. Hodson, *List of the Officers of the Bengal Army, 1758–1834* (London: Constable, 1927); Cracklow the son is mentioned in Clark's *East India Reporter and Army List* in the years from 1852 until 1862, and both officers are noted in F. W. Stubbs, *List of Officers Who Have Served in the Regiment of the Bengal Artillery* (London: Allen, 1892). Cracklow the son is noted in F. W. Stubbs, *History of the Organization, Equipment and War Services of the Regiment of Bengal Artillery,* vol. III (London: Allen, 1895). A few records of the boyhood of the younger Cracklow in Brighton, England, are extant at the County Record Office, County of Bedford; records of his life in Cheltenham after retirement from the army in 1864 are in the County Records Office, Gloucester. For the younger Cracklow's Addiscombe record, see Addiscombe Cadet Papers, 1840–1849, IOL, L/Mil/9/221 and 341; see also L/Mil/10/53–54. For the "military drawing" project, see *Times* (London), December 13, 1851.

16. Frederick S. Roberts, *Forty-one Years in India,* 2 vols. (London: Bentley, 1897). George W. Forrest, *The Life of Lord Roberts* (London: Cassell, 1914). W. H. Hannah, *Bobs, Kipling's General: The Life of Field-Marshall Earl Roberts of Kandahar, V.C.* (London: Cooper, 1972). David James, *Lord Roberts* (London: Hollis & Carter, 1954). The Roberts mutiny letters were published under his name by his daughter: Frederick S. Roberts, *Letters Written during the Indian Mutiny* (London: Macmillan, 1924).

17. Roberts, "I will go willingly," *Letters,* pp. xvii–xix. For Addiscombe comparisons, see A. Lawrence Lowell, *Colonial Civil Service: The Selection and Training of Colonial Officials in England, Holland and France* (New York: Macmillan, 1900), p. 325.

18. The Arthur Lang papers are held by the Department of Manuscripts, British Library (Add 43818–25; 43973). The Lang mutiny letters were published in full in *Journal of the Society for Army Historical Research* 9 (January 1930), 1–27, (April 1930), 73–97, (October 1930), 189–213; 10 (April 1931), 69–109, (July 1930), 129–143, (October 1931), 195–206; 11 (January 1932), 1–25. These papers will be cited here as *SAHR.* Lang's biographer is quoted from 11:22.

19. Roberts, "I should be ashamed," *Letters,* p. xix. The graduation exercises reported in *Times* (London), December 13, 1851. The paragraphs that follow are from this source also.

20. W. H. Fitchett, *The Tale of the Great Mutiny* (London: Smith, Elder, 1901), p. 97.

Chapter 2. "Curry and Rice"

1. Roberts, *Forty-one Years,* I, 1. Transportation to India in the mid-nineteenth century is described by H. L. Hoskins in *British Routes to India* (London: Cass, 1928). For analysis of communication by letter in this period, see B. B. Misra, *Postal Communications in India* (Manchester: Manchester University Press, 1959); John K. Sidebottom, *The Overland Mail* (London: Allen & Unwin, 1948); *Encyclo-*

pedia of British Empire Postage Stamps, vol. III (London: Robson, Lowe n.d.); D. R. Martin, *Numbers in Early Indian Cancellations, 1855–1884* (London: Robson, Lowe, 1970).

2. T. A. Heathcote, *The Indian Army: The Garrison of British Imperial India, 1822–1922* (New York: Hippocrene Books, 1974), p. 118.

3. The Thomas Watson papers also are unpublished; the manuscript papers are in IM. Quotations in text on Watson's appointment are from IOL, L/Mil/9/225/314; there is additional biographical material at IOL, L/Mil/10/79 (p. 55), 86 (p. 63), 95 (p. 36); and L/AG/23/7/18.

4. Arthur Lang's biographical data from *SAHR,* 9:3–8; 11:22–25. See also *Royal Engineers Journal* 24 (1916), 165; "Lieutenant Lang's Diary," *Blackwood's Magazine* 316 (1974), 543.

5. Philip Woodruff [pseud. of Philip Mason], *The Men Who Ruled India,* 2 vols. (London: Cape, 1953–1954), I, 336.

6. Ibid., pp. 339–340.

7. Charles Aitchison, *Rulers of India: Lord Lawrence* (Oxford: Oxford University Press, Clarendon Press, 1892), p. 62.

8. Vivian Majendie, *Up among the Pandies* (London: Routledge, Warne & Routledge, 1859), pp. 44–45.

9. Oliver Jones, *Recollections of a Winter Campaign in India* (London: Saunders & Otley, 1859), pp. 122–128.

10. S. N. Sen, *Eighteen Fifty-seven* (Delhi: Ministry of Information & Broadcasting, Government of India, 1957), p. 25.

11. George Bourchier, *Eight Months' Campaign against the Bengal Sepoy Army during the Mutiny of 1857* (London: Smith, Elder, 1858).

12. Roberts, *Letters,* pp. 34–35.

13. J. R. J. Jocelyn, *The History of the Royal and Indian Artillery in the Mutiny of 1857* (London: Murray, 1915), pp. 433–434.

14. Joseph Jobe, *Guns: An Illustrated History of Artillery* (Greenwich, Conn.: New York Graphic Society, 1971), pp. 142–143. Fairfax Downey, *Cannonade* (Garden City, N.Y.: Doubleday, 1966), p. 105. For a general description of the Bengal Artillery equipment during this period see Stubbs, *History of the Bengal Artillery,* III, 549–584.

15. Jones, *Recollections of a Winter Campaign,* pp. 62–63, 122–128. The Cracklow quotation is from his letter of March 6, 1857, IM.

16. Woodruff, *The Men Who Ruled India,* I, 314.

17. I. T. Prichard, *The Administration of India from 1859 to 1868: The First Ten Years of Administration under the Crown,* 2 vols. (London, Macmillan, 1869), I, 181–182.

18. For the history of flogging in the British military services in the first half of the nineteenth century, see E. L. Woodward, *The Age of Reform, 1815–1870* (Oxford: Oxford University Press, 1938), p. 257. The differing treatment of British and Indian troops in India is described in Philip Mason, *A Matter of Honour: An Account of the Indian Army, Its Officers and Men* (New York: Holt, Rinehart & Winston, 1974), pp. 202–203. For public school bullying, see John Chandos, *Boys Together: English Public Schools, 1800–1864* (New Haven: Yale University Press, 1984). The Stephen quotation, ibid., pp. 326–327. Quotation on "draconian" rule of William

Hodson, ibid., p. 97. Quotation on army officer beating a servant, anonymous letter to Lt. P. Vans Agnew, May 23, 1803, IM.

19. Cracklow on housing, March 6, 1857, IM. Woodruff, *The Men Who Ruled India,* I, 325.

20. National Archives of India, Government of India, Index to Foreign Department Proceedings for the Years 1850–1859, Sialkot, F.C. 69–70, 165–168, 212–213, 221–223.

21. Lang on dances, December 23 and 26, 1856; "pucka Executive," April 6, 1857, SAHR. Sarah Watson on health, January 25, 1857, IM. Thomas Watson on attitude about Sialkot, ibid. Roberts's description of his leave, *Forty-one Years,* I, 38–39. Cracklow's description of his leaves, October 21, 1854, and June 3, 1856, IM.

22. Sen, *Eighteen Fifty-seven,* p. 23. Julius George Medley, *A Year's Campaigning in India from March 1857 to March 1858* (London: Thacker, 1858), p. 197. George F. Atkinson, *"Curry and Rice,"* or the Ingredients of a Social Life at "Our Station" in India (London: Day, n.d.), chap. entitled "Our Judge."

23. Thomas Frost, ed., *Complete Narrative of the Mutiny in India, from Its Commencement to the Present Time,* 3d ed. (London: Read, 1858), p. 29.

24. Gwyn Harries-Jenkins, *The Army in Victorian Society* (London: Routledge & Kegan Paul, 1977), p. 147.

25. For discussion of "black lust" in the Jamaican insurrection, see Douglas A. Larimer, *Colour, Class and the Victorians: English Attitudes to the Negro in the Mid-Nineteenth Century* (Leicester: Leicester University Press, 1978), pp. 182–184.

26. Micaiah Hill to Rev. G. Burden, October 22, 1822, IM.

Chapter 3. Devil's Wind

1. The statement of the inspector-general in regard to the grease on the cartridges, dated January 29, 1857, is reprinted in full in Francis C. Maude, *Memories of the Mutiny with Which Is Incorporated the Personal Narrative of John Walter Sherer,* 2 vols., 2d ed. (London: Remington, 1894), I, 509.

2. Cracklow on the beginning of the mutiny, May 22, 1857, IM.

3. Roberts's quotations, *Letters,* pp. 2–5.

4. Lang on "hoi Polloi," April 5, 1857; "terrible example," April 8; idiotic caste rules, April 15; Edwardes, April 26; Meerut meeting, May 12; disarming, May 13; Montgomery at house, May 14; "exciting time" and "daft with fright," May 18; "croakers," June 1; "like a fair," June 7, "patience," June 8; gallows, June 9, *SAHR.*

5. Bourchier, *Eight Months' Campaign,* pp. 2–5. Roberts on amir of Kabul, *Letters,* pp. 39–40.

6. Sarah Watson on "tiffin," January 22, 1857; "knocked up," January 25; "a coquette," February 28; violent feelings, June 4; "act of justice," June 30; "hide under shadow," July 1; house "cheerful," July 5; "comfort of scriptures," June 15, IM. Harcourt S. Anson (ed.), *With H.M. 9th Lancers during the Indian Mutiny: The Letters of Brevet-Major O. H. S. G. Anson* (London: Allen, 1896), p. 6. Thomas Watson on "burning feelings," June 26, IM. Sarah Watson on "misled and unoffend-

ing," June 9, IM. Bourchier, *Eight Months' Campaign*, p. 3. George W. Forrest, *History of the Indian Mutiny*, 3 vols. (Edinburgh: Blackwood, 1904), I, 5.

7. Roberts on "confidence," *Letters*, pp. 9–10.

8. National Archives, Government of India, Foreign Proceedings (Military), John Lawrence to Native Officers and Sepoys of the 4th N.I., August 11, 1857, Secret 408–411, December 18, 1857.

9. Roberts on "drum head," *Forty-one Years*, I, 123. William Butler, *The Land of the Veda, Being Personal Reminiscences of India, Its People, Castes, Thugs and Fakirs, Its Religion, Mythology, Principal Monuments, Palaces and Mausoleums, Together with Incidents of the Great Sepoy Rebellion and Its Results to Christianity and Civilization* (New York: Nelson & Phillips, 1875), p. 314.

10. Cracklow's description of "blowing from guns," June 10, IM. *Narrative of the Indian Revolt from Its Outbreak to the Capture of Lucknow by Sir Colin Campbell* (London: Vickers, 1858), p. 142.

11. Roberts, *Letters*, p. 12.

12. Cracklow on Chamberlain, June 10; "Jack Vetch," July 1, IM.

13. George Malleson, *Kaye's and Malleson's History of the Indian Mutiny of 1857–8*, II, 368–369.

14. Lang on movable column, June 9; "croakers," June 8; "croaking cowards" and "not a nigger," June 2; "never slaves," June 15; "Cortez or Pizzaro," June 17; "poor, frightened ladies," June 18, *SAHR*. Cracklow on Delhi news, May 27; Gwalior mutiny, August 10, IM. Sen, *Eighteen Fifty-seven*, p. 291. Lang on Boileau family and "inoffensive Hindoo," June 18; walls with ladies, June 22; "dawdling cantonment," June 23; "suicide," June 25; "too comfortable" and "careless station," June 30; *Friend of India*, July 5, *SAHR*.

15. Gregory Rich, *The Mutiny in Sialkot, with a Brief Description of the Cantonment from 1852–1857* (Sialkot: Handa Press, 1924), pp. 11–12, 53–57.

16. Sarah Watson on Sialkot, July 5; loss of property, July 19; levy and wretches, July 24; "imprudent," August 2; "enemies," October 21, IM. Thomas Watson on Caulfield, November 31 [*sic*], IM. J. Cave Browne, *The Punjab and Delhi in 1857*, 2 vols. (Edinburgh: Blackwood, 1861), II, 68.

17. Cracklow on "went to General," July 13, 1857, IM. Bourchier, *Eight Months' Campaign*, pp. 13–14, 17, 20. Cave Browne on Nicholson, *The Punjab and Delhi*, II, 74–75; "gnashing of teeth," ibid., II, 98. Nicholson's order on the river crossing in his letter to Dickson, July 13, 1857, National Army Museum (London), ms. 6807–45199.

18. National Archives, Government of India, R. Montgomery to A. Brandreth, August 10, 1857, Secret 408–411, December 18, 1857.

19. Cracklow on "buggies," July 28, 1857; IM. Roberts on appointment to quartermaster post, *Letters*, p. 19.

20. Lang on Sialkot mutiny and "old muffs," July 10; Boileau quarters, July 12; Lahore as "capital," July 14; engagement, July 16; "twaddle," July 2; parting, July 28; meetings with Cracklow and Bourchier, July 25 and 26; "no carpet-Knight," July 26; meeting with Roberts. July 28, *SAHR*. Cracklow on river crossings, July 28, IM.

21. Roberts on his wounding, *Letters,* p. 25; "officers being killed," ibid., p. 28.

22. Bourchier on his leave, *Eight Months' Campaign,* p. 35. Cracklow on Bourchier's return, August 10, IM. Thomas Watson on Sialkot house, June 26; "nervous" about command, July 30, IM. Sarah Watson on leave, August 7, IM.

Chapter 4. The Battle for Delhi

1. Roberts on "formidable" Delhi, *Letters,* p. 19; "melancholy," ibid., p. 27.

2. Ibid., p. 48.

3. Cracklow on walled gardens and "creeping," August 26, IM.

4. "Letters from Lieutenant Edward Chamier to General Sir James Outram," November 24, 1857, privately printed, circa 1858, p. 25, IOL. Robert Henry Wallace Dunlop, *Service and Adventure with the Khakee Ressalah, or Meerut Volunteer Horse, during the Mutinies of 1857–58* (London: Bentley, 1858), pp. 138–139.

5. Cracklow on artillery officers, August 26; "without obligation," August 10, IM. Roberts on the Victoria Cross, *Letters,* p. 29. There is further information on the Victoria Cross in John Smyth, *The Story of the Victoria Cross, 1856–1963* (London: Muller, 1963); Rupert Stewart, *The Victoria Cross: The Empire's Role of Valour* (London: Hutchinson, 1928). Lang on "jungly garden," July 30; "infernal machine," August 4; disloyalty of servants, August 8; work steeling mind, August 13; building own works, August 22; beauty of tents, July 28, *SAHR.*

6. Anson, *With H.M. 9th Lancers,* p. 53. Lang on "ground once ours," August 22; mustering courage, August 14, *SAHR.* Roberts on General Wilson, *Letters,* p. 41, and *Forty-one Years,* I, 213–214.

7. "Towering form of Nicholson," Cave Browne, *The Punjab and Delhi,* II, 152. "Chivalry" at Najafgarh, James Burnie Lind, "Jim's Experiences during the Mutiny of 1857–58," p. 52, Ms. 5105–89, National Army Museum (London). Cracklow on cleanup, September 11, IM. Roberts on visit to Nicholson, *Letters,* p. 50. Cracklow on "old Nick," August 10, IM. Roberts on artillery officers, *Letters,* p. 35.

8. Jocelyn, *History of the Royal and Indian Artillery,* p. 116.

9. Cracklow on breach, September 11, 1857, IM. Roberts on "*the* Battery," *Letters,* p. 53. Cracklow on "good spirits," August 10, IM. Lang on "sharpening swords," September 11; "no nonsense," September 12; glacis, September 13, *SAHR.* Medley, *A Year's Campaigning in India,* pp. 98–99.

10. Cracklow on "plucky Pandies," September 11, IM. Roberts on "few will be spared," *Letters,* p. 37. Archdale Wilson report in Malleson, *Kaye's and Malleson's History,* IV, 2.

11. National Archives, Government of India, Secret 408–411, December 18, 1857, quoting *Delhi News* of August 7, 1857; ibid., Secret 23, October 30, 1857, quoting *Delhi News* of September 2, 1857.

12. Michael Edwardes, *Battles of the Indian Mutiny* (New York: Macmillan, 1963), p. 39.

13. Cracklow on "brutes," and account of the attack, September 22, IM. Lang's story of the attack, September 14, *SAHR.*

14. On "faulty formation," P. R. Innes, *The History of the Bengal European Regi-*

ment, *Now the Royal Munster Fusiliers, and How It Helped to Win India* (London: Simpkin, Marshall, 1885), p. 484. Lawrence's description of attack of Fourth Column, National Archives, Government of India, R. C. Lawrence to Military Secretary, Lahore, October 5, 1857, Secret 448, December 18, 1857. Henry Knollys, *Life of General Sir Hope Grant,* 2 vols. (Edinburgh: Blackwood, 1894), I, 249.

15. Lawrence and Dwyer quotations, Government of India, National Archives, R. C. Lawrence to Military Secretary, Lahore, October 5, 1857, Secret 448, December 18, 1857. "Poet Laureate" quotation, A. R. D. Mackenzie, *Mutiny Memoirs, Being Personal Reminiscences of the Great Sepoy Revolt of 1857* (Allahabad: Pioneer Press, 1891), p. 91. "Costly heroics" and William Hodson description, James Leason, *The Red Fort* (New York: Reynal, 1956), p. 322.

16. William Hodson as *beau ideal,* Sen, *Eighteen Fifty-seven,* p. 99. Fred Roberts on Fourth Column, *Letters,* p. 63.

17. Lang on Kabul Gate attack, September 14, *SAHR*. Anson, *With H.M. 9th Lancers,* p. 154. Cracklow on cowardice, September 22, IM.

18. Telegrams from National Archives, Government of India, J. D. MacPherson to Chief Commissioner's Office, Lahore, September 13, 15, 18, 19, 1857, Secret 75, October 30, 1857. Cracklow on drinking, September 22, IM. William Hodson on "demoralized" men, George H. Hodson, *Twelve Years of a Soldier's Life in India, Being Extracts from the Letters of the Late Major W. S. R. Hodson* (London: Parker, 1859), p. 296. Lang on torture, September 17, *SAHR*. Roberts on drinking, *Letters,* p. 64, and *Forty-one Years,* I, 243. "Deplorable" breaking of bottles, Edwardes, *Battles of the Indian Mutiny,* p. 49. Bourchier on drinking, *Eight Months' Campaign,* p. 70.

19. Roberts on "portmanteau," *Letters,* p. 59; Nicholson, ibid., p. 64; Burn Bastion, ibid., pp. 66–67. Lang on his meeting with Roberts, September 19, *SAHR*. Roberts on two native women, *Letters,* p. 60; king's son, ibid., p. 37. Lieutenant McDowell's report on the killing of the princes, Hodson, *Twelve Years of a Soldier's Life,* p. 310. William Hodson on "seizing and destroying" the princes, ibid., p. 297. Roberts on Hodson, *Forty-one Years,* I, 250; capture of the palace, *Letters,* p. 68.

20. Forrest, *History of the Indian Mutiny,* I, 150–154. Roberts on brevet majority, *Letters,* p. 69. Bourchier on "bigotry," *Eight Months' Campaign,* p. 75.

Chapter 5. Agra's Smug Garrison, Cawnpore's Well

1. Cracklow on visit to general, September 25, IM. Roberts on "handsome," *Letters,* p. 73. Lang on the march, September 25 and 27; "soldiers' life," October 16, *SAHR*. Roberts's description of Delhi streets, *Forty-one Years,* I, 258–259.

2. Bourchier on "Musselmen," *Eight Months' Campaign,* pp. 78–84. Roberts on "bad district," *Letters,* p. 75.

3. National Archives, Government of India, A. Brandeth to G. F. Edmonstone, Secret 440–443, October 9, 1857; ibid., Secret 447, December 18, 1857.

4. George Cracklow's role in the Battle of Bulandshahr, see "Lieutenant G. Cracklow, Commanding 2nd Troop, 3rd Brigade, Horse Artillery to Captain C. H. Blunt, Commanding in Charge," reprinted in G. W. Forrest (ed.), *Selections from*

the Letters, Dispatches and Other State Papers Preserved in the Military Department of the Government of India, 1857–58, 3 vols. (Calcutta: Military Department Press, 1893), III, p. ix. See also Bengal General Orders, July-December 1857, No. 1627, December 23, 1857, IOL; Jocelyn, *History of the Royal and Indian Artillery,* pp. 134–135. Thomas Benson Laurence, *Six Years in the North-West, from 1854 to 1860, Being Extracts from a Private Diary, with a Glimpse of the Rebellion of 1857–1858* (Calcutta, 1859), p. 42. Roberts on Nicholson's horse, *Letters,* p. 73. Lang on the timorousness of troops, September 28, *SAHR.*

5. Quotations on killing of the wounded men from "Diary of Private Frederick Potiphar," p. 56, 7201–45–2, National Army Museum (London). Malleson on "their dash," *Kaye's and Malleson's History,* IV, 13.

6. Cracklow, "just commencing," October 18, IM. Lang on Malagarh Fort, September 29; explosion leading to the death of Home, October 1, *SAHR.*

7. Bourchier on Khurja, *Eight Months' Campaign,* p. 91. Roberts on Khurja, *Forty-one Years,* I, 264.

8. Roberts, *Forty-one Years,* I, 266–267.

9. Roberts's intelligence reports on Agra, *Letters,* p. 79. Bourchier on Agra inhabitants, *Eight Months' Campaign,* p. 95. Roberts on "dirty looking lot," *Forty-one Years,* I, p. 270. "Dreadful looking men," C. Raikes, *Notes on the Revolt in the North-West Provinces of India* (London: Longmans, Brown, Greene, Longmans & Roberts, 1858), pp. 69–70. Lang on "good Sikhs" and "coffee shop," October 10, *SAHR.* Roberts on his faulty intelligence, *Letters,* p. 83; his report to Colonel Becher, ibid., appendix, p. 163. Bourchier on "fat old gentleman," *Eight Months' Campaign,* p. 107. Roberts on the Taj picnic, *Letters,* p. 82. Lang on "jolly picnic," October 13, *SAHR.*

10. Thomas Watson on "this dull place," October 15, IM. Sarah Watson on his companions, October 3, IM. Thomas Watson on "no wish to mix," November 23, IM. Sarah Watson on the move to Kupowlie, October 10; feeling "most alone," October 21, IM. Thomas Watson on "stranger among strangers," October 15; Delhi houses, November 23, IM. Sarah Watson on "Christian man," October 16; attempted conversion, December 12; Seaton column, December 14, IM. Thomas Watson on lack of a dooly, November 18, IM.

11. Edwardes, *Battles of the Indian Mutiny,* p. 66.

12. Ibid.

13. "Depositions taken at Cawnpore, under the direction of Lieutenant-Colonel G. W. Williams, Commissioner of Military Police, North-Western Provinces," in Forrest, *Selections,* III, xliv.

14. "Receptacle was far too small," Maude, *Memories of the Mutiny,* I, 208. Though the sixty-two witnesses in the "Williams" hearings did produce conflicting testimony on many points, this story of the children was mentioned by several of them: "Depositions taken at Cawnpore."

15. Quotation on childrens' feet, T. Gowing, *A Soldier's Experience or a Voice from the Ranks, Showing the Cost of War in Blood and Treasure: A Personal Narrative of the Crimean Campaign, from the Standpoint of the Ranks; the Indian Mutiny and Some of Its Atrocities; the Afghan Campaigns of 1863; Also Sketches of the Lives and*

Deaths of Sr. H. Havelock, K.C.B. and Captain Hedley Vicars, Together with Some Things Not Generally Known, by One of the Royal Fusiliers (Nottingham: Forman, 1899), p. 288.

16. Malleson, *Kaye's and Malleson's History*, IV, 301.

17. The story of General Wheeler's daughter has been reprinted in a number of places; I have quoted from Charles Ball, *The History of the Indian Mutiny: Giving a Detailed Account of the Sepoy Insurrection in India; and a Concise History of the Great Military Events Which Have Tended to Consolidate British Empire in Hindostan,* 2 vols. (London: London Printing & Publishing Co., 1858), I, 344. For Williams quotation on "most searching and earnest enquiries," see Forrest, *History of the Indian Mutiny,* I, 479; Malleson, *Kaye's and Malleson's History,* II, 281.

18. R. Montgomery Martin, *The Indian Empire,* 3 vols. (London: London Printing & Publishing Co., 1858), II, 449. John William Kaye, *History of the Sepoy War in India, 1857–1858,* 3 vols. (London: Allen, 1870), II, 270.

19. Edwardes, *Battles of the Indian Mutiny,* p. 67.

20. Cracklow on Cawnpore well, October 28, IM. Roberts's views, *Letters,* pp. 87, 91. Lang's words and sketch, October 28, *SAHR.* Bourchier on "everyone with a black face," *Eight Months' Campaign,* p. 122.

21. R. C. Majumdar, *British Paramountcy and Indian Renaissance* (Bombay: Bharatiya Vidya Bhavan, 1963), part I, p. 592.

22. Ball, *History of the Indian Mutiny,* I, 390. For a different version of Neill's order see W. Gordon-Alexander, *Recollections of a Highland Subaltern* (London: Arnold, 1898), pp. 38–39; Malleson, *Kayes's and Malleson's History,* IV, 300.

23. W. Forbes-Mitchell, *Reminiscences of the Great Mutiny, 1857–59* (London: Macmillan, 1893), pp. 19–20.

24. Roberts on "10 years older," *Letters,* p. 92. Lang on "my duty," October 16; his sunstroke, October 22, *SAHR.* Cracklow on "errant cowards," November 10; "game of long bowls," November 20, IM.

Chapter 6. Lucknow—the First Battle

1. Cracklow on Havelock, November 10, IM. Havelock on liquor, Edwardes, *Battles of the Indian Mutiny,* p. 83. Ingles quotation, ibid., p. 94. "Tough old buck," Christopher Hibbert, *The Great Mutiny, India, 1857* (New York: Viking Press, 1978), p. 333. The "Sir Crawling Camel" moniker can be found in several places; see ibid., p. 334.

2. Gordon-Alexander, *Recollections of a Highland Subaltern,* p. 209.

3. Jones, *Recollections of a Winter Campaign,* pp. 60–61.

4. Bourchier, *Eight Months' Campaign,* p. 129. Gordon-Alexander, *Recollections of a Highland Subaltern,* p. 46.

5. Forbes-Mitchell, *Reminiscences of the Great Mutiny,* p. 30. Lang on the killing of the water carrier and the Roberts skirmish, November 2, *SAHR.* Roberts on this incident, *Letters,* p. 97.

6. *Blackwood's Magazine,* October 1858.

7. Forbes-Mitchell, *Reminiscences of the Great Mutiny,* pp. 33–34.

8. Lang on monkeys, November 14, *SAHR*.

9. Cracklow on "Pandy cowardice," December 2, IM. Forbes-Mitchell report on Lieutenant Mayne, *Reminiscences of the Great Mutiny*, pp. 44–45.

10. Roberts's description of Maynes's death, *Letters*, pp. 104–105, and *Forty-one Years*, I, 313.

11. Hugh Henry Gough quotation from *Old Memories* (Edinburgh: Blackwood, 1897), pp. 161–162. See also *Blackwood's Magazine*, October 1858.

12. Fitchett, *Tale of the Great Mutiny*, pp. 219–220. Gordon-Alexander, *Recollections of a Highland Subaltern*, p. 69. See also Forrest, *History of the Indian Mutiny*, II, 294.

13. Roberts describes the Blunt charge in *Letters*, p. 103, and *Forty-one Years*, I, 322.

14. Roberts, *Forty-one Years*, I, 323.

15. Forrest, *History of the Indian Mutiny*, II, 146.

16. *Blackwood's Magazine*, October 1858.

17. Malleson, *Kaye's and Malleson's History*, IV, 129. Gordon-Alexander has a different version, with the Highlanders playing a larger role: *Recollections of a Highland Subaltern*, pp. 85–90; he places Blunt near the breach but believes the latter misidentified the man who made the "Harlequin leap."

18. Roberts on the taking of the Secundrabagh, *Forty-one Years*, I, 325–326. Cracklow on the breaching, December 2, IM.

19. Lang on the Secundrabagh attack, November 16, *SAHR*.

20. Bourchier, *Eight Months' Campaign*, p. 143. Roberts, *Letters*, p. 104.

21. Edwardes, *Battles of the Indian Mutiny*, p. 110.

22. Forbes-Mitchell, *Reminiscences of the Great Mutiny*, p. 78.

23. Bourchier, *Eight Months' Campaign*, p. 145. Lang on Peel's gun, November 16, *SAHR*. Gordon-Alexander, *Recollections of a Highland Subaltern*, p. 141.

24. Cracklow on "regular bolt," December 2, IM. Lang on "shame," November 24, *SAHR*. H. W. Norman, *Lecture on the Relief of Lucknow* (Simla: Station Press, 1867), p. 24. Maria Germon, *Journal of the Siege of Lucknow*, ed. Michael Edwardes (London: Constable, 1958), p. 122.

25. Cracklow on the evacuation, December 2, IM.

26. Roberts on ladies, *Forty-one Years*, I, 346. Gordon-Alexander on "fearful stench," *Recollections of a Highland Subaltern*, p. 141. Lang on "ladies and children interspersed," November 24, *SAHR*.

27. Lang on "gypsying," November 25, *SAHR*. Cracklow on women as "encumbrance," December 2, IM. Roberts on the evacuation, *Letters*, p. 106 (see also Countess Roberts's footnote here).

28. National Archives, Government of India, Secret 83, December 18, 1857.

29. Forrest, *History of the Indian Mutiny*, II, 221–222.

30. Malleson, *Kaye's and Malleson's History*, IV, 196.

31. Forrest, *History of the Indian Mutiny*, II, 226.

32. Cracklow on pursuit, December 16, IM. Gough, *Old Memories*, p. 177.

33. Cracklow on the future, December 2, IM. Roberts on his desire for a leave, *Letters*, p. 119. Lang on Royal Engineers and staying in the engineers, December

13, *SAHR*. Quotations on Bithoor well, Knollys, *Life of General Sir Hope Grant*, I, 315.

Chapter 7. Skirmishes, Banners, and Crosses

1. H. H. Stansfeld, MS, December 16, 1857, 7606–43, National Army Museum (London).

2. Cracklow on Christmas dinner, December 30, IM. Lang on Cracklow's hunting, December 25 and 28; women and children at Etawah, December 29, *SAHR*. Bourchier on this incident, *Eight Months' Campaign*, p. 180. Lang on cutting women and children with tulwars, December 29, *SAHR*.

3. Thomas Watson on the two Seaton battles, December 14 and December 17, IM.

4. Sarah Watson on *"fatigue,"* December 14, IM. Thomas Watson on leaving men, December 28; comments after leaving, January 10, 1858, IM.

5. Cracklow on Royals being left behind, January 9, 1858, IM. Lang on troops from the Crimea, December 15, 1857, *SAHR*. Roberts on "battles in every shape," *Letters*, p. 112; Colin Campbell, ibid., p. 116; "masters of India," ibid., p. 119.

6. Cracklow on Fatehgahr, January 9, IM. Roberts on capturing standard, *Letters*, p. 134.

7. Malleson, *Kaye's and Malleson's History*, IV, 214.

8. Rudyard Kipling, typescript report concerning Colonel Fielden in letter to Lady Roberts, December 27, 1929, 5504/71 and 72, National Army Museum (London). Jones, *Recollections of a Winter Campaign*, p. 80.

9. Jones, *Recollections of a Winter Campaign*, pp. 88–90.

10. Majendie, *Up among the Pandies*, p. 58.

11. Anson, *With H.M. 9th Lancers*, p. 231.

12. Roberts on dead bodies of husbands, *Letters*, p. 140. Jones, *Recollections of a Winter Campaign*, p. 145.

13. Cracklow on beating a native, February 10; leave in 1862, March 4, IM.

14. Roberts on royal gunners, *Letters*, p. 128; brevet majority, ibid., p. 134.

15. Cracklow on passage money, January 9, IM. Roberts on prize money, *Letters*, p. 133. Cracklow on dog Meg, January 9, IM.

16. Cracklow on Campbell strategy, January 25 and February 10 and 14, IM. Lang on Campbell, February 21, *SAHR*. Roberts on the Victoria Cross, *Letters*, pp. 134, 142.

17. Thomas Watson on "pushing one's way," January 10; talk with General Grant, January 11; appointments, January 19; staying in tent alone, January 17 and 19; Bourchier's and FitzGerald's coldness, January 20; his brother John, January 21; marching away from mother, February 7, IM.

18. Sarah Watson on "own class of life," January 22; complaints about breakfast, February 3; move to Simla, March 4 and 5; the Sialkot house, January 1, IM.

19. Cracklow on Victoria Cross, February 14, IM. Smyth, *The Story of the Victoria Cross*, pp. 15, 457.

20. William Howard Russell, *My Indian Mutiny Diary*, ed. Michael Edwardes

(London: Cassell, 1957), p. 42. Lionel Dawson, *Squires and Sepoys, 1857–1958* (London: Hollis & Carter, 1960), pp. 90–91.

21. Gordon-Alexander, *Recollections of a Highland Subaltern*, p. 100. Knollys, *Life of General Sir Hope Grant*, I, 331.

22. Cracklow on task at Lucknow, February 10, IM.

Chapter 8. The Final Battle for Lucknow

1. Cracklow on siege train, March 4, IM. Lang on same, March 3, *SAHR*.

2. Thomas Watson on "watching by glass," March 2; the enemy firings, March 5, IM.

3. Knollys, *Life of General Sir Hope Grant*, p. 344.

4. Russell, *My Indian Mutiny Diary*, pp. 55–56.

5. Malleson, *Kaye's and Malleson's History*, IV, 257. Majendie, *Up among the Pandies*, pp. 163–164.

6. Fitchett, *Tale of the Great Mutiny*, p. 354. Roberts, *Letters*, p. 145.

7. Cracklow on "licking," March 12, IM. Majendie, *Up among the Pandies*, p. 174. Jocelyn, *History of the Royal and Indian Artillery*, p. 280.

8. Majendie, *Up among the Pandies*, pp. 187–188. Russell, *My Indian Mutiny Diary*, p. 87.

9. Jones, *Recollections of a Winter Campaign*, p. 169.

10. Lang on Hodson's death, March 11, *SAHR*. Roberts on Hodson, *Letters*, p. 146, and *Forty-one Years*, I, 404. Russell, *My Indian Mutiny Diary*, p. 93. Forbes-Mitchell, *Reminiscences of the Great Mutiny*, p. 215.

11. Russell, *My Indian Mutiny Diary*, p. 90. Lang on shells falling short, March 11, *SAHR*. Jones, *Recollections of a Winter Campaign*, pp. 169–172.

12. Cracklow on Iron and Stone bridges, March 12, IM. Majendie, *Up among the Pandies*, pp. 192–196, 199–200, 205–206, 217, 221–225.

13. Majendie, *Up among the Pandies*, pp. 230–231.

14. Lang on mutineers killing one another, March 14, *SAHR*.

15. Edwardes, *Battles of the Indian Mutiny*, p. 131. Roberts, *Forty-one Years*, I, 406. Innes, *History of the Bengal European Regiment*, p. 522.

16. Malleson, *Kaye's and Malleson's History*, III, 252–256; IV, 281.

17. Thomas Watson on "not firing a shot," March 14; "uncomfortable place," March 15; "Lucknow is taken," March 18; looting, March 21, IM.

18. Cracklow on looting, March 28, IM.

19. Russell, *My Indian Mutiny Diary*, pp. 101, 103–104.

20. Forbes-Mitchell, *Reminiscences of the Great Mutiny*, p. 221.

21. Majendie, *Up among the Pandies*, p. 201. Jones, *Recollections of a Winter Campaign*, p. 197.

22. Forbes-Mitchell, *Reminiscences of the Great Mutiny*, p. 228.

23. Gordon-Alexander, *Recollections of a Highland Subaltern*, p. 284.

24. Majendie, *Up among the Pandies*, pp. 244–245.

25. Lang on Elliot Brownlow, March 17 and 25, *SAHR*. Typescript of mutiny letters of Col. H. P. Pearson, MS, EUR, C321, IOL. James Aberigh-MacKay, *From*

London to Lucknow: With Memoranda of Mutinies, Marches, Flights, Fights, and Conversations, to Which Is Added an Opium-Smuggler's Explanation of the Pieho Massacre by a Chaplain in H.M. Indian Service, 2 vols. (London: Nisbet, 1860), II, 444–445.

26. Cracklow on "heartily sick," March 28, IM. Roberts on his Victoria Cross, promotions, and a possible leave, *Letters,* pp. 154–156, and *Forty-one Years,* I, 411.

Chapter 9. Small, Nasty Mop-ups

1. Cracklow on attacking villages, May 16, IM.

2. Jocelyn, *History of the Royal and Indian Artillery,* p. 373. Malleson, *Kaye's and Malleson's History,* IV, 380. Cracklow on Adrian Hope death, April 25, IM.

3. Cracklow on battle at Simri, May 16, IM. Majendie, *Up among the Pandies,* p. 283.

4. Knollys, *Life of General Sir Hope Grant,* I, 358.

5. Forbes-Mitchell, *Reminiscences of the Great Mutiny,* 242.

6. Majendie, *Up among the Pandies,* p. 267.

7. Ibid., pp. 292–293.

8. Cracklow on "life is terrible," June 9; the "Royals," May 30, IM.

9. Thomas Watson on appointment as provost marshal, April 17, 19, and 21, IM. Sarah Watson's reply, April 25, IM. Thomas Watson on clubbing with minister, May 1 and 9; Europeans in the sun, May 25; his eleven servants, June 8, IM. Sarah Watson on Mrs. Scott, June 4; Mrs. Money, June 11 and 23, IM.

10. Cracklow on battle at Nawabgunge-Barabanki, June 22, IM. Grant's account, Edwardes, *Battles of the Indian Mutiny,* p. 140.

11. Cracklow on Nawabpuje and the Royals, July 19; homesickness and getting out of the service, August 22; being put in charge and Money, October 26, IM.

12. Knollys, *Life of General Sir Hope Grant,* I, 346.

13. National Archives, Government of India, J. D. Forsyth to G. F. Edmonstone, May 22, 1858, Secret 52–55, June 25, 1858.

14. Cracklow on "miserable Raja," November 27, IM.

15. National Archives, Government of India, R. A. Princep to R. N. Cust, January 7, 1859, F.C. 645–646, February 25, 1859.

16. Thomas Watson on meeting with General Grant, July 9 and 14; "Athletic Society," July 14, IM. Sarah Watson on walking with a dog, July 10, IM. Thomas Watson on difficulties with Mrs. Money, August 9 and September 4; the best tent, September 4 and 19; buggy, May 20 and June 3, IM. Sarah Watson on proselytizing, July 16; natives, September 23, IM. Thomas Watson on "Sir Lawrence," August 23; shunning society, August 21 and September 14; secret cause for not getting appointment, September 25; new command a "queer lot," October 17, IM.

17. Forrest, *History of the Indian Mutiny,* III, 511.

18. Thomas Watson's citation for Rampore battle, G.O.C.C., January 15, 1859. Thomas Watson on losing his post, December 5, IM. Sarah Watson on no one understanding her as well as Thomas, undated fragment, N33, IM.

19. Cracklow on trip to Umballa and Simla, February 28 and May 12, 1859, IM.

Chapter 10. A Mutiny's Legacy

1. Roberts on his mother and father, *Forty-one Years,* I, 450. See also James, *Lord Roberts,* p. 55; Forrest, *The Life of Lord Roberts,* p. 40.

2. James, *Lord Roberts,* p. 241.

3. Rudyard Kipling's "Bobs" has been printed in a number of places; see ibid., pp. 241–243. Roberts's horse Vonolel is discussed in ibid. at pp. 246, 260.

4. Ibid., p. 485.

5. Cracklow on "becoming a barbarian" and women quarreling, May 25, 1860; suicide, June 27; fall from horse, July 14; paralysis, November 2 and 3, IM. His will is dated February 17, 1870, Cheltenham, County Gloucester; his pension is noted in Bengal Military Fund Ledger, IOL, L/AG/23/6/8, p. 165.

6. Lang's obituary is in *Journal of the Society for Army Historical Research* II (1932), 22; and in *Royal Engineers Journal,* October 1916, p. 165.

7. Thomas Watson's service record is listed in IOL, L/AG/23/7/18, p. 28.

8. Chandos, *Boys Together,* p. 320.

9. David Roberts, *Paternalism in Early Victorian England* (New Brunswick, N.J.: Rutgers University Press, 1979), p. 277.

10. There are a number of editions of Thomas Hughes's *Tom Brown's Schooldays,* first published by Macmillan in 1856. I have drawn on the Penguin edition, 1971. Chandos on "Dickensian suppression," *Boys Together,* p. 290.

11. Peter Gay in Charles B. Strozier and Daniel Offer, *The Leader: Psychohistorical Essays* (New York: Plenum Press, 1985), p. xii. David E. Stannard, *Shrinking History: On Freud and the Failure of Psychohistory* (New York: Oxford University Press, 1980), p. 156. See also Gay's book *Freud for Historians* (New York: Oxford University Press, 1985).

12. A place to start on leadership studies is James MacGregor Burns, *Leadership* (New York: Harper & Row, 1978). The older classic studies of leadership have been supplemented by a number of recent books: Michael Maccoby, *The Leader* (New York: Simon & Schuster, 1981); William E. Rosenbach and Robert L. Taylor, eds., *Contemporary Issues in Leadership* (Boulder, Colo.: Westview Press, 1984); Warren Bennis and Burt Nanus, *Leaders: The Strategies for Taking Charge* (New York: Harper & Row, 1985); Bernard M. Bass, *Leadership and Performance beyond Expectations* (New York: Free Press, 1985); John P. Kotter, *Power and Influence* (New York: Free Press, 1985); Edgar H. Schein, *Organizational Culture and Leadership: A Dynamic View* (San Francisco: Jossey-Bass, 1985).

13. Daniel Coleman, "Successful Executives Rely on Own Kind of Intelligence," *New York Times,* July 31, 1984, pp. C1, 11.

14. Nicholas Wollaston, "India: The Imperial Summer," in George Perry and Nicholas Mason, eds., *The Victorians: A World Built to Last* (New York: Viking, 1974), pp. 64–65.

Appendix: An Essay on Historical Method

1. The reader is referred to the extensive content analysis bibliography that ends the appendixes (Bibliography for the Content Analysis Project).

2. Philip J. Stone, Dexter C. Dunphy, Marshall S. Smith, and Daniel M. Ogilivie, *The General Inquirer: A Computer Approach to Content Analysis* (Cambridge: MIT Press, 1966). Edward Kelly and Philip J. Stone, *Computer Recognition of English Word Senses* (Amsterdam: North-Holland, 1975).

3. Ithiel de Sola Pool, *Trends in Content Analysis: Summary* (Urbana: University of Illinois Press, 1959), p. 194.

4. Donald P. Spence, "Lawfulness in Lexical Choice: A Natural Experiment," *Journal of the American Psychoanalytic Association* 28 (1980), 115. The extensive bibliography of the Stanley Rosenberg group at the Department of Psychiatry, Dartmouth Medical School is noted in Bibliography for the Content Analysis Project.

5. *The General Inquirer* outlines the hand-scoring system of content analysis for achievement motivation on pp. 191–206. David C. McClelland's initial effort on achievement motivation was *The Achieving Society* (Princeton: Van Nostrand, 1961; 2d ed., 1976). See also McClelland's *Power: The Inner Experience* (New York: Wiley, 1975); his recent book *Motives, Personality, and Society: Selected Papers* (New York: Praeger, 1984); his book with David G. Winter, *Motivating Economic Achievement* (New York: Free Press, 1969); and Winter's book *The Power Motive* (New York: Free Press, 1973).

6. The original Brown University study was first published in Henry Kucera and W. Nelson Francis, *Computational Analysis of Present-Day American English* (Providence: Brown University Press, 1967). This study was updated in W. Nelson Francis, Henry Kucera, and Andrew W. Mackie, *Frequency Analysis of English Usage: Lexicon and Grammar* (Boston: Houghton Mifflin, 1982).

7. Peter Mark Roget, *Thesaurus of English Words and Phrases, Classified and Arranged so as to Facilitate the Expression of Ideas and Assist in Literary Composition* 2d ed. (London: Longman, Brown, Green, & Longmans, 1853). George Crabb, *English Synonymes, with Copious Illustrations and Explanations, Drawn from the Best Writers* (New York: Harper & Bros., 1850).

Appendix: Statistical Note

1. Michael R. Anderberg, *Cluster Analysis for Applications* (New York: Academic Press, 1973).

2. See ibid. for further details.

3. S. Geisser, "Posterior Odds for Multivariate Normal Classifications," *Journal of the Royal Statistical Society* 26 (1964), 69–76. R. A. Eisenbeis and R. B. Avery, *Discriminant Analysis and Classification Procedures* (Lexington, Mass.: Heath, 1972).

4. Henry Kucera and W. Nelson Francis, *Computational Analysis of Present-Day American English* (Providence: Brown University Press, 1967). Alvar Ellegard, *The Syntactic Structure of English Texts: A Computer-Based Study of Four Kinds of Text in the Brown University Corpus,* Gothenburg Studies in English 43 (Gothenburg: Acta Universitatis Gothoburgensis, 1978).

Index